Surveys in Experimental Economics

Contributions to Economics

http://www.springer.de/cgi-bin/search_book.pl?series=1262

Hagen Bobzin
Indivisibilities
1998. ISBN 3-7908-1123-8

Helmut Wagner (Ed.)
Current Issues in Monetary Economics
1998. ISBN 3-7908-1127-0

Peter Michaelis/Frank Stähler (Eds.)
Recent Policy Issues in Environmental and Resource Economics
1998. ISBN 3-7908-1137-8

Jessica de Wolff
The Political Economy of Fiscal Decisions
1998. ISBN 3-7908-1130-0

Georg Bol/Gholamreza Nakhaeizadeh/ Karl-Heinz Vollmer (Eds.)
Risk Measurements, Econometrics and Neural Networks
1998. ISBN 3-7908-1152-1

Joachim Winter
Investment and Exit Decisions at the Plant Level
1998. ISBN 3-7908-1154-8

Bernd Meyer
Intertemporal Asset Pricing
1999. ISBN 3-7908-1159-9

Uwe Walz
Dynamics of Regional Integration
1999. ISBN 3-7908-1185-8

Michael Carlberg
European Monetary Union
1999. ISBN 3-7908-1191-2

Giovanni Galizzi/ Luciano Venturini (Eds.)
Vertical Relationships and Coordination in the Food System
1999. ISBN 3-7908-1192-0

Gustav A. Horn/Wolfgang Scheremet/ Rudolf Zwiener
Wages and the Euro
1999. ISBN 3-7908-1199-8

Dirk Willer
The Development of Equity Capital Markets in Transition Economies
1999. ISBN 3-7908-1198-X

Karl Matthias Weber
Innovation Diffusion and Political Control of Energy Technologies
1999. ISBN 3-7908-1205-6

Heike Link et al.
The Costs of Road Infrastructure and Congestion in Europe
1999. ISBN 3-7908-1201-3

Simon Duindam
Military Conscription
1999. ISBN 3-7908-1203-X

Bruno Jeitziner
Political Economy of the Swiss National Bank
1999. ISBN 3-7908-1209-9

Irene Ring et al. (Eds.)
Regional Sustainability
1999. ISBN 3-7908-1233-1

Katharina Müller/Andreas Ryll/ Hans-Jürgen Wagener (Eds.)
Transformation of Social Security: Pensions in Central-Eastern Europe
1999. ISBN 3-7908-1210-2

Stefan Traub
Framing Effects in Taxation
1999. ISBN 3-7908-1240-4

Pablo Coto-Millán
Utility and Production
1999. ISBN 3-7908-1153-X

Frank Riedel
Imperfect Information and Investor Heterogeneity in the Bond Market
2000. ISBN 3-7908-1247-1

Kirsten Ralf
Business Cycles
2000. ISBN 3-7908-1245-5

Michele Bagella/ Leonardo Becchetti (Eds.)
The Competitive Advantage of Industrial Districts
2000. ISBN 3-7908-1254-4

continued on page 268

Friedel Bolle
Marco Lehmann-Waffenschmidt
(Editors)

Surveys in Experimental Economics

Bargaining, Cooperation and Election Stock Markets

With a Preface by Reinhard Selten

With 16 Figures and 58 Tables

Physica-Verlag
A Springer-Verlag Company

Series Editors
Werner A. Müller
Martina Bihn

Editors
Professor Dr. Friedel Bolle
Europa-Universität Viadrina
Wirtschaftswissenschaftliche Fakultät
Lehrstuhl VWL, insbesondere Wirtschaftstheorie
Große Scharrnstraße 59
D-15230 Frankfurt/Oder
Germany
bolle@euv.frankfurt-o.de

Professor Dr. Marco Lehmann-Waffenschmidt
Technische Universität Dresden
Fakultät für Wirtschaftswissenschaften
Managerial Economics
Mommsenstraße 13
D-01062 Dresden
lw@rcs.urz.tu-dresden.de

ISSN 1431-1933
ISBN 3-7908-1472-5 Physica-Verlag Heidelberg New York

Cataloging-in-Publication Data applied for
Die Deutsche Bibliothek – CIP-Einheitsaufnahme
Surveys in experimental economics: bargaining, cooperation and electronic stock markets; with 58 tables / Friedel Bolle; Lehmann-Waffenschmidt (ed.) With a pref. by Reinhard Selten. – Heidelberg; New York: Physica-Verl., 2002
(Contributions to economics)
ISBN 3-7908-1472-5

Physica-Verlag Heidelberg New York
a member of BertelsmannSpringer Science+Business Media GmbH

Softcover Design: Erich Kirchner, Heidelberg

SPIN 10866050 88/2202-5 4 3 2 1 0 – Printed on acid-free and non-aging paper

Preface

Experimental economics is now a well established field. Laboratory experimentation has changed our view of human economic behaviour. The confidence in the descriptive validity of unbounded rationality has been shattered. Moreover, it becomes more and more clear that minor revisions of existing theory are not sufficient. Radical new departures are necessary. The non-optimising character of human decision making has to be taken seriously.

In this situation it is important to gain an overview over the surprising wealth of empirical facts revealed by experimental economics. There is a need for surveys which provide guidance to the experimenter and to the theorist. Unfortunately, writing such papers is hard and demanding work. It is more gratifying to report on one's own work rather than of that of others. I am grateful to the editors and the authors of this work for their effort of bringing together survey papers on three areas of research in experimental economics.

German experimental economics has a tradition which goes back to the beginnings of the field. More than elsewhere, exploratory experimentation was used in order to gain insights into the structure of boundedly rational economic behaviour. Nevertheless rigorous standards of statistical evaluation were not neglected. Most of the contributors to this work are native speakers of German, even if they write in English in order to reach a world wide audience. It is my pleasure to see that experimental economics is still strong in the German language area and that the good traditions are still living.

Undoubtedly, this book deserves to be recognised as a valuable source of information on the state of the art in the field. It is highly recommendable to everybody with an interest in experimental economics. The book does not only present surveys but also critical remarks of discussants. This attractive special feature reminds us of the fact that nothing in science is completely uncontroversial.

It cannot be the task of a preface to attempt a detailed appraisal. The attention of the thorough but impatient reader of the whole book should not be strained too much and should be permitted to shift to the much more informative introduction as soon as possible. It remains to express my warmly felt hope for a full success of this book.

Bonn,
February 2002

Reinhard Selten

Contents

1 Introduction

Friedel Bolle and Marco Lehmann-Waffenschmidt

In some social sciences laboratory experiments have a long tradition. Compared with, for example, psychology experimental economics started lately but has experienced a steadily increasing attention by the economic profession in the last years. Apparently experiments open up a promising gate to generate and evaluate behavioral hypotheses particularly for economic problems, too. In fact, the experimental approach in economics has taken the lead concerning questions of personal and joint decision making. Not surprisingly for many economists, however, the experimental evidence in a number of cases has been inconsistent with the well-known theoretical claims of standard economics, particularly of game theory. This has raised the fundamental problem of how to deal with an empirical evidence which is – at least partly – conflicting with established theoretical results.

To be sure, experimental economists often had to face the reproach of presenting facts without theory. This leads to the methodologically, and historically, interesting problem of how empirical findings, conflicting with the predominant theoretical approach, should, or did in history, be dealt with by the scientists involved. Though it may seem to be a natural answer at first glance, the idea turns out to be too simple to replace an established theoretical framework, which has found not to be in line with certain empirical findings by a new one fitting the data better. Of course, an editorial introduction like this one is not the place where this fundamental question could be exhaustively discussed. Thus we confine ourselves with the observation that in their self-understanding so far most experimental economists do not see their field in an irreconcilable rivalry, nor in a substitutional relationship, to other related fields from mainstream economics. Nor do they see it as an endeavour to "repair" mainstream economics' deficiencies and fallacies. Of course, all research activities in the experimental field hope to contribute to a positive theory of human behavior which, at last, should emerge from the large and steadily growing body of behavioral regularities that we get more and more conscious of.

The first economic experiments were already conducted in the middle of the last century. One may quarrel about the "real beginning" of economic experiments, but at least after Mosteller's and Nogee's (1951) and Allais' (1953) work on risky choices[1] it became clear that experiments might open up a new research field. During the sixties some centres developed in the economic profession's research landscape where systematic investigations in experimental economics started. But only in the late seventies economists really got to be acquainted to the idea of empirical investigations in the laboratory.

[1] Mosteller, F., and Nogee, P. 1953 : "An experimental measurement of utility." Journal of Political Economy 59, 1951, 371-404. Allais, M. "Le comportement de l'homme rationnel devant le risque: Critique des postulats et axiomes de l' école americaine." Econometrica 21, 503-46.

German experimental research was initiated by a group of young economists under the tutorship of Heinz Sauermann in Frankfurt (Main) where regular economic experiments started in the sixties. There also took place the world wide first international conference on Experimental Economics in 1971. In 1977 the GEW (Gesellschaft für Experimentelle Wirtschaftsforschung) was founded[2]. Practically all German experimentally working economists have their "father", or "grandfather", in this group. All the time the GEW has been an important tie for the spreading activities of the group, for gathering and communication. Meanwhile it is a market place where young experimenters can exchange ideas: in the newsletter, on the homepage (www.gew.de), and during the annual conferences of the GEW.[3]

The development process of Experimental Economics was accompanied by methodological progress in Game Theory (Selten's (1965, 1975) subgame-perfectness and trembling hand perfectness, Harsanyi's (1967/68) conceptualisation of games with incomplete information, Kreps and Wilson's (1982) Sequential Equilibrium etc.) and fruitful applications of this new body of theories to a wide area.[4] A new generation of microeconomists in the last quarter of the 20th century not only created "New Industrial Economics" and other "new approaches" to old disciplines, but they also became aware of the necessity to develop a positive theory of behavior –

[2] Founding members have been Otwin Becker, Rudolf Richter, Heinz Sauermann, Reinhard Selten, Reinhard Tietz, Horst Todt, Ulrike Vidmajer and Hans-Jürgen Weber.

[3] After the first Conference on Experimental Economics had been held by Heinz Sauermann in 1971 in Kronberg near Frankfurt (cf. H. Sauermann. Ed., series Contributions to Experimental Economics, Vol. 3, (Mohr) Tübingen 1972), the second Conference took place in 1977 (vgl. Vol. 7 of the series, Bargaining Behavior, and Vol. 8, Coalition Forming Behavior), the third in 1982 after Sauermann's death (cf. R. Tietz (Ed.), Aspiration Levels in Bargaining and Economic Decision Making, (Springer) Berlin u.a. 1983), the fourth in 1986 (cf. R. Tietz, W. Albers, R. Selten (Eds.), Bounded Rational Behavior in Experimental Games and Markets, (Springer) Berlin u.a. 1988.), the fifth in 1992 in Frankfurt, and from 1992 on the Conferences of the GEW were held annually. Inspired by the steadily diminishing distances of the conference dates Reinhard Tietz at the 4th conference presented a model of "bounded rational conference behavior" (see R. Tietz, Experimental Economics: Ways to Model Bounded Rational Bargaining Behavior, in Tietz et alii, 1988, FN, pp. 3 and 5, see also R. Tietz, "30 Jahre Experimentelle Wirtschaftsforschung in Frankfurt", Frankfurter Arbeiten zur Experimentellen Wirtschaftsforschung, A27, Frankfurt, December 1989.) Particularly the predicted regime switch in 1992 to an annual conference rhythm has become real. Since 1990 the "Heinz-Sauermann-Preis" is awarded by the GEW in a two-years rhythm to young experimenters for the best PhD-thesis.

[4] Selten, R. 1965: "Spieltheoretische Behandlung eines Oligopolomodells mit Nachfrageträgheit", Zeitschrift für die gesamte Staatswissenschaft 12, 301–324. Selten, R. 1975: "Reexamination of the Perfectness Concept for Equilibrium Points in Extensive Games", International Journal of Game Theory 4, 25-55. Harsanyi, J. C. 1967/68: "Games with Incomplete Information Played by 'Bayesian' Players", Part I: The Basic Model, Part II: Bayesian Equilibrium Points, Part III: The Basic Probability Distribution of the Game, Management Science 14, 159-182, 320-334, 486-502. Kreps, D. M./Wilson, R. 1982: "Sequential Equilibria", Econometrica 4, 863-894

a theory which can only emerge from many years of patient and scrupulous work in the laboratory, as well as in the field.

Game theory particularly makes us aware of two important characteristics of normative theories. The first is the fact that "rational behavior" is no quasi natural concept, but is highly dependent on definition. All the different concepts of "equilibria" and "solutions" are attempts to define rationality, and there is no apparent superior concept among all these proposals. The second characteristic is the complexity of thinking, which is necessary in seemingly simple everyday situations as for instance negotiating the price of a used car.

This requires finding out more about the ability of men to solve problems, in new as well as in routine situations. The danger at underestimating men's abilities is perhaps as large as overestimating them. Experimental investigation seems to be the only way to successfully approach this question. So it is understandable that – contrary to physics, for example – in economics there is no clear distinction between theorists and experimentalists. Instead, many current researchers are working in both fields. The most prominent among these is Reinhard Selten, who won the Nobel Price in 1994 for his game theoretical work and who is one of the "founding fathers" of Experimental Economics in Germany.

Naturally in a field, which has undergone such a dynamic development as experimental economics in the last decade, the body of knowledge changes very quickly. Thus, the need for an overview seems understandable. To be sure, there exists already a number of survey contributions on this topic, from which, first and foremost, the Handbook of Experimental Economics (edited by Kagel and Roth) should be mentioned here. Accordingly, the present book is not aimed at providing an all–embracing overview of this steadily expanding field. We instead confine ourselves to gather state of the art survey articles on three major topics of experimental economics which, moreover, seem to be of particular interest not only to experimentalists but also to other social scientists: bargaining, cooperation and election markets.

To give the reader the opportunity to experience the lively discourse in experimental economics and to provide him or her with an information base, which is as broad as possible we have added to each one of the survey articles a detailed comment by an expert in the field. Moreover, the book also reflects another characteristic of the field of experimental economics, which may be identified as one of the sources of its dynamics and vitality: the mix of younger, yet less well–known, authors and of scientists who are already established in the field.

The first part of this volume *"Bargaining Behavior"* contains a survey by Werner Güth *"Negotiation Rules and Bargaining Behavior – What Is Known and What Needs to Be Further Explored?"* where he concentrates mainly on experiments where non–cooperative game theory serves as benchmark, and a survey by Axel Ostmann *"Coalitions in Multilateral Negotiations: Aspirations, Agreements, and Outcomes"* on the experiments in the cooperative domain. A comment by Friedel Bolle *"Of Models and Men"*, which is not directed solely to the surveys, but to experimental investigation of bargaining behavior in general, completes the first part.

As Werner Güth emphasizes, cooperation requires bargaining if those who want to cooperate have conflicting interests about the possible result (often the distribution of the profit from cooperation). So, all existing societies (human as well as animal) can be regarded as success stories not only with respect to cooperation, but also concerning bargaining. This point of view makes bargaining one of the central problems of all social sciences.

Empirical research on bargaining may rely on field studies, or on experiments. As the first cannot be discussed here, we are interested in what the main results of the latter are. The first and most important finding is that at least at first glance normative models of bargaining contribute neither to our understanding of the bargaining process nor to a reliable prediction of bargaining results. On the contrary: the most stable patterns of behavior can be formulated as predictable deviations from game theoretic equilibria.

For finite horizon alternating offer games (including Ultimatum Bargaining) Güth finds that, compared with the game theoretical equilibrium prediction,

- offers are more generous (than equilibrium offers)
- equilibrium offers are (often) rejected
- participants do not rely on backward induction if the horizon is larger than two rounds.

The first two points show that standards of (equal) distribution do play a decisive role in bargaining. Also for experiments in the framework of cooperative game theory, where bargaining power is determined by superior possibilities to contribute to highly productive coalitions, Güth observes that power is often overruled by social norms.

As a consequence Güth pleads to pay more attention to individual characteristics and to the social context and framework of decisions. Individual characteristics can be measured for instance by standardized questionnaires, available from psychology, by measuring risk aversion, or by eliciting the inclination to contribute to charitable organizations, etc.

Axel Ostmann's contribution to Part I of this volume is concentrated on experiments where subjects can (limitedly or unlimitedly) communicate, can try to coordinate their actions, can exchange threats and promises and finally can (sometimes) commit on certain options. This is the environment, where cooperative game theory should apply. Thus, consequently it is mainly this body of solution concepts, which serves as a benchmark to evaluate experimental behavior.

In principle, Ostmann supports Güth's evaluation but, of course, he adds a lot of details in his field of specialization. One question, in particular in majority games, is whether or not "resource illusion" matters, i.e. whether players with the same possibilities to support winning coalitions, but different shares of votes, receive on average the same payment or not. The result is: Resource illusion does exist, but it often vanishes when the players become more experienced.

In simple majority games with equal players, surprisingly often unequal payoff configurations result. Another often observed deviation from all game theoretic equilibrium concepts are oversized final coalitions. This result, also to be found in other experimental situations, certainly needs an explanation of its own. A convincing idea is that superfluous members stabilize the coalition because all (or many) of the members thus have no power to threaten leaving the coalition.

Perhaps the most convincing concept of cooperative game theory is the core, provided it is not empty and not too large. But even if the core consists only of a single pay-off configuration it is possible that empirical results are completely different. In games with one veto player, we have a structure similar to ultimatum bargaining. The core concept predicts that the veto player should get "the whole cake", but as in ultimatum bargaining experiments, he usually succeeds in getting only 70% or less.

Ostmann emphasizes that there is a lot of regularities in the results, but always also exceptions. For example, often coalitions emerge with the largest average pay-off per member. But this is not always true. As Güth observes in experiments with "non–cooperative situations" it is found that a lot depends on framing and context. But, in addition, Ostmann doubts whether using exclusively the approach of cooperative game theory is promising at all. One problem is that often it is questionable whether a well-defined characteristic function can be established. However, more severe is his general suspicion that the final pay-off structure is largely influenced by the process in which it is reached, i.e. non–cooperative aspects seem to play a crucial role also in cooperative environments.

So, in a way, both surveys end with similar conclusions: the game structure alone usually is not enough to predict results. More has to be known about the influence of context, of framing, of individual characteristics, and of culture. In addition, viewed from both sides, "cooperative" and "non–cooperative" bargaining should not be kept apart, but should be investigated for common characteristics.

In his comment on experimental economics in general and bargaining experiments in particular, Friedel Bolle proposes that research efforts should more often be directed to the question how personal models of a situation emerge. The application of game theory to "objective" situations cannot result in satisfactory predictions – not even for benchmark purposes – when subjects make their decisions with an environment in mind completely different from that of the experimenter. In addition, Bolle proposes to pay more attention to the topic of signalling. In real bargaining situations, which often take place under "rather incomplete" information, signalling may play an eminent role. Of special interest is the *creation* of reliable signals.

The second part *"Cooperative Behavior"* of this volume comprises contributions from three major areas of application of the cooperation issue: public goods, environmental commons, and labour economics.

Voluntary contributions by subjects in a public goods provision may well be considered one of the most natural fields of experimenting with cooperative behavior. In fact, public goods experiments detected the limitations of standard economic theorizing in a convincing way: in experiments subjects did not show the selfish behavior predicted by standard economics. In her paper *"Cooperation in Public Goods Experiments"* Claudia Keser presents a systematic survey on public goods experiments with a special focus on the question how to explain the relative robustness of voluntary contributions beyond the standard game-theoretic prediction.

Keser identifies two major motivational reasons: reciprocity and conditional cooperation, where a subject makes her cooperative behavior dependent on the cooperative behavior of the others. Thus, the decline of cooperation in a population where free-riders coexist with conditionally cooperative subjects can consistently be explained. Consequently, the opportunity to punish non–cooperative players or to migrate to cooperative communities turns out to be an effective measure to increase the level of cooperation willingness in populations. These findings also shed new light on the role of the government in the provision of public goods. Indeed, the importance of governmental interventions to enforce cooperative behavior appears to be of much less importance than what is usually claimed by standard economic theory. This has been explored in a number of experiments by Keser and co-authors. As an issue where further experimental research would be desirable Keser mentions the question to what extent a lump-sum tax counteracts voluntary contributions to a public good project.

In his comment Claude Montmarquette particularly appreciates Keser's own approach in public goods experiments. He identifies her merits in the systematic investigation of the true motivations of voluntary contributions by subjects using different experimental settings. A little criticism is due to the fact that in her discussion of reciprocity Keser omits Axelrod's and Becker's pathbreaking contributions. Pursuing these lines of thought one would arrive at the hypothesis that efficiency is more due to market structure than to the agents' individual preferences and capabilities which is Keser's focus. Indeed, experimental evidence seems to confirm this latter hypothesis. Consequently, in Montmarquette's eyes future experimental work should concentrate more on market restrictions than on adding further elements to the utility function.

An issue, which is closely related to cooperation in public goods, is the (environmental) common's dilemma. In his contribution *"Cooperation in Environmental Commons"* Axel Ostmann first resumes the omnipresence as well as the general structure of the (environmental) common's dilemma using historical quotations by philosophers and novelists. After describing the formal structure of the common's problem which has served as a starting point for experimental studies on this issue Ostmann reports and discusses the experimental evidence on two measures which help to overcome, or at least to ease, the common's dilemma: communication and sanctions. In the fifth section of his paper Ostmann considers the common's dilemma in the framework of dynamic games ("dynamic commons"). Experimental evidence shows that in order to avoid a quick and complete depletion of a resource in a dynamic setting, additional measures are necessary. The more actual stimuli and incentives are, the more they govern an actor's behavior. Thus suitable measures like praise and reproach, or information on the state of a common pool resource can enhance the resource misuse problem. In his conclusions Ostmann, however, paints a differentiated picture of possible solutions to the common's dilemma. In the lab real agents show fairly different behavior – some are influenced by institutions and incentives, some are not – , particularly in a dynamically changing or stochastic environment, or if for instance sanctions are perceived as unfair. But in accordance with the evidence from public goods experiments some agents, fortunately, perform even better than explainable by the imposed incentive structure. As Ostmann concludes, these findings show the need for a better understanding of the interaction of situational characteristics and of the personal characteristics of the agents in a complex environmental common's dilemma situation.

Andrew Muller acknowledges in his comment the contribution by Ostmann as an overview over an important applied topic of experimental economics. Muller focuses on the fact that common property experiments in their results substantially differ from those of public goods experiments. While public goods experiments usually show a positive cooperation shift, common's dilemma experiments show a negative one. The explanation may lie in framing effects and interior equilibrium characteristics of the experimental settings. Muller concludes that the laboratory data suggest that small stable communities are likely to manage the common's problems successfully, but ethnically or geographically divided societies are not.

Simon Gächter's and Ernst Fehr's survey *"Experiments and Labour Economics"* convincingly advocates the use of laboratory experiments to evaluate labour market theory. The authors start from the observation that employment relations such as wage determination, effort incentives, or unionisation are frequently governed by incomplete contracts. Thus it appears to be of natural interest to study various mechanisms and attitudes together with their impacts, which may fill in the contract enforcement gap: reciprocity, motivation and incentives schemes as well as labour market institutions. This makes it also comprehensible to the reader why the paper figures under the headline "cooperative behavior" in this book. Moreover, as the behavioral aspect is essential for this study, the laboratory experimental approach appears to be natural for an effective analysis of these issues. Thus, in their paper the authors review a large number of relevant laboratory experiments. Indeed, many of these have been conducted by the authors themselves.

Much evidence turns out to be gained from stylised strategic interaction schemes, for instance the dictator or the ultimatum game. It is of major concern to the authors to investigate how the evidence – theoretical as well as experimental – from those elementary stylised strategic interaction schemes can be transferred to the more complex questions that arise from labour relations. The authors finally come to the conclusion that the experimental approach provides a valuable way to work empirically on the subject. As they argue it is in the best sense complementary to conventional empirical methods like case studies, interview and other field studies or statistical and econometric analysis. Furthermore, experiments also in this field not only allow to test hypotheses and theories, but also contribute to refine them.

Manfred Königstein's comment emphasizes the innovative potential of introducing the experimental method into labour economics. Complex human relationships like labour relations require a multiple scientific approach, and the experimental approach turns out to be a most fruitful one. In Königstein's eyes the paper by Gächter and Fehr comprises in a systematic and informative way the actual state of experimental evidence in this area.

In its third part *"Election Markets and Experimental Stock Markets"*, the perspective of this volume turns to another type of experimental design. Experimental economics usually takes place in the lab. This is done with the hope, of course, to gain insights, which prove to be robust, or, at least, to be in some sense useful in the real environment of the social interaction or decision from which the experimental design has been idealized. To put it into more formal terms, the experimental design should be a homomorphic image of the real interaction, or decision process, under consideration. But there is a type of experiment where the link to the real subject to be analyzed is very close: the so-called "electronic election markets", or political stock markets. Strictly speaking, electronic election markets are not laboratory experiments meeting the strict experimental quality standards because of their complexity and their non–replicability, but they are "field experiments". Recently this branch of experimental economics has received increasing attention, not only within the experimental community. This is at least partly due to their sometimes surprising successes in predicting real political election outcomes in the past. In fact, incentive driven electronic election markets several times outperformed conventional prediction instruments like public opinion polls or statistical forecasting models. The final part of the volume *"Election Markets and Experimental Stock Markets"* presents three survey contributions on this subject.

The first contribution by Brüggelambert and Crüger *"Election Markets. Experiences from a Complex Market Experiment"* surveys and evaluates the evidence from five computerized election markets, which were conducted in Germany from 1990 to 1998. As a point of theoretical reference for their evaluation the authors use the path-breaking paper by Forsythe et al. from 1992. Though Brüggelambert and Crüger corroborate the undeniable merits of election markets in forecasting election outcomes, they do not find a superiority of the election market method for their case studies. Instead, they plead for a broader assessment of this method. This means that election markets should be evaluated more generally to detect regularities in the way institutions influence human decision behavior. Authors own experiments confirm this judgement. Particularly, the "marginal trader" hypothesis, which should explain theoretically the experimental evidence of election markets, could not be validated by the evidence of the German election events under consideration.

Michael Berlemann questions in his comment on the survey by Brüggelambert and Crüger whether the authors have applied the appropriate method to test the superiority of the election market method. Together with the fact that the American election markets had been excluded from the analysis, this argument challenges the pessimistic conclusion by Brüggelambert and Crüger on the forecasting superiority of the election stock market method. Moreover, Berlemann gives an explanation for the experimental evidence, which is surprising in the eyes of the authors that experienced traders do no better than inexperienced ones.

Due to its complex structure, the election markets approach admits more far-reaching conclusions than forecasting election outcomes. In their paper on *"Expectations and Rational Actions in an Experimental Financial Market"* Forrest Nelson, pioneer of the election markets approach, and Reinhard Tietz, pioneer of the election markets approach in Germany, report on how to tackle one of the most fundamental and intricate problems of economic reasoning using the election markets approach: to test the coincidence of subjects' behavior and expectations under conditions of uncertainty. In this paper the authors give a prolific rounding off to the survey by Brüggelambert and Crüger basing on a famous election market experiment and suggesting a promising field of application. At the heart of the study lies an early political election market experiment in Germany conducted by the authors at the university of Frankfurt/Main shortly after the German reunification on October 3, 1990. In these weeks German political parties for the first time competed for seats in the new "Bundestag" in the federal election on December 2. With their contribution the authors strive for a more far-reaching application of the election market approach than just to predict the outcome. Their focus lies on the investigation of the consistency between expectations and actual transactions of traders. Naturally questions like this one are hard to examine since expectations cannot be observed directly. Nelson and Tietz interpret their experimental setting as a finance market setting which reveals possible discrepancies between the traders' expectations and transactions by differences between the computable optimal transactions with respect to profit seeking and the observed ones. The authors are well aware of different possible sources of bounded rational behavior of traders in markets like e.g. risk averse attitudes, incomplete information, strategic behavior or transactions costs. Nelson and Tietz find that only 40 percent of observed market actions are optimal ones, given the traders' expectations, 30 percent are sub-optimal, but consistent, and another 30 percent are inconsistent.

Though this seems to exhibit a great deviation from rational behavior at the first glance, things become different when looking more closely. Indeed, the authors are able to explain the observed sub-optimal, or inconsistent, transactions by the traders to a great deal by further restricting circumstances (e.g. liquidity restrictions) and purposes different from that of profit seeking (e.g. personal preferences for a certain political party). Finally, Nelson and Tietz provide a classification of seemingly inconsistent behavior. For instance, they find that purchases seem to be more consistent with expectations than sales, that transactions get the more rational the closer the election event came, that transactions involving small parties are more rational than those involving large parties, or that traders' favourite parties are treated by them differently from the other ones.

In his comment Michael Berlemann appreciates the approach by Nelson and Tietz to assess the degree of rationality and to classify the determinants of (ir)rational actions of traders in a market. However, he also mentions some criticisms on the authors' conclusions about irrationality. Berlemann argues that the degree of irrationality would decrease when certain market transactions (arbitrage transactions), which were excluded by Nelson and Tietz from the sample, would be included again. Furthermore, transactions driven by speculative motives are classified as irrational by Nelson and Tietz, but should in Berlemann's eyes be treated as fully rational since they base upon the profit seeking motive. In his opinion also traders who did not express an expectation for each party should not be eliminated from the analysis since these traders usually feel well informed about certain parties, but do not know much about the other ones. This would suggest to study whether these traders are inclined to trade more in shares of parties they know well and they revealed an expectation on.

If the method of electronic stock markets really provides a powerful forecasting method on the outcomes of political elections, then it should also be applicable to other processes with similar characteristics. Jörg Bochow, Peter Raupach and Mark Wahrenburg report in their paper *"What Do Market Makers Achieve? Evidence from a Large Scale Experimental Stock Market"* on an application in the realm of sports: on the soccer World Cup 1998. This stock market experiment has been motivated by a securities' stock market problem and realized several achievements:

- It was a large scale experiment (more than 50.000 people participated via the internet)
- It allowed for gaining insights in the influence of institutions, or say market structures, on decisions and forecasting quality (three different trading mechanisms were employed)
- The findings can be applied to real stock markets (how to provide a satisfactory level of liquidity? Are market makers a solution?)

The evidence from the experiment shows that market makers improve liquidity significantly, and it furthermore admits to identify a certain type of market maker as superior in this respect (competitive market makers perform better than monopolistic market makers). Moreover, market making in the experimental evidence appears to be effective in ensuring a quick reduction of the bid-ask spread after new information has arrived at the market.

In his comment, Michael Berlemann emphasizes that in Bochow's et al. soccer World Cup experiment the situation for participants was significantly different from election markets in that the information about the final value of a contract was revealed in a piecemeal way in the course of time through the results of the consecutive matches. Another difference is due to the different motivation by the traders in this experiment compared with the motivation of voters in an election market. All these differences lead to distortions in relation to pure election stock markets experiments and make it hard to relate the design and the evidence to real-world financial or election situations as well as to standard election market experiments.

At the end of this introduction we have to thank everybody who has contributed to the formation of this volume. First and foremost, thanks are due to our authors who all complied with our ideas on which kind of survey to contribute to this volume. On the other hand, and not less important, the Physica–Verlag provided the proper preconditions for realizing the experiment of publishing a volume on surveys in experimental economics. This is gratefully acknowledged.

Frankfurt (Oder),
Dresden,
October 2001

Friedel Bolle
Marco Lehmann-Waffenschmidt

Part I

Bargaining Behavior

2 Negotiation Rules and Bargaining Behavior*

What Is Known and What Needs to Be Further Explored?

Werner Güth

Abstract. Our programmatic review discusses the empirical support of the normative theory of bargaining which is an application of (non-) cooperative game theory and whose predictions depend more or less crucially on the specific rules of bargaining. Unfortunately, little is known about the rules of bargaining, i.e. there is a lack of empirical research concerning this type of institutional economics. An interesting, but hardly satisfactory alternative to such empirical research, namely to derive the rules of bargaining, is illustrated with a help of a simple example. From empirical, mostly experimental results we draw some general conclusions how one might proceed when developing the behavioral theory of bargaining.

2.1 Introduction

When people cooperate, they mostly determine the terms of social exchange by bargaining. Only in highly special institutional set ups like a modern stock or commodity exchange such kind of strategic interaction is avoided. (Predetermined prices in supermarkets can be viewed as a special form of bargaining tactics, namely as preemption by early commitments.) Thus bargaining is no specific problem of economics, but rather of the social sciences in general. Bargaining problems are studied, for instance, in (inter)national politics (peace negotiations, coalition formation in parliaments), in (social) psychology (when starting or dissolving joint ventures), in sociology (when forming collectives to bargain collectively like in the case of trade unions, parties, or environmental organizations), and also in biology and ethology (e.g. the coalition formation by chimpanzees, see de Waal, 1982).

Like in other fields of economics bargaining theory has been studied initially by presupposing (common knowledge of) rationality. In essence this renders bargaining theory an application of game theory. As a consequence one encounters two tasks, namely to model a bargaining situation as a game and to solve the bargaining game. The institutional knowledge required by the first task depends on the **game form**, e.g. the extensive, the normal or the characteristic function form. Whereas the first two ask for the most detailed kind of information, the latter needs much less details.

An institutionally richer bargaining model is not necessarily a better one. If the predictions depend on many institutional details, everything becomes context dependent. Institutional details like individual beliefs and preferences etc., which are usually unobservable, may even question the possibility to develop generally accepted models. One could speak of a curse or trap of institutional economics if it

* This study has been inspired by Wulf Gärtner whose encouragement is gratefully acknowledged.

wants to rely on such details. Although we presently experience the high time of extensive form modelling (the so called **noncooperative approach to bargaining**), there may come a revival of **cooperative models of bargaining** whose predictions are more robust, i.e. less sensitive to subtle institutional details.

In our view, only the observable and actually used **rules of bargaining** can be the – nevertheless – challenging task of empirical research, e.g. in institutional economics. There are certain areas, e.g. in legislative bargaining (see Baron and Ferejohn, 1987) and labour economics (see Franz, 1991) where the rules of bargaining are partly even codified and where a lot is known about the formal negotiation procedure (one, however, has to be aware that there may be also informal meetings or preplay communication and, of course, unobservable aspects like individual beliefs or preferences). In general too little is known about how people bargain: Who takes the initiative, when do parties commit finally, what do parties know when deciding, how do they evaluate certain outcomes, ...? All these questions have to be answered before one can specify a detailed bargaining model — definitely a challenging task of empirical research. The necessarily incomplete answers will require many efforts by many scholars.

An alternative to finding out empirically the rules of bargaining is to derive them. We mention and illustrate two approaches, **endogenous timing**, which determines later rules of bargaining by earlier choices, and **indirect evolution** which first studies how bargaining rules determine bargaining outcomes and then derives the evolutionarily stable rules of bargaining. Such approaches also require models, e.g. endogenous timing a more encompassing game which does not only model the negotiation process, but also how parties decide about certain aspects of the negotiation process beforehand. In indirect evolution one has to specify an evolutionary model allowing to study the evolution of bargaining rules.

Another type of empirical research is to explore behavior in a given bargaining game, i.e. for a given set of rules of bargaining. Here for some simple, mostly extreme cases of bargaining rules a lot is known thanks to experimental research (see Roth, 1995, for a recent, but non-exhaustive survey). We review some stylized facts from such research without claiming completeness. Such experimental results may shed some light on the acceptability of specific rules of bargaining and what they imply for a behavioral theory of bargaining which substitutes (common knowledge of) perfect decision rationality by taking into account the cognitive limitations of human decision makers.

In section 2 we first review the strategic bargaining approach and its empirical support. This points to an (empirical) research question, namely which rules of bargaining are actually used in practice. A theoretical alternative to this empirical institutional approach is to derive the rules of bargaining for which we provide an example in section 3. A further alternative is to rely on bargaining models which pay less attention to subtle details of bargaining rules like cooperative bargaining theory discussed in section 4. When concluding (section 6) we briefly discuss intrapersonal decision conflicts and summarize our findings.

To avoid any misunderstanding when reading the following sections one should keep the following **convention** in mind: (Bargaining or negotiation) **Rules** always refer to the game theoretic model, i.e. rules are the rules of the game. **Behavioral patterns** or **regularities** can at best reflect **norms**, i.e. they always refer to behavior. Thus rules capture the structure of the situation whereas behavioral norms reflect empirically validated or (often) normatively justified behavioral regularities. Rules may influence which norms are applied by decision makers, but they must not do so.

2.2 Strategic bargaining

Bargaining problems are special situations with strategic interaction. Thus normative bargaining theory is just a special field of applied game theory. Correspondingly its two main tasks are

- to model bargaining situations as games and
- to solve these bargaining games.

Let us first ask in which sense bargaining games are special games. Clearly, bargaining means to arrange some joint activities in a mutually profitable way, i.e. bargaining games are **non-zero sum games**. In most situations bargaining is also **non-anonymous** and allows for **free communication**. For a game theoretic analysis the latter two aspects are, however, inessential like cheap talk-preplay communication. Thus by concentrating on bargaining games one hardly gains any structural information except for the non-zero sum property which, of course, rules out concepts like maximin-strategies and the (direct, for an indirect use see Nash, 1953) use of saddle point-theorems (von Neumann and Morgenstern, 1944).

Conversely, one can ask whether every kind of cooperation requires to bargain. That this needs not to be true can be illustrated by

Sender-Receiver-Games Let $\Omega = \{w_1, ..., w_T\}$ denote the finite set of states $w \in \Omega$ of the world with $T \geq 2$. Whereas the sender S observes the true state $w \in \Omega$ of the world, the receiver R must choose the action $a \in A$ yielding the same (expected) utility $u(a,w)$ for both players R and S. Before choosing $a \in A$ player R receives a message $m \in M$ sent to him by S. For the sake of simplicity let us assume that there are as many different messages as states of the world, i.e. $|\Omega| = |M| = T$, and that for every two distinct states $w', w'' \in \Omega$ of the world the optimal actions $a'(w'), a''(w'') \in A$ are different what implies $|A| \geq T$.

Effective Cooperation in Sender-Receiver-Games requires only a kind of language $m(w)$ in the sense that for all $w \in \Omega$ sender S can signal by m the actually prevailing state w. Given such a language receiver R will choose the optimal action for all messages $m \in M$ by decoding it correctly. Clearly, one will not speak of bargaining if people just communicate in such an elementary way, i.e. cooperation per se does not lead to bargaining. Whether and how such an elementary language develops can be analysed in an evolutionary way (Blume, Kim, and Sobel, 1993, Wärneryd, 1993).

An elementary way of bargaining is **ultimatum bargaining** where one party confronts one or many other parties with a take it or leave it-offer how to split the pie (a positive monetary amount) c, i.e. either the ultimatum proposal is accepted or conflict results (see Güth, 1976, for an early discussion). In case of many responders one can distinguish the case of veto-responders in the sense that any responder can induce conflict as well as the cases where an individual responder cannot do so. We just introduce the former case more formally.

Ultimatum Bargaining with Veto-Responders Let $\varepsilon\,(>0)$ be the smallest monetary unit and $c = K\varepsilon$ with $K > n$. Proposer P first chooses an offer $(r_1,...,r_n)$ to all n responders R_i such that $r_1 + ... + r_n \leq c$ and $r_i \geq \varepsilon$ for $i = 1,...,n$ are all integer multiples of ε. Knowing either the whole vector $(r_1,...,r_n)$ or only his own offer r_i every responder R_i can either accept the offer or reject it. If all n responders accept, each of them receives r_i and proposer P the residual amount $c-(r_1+...+r_n)$. Otherwise all players receive 0-payments, i.e. conflict results.

According to the **non-cooperative approach to bargaining** (Nash, 1953) cooperation should be justified as **equilibrium behavior** in bargaining games, i.e. the parties' bargaining behavior should be mutually optimal (Cournot, 1838; Nash, 1950). Now equilibrium behavior does not necessarily imply rational behavior. For $n \geq 2$ any behavior such that all responders reject all offers is, for instance, an equilibrium.

Rejecting a positive offer r_i appears like an economic suicide by responder R_i. In game theoretic terminology: All responder strategies prescribing the rejection of some positive offers are **dominated**, i.e. there are other strategies which are never worse and sometimes better. Thus according to this more basic rationality requirement all offer vectors will always be accepted what renders the **minimal offer vector** $(r_1,...,r_n) = (\varepsilon,...,\varepsilon)$ as optimal for P.

One important experimental result (see the early study by Güth, Schmittberger, and Schwarze, 1982, and the survey by Roth, 1995) is that responders will not always accept positive offers and that this is anticipated by proposers P who offer substantially more than ε to responders. One reaction to such empirical findings is to introduce additional arguments of players' utilities like an aversion against inequality in one's own disfavor (Bolton, 1991, Bolton and Ockenfels, 2000, Fehr and Schmidt, 1999), envy (Kirchsteiger, 1994), a desire for reciprocity (Rabin, 1993), or other repairs of the game (Geanakoplos, Pearce, and Stacchetti, 1989). In this research tradition of game fitting exercises or neoclassical repairs (Güth, 1995) empirical findings help to provide an empirically sound game theoretic representation of a bargaining situation, but do not question the assumption of rational behavior.

What ultimatum bargaining with $n \geq 2$ illustrates is that an equilibrium of some bargaining game does not necessarily imply cooperation. One rather must select between equilibria either by **refining the equilibrium** notion, e.g. by requiring an equilibrium in undominated strategies (for other attempts see van Damme, 1983) or by applying concepts of **equilibrium selection** (Nash, 1953; Harsanyi and Selten, 1988; Güth and Kalkofen, 1989).

Usually refinement concepts still allow for (generic) multiplicity of equilibria. A game may have, for instance, **multiple strict equilibria** in the sense that every player would lose by deviating unilaterally. An influential development in bargaining theory has been to avoid this troublesome ambiguity by studying bargaining games where the appropriately refined equilibrium is unique (see Ståhl, 1972, Krelle, 1976, and – most elegantly – Rubinstein, 1982). Unfortunately, this advantage is easily lost when imposing realistic assumptions like discreteness (see van Damme, Selten, and Winter, 1990). There is also the danger of imposing convenient albeit unrealistic rules rather than trying to model a bargaining game in a way which closely resembles the actually applied rules.

Alternating Offer-Bargaining Let parties $i = 1,2$ divide the unit amount of completely divisible money by alternating in offering, i.e. party 1 offers in all odd periods $t = 1,3,5,...$ and party 2 in all even periods $t = 2,4,6,...$ an amount y_t with $0 \leq y_t \leq 1$ to the other party. If the offer is accepted, the other party j receives $\delta_j^{t-1} y_t$, whereas the offering party i gets $\delta_i^{t-1}(1-y_t)$ where the discount factors δ_1 and δ_2 must satisfy $0 < \delta_1, \delta_2 < 1$. If no offer is ever accepted, both players 1 and 2 receive 0-payments.

Rubinstein (1982) has shown that there exists only one **subgame perfect equilibrium** (prescribing equilibrium behavior not only for the game itself, but also for all its subgames, i.e. its informationally closed substructures) in alternating offer-bargaining. Its offers are

$$y_t^* = \begin{cases} \frac{\delta_2(1-\delta_1)}{1-\delta_1\delta_2} \text{ if } t \text{ is odd} \\ \\ \frac{\delta_1(1-\delta_2)}{1-\delta_1\delta_2} \text{ if } t \text{ is even.} \end{cases} \tag{2.1}$$

Such and better offers are accepted whereas worse offers are rejected.

An **infinite horizon** is, of course, a theoretical idealization which cannot be, for instance, experimentally implemented (see Weg, Rapoport, and Felsenthal, 1990). It is therefore a desirable property of the above solution (Rubinstein, 1982) that the solutions of alternating offer-bargaining games with finite horizon T (the last round T is then like in ultimatum bargaining) converge to it for $T \to \infty$. What the experimental results (see Güth, 1995, and Roth, 1995, for surveys) reveal is that the game theoretic solution has little empirical appeal in the sense that

- offers differ systematically from y_t^*,
- offers are rejected even when they are more generous than y_t^*,
- participants do not rely on backward induction if the horizon is longer than two rounds (they do not even ask for the necessary information, see Camerer et al., 1993) and/or if this would induce a very biased distribution (Güth and Tietz, 1990),
- strategically irrelevant aspects, e.g. party 1's discount factor δ_1 in case of only two rounds of negotiation ($T = 2$), influence behavior (Ochs and Roth, 1989).

Using alternating offer-bargaining in applications (see, e.g., Bester, 1988) questions the empirical validity of such studies. The frequent use of take it or leave it-offers in principal-agent-models (e.g. Holmstrom, 1979) should induce us to doubt their practical relevance. By such models one only avoids to select among equilibria. A model where this problem is crucial is

Independent Offer-Bargaining In all periods $t = 1,2,3,...,T$ both parties $i = 1,2$ independently choose their own demand d_t^i with $0 \leq d_t^i \leq 1$. The offer y_t^j for party j, implied by i's demand d_t^i, is then $y_t^j = 1 - d_t^i$. If for the first time $d_t^1 + d_t^2 \leq 1$, these demands are accepted and both parties $i = 1,2$ receive $\delta_i^{t-1} d_t^i$, i.e. the discounted demand. If this never happens, both parties receive 0-payments.

Assume that T is finite and consider the last round $t = T$ of independent offer-bargaining. Clearly, all demand vectors (d_T^1, d_T^2) with $0 < d_T^1, d_T^2 < 1$ and $d_T^1 + d_T^2 = 1$ are strict equilibria of these subgames what illustrates why one has to rely on equilibrium selection. Nash (1950 and 1953) suggested (by providing convincing axioms and a constructive selection method) the solution maximizing the product of the dividends $\delta_i^{T-1} d_T^i$ and $\delta_j^{T-1} d_T^j$ what yields $d_T^1 = d_T^2 = \frac{1}{2}$ and thus an agreement in the last round T.

For earlier rounds $t < T$ let d_{t+1}^i and d_{t+1}^j with $0 \leq d_{t+1}^i, d_{t+1}^j \leq 1$ and $d_{t+1}^i + d_{t+1}^j = 1$ be the solution offers if no agreement would be reached in round t, but only in period $t+1$. Thus the dividends in round t are $d_t^j - \delta_j d_{t+1}^j$ and $d_t^i - \delta_i d_{t+1}^i$. Maximizing their product requires $d_t^i + d_t^j = 1$ and

$$d_t^i = \frac{1}{2} - \frac{\delta_i}{2} + \frac{\delta_i + \delta_j}{2} d_{t+1}^i \text{ for } i = 1,2. \tag{2.2}$$

Given the initial values $d_T^1 = d_T^2 = \frac{1}{2}$ this difference equation allows to compute all demands d_t^i for all periods $t = 1,2,3,...,T$ and both parties $i = 1,2$ by backward induction.

What one actually derives in this way is the subgame consistent bargaining solution suggested by Nash (1950 and 1953). Here **subgame consistency** means that one does not only require this solution for the T-round bargaining game itself, but also for all its subgames (see Selten and Güth, 1982, for a more complex bargaining model based on the well-known accelerator-multiplier macroeconomic model as studied by Hicks, 1949, and Samuelson, 1939).

To illustrate the different implications of alternating offer- and independent offer-bargaining consider $T = 1$ for which alternating offer-bargaining boils down to ultimatum bargaining with $y_1^1 = 0$ whereas independent offer-bargaining implies an equal division with $d_1^1 = d_1^2 = \frac{1}{2}$.

For $T = 2$ alternating offer-bargaining prescribes an initial offer $y_1^1 = 1 - \delta_2$ whereas independent offer-bargaining requires initial demands $d_1^i = \frac{1}{2} - \frac{\delta_i}{4} + \frac{\delta_j}{4}$ for $i = 1,2$. According to the latter result one party gets at most $\frac{3}{4}$ of the unit amount, whereas the former result allows for all possible distributions. For $T = 2$ and alternating offer-bargaining δ_1 is strategically irrelevant whereas both discount factors matter in case of independent offers.

Although experimental studies of independent offer-bargaining seem to have concentrated on $T = 1$ (see Nydegger and Owen, 1975, and Malouf and Roth, 1981), one can reasonably expect that both discount factors will matter when $T > 1$. Discount factors strongly influence the payoff expectations of later agreements and – contrary to the game theoretic prediction – parties often do not achieve an agreement immediately, i.e. in round 1.

2.3 On the rules of bargaining

What we have learned above is that the game theoretic bargaining solutions usually fail to predict actual bargaining behavior and that the game theoretic prediction crucially depends on the rules of bargaining. Thus even if game theory would predict bargaining behavior, one would have to know the empirically used negotiation rules (experimentally these rules can be – at least partly – controlled by the experimental design). In this section we want to discuss how one might be able to narrow down the rules of bargaining.

What one needs are empirical studies focusing on institutional aspects like the process structure of negotiations, the information conditions and the preferences of the negotiators (partly such attempts can be found in Mautner-Markhof, 1989, Murnighan, 1991 an 1992, Young, 1991, Raiffa, 1997). Typically such research can be found in legislative bargaining (Baron and Ferejohn, 1987) or labour economics (e.g. Franz, 1991) where established – and sometimes even codified – rules exist. Of course, even such well established rules may not suffice to define unambiguously a strategic bargaining game since they usually do not specify the beliefs nor the preferences of the interacting parties. Nevertheless stylized facts concerning when a party decides what can certainly narrow down considerably the range of possible bargaining games and of possible bargaining outcomes. Here we can only argue for empirical studies of the rules of bargaining as important research in institutional economics. For such studies statistical yearbooks will not offer many hints since one cannot deduce the rules unambiguously from observed behavior.

Quite often the party who takes the initiative, e.g. by finding out about some form of cooperation, may determine the way of bargaining. An employer, offering a job, will often also determine the wage as well as other aspects which then a potential employee can only accept or reject, i.e. the employer assumes the role of the proposer in ultimatum bargaining. In such situations the rules of bargaining should be optimal for the one taking the initiative.

A further alternative is to derive the rules of bargaining. Generally one can distinguish two methods of deriving the rules of (bargaining) games. One way is to model the way in which the interacting parties determine the rules of later bargaining, i.e. one must specify rules for committing to the rules of bargaining. With respect to rules concerning the timing of decisions this type of research is usually summarized as studies of **endogenous timing** (see van Damme and Hurkens, 1996). More generally, one can speak of **strategic commitment** to later rules (for the case of preferences see Rotemberg, 1994).

An alternative, although related method is **indirect evolution**. Here one first derives the outcome for all possible (bargaining) rules and determines then the evolutionarily stable rules, i.e. those rules which survive in the evolutionary game with possible rules as strategies. Our example can be interpreted as an application of both methods although usually the two methods pose different modelling challenges, namely an **overall game** for committing to later rules, respectively an **evolutionary framework** to analyse the evolution of (bargaining) rules (see Dufwenberg and Güth, 1997, for a detailed comparison of the two methods). We determine whether or not bargainers commit to final offers sequentially or simultaneously, i.e. independently what explains why we refer to it as the

Alternating or Independent Offer-Model The two parties $i = 1,2$ must first decide between P(reemption) and W(ait) where P means that one commits before the amount c to be distributed is randomly determined. The decisions are then publicly announced. If both parties have chosen P, they must then independently decide about their own demands d_1 and d_2, respectively, where they only know that $c \in [0,1]$ is randomly selected according to the uniform density. If both parties have chosen W, they determine their demands independently knowing the realization c. If only one uses P, this party commits to a demand before c is chosen, whereas the other waits till c is known and P's demand has been announced. Whenever $d_1 + d_2 \leq c$ each party i receives its demand d_i; otherwise both receive nothing.

This model does not impose a process structure, but leaves it open. These parts of the rules of bargaining should be derived and not exogenously predetermined. In case of (W,W) we apply the solution, suggested by Nash (1950 and 1953), relying on maximizing the product of dividends, i.e. on the solution $d_1^* = d_2^* = c/2$ for all $c \in [0,1]$. The solution for (P,P) is the unique equilibrium $d_1^* = d_2^* = 1/3$. Similarly, one derives the solution $d_P^* = 1/2$ and $d_W^* = \max\{c - d_P, 0\}$. Here d_P^* denotes the strategy of the party which precommits (has chosen P) and d_W^* the strategy of the party which waits till the realization of c (see Güth and Ritzberger, 2001, for a much more general analysis).

With the help of these results the timing dispositions can be analysed by the bimatrix in table 2.1 which lists for any timing dispositions P or W of parties 1 and 2 the expected profits of both parties in the natural order. In the tradition of endogenous timing this symmetric bimatrix game is just the **truncation** (the early decision game when one anticipates rational decisions on later bargaining stages). In view of indirect evolution this bimatrix game would be interpreted as an **evolutionary game** with timing dispositions as strategies whose evolution is to be investigated. Fortunately, these differences in interpretation do not matter for this bimatrix game since W dominates P (if the other party uses P the timing disposition W yields a higher expected profit; if the other party uses W, the timing disposition W is not worse than P). This renders the vector (W,W) as the only result – as part of the players' rational behavior in view of endogenous timing, as an implication of evolutionary stability in view of indirect evolution.

Table 2.1. The expected profits for the timing positions

1 \ 2	P	W
P	$\frac{1}{9}, \frac{1}{9}$	$\frac{1}{4}, \frac{1}{8}$
W	$\frac{1}{8}, \frac{1}{4}$	$\frac{1}{4}, \frac{1}{4}$

Can parties actually influence when to commit to a final demand? There is no or very little influence when such negotiations occur rather regularly. Trying to deviate from standardized rules of bargaining might ruin one's reputation and the future possibilities to engage in mutually profitable cooperation. One can, of course, investigate timing commitments experimentally. It is, for instance, obvious how to perform experiments based on the above alternating or independent offer-model (see Güth, Marchand, Rullière and Zeiliger, 2000, who confront their participants with three different distributions other than the uniform one in order to avoid the degeneracy of the bimatrix above).

2.4 Stable outcomes of bargaining

Whereas strategic bargaining relies on detailed models of bargaining processes stable outcomes of bargaining just look at bargaining outcomes, e.g. in the form of likely payoffs from bargaining. To do so one does not specify individual strategies, but captures only the set of possible agreements for all possible coalitions. In case of unrestricted side payments the conventional tool is the **characteristic function** $v(C)$ assigning to every coalition C of interacting parties $i = 1, ..., n$ the utility/payoff sum $v(C)$ which C can distribute among its members. Examples are, for instance, the

Apex Game with $n \geq 4$ and $v(C) = 1$ if $1 \in C$ and $|C| \geq 2$ or if $C = \{2, ..., n\}$ and $v(C) = 0$ otherwise.
Excess Labor Economy with $n \geq 3$ and $v(C) = 1$ if $1 \in C$ and $|C| \geq 2$ and $v(C) = 0$ if $1 \notin C$;
Majority Voting with $v(C) = 1$ if $|C| > n/2$ and $v(C) = 0$ for $|C| \leq n/2$.

In the Apex-game the Apex (player 1) needs only one partner to achieve the maximal joint profit, normalized to 1, whereas without him all other players are needed. Player 1 of the excess labor economy can be viewed as a capitalist who can hire players 2 to n as workers with the same unit productivity if employed as the only worker. The workers alone, i.e. without the capitalist, are unproductive since they need the machinery, owned by player 1. Majority voting assumes that the majority takes it all, i.e. leaves nothing for the minority of players.

An outcome for a characteristic function $v(C)$ for all coalitions $C \subseteq \{1,...,n\}$ with $C \neq \emptyset$ can be described as a **configuration** $(C_1,...,C_T;u_1,...,u_n)$ of disjoint coalitions $C_1,...,C_T$ with $C_1 \smile ... \smile C_T = \{1,...,n\}$ and a payoff vector $(u_1,...,u_n)$ specifying a payoff u_i for every player $i = 1,...,n$. If $v(C)$ is **superadditive**, i.e. if $v(C') + v(C'') \leq v(C' \smile C'')$ for all disjoint coalitions C' and C'', one usually requires $T = 1$, i.e. that the **grand coalition** $\{1,...,n\}$ forms. Clearly, all three examples above are superadditive. In the following we confine ourselves to such simple constellations.

Stable outcomes are configurations satisfying certain stability requirements like
Individual Rationality requiring $u_i \geq v(\{i\})$ for $i = 1,...,n$;
Efficiency meaning $u_1 + ... + u_n = v(\{1,...,n\})$ due to superadditivity;
Group Rationality demanding $\sum_{i \in C} u_i \geq v(C)$ for all C with $\emptyset \neq C \subset \{1,...,n\}$.

Unfortunately, even such basic and intuitive stability requirements may already be inconsistent. Majority voting in case of $n = 3$ requires, for instance,

$$u_i + u_j \geq 1 \text{ for all coalitions } \{i,j\} \text{ with } i \neq j \tag{2.3}$$

because of group rationality and thus

$$u_1 + u_2 + u_3 \geq 3/2 \tag{2.4}$$

contradicting the efficiency requirement $u_1 + u_2 + u_3 = 1$. The **core**, i.e. the set all stable outcomes satisfying individual and group rationality as well as efficiency can thus be empty (see Edgeworth, 1881, for an ingenious and early analysis of the core of replica-exchange economies). In the Apex-game the core is also empty. For the excess labor economy it consists of a unique payoff vector, namely the payoff vector $(1,0,...,0)$ giving all the profit to the capitalist player 1.

A configuration specifies both, the coalitions which form, e.g. the grand coalition, and how they divide what they can assure to its members. If this is impossible, e.g. if the core is empty, one may restrict one's ambition to only predicting the payoff u_i for the members of coalition C in case it forms. Such a concept is the **quota vector** which specifies aspiration levels $(u_1,...,u_n)$ satisfying

$$\sum_{i \in C} u_i = v(C) \tag{2.5}$$

for all coalitions C which are not excluded. The quota-vector of the Apex-game is $\left(\frac{n-2}{n-1}, \frac{1}{n-1}, ..., \frac{1}{n-1}\right)$ and of majority voting with $n = 3$ the vector $\left(\frac{1}{2}, \frac{1}{2}, \frac{1}{2}\right)$. For the excess labor economy it is the vector $(1,0,...,0)$.

Experimentally the quota prediction is questionable. It fails in case of extreme payoff distributions like in the labor excess economy with $n = 3$ where the two "workers" will get more than the competitive wage 0. Often players try to be in the actually forming coalition by "committing" to a lower aspiration than their quota (see Albers and Laing, 1991).

Let $u' = (u'_1,...,u'_n)$ and $u'' = (u''_1,...,u''_n)$ be two configurations with $T = 1$. We say that u' **dominates** u'' (via the coalition C) if there exists a coalition C with $\emptyset \neq$

$C \subset \{1,...,n\}$ such that $\sum_{i \in C} u'_i \leq v(C)$ and $u'_i > u''_i$ for all members i of coalition C. Clearly, any inefficient payoff vector $u = (u_1,...u_n)$ with $u_1 + ... + u_n < v(\{1,...,n\})$ is dominated since the grand coalition can give more to every player $i = 1,...,n$. Similarly, $u_i < v(\{i\})$ would imply that u is dominated. Thus the core is the set of undominated payoff vectors $(u_1,...,u_n)$.

Since the core may be empty, one may want to allow dominated payoff vectors as stable outcomes. A suggestion by von Neumann and Morgenstern (1944) are the

Stable Sets $U = \{u = (u_1,...,u_n)\}$ of individually rational and efficient payoff vectors satisfying

- internal stability (no $u \in U$ is dominated by another payoff vector in U) and
- external stability (for every $u' \notin U$ there exists a payoff vector $u \in U$ dominating $u' = (u'_1,...u'_n)$).

A stable set for majority voting with $n = 3$ is, for instance, given by $U = \{(\frac{1}{2},\frac{1}{2},0),(\frac{1}{2},0,\frac{1}{2}),(0,\frac{1}{2},\frac{1}{2})\}$. Of course, a stable set must contain the non-empty core, i.e. one must have $(1,0,...,0) \in U$ for any stable set of the excess labor economy. The set $\{(1,0,...,0)\}$ is, however, not externally stable since $(1,0,...,0)$ does not, for instance, dominate $(0,\frac{1}{n-1},...,\frac{1}{n-1})$. In the Apex-game the set

$$U = \left\{u : u_1 = \frac{n-2}{n-1}, u_i = \frac{1}{n-1} \text{ for some } i = 2,...,n \text{ or } u = \left(0,\frac{1}{n-1},...,\frac{1}{n-1}\right)\right\} \tag{2.6}$$

is stable: Obviously, no $u \in U$ is dominated by another payoff vector u' in U, i.e. U is internally stable. Furthermore, a payoff vector $u \notin U$ is dominated by $u' \in U$ with $u'_1 = \frac{n-2}{n-1}$, $u'_j = \frac{1}{n-1}$ for some j if $u_1 < \frac{n-2}{n-1}$ and by $u' = (0,\frac{1}{n-1},...,\frac{1}{n-1}) \in U$ if $u_1 > \frac{n-2}{n-1}$ what proves the external stability of U for Apex-games.

Let u' and u'' be two individually rational and efficient payoff vectors. When u' dominates u'' via the coalition S, i.e. $u'_i > u''_i$ for all $i \in S$ and $\sum_{i \in S} u'_i \leq v(S)$, one can say that u' qualifies as an **objection** against u''. A **counter objection** against an objection u' against u'' via coalition S is an individually rational and efficient payoff vector $\hat{u}$ dominating u' via the coalition T and satisfying $\hat{u}_i > u''_i$ if $i \in T$ and $i \notin S$. The set of all individually rational and efficient payoff vectors for which there exists a counterobjection to any objection is the **bargaining set** (Aumann and Maschler, 1964) which is never empty and, of course, contains the core if non-empty. Bargaining sets can be viewed as intermediate stability concepts since they do not accept every objection like the core and allow for counterobjections to objections, but not for countercounterobjections to counterobjections. The sequence "proposal followed by objection followed by counterobjection" may reflect aspects of procedural rules (Osborne and Rubinstein, 1990), but in a rather arbitrary way.

Here we do not want to discuss this concept in more detail (for an evaluation of its predictive success see Maschler, 1978, and Selten, 1985). We also neglect the so-called **value concepts** which define a unique payoff vector as stable (see Shapley, 1953, and Schmeidler, 1969).

2.5 The merits of cooperative game theory

Compared to strategic bargaining games it is much easier, but not necessarily easy to find out the characteristic function $v(C)$ of a bargaining situation. One does not have to specify what a party decides when, what it knows when deciding etc. All what is needed are the possible payoff vectors for every coalition C. To derive $v(C)$ on an oligopoly market where the worst behavior of other sellers is that they sell as much as possible, one would, for instance, have to know in addition to the demand and cost functions only the total capacity of all non-members for coalition C. This is by no means an easy task of empirical research, but can – more or less convincingly – be done, e.g. by relying on capacity utilization data (see Sachverständigenrat zur Begutachtung der gesamtwirtschaftlichen Entwicklung, 1997).

Although nowadays there are more experiments of strategic than of characteristic function bargaining, the latter type of experiments was very prominent during the beginning phase of experimental game theory (see, for instance, the respective contributions in Sauermann, 1967 - 1978). Stability analysis often does not capture what is empirically relevant. One example is the **norm of fairness** requiring payoff vectors with equal payoffs. Selten (1985) has therefore suggested a modified stability concept which only allows for – in this sense – fair objections and which is more in line with the experimentally observed behavior.

Since the predictions of cooperative game theory are less sensitive to subtle details concerning the rules of bargaining, one can claim its wider applicability (see, for instance, Aumann, 1996). This hope could be substantiated by **social norms** which are obeyed regardless of strategic aspects and which may be captured by the underlying axioms or stability requirements. If cooperative solutions rely, for instance, on symmetry invariance (e.g. Nash, 1953; Shapley, 1953; Schmeidler, 1969), the strong support of equity theory (e.g. Homans, 1961, Selten, 1978, and Güth, 1994) might confirm also the predictions of cooperative solution concepts.

Unfortunately, cooperative concepts often do not essentially restrict the possible bargaining results. Sometimes they only exclude conflict if this is the only inefficient payoff vector like in ultimatum bargaining. Other (value-)concepts always predict a unique payoff vector, but are confirmed only in rare situations. The fact that strategic aspects are often neglected in decision making has to be clearly distinguished from the claim that strategic aspects do not matter at all. They often influence bargaining behavior, but strategic considerations have to compete with other forces on decision making like the desire to obey social norms, e.g. the norm of reciprocity (see Young, 1986).

A behavioral theory of bargaining thus will have to pay attention to strategic aspects as well as to non-strategic aspects which are not reflected by monetary incentives. Decisions emerge by cognitive processes where all these aspects can be more or less suppressed as claimed by the psychological theory of cognitive dissonance (Festinger, 1957). The assumption of predetermined and complete preferences may be maintained in economic textbooks, but has no appeal for actual decision makers who have to determine not only their choices, but also what they really care for. Cooperative game theory might often account for the result of such decision processes and one might hope to find more or less precise conditions when this will happen, but it often will fail either by making too vague predictions or by being empirically falsified. Typically it should be helpful in complex bargaining situations with unclear procedural rules, but strong norms of behavior which – hopefully – are captured by some notion of stability.

2.6 Final remarks

Bargaining is necessary if cooperation requires several actors with at least partially conflicting interests. Via bargaining one aims at a coordinated behavior of the different parties what usually means that each party gains by such cooperation, but also than no single party achieves its optimal result. Thus bargaining is typically an interpersonal coordination process involving concessions and compromises.

It has long be recognized (Plato, 1941) that conflicting interests do not necessarily need different individuals. Quite often also individual decision makers are not sure which of their conflicting interests should guide their behavior. Such problems typically arise in dynamic decision making, e.g. when present and future needs are competing like in saving or investment decisions and, most dramatically, when yielding to addiction (see, for instance, Modigliani and Brumberg, 1954, for studies of saving behavior and Becker and Murphy, 1988, for a study of addiction).

Game theory has been developed to analyse social interaction. Thus to explore intrapersonal bargaining in the sense of having to coordinate between competing interests intrapersonal decision conflicts should be transformed into interpersonal ones (see Frank, 1996, for a game theoretic interpretation of the conflict between "passion" and "reason" as discussed by Plato, 1941). This, however, requires to invent the rules of intrapersonal bargaining where the empirical evidence supporting cognitive dissonance theory (see Festinger, 1957) might offer some guidance. Although the idea to transform intrapersonal decision conflicts into interpersonal bargaining games is intriguing, a normative analysis of such bargaining problems appears rather questionable.

There are other surveys of bargaining theory, e.g. Bester (1989), Osborne and Rubinstein (1990). Here an attempt has been made to discuss bargaining theory in light of the available evidence and to outline the type of empirical research needed. Quite often this empirical research will not be of the traditional form, e.g. of analysing the data of statistical yearbooks or experimental data for given bargaining rules. What we suggest is an empirical institutional approach to find out the negotiation rules on which people rely. One has to expect that this is context dependent, i.e. there will not be a simple general answer. Some studies in labor economics and in public decision making can be seen as first steps in finding out the rules of bargaining in certain domains.

There is no need to complain that so little is known and that the task of empirical research is tremendous. Bargaining is an overwhelming aspect of human, but not only of human (see de Waal, 1982) life. It is not to be expected that there ever will be complete answers. This should, however, not prevent us from going on with research: Although doctors will never be able to guarantee eternal life, we still consult them and are thankful for the little help they can provide. In the same way bargaining research will be unable to give unambiguous recommendations for all possible bargaining problems, but it should be helpful sometimes.

References

1. Albers, W. and J. D. Laing (1991): Prominence, Competition, Learning, and the generation of offers in computer-aided experimental spatial games, *Game Equilibrium Models*, Berlin: Springer-Verlag, 141 - 185.
2. Aumann, R. J. (1996): On the state of the art in game theory: An Interview with Robert Aumann, in: *Understanding strategic interaction - Essays in Honor of Reinhard Selten*, W. Albers, W. Güth, P. Hammerstein, B. Moldovanu, E. van Damme (eds.), Berlin - Heidelberg: Springer-Verlag, 8 - 34.
3. Aumann, R. J. and M. Maschler (1964): The bargaining set for cooperative games, in: *Advances in game theory*, M. Dresher, L. S. Shapley, A. W. Tucker (eds.), Princeton, N. J.: Princeton University Press.
4. Baron, D. P. and J. Ferejohn (1987): Bargaining and agenda formation in legislatures, *American Economic Review*, 77 (2), 303 - 309.
5. Becker, G. S. and K. M. Murphy (1988): A theory of rational addiction, *Journal of Political Economy*, 96, 675 - 700.
6. Bester, H. (1988): Bargaining, search costs and equilibrium price distributions, *Review of Economic Studies LV*, 201 - 214.
7. Bester, H. (1989): Non-cooperative bargaining and imperfect competition: A survey, *Zeitschrift für Wirtschafts- und Sozialwissenschaften*, 109, 265 - 286.
8. Blume, A., Y.-G. Kim, and J. Sobel (1993): Evolutionary stability in games of communication, *Games and Economic Behavior*, 5 (4), 547 - 575.
9. Bolton, G. (1991): A comparative model of bargaining: Theory and evidence, *American Economic Review*, 81, 1096 - 1136.
10. Bolton, G. and A. Ockenfels (2000): ERC - A theory of equity, reciprocity and competition, *American Economic Review*, 90 (1), 166-93.
11. Camerer, C. F., E. J. Johnson, T. Rymon, and S. Sen (1993): Cognition and framing in sequential bargaining for gains and losses, in: *Frontiers of game theory*, K. Binmore, A. Kirman, and P. Tani (eds.), Cambridge Mass.: MIT Press, 27 - 47.
12. Cournot, A. (1838): *Recherches sur les principes mathématiques de la théorie des richesses*, Paris: L. Hachette.
13. de Waal, F. (1982): *Chimpanzee politics*, London.
14. Dufwenberg, M. and W. Güth (1999): Indirect evolution versus strategic delegation: A comparison of two approaches to explaining economic institutions, *European Journal of Political Economy*, 15, 281 - 295.
15. Edgeworth, F. (1881): *Mathematical Psychics*, London: Kegean.
16. Fehr, E. and K. Schmidt (1999): A theory of fairness, competition and cooperation, *Quarterly Journal of Economics*, 114 (3), 817 - 68.
17. Festinger, L. (1957): *Theory of cognitive dissonance*, Evanston, Ill.: Roar.
18. Frank, B. (1996): The use of internal games: The case of addiction, *Journal of Economic Psychology*, 17, 651 - 660.
19. Franz, W. (1991): *Lohnbildung, Lohnrigiditäten und Lohnstrukturen*, in: Arbeitsmarktökonomie (Chapter 8), Berlin: Springer-Verlag.

20. Geanakoplos, J., D. Pearce, and E. Stacchetti (1989): Psychological games and sequential rationality, *Games and Economic Behavior*, 1 (1), 60 - 79.
21. Güth, W. (1976): Towards a more general analysis of von Stackelberg-situations, *Zeitschrift für die gesamte Staatswissenschaft*, 1976, 592 - 608.
22. Güth, W. (1994): Distributive justice - A behavioral theory and empirical evidence, in: *Essays on Economic Psychology*, H. Brandstätter and W. Güth (eds.), Berlin - Heidelberg: Springer-Verlag, 153 - 176.
23. Güth, W. (1995): On ultimatum bargaining - A personal review, *Journal of Economic Behavior and Organization*, 27, 329 - 344.
24. Güth, W., R. Schmittberger and B. Schwarze (1982): An experimental analysis of ultimatum bargaining, *Journal of Economic Behavior and Organization*, 367 - 388.
25. Güth, W. and B. Kalkofen (1989): Unique solutions for strategic games - Equilibrium selection based on resistance avoidance, *Lecture Notes in Economics and Mathematical Systems*, No. 328.
26. Güth, W. and R. Tietz (1990): Ultimatum bargaining behavior - A survey and comparison of experimental results, *Journal of Economic Psychology*, 11 (3), 417 - 449.
27. Güth, W., N. Marchand, J.-L. Rullière, R. Zeiliger (2000): Preempt to wait! An experimental study of endogenous timing in bargaining, *Discussion Paper 160,* Humboldt University of Berlin.
28. Güth, W, K. Ritzberger (2001): On the Nash Bargaining Solution with Noise, Max-Planck-Institut zur Erforschung von Wirtschaftssystemen, Jena.
29. Harsanyi, J. C. and R. Selten (1988): *A general theory of equilibrium selection in games*, Cambridge Mass: M.I.T. Press.
30. Hicks, J. R. (1949): *A Contribution to the theory of the trade cycle*, New York: Oxford University Press.
31. Holmstrom, B. R. (1979): Moral hazard and observability, *Bell Journal of Economics*, 10 (1), 74 - 91.
32. Homans, G. C. (1961): *Social behavior: Its elementary forms*, New York.
33. Kirchsteiger, G. (1994): The role of envy in ultimatum games, *Journal of Economic Behavior and Organization*, 25, 373 - 389.
34. Krelle, W. (1976): *Preistheorie, I. Teil: Monopol und Oligopoltheorie*, 2. Aufl., Tübingen: Mohr-Verlag.
35. Krelle, W. (1976): *Preistheorie, II. Teil: Theory des Polypols, des bilateralen Monopols (Aushandlungstheorie), Theorie mehrstufiger Märkte, gesamtwirtschaftliche Optimalitätsbedingungen*, Spieltheoretischer Anhang, 2. Aufl., Tübingen: Mohr-Verlag.
36. Malouf, M. W. K. and A. E. Roth (1981): Disagreement in bargaining. An experimental study, *Journal of Conflict Resolution*, 25, 329 - 348.
37. Maschler, M. (1978): Playing an n-person-game - An experiment, in: *Coalition Forming Behavior, Contributions to Experimental Economics*,Vol. 8, H. Sauermann (ed.), Tübingen: J. C. B. Mohr, 231 - 328.
38. Mautner - Markhof, F. (1989): *Processes of International Negotiations*, Boulder: Westview Press.
39. Modigliani, F. and R. Brumberg (1954): Utility analysis and the consumption function: An interpretation of cross-section data, *Post-Keysian Economics*, Keneth K. Kurihara (ed.), New Brunswick, N. J., Rudgers University.
40. Murnighan, J. K. (1991): *The dynamics of bargaining games*, Englewood Cliffs, N.J.: Prentice Hall.
41. Murnighan, J. K. (1992): *Bargaining games: A new approach to strategic thinking in negotiations*, William Morrow.

42. Nash, J. F. (1950): The bargaining problem, *Econometrica*, 18, 155 - 162.
43. Nash, J. F. (1953): Two-person cooperative games, *Econometrica*, 21, 128 - 140.
44. Nydegger, R. V. and G. Owen (1975): Two person bargaining: An experimental test of the Nash axioms, *International Journal of Game Theory*, 3, 239 - 349.
45. Ochs, J. and A. E. Roth (1989): An experimental study of sequential bargaining, *The American Economic Review*, 79, 355 - 384.
46. Osborne, M. J. and A. Rubinstein (1990): *Bargaining and markets*, San Diego, California: Academic Press.
47. Plato (1941): *The Republic of Plato*, translated by Francis MacDonald, Cornford/London/Oxford/New York: Oxford University Press.
48. Rabin, M. (1993): Incorporating fairness into game theory and economics, *American Economic Review*, 83, 1281 - 1302.
49. Raiffa, H. (1997): *Lectures on negotiation analysis*, Cambridge Mass.: Program on Negotiation Clearinghouse/Havard Law.
50. Rotemberg, J. (1994): Human relations in the workplace, Journal of Political Economy, 102 (4), 684 - 717.
51. Roth, A. E. (1995): Bargaining experiments, in: *Handbook of Experimental Economics*, J. H. Kagel and A. E. Roth (eds.), Princeton, N.J.: Princeton University Press, 253 - 348.
52. Rubinstein, A. (1982): Perfect equilibrium in a bargaining model, *Econometrica*, 50, 97 - 109.
53. Sachverständigenrat zur Begutachtung der gesamtwirtschaftlichen Entwicklung (1997): *Wachstum, Beschäftigung, Währungsunion – Orientierungen für die Zukunft*, Jahresgutachten 1997/98, Anhang: Tabelle A1 (S. 255): Produktionspotential, Bruttoinlandsprodukt und Auslastungsgrad, Stuttgart: Metzler-Poeschel.
54. Samuelson, P. (1939): Interactions between the multiplier analysis and the principle of acceleration, *Review of Economic Statistics*, 21, 75 - 78.
55. Sauermann, H. (1967 - 1978): *Contributions to experimental economics*, Vol. 1 - 8, Heinz Sauermann (ed.), Tübingen: J. C. B. Mohr.
56. Schmeidler, D. (1969): The nucleolus of a characteristic function game, *SIAM Journal of Applied Mathematics*, 17, 1163 - 1170.
57. Selten, R. (1978): The equity principle in economic behavior, in: *Decision Theory and Social Ethics, Issues in Social Choice*, H. Gottinger and W. Leinfellner (eds.), Dordrecht: Reidel, 289 - 301.
58. Selten, R. (1985): Equal division payoff bounds for 3-person characteristic function experiments, in: *Aspiration levels in bargaining and economic decision making*, R. Tietz, W. Albers, R. Selten (eds.), Berlin: Springer-Verlag, 265 - 275.
59. Selten, R. and W. Güth (1982): Game theoretical analysis of wage bargaining in a simple business cycle model, *Journal of Mathematical Economics*, 177 - 195.
60. Shapley, L. S. (1953): A value for n-person games, in: Contributions to the theory of games II, H. W. Kuhn and A. W. Tucker (eds.), *Annals of Mathematical Studies Series*, 28, Princeton, N.J.: Princeton University Press, 307 - 317.
61. Ståhl, I. (1972): *Bargaining theory*, Stockholm: Economic Research Institute.
62. van Damme, E. (1983): *Refinements of the Nash Equilibrium Concept*, Heidelberg, New York: Springer Verlag.
63. van Damme, E. and S. Hurkens (1999): Endogeneous Stackelberg Leadership, *Games & Economic Behavior*, 28 (1), 105 -29.
64. van Damme, E., R. Selten, and E. Winter (1990): Alternating bid bargaining with a smallest money unit, *Games & Economic Behavior*, 2 (2), 188 - 201.
65. von Neumann, J. and O. Morgenstern (1944): *Theory of games and economic behavior*, Princeton N.J.: Princeton University Press.

66. Wärneryd, K. (1993): Cheap talk, coordination, and evolutionary stability, *Games and Economic Behavior*, 5 (4), 532 - 546.
67. Weg, E, A. Rapoport, and D. S. Felsenthal (1990): Two-person bargaining behavior in fixed discounting factors games with infinite horizon, Games and Economic Behavior, 2, 76 - 95.
68. Young, G. A., Jr. (1986): Patterns of threat and punishment reciprocity in a conflict setting, *Journal for Personality of Social Psychology*, 51, 541 - 546.
69. Young, P. H. (1991): *Negotiation analysis*, Ann Arbor: University of Michigan Press.

3 Coalitions in Multilateral Negotiations

Aspirations, Agreements, and Outcomes

Axel Ostmann

Abstract. For most negotiations we can assume that participants or parties like to establish results more favourable than attainable without communication. In this survey it is assumed that all parties meet at one place to freely discuss how to establish cooperation by coalition formation and how to share the gains of cooperation. The formal analysis of the incentive structure of such settings is based on game theoretical methods including the field of cooperative game theory. Observations from a variety of experimental scenarios are compiled and evaluated. The experimental scenarios considered include characteristic function scenarios and matrix scenarios. For matrix scenarios we distinguish the binding agreement environment and the non-binding agreement environment.

3.1 A coalition game derived from a matrix game

A popular game-theoretical model for demonstrating efficiency losses in situations without the possibility to establish agreements is given by the famous prisonners' dilemma. Let me recall a symmetric multi-person version of this **matrix** (or normal form) **game**.

Table 3.1. 7-PD

	6C	5C	4C	3C	2C	1C	0C	
C	**6**	5	4	3	2	1	**0**	↓
D	7	6	5	4	3	2	**1**	⋆

There are two choices C and D for an individual actor. The entries in table 3.1 refer to payoffs. In case the actor's choice is C and he or she faces x C-choices of the partners the payoff is found in the cell (C, xC). Correspondingly payoffs in case of a D-choice are found in the D row of the table. It is clear (and indicated in the last column) that given any set of partners' choices D is a best reply guaranteeing the maximum payoff.

A vector of choices, the individual components of which are best reply to the vector of the remaining components, is called a (Nash-)equilibrium. In our case 7D is the only equilibrium. Individually there is no incentive to deviate from such a constellation. But the corresponding result with one unit payoff for everybody is highly inefficient. A choice vector maximising the sum of all individual payoffs is called welfare optimum. In our case the maximal total payoff can be attained for the choice vector 7C. This is why the C-choice often is called the cooperative choice.

Reading from the table and multiplying by 7 we find a total payoff of 42 at the welfare optimum and of 7 in equilibrium. Let us consider another payoff situation deriving from choices 5C. C-actors get 4 units each and D-actors 6. Total payoff is 32.

Let us now assume, that in a respective situation it would be possible to communicate before actors have to make choices. In this case the non-cooperative game-theoretical model has to be enriched with respective cooperative game-theoretical components. Meeting for a **round-table** actors may detect, that a group of cooperators can guarantee for ist members some value, whatever the outgroup may do. It is clear that in our case total per head is maximal for the grand coalition. Considering the case of five cooperators as above, we calculate a guaranteed value of 20 (this correspondts to the worst case scenario of the decision vector 5C).

Let us represent actors by elements of the set $N = \{1,\ldots,7\}$. Subsets of N are called coalitions. N itself is called the grand coalition. Similarly as above we get (alpha-)values $v_\alpha(S)$ for every coalition S, for our case summarised in table 3.2. An alpha-value represents what the respective coalition can guarantee to itself without the good will of its opposition.

A pair (N,v) of a grand coalition N and a so-called characteristic function v assigning a value to every subset of N is called a cooperative game or a **coalition game**. Up to (including) section 3.4 we deal with values that are numbers. This case is called the transferable utility (TU) case, because we assume that the members of a coalition S are free to distribute the amout $v(S)$ in shares whichever they agree upon. In a later section we also will deal with the more general non-transferable utility case.

Table 3.2. Characteristic function $v = v_\alpha$ derived from the 7-PD

$\#S$	0	1	2	3	4	5	6	7
v	0	1	2	6	12	20	30	42
$\partial_i v$		1	2	4	6	8	10	12

Let us return to our TU example with values being numbers. In the last row of table 3.2 entries show marginal values $\partial_i v$, i.e. the value added by one additional member. In our case we get a characteristic function which is convex, i.e. marginal values increase with coalition size. The convexity property is also typical for games derived from common pool resources and oligopolies (see [O9], this volume), and has important consequences for the availability and the properties of cooperative solutions.

In this chapter the question is rised how subjects deal with **laboratory situations** in which they have the task to negotiate for alliances and agreements under an incentive structure the coalitional issues of which can be represented by a coalitional game. Cooperative game theory is used to analyse the given incentive structure and to compare experimental results with theoretical standards. To my knowledge the first experiments dealing with a coalition game was Kalisch et al. in 1952 [KMNN].

Especially in social psychology there is a rich literature dealing with coalition games (cp. [CE]). Nevertheless it is not easy to compile the experiences made as it has been noted by Kahan and Rapoport 1984, p.249:

> "Creating an experimental game to study coalition formation behavior is no straightforward task, and virtually every investigator has his own idiosyncratic approach."

And Zwick & Rapoport 1985, p.345 add:

> "When several methodologies are employed, problems of comparison and integration arise, because the subjects interpretations of the task, their motivations, their aspirations, and consequently the ensuing negotiations are affected by the experimental formulation of the task."

The following report focuses on **experimental conditions** comparable to those stated in Selten 1972: full information, strong (monetary) motivation, one-shot play, face-to-face communication, open (=public), unrestricted, and unstructured communication, absence of precoalition commitment power. Let us refer to this framework as **standard conditions**. Sequencing procedures for bargaining, often implemented in computerised bargaining, usually show strategic features that may be better represented in extensive form modelling. In contrast to standard conditions restricted communication setups - restricting the type of communicative acts, the communication channels, the number of addressees, time pressure, etc. - introduce several obstacles to establish the cooperation; on the other side it is clear that under standard conditions beside the game structure communicative competences like talkativeness, personal characteristics like appearance, and socio-emotional behavioural directions like friendlyness may play an eminent role.

Refering to the computer-restricted communication conditions of for example the North Carolina research programm in the 70s Michener and Potter state ([MP], p.741):

> "The paradigm prevents subjects from communicating in their own terms, and it filters out meaning transmitted by subtle word choice, nonverbal gestures, and eye contact. These restrictions may prevent subjects from communicating their seriousness, their willingness (or unwillingness) to bargain flexibly, the finality of their offers, and the like."

Deciding under this statement for standard conditions has far reaching consequences for the recording during experiment and for the respective data analysis. If we are interested in explaining behaviour and the observed acts and results are not conform with specific game-theoretical concepts for an explanation of such variation we have to deal with verbal data and maybe with video records too.

Throughout this chapter coalition games are used to represent the incentive structure and the interdepence between conflict partners that meet for a multilateral face-to-face negotiation with public unrestricted communication. With the exception of subsection 3.4.2 it is also assumed that whenever the conflict partners establish an agreement the implementation of it will be guaranteed. The corresponding setting often is called a binding agreement or binding contract environment. But before we can deal with specific experimental setups in section two some basic concepts are introduced.

3.2 Basic concepts for coalition games

3.2.1 Proposals and arguments

A part of the negotiation process can be described in game-theoretical terms. Actors may claim, propose, agree or deny, and can exchange arguments. Proposals can be seen as potential agreements. In the coalition game model proposals and agreements are represented by pairs (S,x), S being a coalition and x an S–vector of numbers summing up to the value $v(S)$ of coalition S.

A common argument against (N,x) rises from $v(S) > \Sigma\{x(i); i \in S\}$ for some coalition S. In this case it can be said, that x means a loss for the members of S because they can guarantee themselves larger shares than according to x.

For any vector y let us define $y(S) := \Sigma\{y(i); i \in S\}$. With this definition the virtual loss refered in the above argument can be written as $e(x,S) := v(S) - x(S)$; usually $e(x,S)$ is called the excess of x at S.

The game-theoretic solution concept deriving from such kind of argumentation is the **core**. In this section let us restrict ourselves to the core for the grand coalition. This set is defined by the property "no loss" or formally:

$$C(v) := \{x \in N\text{–vector}; e(x,S) \leq 0 \text{ for all coalitions } S \text{ and } v(N) = x(N)\}. \quad (3.1)$$

Note "all coalitions" include the singletons: $v(\{i\}) \leq x(i)$.

Calculations refering to the uniquely solvable equation system

$$\{v(S) = q(S);\ \#S = n-1\} \quad (3.2)$$

for the so-called **quota** vector q show that individual claims $q(i)$, $i \in N$ can be based on "no loss" arguments too. Every core element x has to be weakly larger than q (formally: $q(i) \leq x(i)$ for all i). For our specific example, the 7-PD coalition game, the core is not empty - as it is for every convex game ("the maximum claim can be based on the largest coalitions"): the symmetric system $\{v(S) = 30; ...\}$ yields $q(i) = 5$ for every member. Since the value $v(N)$ of the grand coalition is larger than the sum $q(N)$ of the quotas all claims can be satisfied simultaneously. We get the core as convex hull of the N-vector of the exteme points of type "one individual gets all what remains" (5,...,5,12,5,...,5).

There are also important cases in which such claims cannot be satisfied simultaneously. The most simple cases derive from voting settings. More general, but generating the same class of games ("**weighted majority games**"), are scenarios in which actors i are endowed with maybe different amounts of a resource $m(i)$ and in which a cooperative or a team S has to have a joint amount $m(S) := \Sigma\{m(i); i \in S\}$

surpasing a certain threshold μ at its disposal to become productive. The simplest example is the three person majority game $(\mu;m) = (2;1,1,1)$: for a positive decision, two of the three individual votes are needed. The game induced—$v(S) = 1$ whenever $\#S > 1$ and $v(S) = 0$ in the other cases—shows quotas of one half each and an empty core correspondingly (such claims cannot be satisfied simultaneously). Similarly every weighted majority game has the empty core property excepted those in which single can veto a decision.

In case of an empty core negotiators have to present other kinds of arguments that open a way out. Two possible solutions may come into mind. First, what about smaller coalitions to form? Second, what about compromising by accepting some fairly balanced loss?

Suppose a **non-grand coalition** is about to be formed. In case of an empty core the opposition (i.e. the out-group) always can entice some members from the former coalition. No coalition is stable if everybody can be persuade to leave a coalition by offering a larger payoff. Since we can observe in corresponding instable situations small and effective coalitions (for example a minimal winning coalition of a weighted majority game) are formed it is at least in part an empirical task to detect by what rules the chains of proposals can be brought to a stop. Note that in case of an empty core also the following is true: the most effective coalitions are also the most instable ones, i.e. the ones with the smallest number of members to move to the opposition. An outline, motivation, and discussion of rules explaining observed chains of proposals can be found in [Al2].

The second idea is to rely on another standard of argumentation: searching for a **fair compromise**. Let us assume that this compromise is searched for the grand coalition. Game theory provides different concepts for such a task. Here let us only deal with the kernel and the nucleolus. Both concepts are also based on the above virtual losses $e(x,S)$. In case of the search for the nucleolus the decreasingly ordered 2^n-vector of losses for all coalitions is lexicographically minimised. The result is an unique N-vector called the nucleolus. By construction the nucleolus has the property to simultaneously minimising losses. In case of the kernel the idea is to balance losses within all possible pairs of partners. After balancing, nobody can reproach somebody with getting an advantage compared to oneself. Let $T(i,j)$ be the set of coalitions such that i is member in S but j not. Moreover let $s(i,j,x) := \max\{e(x,S); S \in T(i,j)\}$. Then refering to the respective maximiser can be interpreted as i's "best argument" against j. In case $s(i,j,x) > s(j,i,x)$ the actor represented by i can feel disadvantaged. The kernel is defined (here only for the grand coalition) as the set of all vectors that are without such advantages or in case of an advantage of i over j this has to be justified by a share $x(j)$ of j that cannot be lowered because its equality to j's individual value $v(\{i\})$. It can be shown that the nucleolus is element of the kernel. In case of an non-empty core the kernel is a subset of the core.

All classical game-theoretic solution concepts (with maybe the exception of the von Neumann solution) are based on a kind of negative thinking or say stability test. Payoff constellations are tested if they could serve as solution. For the core positive excesses are valid objections, for the kernel the lack of balance. A more sophisticated mechanism of objections and counter-objections is characterising the solution concept bargaining set.

As mentioned before weighted majority games can be seen as threshold production games with one resource. Before ending this subsection let us consider an example of another simple game (coalition games are called **simple** if the characteristic function only allows for two different values, in the TU-context usually normalised to 0 and 1, interpreted as losing and winning, inproductive and productive, etc.). In this game we refer to 6 actors, $N = \{A, B, ..., F\}$ and to two resources say fertile soil (land) and water. Production is possible if at least one unit water and five units land are at disposal. Table 3.3 shows the endowment of the actors:

Table 3.3. "Water and land"

	A	B	C	D	E	F
water	1	0	0	0	0	1
land	2	3	2	1	1	0

A coalition S is winning ($v(S) = 1$) if one of the following minimal winning coalition is enclosed in S: AB, ACD, ACE, BCF, BDEF. Calculations show that the kernel contains only one point, the nucleolus, which is given by (2,3,2,1,1,0)/9. Note that F's share according to the nucleolus is zero. It is clear that in negotiations nobody in such a rôle would accept a zero payoff. On the other side it is clear that in a chain of proposals F's opponents for every positive value can argue for lowering F's share. In our case the opponents can do it without F, but there are extreme games - games with veto players - in which the strong players need to get the cooperation of players that get a zero-share according to all these standard concepts: core, kernel, nucleolus. As an example consider the smallest veto game: $N = \{A, B, C\}$ and minimal winning coalitions AB and AC. All of the above mentioned types of argumentation allow for a ruinous competition between the both weak ones.

3.2.2 Coalition structure and final results

An agreement or contract (x, S) is not the adequate concept to describe a result of a negotiation. Usually a result is represented by a so-called payoff configuration $(x, \underline{B})$ specifying an n-vector of individual payoffs and a coalition structure $\underline{B}$ satisfying $v(B) = x(B)$ for all coalitions $B \in \underline{B}$ (a coalition structure is a set of disjoint coalitions the union of which is the grand coalition). Behind this definition there is the idea that every negotiator can sign at most one contract. In these terms **breakoffs** without any agreement can be represented by the pair $(\underline{v}, \underline{I})$, $\underline{v} := (v(\{1\}), ..., v(\{n\}))$ and $\underline{I} := \{\{1\}, ..., \{n\}\}$. In $(\underline{v}, \underline{I})$ everybody stays alone and receives the corresponding individual base value ($\underline{v}$ sometimes is called threat point).

Grand coalition agreements (x, N) can be easily transformed in results $(x, \underline{N})$, $\underline{N} := \{N\}$. A game is said to exhibit the **one-stage property** if all payoffs are determined whenever one (non-trivial, feasible) contract is signed. In such a case the contract (y,S) can be translated into $((y,\underline{v}_{N-S}),\underline{S})$, $\underline{S} := \{S\} \cup \{\{i\}; i \in N-S\}$. Examples of such games are all three-person games and all superadditive simple games (a game is superadditive if a merger of two disjoint coalitions has a larger value than the sum before). In games without the one-stage property it can be argued that the order of the agreements which constitute the coalition structure may exert a considerable strategic influence. The first contract (x,S) alters the incentive structure between the remaining partners in so far as they may lose important alternatives dependent on some members on S.

Solution concepts (both set- and point-valued) refering to the grand coalition have been generalised for other coalition structures (see [AD]). The solution elements w.r.t. a specific coalition structure now have to be payoff configurations with the same coalition structure as second component.

As a first example let us consider the nucleolus for the weighted majority game $(\mu;m) = (4;3,1,1,1,1)$ - called 5-person apex game. By using the one-stage property we can restrict our calculations to 5 types of winning coalitions S and the induced coalition structures $\underline{S}$. In table 3.4 the nucleolus for the coalition structures $\underline{S}$ are listed (shares for outsiders are zero).

Table 3.4. Nucleolus of the 5-apex game for coalition structures $\underline{S}$

m(S)	7	6	5	4	4
weights within S	(3,1,1,1,1)	(3,1,1,1)	(3,1,1)	(3,1)	(1,1,1,1)
nucleolus	(3,1,1,1,1)/7	(3,1,1,1)/6	(1,1,1)/3	(1,1)/2	(1,1,1,1)/4

Beside the classical game-theoretical solution concepts (core, bargaining set, kernel, nucleolus) especially experimentalists have introduced several other solution concepts in order to get a better fit with observed behaviour. The most simple of these concepts are the **equal share** and the **equal surplus** solutions. Both concepts are single valued for every coalition structure. For equal share we assume that we forget about all possible arguments that can be found for differentiating between coalition members. Formally: $(x,\underline{B})$ is an equal share solution iff $x(i) = 1/\#B$ for $i \in B \in \underline{B}$. Instead of forgetting about all subcoalitional arguments the equal surplus solution forgets about all coalitional arguments but the one-member arguments, i.e. the individual values $v(\{i\})$. By expanding the base vector of individual values $\underline{v}$ to a game (let us call this game the **base measure**)

$$\underline{v}(S) := \Sigma\{\underline{v}(i); i \in S\} \tag{3.3}$$

we can decompose a given game v into the base measure $\underline{v}$ and the **surplus game** v' (usually called normalised game): $v = \underline{v} + v'$. In this notation the equal surplus solution is the sum of the base vector and the equal share solution of the surplus game. In contrast to equal shares the equal surplus solution respects the (minimum) standard of "individual rationality" (nobody should be worser off than what (s)he will get without any cooperation).

As an **example** let us consider the following three-person game:

$$\underline{v} = (8,10,24), v(\{1,2\}) = 98, v(\{1,3\}) = 68, v(\{2,3\}) = 48, v(N) = 148, \quad (3.4)$$

or in short: $v = [8,10,24,98,68,48,148]$. We get

$$q = (59,39,9) \quad \text{and} \quad v' = [0,0,0,80,36,14,106]. \quad (3.5)$$

The quotas q' of the surplus game are $q' = (51,29,-15)$. Note that the third quota is negative.

Kernel (but also the nucleolus) are based on **excess balancing**. For the kernel (of the grand coalition) we can get a sequence of sets of coalitions, that are used as best arguments (i.e. showing the largest excesses). In our example the kernel (for the grand coalition) coincides with the nucleolus (65.5,45.5,37).

Table 3.5. Excesses for the grand coalition nucleolus (65.5,45.5,37)

S	{1}	{2}	{3}	{1,2}	{1,3}	{2,3}	N
e(S,.)	-57.5	-35.5	-13	-13	-34.5	-34.5	0

Table 3.5 shows the maximal excess -13 for both the so-called precoalitions $\{1,2\}$ and $\{3\}$; these coalitions are refered to for balancing between the "disputing" pairs $\{1,3\}$ and $\{2,3\}$. The second balancing for the "internally disputing" precoalition $\{1,2\}$ uses the other pair coalitions as best arguments showing an excess of -34.5.

The kernel relies on a characteristic **hierarchical group structure**. It can be generated by starting with the coalition structure of "precoalitions" balancing the maximal excess between individuals of different precoalitions, and refining it step by step (cp. [DM]). The members of a precoalition have common arguments against outsiders. For refining one considers the internal game (usually called reduced game) for each coalition of the structure until all pairs of individuals have found their best arguments. Let us interpret the maximal excess used in a step for pairwise dispute as the step's typical concession level. Then the process starts with the largest concessions to balance and reduces the concession level until all pairwise disputes are solved.

Table 3.6. Nucleolus, equal share and equal surplus

Coalition structure	nucleolus	equal share	equal surplus
$\underline{I}$	(8,10,24)	(8,10,24)	(8,10,24)
$\underline{12}$	(59,39,24)	(49,49,24)	(48*,50*,24)
$\underline{13}$	(44,10,24)	(34,10,34)	(26,10,42)
$\underline{23}$	(8,24,24)	(8,24,24)	(8,17,31)
$\underline{N}$	(65.5*,45.5*,37*)	(49.3*,49.3*,49.3*)	(43,45,59*)

If we interpret a solution concept for coalition structures as an accepted standard how to share the total values it is near at hand to assume that an individual choses the most profitable coalition structure. In table 3.6 these choices are marked by a star. Shenoy [She] examined the respective dynamics if transitions from one coalition structure to another one are motivated by rising individual profits. Considering the attractors of such a process we can interpret the respective coalition structure as **propagated** by the argumentation mode / solution concept under consideration.

Let us call a coalition structure maximal (or exhaustive) if the sum of the values of its coalitions is the maximum attainable for coalition structures. It is easy to show that the core for non-maximal coalition structures is empty. For the core all coalition structures with non-empty core are equivalent and propagated. Other solution concepts show a more complicate behaviour.

Note that in our example for the equal surplus solution the non-maximal coalition structure $\underline{12}$ of the strong pair is propagated. Strong pair? Note that at first glance, i.e. according to the base values the first actor is poorest, but if we apply a concept of strength, based on the surplus values we get the inverse order. After [KMNN] and until [KR1] (in 1977, with computer-restricted communication) there had been no more experiments reported with games that have non-zero base values and more than two actors. The idea that it would be enough to deal zero base values only goes back to an important property of all classical solution concepts the so-called invariance with respect to positive affine transformations of money or in short the strategic invariance. For a given game v, a N–vector m (that is expanded to the measure m by $m(S) = \Sigma\{m(i); i \in S\}$) and some positive number a let us define the transform w of v by $w(S) := av(S) + m(S)$. A solution concept is **strategically invariant** if for all such transforms w the solution concept L evaluated for any coalition structure fulfills the equation $L(w) = aL(v) + m$. The interpretation of this property is that the solution does not depend on the chosen money unit and that it is equivalent to add amounts of money within the game or outside. For a strategically invariant solution concept it is enough to know all solutions of games with zero base values. For all other games we can use the equation $L(v) = \underline{v} + L(v')$. Note that the non-classical equal surplus solution is strategically invariant too.

Strategic invariance is not a valid assumption for real negotiation behaviour as it has been shown in different experiments (we discuss this issue in section 3.3.2) and judgement studies (cp. [Shu] and [WS]). An old idea for explaining the observed significant deviations from strategic invariance is that during the argumentation process the weak rely more on equality standards while the strong prefer power-inclined standards (Uhlich [U] cites from Aristotle's politeia: "equality and justice are always sought by the weaker party, but those who have the upper hand pay no attention to them"). In the literature there are some solution concepts refering to such kinds of disputes with inhomogenous argumentation standards, for example the "bargaining theory" of Komorita and Chertkoff [KC] and Selten's equal division payoff bounds [S3].

Another not strategically invariant solution concept that homogeniously combines excess and equal division arguments is the equal division core introduced by Selten [S1] (cp. [FO]). Alternatively to solution concepts limited rationality approaches provide simple rules to follow for building coalitions and for sharing gains. There are for example the rule to prefer the maximal coalition structure (exhaustion hypothesis) or the order of strength rule for the distribution within a coalition, that forbids that a weaker one receives more than a stronger one (note that not always it is clear how and on what scale to measure "strength") (cp. [S1]).

3.2.3 Aspirations and sequencing of proposals

Attending a face-to-face negotiation relying on a coalition game we usually observe large parts of conversation without any specification of individual shares (cp. [O3]). Nevertheless at some time negotiators typically have to reveal aspirations either directly by claiming or indirectly by accepting or making a proposal. During the bargaining process we usually observe (incompatibly) high initial aspirations and a decrease of individual revealed aspirations with time until some compromise becomes possible. Hidden aspirations like what a person plans to achieve or what is her minimum acceptable usually are not observable for the negotiation partners and observers without additional information sources.

There are several trials to explain the sequencing of proposals (and acceptances and rejections). In contrast to the arguments implicit in the classical solution concepts for sequencing it is to specify what proposal comes next and what terminates the process. In Albers' theory of "ten rules" [Al2] a central element is that proposals are made with reference to "attributed demands" a kind of perceived partners' aspirations. In the simulated proposal sequences of [O6] (locally) best counter-proposals are constructed based on similar updated (revealed) aspirations and hidden minimum aspirations, that limit the possible concessions.

For experimental studies there are some tools to get the additional information on hidden aspirations. Questionnaires can be used before, after, or during the negotiation. When the negotiation is organised in rounds the questionnaires can be extended to written planning report as introduced by Tietz [T]. Beside asking the subjects to fill in a questionnaire we can also observe groups preparing the negotiation rounds. In such a groups setting representatives of the groups meet for bargaining. The representatives are endowed with (for the experimenter) observable hidden aspirations, arguments, and strategies as provided by their groups. The preparing groups technique was used by Hennig-Schmidt for 2-person games [HS2] and by Ostmann, Henss, and Momper [O3] for 3-person games. Bargaining with representatives are usually found to bargain more competitively than nonrepresentatives (cp. [CE], p.477 and [O7] for 3-person characteristic function games) - this may be an effect of the better understanding and preparation, but also of the expectations of the constituents represented as perceived by the representative.

3.3 Characteristic function setups

3.3.1 Committees and other simple games

Nearly all experiments reported are carried out under non-standard conditions (multiplay, restricted communication, and/or non-standard motivation; a discussion how multiplay may alter results, behaviour and norms introduced can be found in [Ko]). Often the conflict scenarios are presented as voting scenarios in a parlament, a company stockholder meeting, or some other committee session. In these experimental scenarios the number of votes becomes focal and usually subjects have to collect some experience until they adapt to the hidden power structure. Different **resource distributions** (and adequate thresholds) can induce the same game. It can be observed the more unexperienced the subjects are the more influencial the given resource distribution becomes for the final result. Especially if subjects in roles that are game-theoretically symmetric get a different payoff or a different chance to be included in a winning coalition then such a difference has no base in the game structure.

Several empirical solution theories focus on the resource distribution given. For example: The famous minimal resource theory of Gamson 1961 [G1] states that there is a norm for deviding the rewards in direct proportion to resources. Moreover, since every person is assumed to maximise his or her share only minimal winning coalitions should be selected.

A large number of experiments are based on a **restricted coalition set** (often motivated by the prejudice of preference for minimal winning coalitions, but sometimes also by practical reason to make the number of coalitions to list shorter). Let $\underline{B}$ be the set of coalitions allowed and v the game given, then $w = v|\underline{B}$ denotes the game defined by $w(S) = v(S)$ if $S \in \underline{B}$ and $w(S) = 0$ in the other case. The usual practice in the early experiments is to formally analyse v while in the experiment subject are confronted with $v|\underline{M}$ or $v|\underline{M}'$, $\underline{M}$ being the set of minimal winning coalitions and $\underline{M}' = \underline{M} \cup \{N\}$. In such a setting it is impossible to use arguments that refer to oversided alternative coalitions. The drastic reduction of alternatives can alter the structure and the solutions of the game considerably (cp. below).

Considering the early reviews [G2] and [KC] it becomes clear that a satisfactory theory was lacking and that there is a strong need for a game-theoretic analysis of the conflict situation imposed on the subjects. The literature of the early days of experimental simple games is full of interesting examples of games with a large variety of different properties. It is also interesting to read how different bargaining strength can be conceptualised (cp. [Ko1], [Mu]). In the following I restrict the attention to the three most frequently used sets of the games considered. These three set are extreme cases with respect to the power distribution: equality, all weak but one, and dependency.

Our first set of games to consider is the set of **simple majority games** $maj(n) = (k; 1, ..., 1)$, $k = (n/2) + 1$ for even n and $k = (n+1)/2$ for odd n. The first series of experiments with $maj(3)$ are reported in [KA] showing that in repeated play subjects adapt more and more to the game-theoretic structure leaving resource illusion. For an even number of players the game is not constant sum, that means it may happen that both the coalition and its opposition are not winning (there some consequences deriving from this fact, esp. concerning the von Neumann solution, cp. [DM], [BW1], and [BW3]). For such a fully symmetric setting often equal treatment solutions are predicted. Contrary to that prediction Buckley and Weston found for n=5 that under face-to-face conditions unequal payoff divisions often occur (29%) and many oversized equal-split agreements are reached (52%) (see [BW4] p.488, cp. [BW2]). Whereas in the non-constant sum case some unequal distributions can also be rationalised by the bargaining set and the von Neumann solution, in this case a justifying game theoretic rationale is not at hand. It is the very merit of the "ten rules" theory of Albers (see [Al2]) that it can explain the unequal treatment between symmetric players in a minimal winning coalition.

A second set of experimental games studied is the set of **apex games** $apex(n) = (n-1; n-2, 1, ..., 1), n > 3$. For apex games the number of minimal winning coalitions is equal to the number of players: every small player "generates" the two person coalition by adding the strong player. The n-th minimal winning coalition is built by all small players. A famous example of a corresponding situation is found for the vote distribution of the last freely elected German Reichstag with Hitler's NSDAP being the strongest player. The game is (324; 288,119,81,73,52,19,6,4,4) = (4;3,1,1,1,1,0,0,0,0) or by deleting dummies simply $apex(5)$.

In the experiments refering to an apex game a resource- or say **contribution-effect** can be observed. For example: Nail and Cole [NC] report for the version (10;8,6,3,2) that the share of the strong varies with the contribution of the partner: forming a coalition with the 6 votes partner results in a 60% share for the strong, with a 3 votes partner in 66% and with the 2 votes partner in 70%. The consequence of such a resource illusion is that coalitions with a costly weak partner are less frequent than coalitions with cheap weak partners (relative frequencies: 0.10, 0.275, 0.425). It is also noticable that in apex games the coalition of the weak is less frequently formed as the mean of the frequency of other minimal winning coalitions (in [NC] 20% with considerable inequalities in payoff).

A second effect reported is the **positional power effect**. The term was introduced by [FRK] to point to the fact that in most games considered a higher number of distinct (non-zero valued, here: winning) coalitions a player may join in guarantees as well to become more frequently included as to get a larger share. In contrary to the contribution effect the positional power effect refers to properties of the game only.

A more refined game-theoretic analysis of the apex games can be found in [Al1]. Refering to an limited rationality approach considering the sequencing of proposals the "ten rules" of Albers [Al2] provide **alternative explanations** of the observed unequal payoff distributions in the coalition of the weak.

Veto games are games with a group of players T that has to be always included in all winning coalitions. The simplest veto games, symmetric and with one veto-player only, are given by $veto(n) = (n+1; n, 1, ..., 1)$. Here the core is single-valued and assignes zero-values for the weak contributors ($core = \{(1,0,...,0)\}$). The situation is an analoge to the extreme dependency in non-cooperative ultimatum games. In such a game (see Güth, this volume). In the simplest version of this game one of the two bargaining partners proposes a distribution (x, y) of a certain amount, say $100 = x + y$. Afterwards the other conflict partner has only the opportunity to accept his share y or to reject. In case of rejection both partners receive nothing. As for the veto-games it can be argued that the strong has to give away only the smallest money unit to the weak for ensuring cooperation. Empirically in both situations results are far from such a normative solution: in most case the weak reject to accept a share larger than 70% for the strong one; and most subjects in the strong role propose less than 70% for themselves. In our cooperative environment we should also consider the fact that forming a union of the weak would transform the game into the symmetric unanimity game with two players, making the union as strong as the veto player before. Even if in our environment **merging** is a non-binding agreement, under the condition of unrestricted face-to-face communication partners may succeed in forming such an union and correspondingly in transforming the game. Up to now there is no game-theoretic bargaining model that includes such more or less informal possibilities to alter the power distribution by merging. In [MuS] experiments with a set of four games with one veto-player varying the (merging) power of the weak was considered. Under secret and restricted communication and multi play conditions the strong received a share of about 90%.

At the end of this section let us consider again the game induced by "water and land". The induced game was introduced by Kravitz [Kr] for an experiment carried out with coalition opportunities restricted to the set of minimal winning coalitions. The game was constructed to distiguish the effect of different sources of strength (cp. also KrI). Under standard conditions the respective game without restrictions was used in [O3], [O4], [O5], and [O7].

Table 3.7. "Water and land"

	A	B	C	D	E	F
min-win included	3	3	3	2	2	2
win included	22	21	18	15	15	16

Comparing pairs of players by strength one may detect (for the unrestricted game) that beside the symmetric pair {DE} all players are of different type. Based on the desirability relation (i is at least as desirable as j if and only if for all coalitions $S\ N-\{i,j\}$ the value for i joining is equal or larger as for j, formally $v(S+i) \geq v(S+j)$) the pairs {A,B}, {C,F}, {D,F}, {E,F}. A and B are strong of different type, F is dependent on B (in the sense that F has no alternative minimal winning coalition without B). D and E are weaker than C. All these relations cannot be represented by a simple count as shown in table 3.7. In consequence for games like this one simply looking for a positional power effect is not the adequate approach. The grand-coalition kernel/nucleolus for this game is (2,3,2,1,1,0)/9 (as in veto games the weak gets nothing) and other cardinal game-theoretical measures of strength can be derived from value-concepts like the Banzhaf- and the Shapley-value. But also refined game-theoretical concepts provide no explanation of the variety of results observed. In [O3] and [O5] simulation techniques based on initial and minimum aspirations are used to generate sequences of proposals, acceptances and rejections until a winning coalition has formed. The very shortcoming of the stylised negotiation process is that in contrary to the observed result over-sized coalitions are almost never formed. In table 3.8 a typical example of an observed sequence of proposals is shown. All of the herein shown proposals refer to oversized coalitions.

Table 3.8. Observed proposals ([O3] p. 258)

proposer	A	B	C	D	E	F
E	40		20	20	20	
B	33	33	33			
A	30	30	30			10
...						
B	40	20	40			
D	37		37	13	13	

Over-sized coalitions generate unnecessarily large losses (excesses), but often have the advantage that they are not so easy to destabilise from outside. The transition from B's first proposal to A's shows no dominance, i.e. payoffs of the members of the new coalition are not in all cases larger than before (this fact contradicts as well classical dynamic concepts as Albers' rule 1 [A2] (bargaining chain)). In our case C or/and D would have to entice away two of the respective partners. Finally they succeed in doing so by refering to an older proposal of E, reducing their aspirations, and acting in solidarity with each other. This behaviour is in the spirit of Albers' rule 4 (sympathy refering to a loyal group). Also for games like this one it has to be asked if players by merging may succeed in transforming the game considerably.

An alternative theory of the possible advantage of oversized coalitions was given by Peleg. In two studies on coalition formation in community parlaments Peleg shows how a dominant player by striving for an oversized coalition can restrain the internal opposition ([P1], [P2]).

In several studies preference structure was added to a simple game. Representing political parties in a one-or multi-dimensional ideological space or issue space, the coalition has to formulate shares to receive by its member indirectly by agreeing to a joint policy that is represented as point or location in the issue space. Experiments with such games have been reported in [AL].

3.3.2 Trilateral and some larger TU games

The large part of experience with TU games has been summarised in the book of Kahan and Rapoport (1984). But most of these experiments have not been carried out under standard conditions, but computer-restricted with subjects separated. Experimental series with unrestricted face-to-face communication are reported in [Ma], [LW], [O6], and [MM1]. The series of [LW] and [MM1] deviate from standard conditions by multiple play (a sequence of 6 resp. of 9 games) and in case of [MM1] by non-monetary motivation.

How the different solution concepts operate on the space of all 3-person games is relatively easy to establish. As shown in [O6] there are not many "types" of games that can be distinguished by precoalition hierarchies of the kernel and by Shenoy's coalition dynamics for the core and the kernel (in total 12 regular types). Experimentally used games cluster in only one of the four regions w.r.t. kernel precoalition dynamics: the case of "quota" games in which the kernel distributes the reminder $v(N) - q(N)$ equally. This case is endowed with a flat hierarchy, just $\underline{N}$ (best arguments are the three pair coalitions). Before the Saarbrücken series 1983-86 (see [O6]) there was not much experience with the cases "two against one" (exceptions: 14 games of type B in an unpublished series of Stoecker and Selten; 14 games of type D, 7 games of type C, and 4 games of type BD in [Ma]).

The general finding was that if available agreements are core solutions. Exception: games equivalent to the simple game veto and other extreme cases. The stylised facts for type C (cf. [O7], p. 95f) are:

a. the smaller the value of the grand coalition, the higher the frequency of pair coalitions, ceteris paribus;
b. the grand coalition is prefered also in case a superadditive game with empty core (types C-ds and C-dc according to [O7]); note that arguing for the inefficient grand coalition has the advantage that nobody has to fear to become excluded and by emptyness of the core every pair agreement can be destabilised from outside;
c. the strongest player is nearly never excluded, but has to pay a price: nearly always the share received is less than prescribed by the kernel; the weakest is the most frequenty excluded player;
d. payoffs in the grand coalition can be approximated by compromising between fairness and equality ([LW] reports a best fit for 0.25 kernel + 0.75 equality for a set of 52 different quota games).

The recently published results of experiments of Michener and Myers with nine different superadditive games showing an empty core (type C-ds) are in line with the above stylised facts only with respect to the coalition structure and not with respect to payoffs. About half of the observed coalition structures are pair structures (155 of 324), and in only 22 of them the strong player is isolated. Remarkably payoffs show only small deviations from the kernel.

Already the early experiments of [KMNN] use games with non-zero values. The first systematic explorations of games with non-zero base values are reported in [KT] and [KR1] (the first setup deviates from standard conditions by triple play, the second also by computerised restricted communication). While [KT] found no significant differences within the sets of strategically equivalent games [KR1] compared strategically equivalent variants showing clear differences, but also some irregularities not easy to interpret. The design of [KR1] compares two strategically equivalent variants of 5 games; the corresponding systematic variation concerns the relation of the order of base values and the order of quotas: "In variation S (same relationship) the values of the 1-person coalition were set in direct relationship to the players' quotas ... In variation R (reversed relationship) the inverse relationship was used" ([KR1] p.102). In [He] Henss reanalysed the [KR1] data by considering the relation of base-value order and normalised quotas, interpreted as "pure bargaining strength". Using this "normalised" definition of strength the stilised facts given above can be extended without irregularities: the strongest players is seldomly excluded and has to sacrifice some share of the normatively substantiated payoff for becoming member. Moreover the amount to sacrifice is less under the condition S than under R. Indeed the Saarbrücken data reported in [O7] strongly support these rules (cp. hypotheses RO and RI ibd.).

In a series of papers Selten compared data from different data sets including face-to-face settings ([S1], [SKr], [S4], [S7]). The respective meta-analyses largely rely on measuring the success of a variety of descriptive set-valued solution concepts (for a discussion of the properties of the respective measure of success see [Ra] and [S5]).

Adding one more player makes the theoretic analysis a much harder task. Thus it would be fine to detect a simple limited rationality rule that governs a great deal of results observed. Indeed,

> "in many coalition experiments, the coalition with the largest payoff per member occurs most frequently, and the reward division is close to an equal split" ([MK], p.721).

Suggested by this observation an easy rule of thumb for predicting results would be the rule "maximising equal shares" (MES rule, cp. [MK] and [S1]). Despite some support for this rule for some games it was also reported that "such coalitions are not always most frequent, however, and payoff divisions deviate considerably from equal shares" ([MK], p.721).

Admitting multiple values for a formerly (restricted) simple game we can easily design interesting characteristic functions. In such a way in the literature generalised apex games are introduced. Such games are multivalued, but only apex coalitions - minimal winning in the apex simple game - have non-zero values. Formally for $apex(n)$ as base game and a "quota" n-vector q by $w(S) := q(S)(apex(n)|M)(S)$ a generalised apex game w is defined (in short: $w = apex(n) * q$). Such games have been studied by [FRK], [Mil], and [MK]. Miller and Komorita [MK] consider a generalised 4-person apex game under non-standard conditions (restricted communication multi play) varying the procedures used. In contrary to the prediction of the bargaining theory of [KC], of the multi play equal excess theory [Ko2], and of the MES rule a strong bias towards the small coalitions was observed. Evidently under certain conditions even inefficient small coalitions are prefered. A theory that may explain the large number of small coalitions and the unequal distribution in the larger coalition of the symmetric players is Albers' theory of "ten rules" for bargaining sequences [Al2]. Nevertheless we can also ask if the small coalition preference is due to the procedure. We may assume that the face-to-face condition would give a fairer chance to build up also larger coalitions.

For the following let us restrict our attention to superadditive games only. For 4-person games the kernel has no more to be single-valued. In fact, exactly for the precoalition hierarchy starting with two pairs as precoalitions the kernel differs from the nucleolus. The full list of cases to distinguish for the kernel and the nucleolus can be found in [Br2] (the author distiguishes 103 cases).

In a recent article [MM2] Michener and Myers present experiments with a set of 24 different 4-person games varying asymmetry (low, high) , existence of core (no, yes), and a third variable with 6 levels. Calculating the quotas for these games reveals that the third variable varies the degree of asymmetry within the strongest pair (6 levels), and that in case of non-empty core the smallest quota becomes negative. The family of games used contains games of different depth of the kernel induced hierarchy. All games with empty core belong to the so-called quota game type (type B2 according to [Br2]) showing a balancing dispute of one step only, let us write [1|2|3|4]. The games with non-empty core start the kernel precoalition hierarchy with "three against one". With the exception of two games (low asymmetry, game 5 and 6) the second step consists in a "two against one" confrontation (type L1 and L5 according to [Br2]), so that a third step is needed to determine the shares of the two strong players ([1|2||3|||4]). For the two exception games the process ends with the second step ([1|2|3||4] and type Q5).

Let us define as 1st level solution the coalition structure propagated by the classical solution concepts, here $\underline{N}$. Turning to a limited rationality view we can assume that in some cases people will not succeed in solving a subdebate. In such a case we can assume that the respective coalition cannot be formed, and instead some best alternative (a reference coalition of maximal excess) will be formed. At the 2nd level coalition $\{1,2,3\}$ may be agreed upon. Q and L differ in the coalitions built at the 3rd level: whereas for Q all other three-person coalitions may come into being for L only $\{1,2,4\}$ or $\{3,4\}$ can be built (coalition structures: $\underline{3}, \{\{1\},\{2\},\{3,4\}\}$ and $\{\{1,2\},\{3,4\}\}$). In table 3.9 we consider the coalition structures reported in [MM2].

Table 3.9. Observed coalition structure

Coalition structures	1st level: $\underline{N}$	$\underline{4}$	$\underline{3}$	$\underline{2}$	$\underline{1}$	others
empty	91	40	10	1	1	1
L1	72	20	3	-	-	1
L5	20	3	-	-	-	1
Q5	21	2	1	-	-	-

Table 3.10. Realised level of coalition structure

Coalition structures	1st level	2nd level	3rd level	others
empty core	91 (1)	52 (4)	-	1 (10)
non-empty core	113 (1)	25 (1)	5 (3)	1 (10)

In brackets: number of admissible coalition structures

The aim of the article [MM2] is to provide a new and better theory for predicting the probability of coalition structures. Instead of dealing with the induced coalition dynamics for older and more classical solution concepts the authors deal with a the new theory (central union) for fitting their data. Nevertheless compared to other theories they introduce some interesting limited rationality concepts.

1. Actors are assumed to form *aspirations depending on the coalition* to join by considering best alternatives refering to the maximal possible marginal value $\partial_i v$.
2. Similarly as for the kernel actors first determine the payoff distribution between the coalitions and afterwards determine the internal distribution.
3. Payoff satisfaction is measured as the received proportion of aspiration. (Remember, the classic concept used for measuring payoff satisfaction refers to the excess e(x,S)).
4. Not all coalition structures can form. Candidates have to be build out of triad: a "central union", a set of potential new members for an "extended union", and the set of the remaining or excluded actors. For being a central union a coalition has show some kind of maximal attractiveness. For being potential new members these actors should not reduce the attractiveness of the coalition.
5. The probability of forming a coalition structure is proportional to the overall acceptance (for the remaining set of candidates). The overall acceptance is a decreasing function of the total of pairwise differences in payoff satisfaction.

The task to predict results is quite different from the task to understand the rules of bargaining. The appeal of limited rationality theory does not lie in the more accurate prediction but in the identification of conditioned rules that drive the process. The appeal of the normative solution theories lies in that they provide standards of comparison and descibe possible consequences by a riguorous analysis of the incentive and interdependence structure. In my view it makes no sense to mix the different tasks. ...

For predicting much simpler "theories" can yield similar goodness-of-fit / deviation scores.

An example for a simple alternative is compromising by "half-fairness half-equality" (0.5 kernel + 0.5 equality). For the grand coalition and the [MM2] data set such a prediction also yields goodness-of-fit in the 90s.

3.4 Matrix setups

3.4.1 Derivation of characteristic functions and game types

In the late 70s in the Wisconsin Research Program matrix games are used to present TU coalition games. In an important controversy ([KR2], [MP]) in 1981 it was clarified that even under binding agreements not all relevant strategic aspects of such a setting can be summarised in one characteristic function. Aumann reflects this fact in the following note:

> "The passage from normal to the characteristic function form is not without pitfalls. Even in the case of games with side payments and transferable utility (the von Neumann-Morgenstern case) it is not generally agreed that the

characteristic function as derived from the normal form by von Neumann and Morgenstern represents the game; this is chiefly because for games that are not constant-sum, it does not always take adequate account of threats." ([Au] 1961, p.19)

Let us reconsider the value function for the 7-PD and let us denote the total payoff for a coalition by the function u. The above calculations for the characteristic function can be expressed in the following formula:

$$v_\alpha(S) := \max\{\min\{u(x,y), y \text{ choices of } N-S\}; x \text{ choices of } S\}. \quad (3.6)$$

Now imagine that S before deciding gets to know how the opposition $N-S$ will decide. Then by reacting a larger value can be attained - formally

$$v_\beta(S) := \min\{\max\{u(x,y), x \text{ choices of } N-S\}; y \text{ choices of } S\}. \quad (3.7)$$

In our case the worst case for a coalition of k members is that no one of the opposition will choose C. It is to show that we get $v_\alpha(S) = v_\beta(S)$. Games with coincidence of alpha and beta values are called **clear games** [J]. For clear games there is no advantage by reacting.

The possible difference between alpha and beta game in not the only obstactle for representing the coalitional strategic features within a unique coalition game. In order to understand a further type of complication let us define a third value by assuming that the opposition $N-S$ will jointly react to an announced strategy of S.

$$v_\gamma(S) := \max\{\min\{u(x,y), y \text{ best reply of } N-Stox\}; x \text{ choices of } S\} \quad (3.8)$$

Our example game exhibits larger gamma values for coalitions with up to 4 members. For determining $v_\gamma(S)$ consider table 3.11.

Table 3.11. Gamma values

#S	0	1	2	3	4	5	6	7
announcement	-	D	-	3D	4C	5C	6C	7C
best reply	7C (42)	6C (30)	5C	4C (12)	3C (18)	all (12)	D (7)	-
$v_\gamma(S)$	0	7	12	18	24	20	30	42

In order to establish full cooperation by gamma argumentation it can make sense to build an intermediate coalition of say 4 members and jointly announce a contract of 4C recommending the remaining conflict partners to adapt with a (joint) best reply. Such cooperative arguments are not representable neither by the alpha nor by the beta game. A similar argument can be found in the above mentioned critique ([KR1] p.729) of the early Wisconsin experiments.

For the further discussion it is good to remember that for coalition games derived from matrix games the characteristic functions represent claims and not values possibly distributed in the final results. It is typical for these games that the forming of one coalition by agreeing to a joint choice has **external effects** on the out-group. Consider for example our simple 7-PD, an agreement of four, while the three other ones do not sign a contract. In the worst case of a total choice of 4C an out-group member gets an individual payoff of 5, a value between the beta and gamma claim. Only in after a grand coalition agreement or a (equivalent) full set of contracts specifying the choice of everybody payoffs are determined.

Contrary to the pure characteristic function setup in case of **no contract** the individual values have not to be realised. In the latter case the non-cooperative equilibrium may become important. In case an equilibrium exists, and a specific equilibrium has been discussed as not too unfavourable (as in our example case) it is reasonable to accept the respective payoffs $E(i)$ as individual minimum claims. Note that $E(i) \geq v_\beta(\{i\})$. During the bargaining the values $E(i)$ can be used by refering to the case of a break off.

Both beta and gamma arguments depend on if the opponents accept the role suggested in the discussion: but during an open discussion such arguments can be used until they are refuted.

Let us extend the concept of **core** in the spirit that "all coalitional claims are satisfied" applying it to the set of respective choice combinations. In our 7-PD example the gamma core is empty - adding the claims of individuals we get a total of 7x7=49 - too large to be paid for.

The analysis becomes more complex if we leave the TU framework. In the **NTU framework** we have to substitute set-valued functions V for v and set-theoretic union and intersection for the max and min operations in the above formulas. Definitions and technique can be found in [Au], [MDC] and [O2]. Let U_S denote the vector-valued payoff-function for coalition S and let ch be the comprehensive hull operator mapping S-vectors a to the set $ch(a) = a - R^S_+$. Then, for example we get

$$V_\beta(S) := \cap\{\cup\{ch(U_S(x,y)), x \text{ choices of } N-S\}; y \text{ choices of } S\} \qquad (3.9)$$

Such sets $V_\beta(S)$ can be interpreted as claims using arguments "for us it is favourable to answer your proposal by ...; if you would propose something else instead, then you cannot lower us below this claim".

As argued above for the TU case also in the NTU case agreements should depend as well on non-cooperative properties of the matrix game as on properties of the different cooperative games induced. Selecting a set of significant properties we can define the type of a game. In the classification given in [O2] the type of a game refers to how alpha-, beta- and gamma-cores are related and on how the intersection of the nonempty ones of the three cores is related to the equilibrium.

Assume that the alpha core is not empty. The intersection of the nonempty cores is called **minimal core** and can be interpreted as the set of all choice vectors that cannot be refuted by a "justified" argumentation mode. A mode of argumentation is revealed as not justified if according to this mode no agreement is possible or mathematically if the respective core is empty. In this view actors in conflicts with empty gamma core have to detect that gamma argumentation is "not justified" in this case and is inadequate for the purpose of reaching an agreement. So they may alter their mode of argumentation. A corresponding behaviour can be postulated in case of an empty beta core. According to the analysis by Moulin [Mo1] for $n = 2$ not both gamma core and beta core are empty. Moulin speaks of an empty gamma core as competition for the first move (announcing renders larger claims, in fact too large claims) and of an empty beta core as competition for the second move (reacting renders larger claims, ...). In case of the empty gamma core there are high incentives to announce actions first for competing disjoint coalitions. Correspondingly the incentives to react to proposals are high for competing disjoint coalitions in case of an empty beta core. Note that for $n > 2$ we can construct games with both gamma and beta core empty, but alpha core not empty (cp. [O2]).

In a second step the above mentioned classification compares the cooperative opportunities with the non-cooperative standards. It is to distinguish between the cases that the matrix game has no equilibrium at all, only coalitionally suboptimal equilibria, or a coalitionally optimal equilibrium (an equilibrium is called coalitionally optimal if it is element of the minimal core). If we consider a negotiation refering to a game with no or only suboptimal equilibria bargainers can be assumed to have the goal to negotiate for getting a better result. Whereas with existence of an equilibrium in case of incompatible aspirations they have also the opportunity of simply coordinating at an equilibrium in case of no equilibrium they may feel to fall into the bottomless. In the third case of an coalitionally optimal equilibrium it should be easy to find an acceptable agreement.

3.4.2 Environments with and without binding agreements

Until this section we assumed that the negotiators can rely on guaranteed implementation of the agreements reached. Negotiations based on matrix games allow for both the binding agreement environment and the non-binding agreements environment. In the binding agreement (or contracting) environment agreements are guaranteed to coincide with final results. In the other type of settings negotiation partners have no means to force everybody to act as agreed. From a theoretical position bound to the fiction of homo oeconomicus it has been argued, that the dispute during the negotiations becomes "cheap talk" and has no further importance. On the other side empirically it can be observed that people do not commit every fraud that would be profitable and without any danger. Often in real life negotiations partners additionally invent methods to establish some implementation control. Here we assume that such paths are not open, but partners really have no means and cannot invent means of binding power.

Imagine the situation after a negotiation refering to our 7-PD game. Assume that the final agreement was 7C, "everybody will cooperate". Experiences with other clear games suggest that in most cases under binding agreement conditions such a contract would be signed. But now, without binding agreements negotiators return back home and now independently everyone has to decide how to act - according to the agreement or deviating from it trying to get some extra profit at the cost of the partners.

Face-to-face negotiations refering to matrix games in a binding agreement environment nearly exclusively have been studied by Michener and his group (with unrestricted communication). For their set of NTU-games they found evidence for a satisfactory fit of the beta-core predictor ([MDC], [MED]; cp. also [MPDM]). To my knowledge non-binding agreement experiments exclusively have been studied at Saarbrücken [O2]. In 1989 the Saarbrücken group directly (i.e. same set of games, standard conditions) compared the behaviour in games without (series 6) and with (series 7) binding agreements. The comparison in table 3.12. shows that the proportion of broken agreements nearly exactly translates to break offs in the binding agreement environment. Would it mean that for our 7-PD no deviations should be expected - certainly not. But with the experience of the games of different types reported in [O2] it can be expected that the instability in a non-binding environment is not smaller than the break off probability.

Table 3.12. Binding vs. non-binding agreements

type	e4	ip	total
not stable (series 6)	7 of 16	6 of 24	13 of 40
break off (series 7)	8 of 16	3 of 24	11 of 40

3.5 Beyond game structure

Game-theoretic modelling of negotiations can represent the focal structures of incentives and interdependences. An analysis of the respective models focuses on properties of the situation and not on characteristics of the specific actors. If actors behaviour is not too far from the assumptions made for a "rational actor" or a "homo oeconomicus" normative or classical solution theories may gain also descriptive relevance. Observations with remarkable deviations from these rationality standards motivated researchers to design various other descriptive solution theories. The aim of such theories is to fit to the results observed and to serve as valuable predictor. Research focussing on this task measures accuracy, success, and/or support of the own preferred theory and some alternative ones. By doing so such research is outcome-oriented and in most cases it gathers no information about the process of negotiation as social interaction and about the individual evaluation and construction of bargaining acts. From the beginning of experimental bargaining research there a warnings against a too simple stimulus - response approach with the game or a little broader the situation as stimulus and the final results as response ([SS1], [SS2]). It has become evident that cultural and psychological variables can play an important role in forming expectancies, behaviour and even results in experimental games. Nevertheless it is not easy to identify the interaction between situational components and such other factors. Up to now most contributions are far from really explaining remarkable deviations from a solution standard. There are cultural variations: for example in what is perceived to be fair; Europeans and

Australians usually show a larger bias to the equality norm than citizens of the US or India not only in their competitive behaviour but also in judgements (cp. [Sh]). There are reports on differences between female and male negotiation success and behaviour (cp. [O8]). Individual differences like personality factors and social orientation have be made responsible for deviations from the standards. Alternatively group constellation measures (how everybody is perceived by his or her partners) have been used to predict results [O5].

We have learnt by observation, that indeed what is attainable refers to the game structure but that the game structure alone is not enough to explain the result. It is of importance how the negotiators introduce their first proposals and to what extent they are prepared to make concessions and to "sell" their concessions. A successful exchange of concessions is base not only on the understanding of the power positions of the partners but also on social competence and adaptation to the common social norms. Furthermore negotiations develop their socio-emotional dynamics. It is of importance if a proposal can be judged as impudence, insolence, or untrustworthyness. Angry partners can become dangerous enemies. Negotiation success is correlated with a role-adapted negotiation style (cp. [OLW]).

References

Al1 Albers, Wulf (1988). Revealed aspirations and reciprocal loyalty in apex games. In R. Tietz, W. Albers, & R. Selten (Eds.), Bounded Rational Behavior in Experimental Games and Markets (pp. 303–316). Lecture Notes in Economics and Mathematical Systems 314. Berlin: Springer.

Al2 Albers, Wulf (1994). Ten rules of bargaining sequences. In U. Schulz, W. Albers, U. Müller (eds.): Social Dilemmas and Cooperation (pp. 429-467). Berlin: Springer.

Al3 Albers, Wulf (1996). Adaptation of aspiration levels. Theory and experiment. In W. Güth et al. (eds.): Understanding Strategic Interaction. Essays in Honor to Reinhard Selten (pp. 345-385). Berlin: Springer.

Al4 Albers, W. (1997). Foundations of a Theory of Prominence in the Decimal System. Part I - Part V. University of Bielefeld, Institute of Mathematical Economics, Working Papers No. 265, 266, 269-271.

AL Albers, W. & Laing, J.D. (1991). Prominence, competition, learning and the generation of offers in a computer aided experimental spatial games. In R. Selten (ed.): Game equilibrium models III. Strategic bargaining (pp. 141-185). Berlin: Springer.

An Antonides, G. (1991). Psychological Variables in negotiations. Kyklos 44, 347-362.

Au Aumann, R.J. (1961). A survey on cooperative games without side payments. In Shubik, M. (ed.): Essays in mathematical economics in honour of Oskar Morgenstern (pp. 3-27). Princeton University Press.

AD Aumann, R.J. & Drèze, J.H. (1974). Cooperative games with coalition structures. International Journal of Game Theory 3, 217-287.

Br1 Brune, S. (1976). On the regions of linearity for the nucleolus and their computation. IMW Working Paper 47. University of Bielefeld.

Br2 Brune, S. (1976). Computation of the nucleolus for superadditive 4-person games. IMW Working Paper 48. University of Bielefeld.

BW1 Buckley, J.J. & Westen, T.E. (1973). The symmetric solution to a five-person constant-sum game as a description of experimental game outcomes. Journal of Conflict Resolution 17, 703-718.

BW2 Buckley, J.J. & Westen, T.E. (1974). Discriminatory solutions to committee decision: some four- and five-person game experiments. Experimental Study of Politics 3, 58.

BW3 Buckley, J.J. & Westen, T.E. (1975). The majority rule game. International Journal of Game Theory 4, 105-112.

BW4 Buckley, J.J. & Westen, T.E. (1976). Bargaining set theory and the majority rule. Journal of Conflict Resolution 20, 481-496.

CBM Carroll, J.S., Bazerman, M.H., & Maury, R. (1988). Negotiator Cognitions. A descriptive approach to negotiators' understanding of their opponents. Organizational Behavior and Human Decision Processes 41, 352-370.

CE Chertkoff, J.K. & Esser, J.K. (1976). A review of experiments in explicit bargaining. Journal of Experimental Social Psychology 12, 464-486.

CA Crott, H.W. & Albers, W. (1981). The equal division kernel: an equity approach to coalition formation and payoff division in n-person games. European Journal of Social Psychology 11, 285-305.

DM Davis, M. & Maschler, M. (1965). The kernel of a cooperative game. Naval Research Logistics Quarterly 12, 223-65

FO Funaki, Y. & A. Okada (1982). Equity core of cooperative games, Working Paper, Tokyo Center for Game Theory.

FRK Funk, S., Rapoport, Am., & Kahan, J.P. (1980). Quota vs. positional power in four-person apex games. Journal of Experimental Social Psychology 16, 77-93.

G1 Gamson, W.A. (1961). A theory of coalition formation. American Sociological Review 26, 373-382.

G2 Gamson, W.A. (1964). Experimental studies of coalition formation. In L. Berkowitz (Ed.): Advances in Experimental Psychology I. New York

HS1 Hennig-Schmidt, H. (1996). Behavior or groups as players in a bargaining experiment. Some results on negotiation processes from a video experiment. Universität Bonn, Sonderforschungsbereich 303. Discussion Paper B-355

HS2 Hennig-Schmidt, H. (1996). How do player groups behave in a bargaining experiment? Some Results on formation and adaptation of aspiration levels. Universität Bonn, Sonderforschungsbereich 303. Discussion Paper B-356e

He Henss, R. (1986). Bargaining strength in three-person characteristic function games with v(i)>0. A reanalysis of Kahan and Rapoport (1977). Theory and Decision 21, 267-282.

HR Horowitz, A.D. & Rapoport, Am. (1974). Test of the kernel and two bargaining set models in four- and five-person games. In An. Rapoport (Ed.): Game Theory as a Theory of Conflict Resolution (pp. 161-192). Dordrecht: Reidel.

J Jentzsch, G. (1984). Some thoughts on the theory of cooperative games. Annals of Mathematical Studies 52, 407-442

KR1 Kahan, J.P. & Rapoport, A. (1977). When you don't need to join: the effects of guaranteed payoffs on bargaining in three-person cooperative games. Theory and Decision 8, 339-362.

KR2 Kahan, J.P. & Rapoport, A. (1981). Matrix experiments and theories of n-person games. Journal of Conflict Resolution 25, 725-732

KR3 Kahan, J.P., Rapoport, A. (1984). Theories of Coalition Formation. Hillsdale: Erlbaum.

KMNN Kalisch, G.K., Milnor, J.W., Nash, J.F., & Nering, E.D. (1952). Some experimental n-person games. In R.M. Thrall, C.H. Coombs, & R.L. Davis (eds.): Decision processes (pp. 301-327). New York: Wiley.

KT Kaufmann, M. & Tack, W. (1975). Koalitionsbildung und Gewinnaufteilung bei strategisch äquivalenten 3-Personen-Spielen. Zeitschrift für Sozialpsychologie 6, 227-245.

KA Kelley, H.H. & Arrowood, A.J. (1960). Coalitions in the triad. Sociometry 23, 231–244.

Kr Kravitz, D.A. (1987). Size of smallest coalition as a source of power in coalition bargaining, European Journal of Social Psychology 17, 1987, 1-21

KrI Kravitz, D.A. & Iwaniscek, J. (1984). Number of coalitions and resources as sources of power in coalition bargaining. Journal of Personality and Social Psychology 47, 534-48.

Ko1 Komorita, S.S. (1977). Negotiating from strength and the concept of bargaining strength. Journal of Theory of Social Behaviour 7, 65-79

Ko2 Komorita, S.S. (1978). Evaluating coalition theories: some indices. Journal of Conflict Resolution 22, 691-706.

Ko3 Komorita, S.S. (1979). An equal excess model of coalition formation. Behavioral Science 24, 369-81.

Ko4 Komorita, S.S. (1984). Coalition bargaining. In L. Berkowitz (Ed.): Advances in Experimental Psychology Vol.18 (pp.186-242). New York

KC Komorita, S.S. & Chertkoff, J.M. (1973). A bargaining theory of coalition formation. Psychological Review 80, 149-162.

LW1 Leopold-Wildburger, U. (1985). Effects of essential offers in 3-person characteristc function games. In M.J. Beckmann et al. (eds.): Methods of Operation Research 54 (pp. 403-413). München: Hain

LW2 Leopold-Wildburger, U. (1992). Payoff divisions on coalition formation in a 3-person characteristc function experiment. Journal of Economic Behavior and Organization 17, 183-193.

LW3 Leopold-Wildburger, U. (1996). The influence of monetary rewards within a three-person experiment. Central European Journal of Operations Research 4, 103-116.

Ma Maschler, M. (1965). Playing an n-person game. Econometric Research Memo Nr.73. Princeton University. (Later version in H. Sauermann (ed., 1978): Coalition forming behavior. Contributions to experimental economics, vol. 8 (pp.231-328). Tübingen: Mohr.)

McGK McGrath, J.E., & Kravitz, D.A. (1982). Group Research. Annual Review of Psychology 33, 195-230.

Me Medlin, S.M. (1976). Effects of grand coalition payoffs on coalition formation in three person games. Behavioral Science 21, 48 61.

Mo1 Moulin, H. (1981). Deterrence and cooperation. European Economic Review 15, 179-193.

Mo2 Moulin, H. (1982). Game theory in the social sciences. New York University Press.

MP Michener, H.A. & Potter, K. (1981). Generalizability of tests in n-person sidepayment games. Journal of Conflict Resolution 25, 733-749.

MPDM Michener, H.A., Potter, K., Depies, C.G., & Macheel, G.B. (1984). A test of the core solution in finite strategy non-sidepayment games. Mathematical Social Sciences 8, 141-168.

MDC Michener, H.A., Dettman, D.C., & Choi, Y.C. (1984). The beta-core solution in cooperative non-sidepayment n-person games. Advances in Group Processes 1, 145-181.

MED Michener, H.A., Ekman, J.M., & Dettman, D.C. (1986). Predictive superiority of the beta-characteristic function in non-sidepayment N-person games. Theory and Decision 21, 99-128.

MS Michener, H.A. & Salzer, M.S. (1989). Comparative accuracy of value solutions in non-sidepayment games with empty core. Theory and Decision 26, 205-233.

MM1 Michener, H.A. & Myers, D.J. (1998). An empirical comparison of probabilistic coalition structure theories in three-person sidepayment games. Theory and Decision 45, 37-82.

MM2 Michener, H.A. & Myers, D.J. (1998). Probabilistic coalition structure theories. An empirical comparison in four-person superadditive sidepayment games. Journal of Conflict Resolution 42, 830-860.

Mil Miller, Ch. E. (1985). Coalition behaviour: Effects of coalition values and monetary stakes. British Journal of Social Psychology 24, 249-258.

MK Miller, Ch. E. & Komorita (1986). Changes in outcomes in coalition bargaining. Journal of Personality and Social Psychology 51, 721-729.

Mu1 Murnighan, J.K. (1978). Strength and weakness in four coalition situations. Behavioral Science 23, 195-202

Mu2 Murnighan, J.K. (1978). Models of coalition behavior: Game theoretic, social psychological, and political perspectives, Psychological Bulletin 85, 1978, 1130-53

MuR1 Murnighan, J.K. & Roth, A.E. (1977). The effects of communication and information availability in an experimental study of a three-person game. Management Science 23, 1336-1348.

MuR2 Murnighan, J.K. & Roth, A.E. (1978). Large group bargaining in a characteristic function game. Journal of Conflict Resolution 22, 299-317

MuS Murnighan, J.K. & Szwajkowski, E. (1979). Coalition bargaining in four games that include a veto player. Journal of Personality and Social Psychology 37, 1933-1946.

NC Nail, P.R. & Cole, St.G. (1985). A critical comparison of bargaining theory and the weighted probability model of coalition behavior. British Journal of Social Psychology 24, 259-266

O1 Ostmann, A. (1985). Erfahrungen mit der Makler-Serie. Experimentelle Drei-Personen-Spiele mit Seitenzahlungen. FRA 96, Dept. of Psychology. University of Saarbrücken.

O2 Ostmann, A. (1988). Limits of Rational Behaviour in Cooperatively Played Normal Form Games. In R. Tietz, W. Albers, & R. Selten (Eds.), *Bounded Rational Behavior in Experimental Games and Markets* (pp. 317-332). Lecture Notes in Economics and Mathematical Systems 314. Berlin: Springer.

O3 Ostmann, A. (1990). On Rationality Issues in the Bargaining Context. Journal of Institutional and Theoretical Economics / Zeitschrift für die gesamte Staatswissenschaft 146, 481-92.

O4 Ostmann, A. (1992). The Interaction of Aspiration Levels and the Social Field in Experimental Bargaining. Journal of Economic Psychology 13, 233-61.

O5 Ostmann, A. (1992). On the Relationship Between Formal Conflict Structure and the Social Field. Small Group Research 23, 26-48.

O6 Ostmann, A. (1994). Aspiration Processing in Multilateral Bargaining - Experiment, Theory and Simulation. In U. Schulz, W. Albers, U. Müller (eds.): Social Dilemmas and Cooperation, 469-494. Berlin: Springer.

O7 Ostmann, A. (1996). Determinants of Bargaining Behaviour in Three-Person Characteristic Function Experiments. Central European Journal of Operations Research 4, 85-101.

O8 Ostmann, A. (1996). Representing Interactional Judgements in Multilateral Bargaining. Small Group Research 27, 450-470.

O9 Ostmann, A. (1999). Cooperation in Environmental Commons. This volume (pp. 138–158).

OLW Ostmann, A. & Leopold-Wildburger, U. (1996). On Styles of Relating to Bargaining Partners. In W. Güth et al. (eds.): Understanding Strategic Interaction. Essays in Honor to Reinhard Selten (pp. 430-443). Berlin: Springer.

P1 Peleg, B. (1980). A theory of coalition formation in committees. Journal of Mathematical Economics 7, 115-34.

P2 Peleg, B. (1981). Coalition Formation in Simple Games with Dominant Players. International Journal of Game Theory 10, 11-33

PD Pruitt, D. & Drews, J.L. (1969). The effect of time pressure, time elapsed and opponents' concession rate on behavior in negotiation. Journal of Experimental Social Psychology 5, 43-60.

PK Pruitt, D & Kimmel: 20 years of experimental gaming. Critique, synthesis, and suggestions for the future. Annual Review of Psychology 28, 363-392.

Ra Rapoport, Am. (1987). Comparison of theories for payoff disbursement of coalition values. Theory and Decision 22, 13-47.

RFP Rapoport, An., Frenkel, O., & Perner, J. (1977). Experiments with cooperative 2x2 games. Theory and Decision 8, 67-92.

RoU Rockenbach (Kuon), Bettina & Uhlich, Gerald: The Negotiation Agreement Area. Universität Bonn, Sonderforschungsbereich 303. Discussion Paper B-126 (1989).

S1 Selten, R. (1972). Equal share analysis of characteristic function experiments. In H. Sauermann (Ed.): Beiträge zur experimentellen Wirtschaftsforschung, Vol. 3 (pp.130-165). Tübingen: Mohr.

S2 Selten, R. (1981). A Noncooperative Model of Characteristic Function Bargaining. In V. Böhm & H. Nachtkamp (Eds.): Essays in Game Theory and Mathematical Economics in Honor of Oskar Morgenstern. Gesellschaft, Recht, Wirtschaft, Vol. 4 (pp. 131-151). Mannheim: Bibliographisches Institut

S3 Selten, Reinhard (1983). Equal Division Payoff Bounds for Three-Person Characteristic Function Experiments. In R. Tietz (Ed.): Aspiration Levels in Bargaining and Economic Decision Making. Lecture Notes in Economics and Mathematical Systems no. 213 (pp. 255-275). Berlin: Springer.

S4 Selten, R. (1987). Equity and coalition bargaining in experimental three-person games. In A.E. Roth (ed.): Laboratory Experimentation in Economics. Six Points of View (pp. 42-98). Cambridge University Press.

S5 Selten, R. (1991). Properties of a Measure of Predictive Success. Mathematical Social Sciences 21, 153-167.

S6 Selten, R. (1992). A Demand Commitment Model of Coalition Bargaining. In R. Selten (Ed.): Rational Interaction (pp. 245-282). Springer.

S7 Selten, R. (1997). Descriptive Approaches to Cooperation. In Sergiu Hart and Andreu Mas-Colell (ed.): Cooperation: Game-Theoretic Approaches, NATO ASI Series, Series F: Computer and Systems Sciences, Vol. 155 (pp. 289-326). Springer.

S8 Selten R. (1998). Aspiration Adaptation Theory. Journal of Mathematical Psychology 42, 191-214.

SKr Selten, R. & Krischker, W. (1983). Comparison of Two Theories for Characteristic Function Experiments. In R. Tietz (Ed.): Aspiration Levels in Bargaining and Economic Decision Making, Lecture Notes in Economics and Mathematical Systems no. 213, Springer-Verlag Berlin, Heidelberg, New York, Tokyo, 1983, pp. 259-264.

SKu Selten, R. & Kuon, B. (1993). Demand Commitment Bargaining in Three-Person Quota Game Experiments. International Journal of Game Theory 22, 261-277.

SS1 Selten, R. & Schuster, K. (1968). Psychological Variables and Coalition Forming Behavior. In K.Borch & J.Mossin (Eds.): Risk and Uncertainty, Proceedings of a Conference held by the International Economic Association (pp. 221-240). London-Melbourne-Toronto-New York.

SS2 Selten, R. & Schuster, K. (1970). Psychologische Faktoren bei Koalitionsverhandlungen. In H. Sauermann (ed.): Beiträge zur experimentellen Wirtschaftsforschung, Vol. II (pp. 99-135). Tübingen.

SU Selten, R. & Uhlich, G. (1988). Order of Strength and Exhaustivity as Additional Hypotheses in Theories for 3-Person Characteristic Function Games. In R. Tietz, W. Albers, R. Selten (Eds.): Bounded Rational Behavior in Experimental Games and Markets. Lecture Notes in Economics and Mathematical Systems no. 314 (pp. 235-250). Berlin: Springer,.

She Shenoy, P.P. (1979). On coalition formation: a game-theoretical approach. International Journal of Game Theory 8, 133-164.

Shu Shubik, M. (1986). Cooperative game solutions. Australian, Indian, and U.S. Opinions. Journal of Conflict Resolution 30, 63-76.

St Stackelberg, H. (1938). Probleme der unvollkommenen Konkurrenz. Weltwirtschaftliches Archiv 48, 95-138.

T Tietz, R. (1975). An experimental analysis of wage bargaining behavior. Zeitschrift für die gesamte Staatswissenschaft 131, 44-91.

TB Tietz, R. & Bartos, O.J. (1983). Balancing of aspiration levels as fairness principle in negotiations. In R. Tietz (ed.): Aspiration Levels in Bargaining and Economic Decision Making. Lecture Notes in Economics and Mathematical Systems no. 213 (pp. 52-66). Berlin: Springer

U Uhlich, G. (1988). An area theory for experimental two-person characteristic function games. Discussion paper B-105. SFB 303. University of Bonn.

WS Wolf, G. & Shubik, M. (1977). Beliefs about coalition formation in multiple resource three-person situations. Behavioral Science 22, 99-106.

ZR Zwick, R. & Rapoport, Am. (1985). Relative Gain Maximization in Sequential 3-Person Characteristic Function Games. Journal of Mathematical Psychology 29, 333-359

4 Comment on Bargaining Behavior

Of Models and Men

Friedel Bolle

4.1 The emergence of models

Reasoning is possible only within models - not "in reality" itself. Reality is too complex to be known completely. Thus not just model builders but "real men" as well have to simplify if they have to decide in a situation with multiple decision possibilities. An appropriate description of the relevant environment is always "simple". Under this aspect, a main task of experimental behavioral sciences should be that of investigating the way in which men "create" an own model of their world.

Up to now, however, experimental scientists often have concentrated on the question how people behave in given well-defined "simple" environments - where one might hope that the subjects and the experimenter's model coincide. Could it be, however, that such an approach is completely misleading, at least in certain areas? Could it be that there are systematic differences between the way an experimenter and his subjects develop their respective models?

If you compare rational behavior as defined by Microeconomic Theory (including Game Theory) with experimental results, you will observe severe discrepancies. In order to arrive at better descriptions you may follow two completely distinct strategies. One is often called a strategy of "neoclassical repairs", i.e. mainly the generalization of the goal function of men by the introduction of such social motives as altruism, reciprocity, or fairness.[1] In terms of an econometric analysis, these repairs add one or several degrees of freedom to the analysis without repairs.

The other strategy, the introduction of bounded rationality, reduces rationality requirements and implies more radical changes. In principle, this adds an infinite number of additional degrees of freedom for the description of behavior. So it is only possible to falsify certain well specified theories of bounded rationality while, faced with so much variability, the general approach can hardly be attacked by empirical findings. This is considerably easier with neoclassical repairs: if you can show that a person's behavior is not influenced by variables describing the status of other

[1] It is difficult to explain to a non–economist why there has been and to some extent still is such resistance to the introduction of such motives. Their existence seems to be self-evident for most people, and outside their profession, not even traditional economists would doubt this. This resistance may be partly explained by the question of how such seemingly disadvantageous motives could evolve. The answer is that they make cooperation possible more often. (See, for example, Bester and Güth, 1998) How successful such approaches can be is shown by Bolton and Ockenfels (2000) and Fehr and Schmidt (1999). One may, however, quarrel about the question which are to most important motives (see Bolle and Kritikos, 2001).

persons, then there is no room for such approaches. Of course, neoclassical repairs and bounded rationality need not compete as better descriptions of behavior. It might also make sense to introduce additional motives in a "boundedly rational way".

There are two components of Bounded Rationality (BR) approaches that should be kept apart. First there is the necessity to simplify the real world, a necessity for all "real" and "model" thinking as I have emphasised at the beginning. One distinction between rational and BR approaches is that the former usually work with a small number of real valued variables while the latter uses a larger number of variables which take only a finite number of values. The selection of such values may, for example, be dominated by prominence principles (see Albers and Albers, 1983).

The other component of BR approaches is the limitation of computation power. But is computation power really limited? And if so, in which way is it limited? If social decision-making were as "simple" as "seeing" or "hearing" then men (and even animals) would have developed a successful strategy for general problem-solving without severe limitations. Imagine for a moment that it has been a vital question for men - say, for several thousand years - to forecast the next values of certain time series[2]. I am sure that under such circumstances, men would be better suited to this task than any statistician equipped with all the computing power in the world. I am convinced of this because the human brain is far more able to detect patterns than any computer program is. The brain is an excellent "computer" if there is enough time for programming, i.e. to learn or to develop an appropriate program by evolution. What makes social decision-making so difficult is its variety! There is no such thing as a finely tuned General Problem Solver (Newell and Simon, 1981) but it seems to me that we respond to variety by means of flexibility. This sounds trivial - but let us see whether it really is trivial.

The German writer Heinrich Spoerl (1937) tells a humorous little story about his father giving him and his friend a problem to solve. The two seven-year-old boys were to tell him the number of squares a certain blanket had. While his friend eagerly began to count, the story-teller used - with a superior grin on his face - a "better" method: he counted the number of squares on both sides of the rectangular blanket and multiplied the numbers. The point of the story was that his friend won the prize because he counted correctly while the story-teller made a mistake in multiplication.

This is a very simple task - too simple for our student subjects - but we may learn from this that even very simple tasks may be represented differently. The friend "sees" the elements which have to be counted as an unstructured set. The story-teller's model of the situation shows a pattern and he is equipped with some knowledge about the properties of such patterns. Thus he could apply a "superior" method. Most tasks are more complicated than this one and thus give more room for different modelling. It is even rather probable that there is some feed-back between model-building and problem-solving. Imagine a very large blanket and imagine someone who started his task by counting the squares. After some time he will

[2] In fact, they have to do this in certain areas, namely in predicting (for a very short time interval, at least) the movement of prey or of an opponent.

probably interrupt his rather lengthy method and search for a better representation of the environment and the task.

Often, this is the point of giving advice to someone in a difficult situation: not just telling her or him what to do but to arrange the stilized facts in a new model which simplifies decision-making. The same is true for aphorisms which often simply require us to take another point of view. "Gott schuf den Menschen nach seinem Bilde, das heißt vermutlich, der Mensch schuf Gott nach dem seinigen"[3] is an example, stemming from the 18th century mathematician and physicist Georg Christoph Lichtenberg (1997).

The problem of decision-making is the large variety of (in particular, social) situations and the even larger variety of mental representations of such situations by the actors involved. This makes it impossible for the human brain to develop routines with high computation power which are well-adjusted to every task. Instead of that, we are capable and ready to adopt different points of view, to take different standpoints not only in similar situation but even in the same situation. This flexibility is the key to successful decision-making in a complicated world.

It is true that psychologists and economists have investigated the influence of representation on decision-making (framing). Prominent examples are the positional order effect (Cooper et al., 1993, Rapoport, 1997), the decomposed Prisoner's Dilemma (Pruitt, 1970, Antonides, 1994) and win/loss representations of the same situation (Twersky and Kahneman, 1986). Dawes (1991) reports about powerful framing effects in the field of public goods provision. This list surely cannot be exhaustive. In every case, however, "framing" is introduced deliberately and explicitly - i.e. experimenters tell their subjects different stories and hope that all end up with models strictly related to these stories. The fact that behavior often varies with the "frame" supports the hypothesis that the internal representation is influenced by frames - but usually it is not clear which internal representation is really used. The excellent overviews in this volume as well as other overviews in the literature (c.f. Roth, 1995, 253 - 342) show that there are experiments on framing but they also show that there is little work on identifying the subjective models used, not to speak of the dynamics of such subjective models.

Let me summarize: *The emergence of subjective models is a difficult and therefore neglected topic in experimental economics. On the other hand, it is clear that the subjective model is the foundation of an explicit description of behavior.*

4.2 The question of valuation

Up to now, we have mainly emphasized the "material" and logical representation of a situation. In many cases, valuations may play an even more important role. Our system of values, sometimes called our utility function, represents a large body of experience, some of which is inherited, some adopted via education, and some based on individual experience, observation, and insight. Economics usually assumes val-

[3] God created man in His image, which probally means that man created God in his.

ues (preferences) to be given. With the exception of learning and habit formation, little has been said by economists about the origin of values.[4]

Nutritious food (usually) tastes good, rotten or otherwise poisoned organic material (usually) tastes, or smells bad. Dangerous situations make us feel uneasy, a kind act by someone else evokes a feeling of thankfulness and obligation, etc. The "wisdom" of such values, feelings and emotions isn't always self-evident and, apparently, our emotions are *not always* wise.[5]

Under such a view, it is plausible that our values should depend heavily on circumstances. Tversky and Simonson (1993) discuss this phenomenon concerning binary choice situations. But we also have a great deal of everyday experience. For example, we allow ourselves to develop erotic or loving emotions more easily towards a single person than to a married or otherwise bound one. While I do my friend a lot of favours, I do not show any altruistic attitude when playing chess with him.

In many situations, and very often in bargaining situations, it is not clear which social norms apply and therefore which values should be adopted by a bargainer. The variety of possible positions and behavioral roles he or she could take is large. Should I be a nice guy? Should I be tough? Should I be fair? Am I expected to be trusting?

In a game of chess, it is clear that I should be tough and nothing else; being characterized as artful because I sacrificed my bishop and then started a successful attack on my opponent's king is meant as approval. But usually things are far less clear. If I bargain on the price of a carpet in an Oriental bazaar, I may hesitate to act simply in a tough manner. Of course, I would not like to pay ten times the price other buyers pay. But perhaps I also think about the production conditions of such a carpet (children's work?) and though there is no direct relation between *this* carpet's price and wages and work conditions, I may have the feeling that there is a *general* relation between market prices and wages. So, as a Kantian, I may hesitate to offer a price which seems ridiculous from a Western point of view. Certainly, it is not necessarily the case that toughness and fairness get their weights *before* the bargaining process starts. The seller knows about the buyer's conflict of norms and tries to exploit it. This is completely different from the viewpoint of most economic models where bargaining results are reached as a consequence of the distribution of power (however this is measured) in connection with selfish preferences. Equally, the bargaining process can be seen as depending on the distribution of values.

What is stated to be one of the main advantages of Experimental Economics[6], namely that - in contrast to reality - we can choose the incentives, is highly doubtful. Providing subjects with certain monetary rewards *influences* their values, but these rewards do not *determine* our subjects' preferences in the experiment. This is

[4] For fresh approaches to this question see Frank (1988), Güth and Kliemt (1998), and Kritikos and Meran (1998).

[5] For a discussion of "Emotional Intelligence" see Goleman (1995).

[6] See, for example, Smith (1991, 1994).

highly evident in Ultimatum Bargaining experiments where explanations based on monetary incentives only are completely misleading.

Let me summarize: *Valuations are condensed knowledge, education, and experience and thus guide behavior. They may be situation-dependent and, they may change in the course of time and with the amount of information.*

4.3 Bargaining strategies

In a world with complete information and complete rationality, bargaining should not need time. Rationality - which is *defined* by the analysing scientist - tells the parties how to act, and as no information can be gained during a lengthy bargaining process, every result (which is foreseen, of course) could be realized as well at once.

Real world as well as laboratory bargaining, however, takes (sometimes a lot of) time. So, we may conclude that either complete information or complete rationality or both are lacking. If we accept the point of view on human decision-making described above we would emphasize the lacking information, in particular about the other's valuation of results.

Incomplete information is introduced also in rational models of bargaining. Under such circumstances the "Bargaining does not need time" result may be confirmed or may be supplemented by additional equilibria without instantaneous agreement (see Bolle, 1996, and several contributions in Roth, 1985). But if we accept the above remarks on models and decisions, such approaches do not at all mirror the real bargaining process.

One difference between "Rational Bargaining Models" and real bargaining situations is that in the latter, "arguments" are exchanged. Every party tries, of course, to provide the others with true, or false, but (for them) advantageous pieces of information - but cheap talk alone is not convincing. So they have to *create signals* which make the submitted information believable. This creation is comparable to R&D activities and therefore cannot be modelled in detail[7]. The information submitted may concern one's own values or it may concern the space of one's strategies available. A negotiator who is representing a group of people or firms may argue, for example, that he has no mandate to bargain on certain issues.

But there are additional fields in which arguments are exchanged. The parties may argue about the correct (or better: appropriate) model of the world to use as a base for bargaining and agreement. In the negotiations about the number of whales to be hunted, there is often no agreement about the number of existing whales, about the minimum number necessary for survival, etc. In negotiations about the reduction of CO_2 emissions, parties who are not interested in any agreement often argue that up to now the hypothesized greenhouse effect has not been proven at all.

A further subject of negotiations often is which norms of behavior should apply, both in moral and in legal terms. Is it *legally* correct for a bank to pressure an 80-years-old women to act as guarantor for her son's loan? If so, is it *morally* correct

[7] This aspect of signaling is emphasized in Bolle (1996).

to garnish her house and expel her from it after her son could not pay his debt? Her lawyer and the bank would surely talk about these aspects as well. In wage negotiations - personal or collective - often arguments of justice and not of power are used. Threatening with outside options often is the *ultima ratio* and not the usual way to negotiate.

Let me summarize: *Negotiations are time-consuming because the parties try to signal their own values and because they try to influence the other parties' view (model) of the situation as well as the other parties' values.*

4.3.1 Investigating bargaining more closely

The overviews of Güth and of Ostmann in this volume show that a lot of research has been done, and has been successful, in finding stable patterns of behavior in certain (especially in simple) bargaining situations such as the Dictator situation, the Alternative Offer situation with a finite number of periods, the Ultimatum Bargaining situation, the Characteristic Function Bargaining situation, and others. There have been many replications of such experiments and we know a lot about the stability of the outcomes and their dependence on monetary payoffs, outside options, informational status, etc.

But we know little about the interior representation of bargaining situations which means that we do not have convincing hypotheses about the emergence of models and the emergence of decisions[8]. Up to now the analysis of bargaining behavior is concentrated (1) on final outcomes, and (2) on intermediate unilaterally proposed outcomes. Little emphasis has been laid on the analysis of (3) the arguments exchanged and (4) the signals created[9] and (5) the content and the dynamics of the interior representation of the situational context.

The problem with this type of analysis is to weigh between two counteracting desiderata. First, to make the situation rich enough to get this type of information at all, and, second, to keep the investigated bargaining situation simple enough to allow the identification of possible influences.

Let me give you three examples of such approaches, namely the videotaped group bargaining experiments by Henning-Schmidt (1996), the e-mail experiments by Bolle et al. (1999) and the investigation of Ostmann and Leopold (1995) on bargaining styles. In the group bargaining experiments the two parties were represented by two or three persons respectively. In order to agree on a common action these persons had to communicate their model of the situation including their beliefs on the values or aspiration levels of the other party. In addition, they had to agree on their own common values. One apparent result is the confirmation of one above view: the "interior" model of the situation is not given and static but it changes in the course

[8] On the latter, see Güth (1999).

[9] Of course, signals can also derived from offers and counter-offers. For example, the question whether initial offers in incomplete information bargaining situations signal true values is investigated by Ockenfels and Selten (1998) and by Bolle et al. (1999).

of the bargaining process because of learning and because of "insight", i.e. thinking about the situation. Such a "dynamic modelling" description of bargaining is emphasized also by Carroll et al. (1998).

In most experiments, arguments with the other party can be exchanged only rather indirectly (by means of proposals). The e-mail experiment by Bolle et al. (1999) tried to investigate just this point in more detail. The results, of course, may depend very much on framing, a question which cannot be settled without making further experiments of this kind. (i) Hardly any discussion on principles of justice took place[10]. (The only negotiation which started with such a discussion, failed in the end.) (ii) There were attempts to submit false information about one's own value (buyers) or about competing offers (seller). (iii) Many sellers tried to terminate the negotiation by an ultimatum, by a "take it or leave it" offer. (iv) No attempt was made to increase the believability of threats and of submitted information by giving promises, taking an oath, or things like that.

In Ostmann and Leopold (1995), bargaining styles were investigated on the basis of videotapes and protocols. The four styles identified (insistence, leadership, cooperation, low profile) can be explained as signalling. The respective person tries to submit believable information about her own values like incentives for cooperation and reciprocity and perhaps also about her abilities.

4.4 Outlook

In my view, the investigation of signalling will be the next big issue in the experimental work on interpersonal decision-making, in particular on bargaining. This requires the experimenter to add channels of communication to those experiments which are traditionally carried out with communication reduced a the minimum, or to restrict communication where - in face-to-face situations - it had been expanded to a maximum. It is important to investigate both of these extreme conditions, but real progress will come from the analysis of experiments where the flow of information between the subjects is richer than the exchange of proposals but, on the other hand, is completely observeable by the experimenter. Some experiments of this kind have been made, but there should be more, and there will be more.

I am sure that important progress will be made in the understanding of signalling during the next few years. We should, however, keep in mind that, in addition to routine signalling, there is something which might be called "creative signalling". Examples of the former are "buying presents[11]", "obeying custom" (or not), "proving strength or intellectual power or sophistication by presenting an example of one's abilities", etc. There are no general examples of creative signalling. The task of creating a signal is like an R&D activity and, thus, can hardly be described in general. Nonetheless, it might be possible to find some regularities in this field as well.

[10] This implies only that in *some* situations such arguments do not play a major role.

[11] See Bolle (1999).

References

Albers, W. and Albers, G. (1983). On the prominence structure of the decimal system, *in* R. Scholz (ed.), *Decision making under uncertainty*, Amsterdam, pp. 271–287.

Antonides, G. (1994). Mental accounting in a sequentional prisoner's dilemma game, *Journal of Economic Psychology* **15**: 351–374.

Bester, H. and Güth, W. (1998). Is altruism evolutionary stable?, *Journal of Economic Behaviour & Organization* **34**: 193–209.

Bolle, F. (1996). Verhandlungen brauchen Zeit. Bemerkungen zur siebzehnten der Masurischen Geschichten von Siegfried Lenz, *Zeitschrift für Wirtschafts- und Sozialwissenschaften* **116**: 395–416.

Bolle, F. (2001). Why to buy your darling flowers, *Theory and Decision* **50**: 1–28.

Bolle, F. and Kritikos, A. (1998). Self-centered inequality aversion versus reciprocity and altruism, Manuscript (revised version), Frankfurt (Oder).

Bolle, F., Baier, A., Buschbom, L., Köhler, A. and Swiniarska, M. (1999). Bargaining under Incomplete Information with e-mail Communication, Diskussionspapier 1998 Frankfurt (Oder), revised version.

Bolton, G. and Ockenfels, A. (n.d.). A Theory of Equity, Reciprocity and Competition.

Carroll, J., Bazerman, M. and Maury, R. (1988). Negotiator cognitions: A descriptive approach to negotiators' understanding of their opponent, *Organizational Behavior and Human Decision Processes* **41**: 352–370.

Cooper, R., De Jong, D., Forsythe, R. and Ross, T. (1993). Forward induction in the Battle-of-the Sexes game, *American Economic Review* **83**: 1303–1316.

Dawes, R. M. (1991). Social dilemmas, economic self-interest, and evolutionary theory, *in* D. Brown and J. Smith (eds), *Recent research in psychology: Frontiers of Mathematical Psychology: essays in honor of Clyde Coombs*, Springer-Verlag, New York.

Fehr, E. and Schmidt, K. (1999). A theory of fairness, competition and cooperation, *Quarterly Journal of Economics* **114**: 817–868.

Frank, R. (1988). *Passions within reason. The strategic role of the emotions*, W.W. Norton & Company, New York/London.

Goleman, D. (1995). *Emotional Intelligence*, Bantam Books, New York et al.

Güth, W. (1988). On the behavioral approach to distributive justice: A theoretical and experimental investigation, *in* S. Maital (ed.), *Applied Behavioral Economics*, Vol. 2, New York University Press, New York, pp. 703–17.

Güth, W. (2001). How do decisions emerge?: Generating ultimatum proposals, *in* F. B., M. Carlberg (ed.), *Advances in Behavioral Economics – Essays in Honor of Horst Todt*, Physica, Heidelberg, pp. 11–24.

Güth, W. and Kliemt, H. (1998). The indirect evolutionary approach: Bridging the gap between rationality and adoption, *Rationality and Society* **10**: 377–399.

Henning-Schmidt, H. (1996). Behavior of groups as players in a bargaining experiment. Some results on negotiation processes from a video experiment, Discussion paper B-335, University of Bonn.

Kritikos, A. and Bolle, F. (2001, Forthcoming). Distributional Concerns: Equity or efficiency oriented?, *Economic Letters*.

Kritikos, A. and Meran, G. (1998). Social Norms, Moral Commitment and Cooperation, *Homo Oeconomicus* **15**: 71–92.

Lichtenberg, G. C. (1997). *In meinem Kopf des Nachts*, Deutscher Taschenbuchverlag, München.

Ockenfels, A. and Selten, R. (1998). An experiment on the hypothesis of involuntary truth-signalling in bargaining, Working paper, University of Magdeburg.

Ostmann, A. and Leopold, U. (1995). On styles of relating to bargaining partners, Working Paper Nr. 35, University of Graz.

Pruitt, D. (1970). Motivational processes in the decomposed prisoner's dilemma game, *Journal of Personality and Social Psychology* **14**: 227–238.

Rapoport, A. (1997). Order of play in strategically equivalent games in extensive form, *International Journal of Game Theory* **26**: 113–136.

Roth, A. E. (1985). *Game-theoretic models of bargaining*, Cambridge University Press, Cambridge.

Roth, A. E. (1995). Bargaining Experiments, *in* J. Kagel and A. Roth (eds), *The Handbook of Experimental Economics*, Princeton University Press, Princeton/New Jersey.

Roth, A. E. and Murnighan, J. K. (1982). The role of information in bargaining: An experimental study, *Econometrica* **50**: 1123–42.

Smith, V. L. (1991). *Papers in Experimental Economics*, Cambridge University Press, New York.

Smith, V. L. (1994). Economics in the laboratory, *Journal of Economic Perspectives* **8**: 113–31.

Spoerl, H. (1937). *Man kann ruhig darüber sprechen*, Piper, München.

Tversky, A. and Kahneman, D. (1986). Rational choice and the framing of decisions, *Journal of Business* **59**: 251–278.

Tversky, A. and Simonson, I. (1993). Context-dependent preferences, *Management Science* **39**: 1179–89.

Part II

Cooperative Behavior

5 Cooperation in Public Goods Experiments

Claudia Keser*

5.1 Introduction

A public good has two distinctive characteristics. Its fundamental characteristic is non-rivalry in consumption. In the words of Samuelson (1954), "each individual's consumption of such a good leads to no subtraction from any other individual's consumption of that good." Another characteristic of a public good is that exclusion from its consumption is difficult. Thus, when it comes to the financing of a public good by private arrangements, individuals face a monetary incentive to free-ride on the contributions of others. According to economic theory, this leads to a Pareto inefficient provision of the public good (e.g., Cornes and Sandler 1986). Social choice theory proposes sophisticated collective decision processes to achieve efficient provision of public goods (see Laffont 1987 for a survey). They are often complicated and difficult to apply. Falkinger (1996) suggested a simple tax-subsidy scheme. In a series of experiments, Falkinger, Fehr, Gächter, and Winter-Ebmer (2000) show that with this mechanism an almost efficient public goods provision can be achieved. But, although this mechanism is easy to apply, it requires a central authority that can enforce taxes.

Actually, the role of government is often justified by the necessity to produce goods and services that the private sector is not inclined to produce, i.e. public goods.[1] Government provision of public goods, financed by lump-sum taxes, is, however, not necessarily more efficient than private provision of public goods (Bergstom, Blume, and Varian 1986, for example, suggest various reasons why private provision would sometimes be more efficient than public provision). We observe many cases of government provision of public goods that do not appear very successful. The public funding of environmental protection measures (e.g., those to comply with the Kyoto protocol), of measures against contagious diseases or of fundamental scientific research are such examples. These are examples relating to public goods which are of global nature. Public goods may also be of local access. Consider, for example, cultural institutions, such as theaters, operas or museums. In countries like France and Germany these cultural institutions are publicly financed.

* I want to thank Roy Gardner, Claude Montmarquette and Carel Vachon for their comments. Thanks are also due to my co-authors Karl-Martin Ehrhart, Roy Gardner, and Frans van Winden. Financial support by the Alexander von Humboldt Foundation (Feodor Lynen Research Fellowship) is gratefully acknowledged.

[1] Another school of thought claims that most of the government expenditures are for the production of private goods that are publicly financed (Aranson and Ordeshook 1981). Montmarquette (1996) estimates that in Canada actually only about 15 percent of the public expenditures are for the provision of public goods.

They often have to put up with a very small budget while their counterparts in the United States, which are largely financed by private donations, do very well. Consider also the public broadcasting service (PBS) in the United States. PBS is a private, nonprofit corporation whose members are America's public TV stations. It provides quality educational programs, products and services for use in homes, schools, and workplaces. It is almost entirely financed by voluntary contributions. In contrast to this, public TV stations in Canada, which are mainly financed by taxes, seem to do less well in quality and budget. They probably could do better with voluntary contributions. Considering the large number of Canadian underwriters to PBS in the United States, we have evidence that Canadians are willing to make voluntary contributions to finance quality broadcasting.

There is a lot of empirical evidence that people are willing to make substantial voluntary contributions to the funding of public goods. Probably, the prediction of economic theory regarding the private provision of public goods is too pessimistic. Experimental economics allows us to examine this question analyzing human behavior in well-controlled public goods situations in the laboratory.

The typical public goods experiment In an experiment, the public good situation is usually presented in an abstract way. Typically, it is a symmetric game with n players. Each player i is endowed with a number of tokens, e, which have to be allocated between two investments, a private and a collective investment. Be x_i the number of tokens that player i allocates to the private investment, and y_i the number of tokens that he allocates to the collective investment, with x_i, $y_i \in \{0,1,2,...,e\}$ and $x_i + y_i = e$. The profit function of player i, $\Pi_i(.)$, which depends on his private investment and the sum of all players' contributions to the collective investment, typically is linear:

$$\Pi_i\left(x_i, \sum_{j=1}^{n} y_j\right) = rx_i + k\sum_{j=1}^{n} y_j \tag{5.1}$$

with the parameters r and k satisfying the constraints (1) $r > k$ and (2) $nk > r$. In other words, each of the investments yields player i a constant return per token. The return per token in the private investment, r, is larger than the individual return per token in the collective investment, k (constraint 1). However, the return of a token in the collective investment for all players together, nk, is larger than the individual return per token in a private investment (constraint 2).

The linearity of the profit function and constraint (1) imply that, in game-theoretic terms, it is a dominant strategy for each player i to contribute all of his endowment to his private investment and nothing to the collective investment: whatever the other players' investment decisions are, his personal profit is always maximized with this strategy. If the game is played T times by the same players, we find the game-theoretical solution by backward induction. In the subgame perfect equilibrium of the game, each player allocates in each round t ($t = 1,\ldots,T$) all of his tokens to his private investment and nothing to the collective investment. However, due to constraint (2), the profit of all players together

is maximized if all of the tokens are allocated to the collective investment. Thus, the group optimum is realized if, in each round t, each player allocates all of his tokens to the collective investment.
Note that, in this game, the return per token contributed to the collective investment, which accrues to each of the players, represents a public good. The game-theoretical solution predicts zero contribution to the funding of this public good—which is collectively inefficient

Ledyard (1995) and Davis and Holt (1994) present extensive surveys of the early experimental studies on voluntary contributions to public goods. They conclude that in the first rounds of the public goods game subjects tend to make considerable contributions to the collective investment. The contribution level decreases, however, over time until it is almost zero by the final round. Many experimental studies replicate these results but also show that the average contribution level depends on several factors. These factors might be parameters of the model or other factors that are irrelevant with respect to the game-theoretic prediction. In a recent survey, Holt and Laury (*forthcoming*) try to explain these so-called *treatment effects* in voluntary contributions experiments by four types of models that incorporate (1) generalized preferences, (2) noisy decision making, (3) evolution and adaptation, or (4) cooperation and signalling.

The major purpose of this article is to present, based on several experiments, an interpretation of subjects' behavior in public goods experiments in terms of cooperation. This article is not meant to present another survey on the literature on public goods experiments. Before focusing on the issue of cooperation, we will show, in Section 2, the robustness of the phenomenon of over–contribution relative to the game-theoretic prediction in two important modifications of the public goods model: first, we consider a public good situation in which each player's dominant strategy is to contribute some of his endowment to the public good (Keser 1996); second, we consider a model where the provision of the public good is uncertain (Dickinson 1998). Then, in Section 3, we will elaborate how reciprocity is used in public goods situations as an instrument to achieve cooperation. I will present the interpretation of subjects' behavior in terms of conditional cooperation given by Keser and van Winden (2000). This interpretation will be complemented by the results of an experiment in which subjects designed complete behavioral plans for playing a public goods game (Keser 2000a). In Section 4, we will discuss the opportunity to punish others individually as another instrument to increase cooperation (Fehr and Gächter, 1999).

A new design of public goods experiments in which the interaction structure is flexible (Ehrhart and Keser 1999, *in preparation*) is presented in Section 5. Players have the opportunity to migrate from one group to another. These experiments allow us to extend our examination of subjects' behavior in public goods situations in two ways: first, we can examine the effect of mobility on the level of voluntary contributions to public goods. Second, these experiments allow us to elucidate aspects of human behavior that remain hidden in experiments with a fixed interaction structure. Both free-riding and conditional cooperation appear to be active principles in the sense that the free-riders seek to take advantage of the contributions of others and that cooperators try to form groups with other cooperators. In Section 6, I will briefly discuss why, in contrast to public goods, cooperative outcomes are more difficult to achieve in common pool resource situations (Ostrom, Gardner, and Walker 1994; Keser and Gardner 1999). Section 7 concludes the article.

5.2 Robustness of the voluntary contributions phenomenon?

The phenomenon of voluntary contributions to public goods when the theory predicts zero contribution is considered a stylized fact. As shown by Isaac, Walker, and Williams (1994), even in very large groups subjects tend to make considerable voluntary contributions. In this Section, I want to present two experimental studies on modifications of the typical public goods game: one where the dominant strategy solution prescribes some contribution to the public good, the other where the public good provision is uncertain. We will see that the voluntary contributions phenomenon is robust also to these modifications.

5.2.1 Partial contribution to the public good is a dominant strategy

The typical public goods game is designed such that each player's dominant strategy is to contribute nothing to the public good. In such a game, if we assume that subjects might err in their decision-making, errors necessarily lead to positive contributions to the collective good. This is due to the fact that the game-theoretical solution of no contribution lies at the border of the strategy space. Thus, the over-contributions that we typically observe in public goods experiments might simply result from subjects' error making (Andreoni 1988, 1995; Rabin 1998).

Therefore, I designed a public goods game that has a dominant strategy solution in the interior of the strategy space. In Keser (1996) I present experimental results on this game with the parameters $n = 4$, $e = 20$, and $T = 25$. It distinguishes itself from the typical public goods game by the fact that the individual profit function is not linear but quadratic in one's private investments. The profit function of player i is

$$\Pi_i\left(x_i, \sum_{j=1}^{4} y_j\right) = 41x_i - x_i^2 + 15\sum_{j=1}^{4} y_j \tag{5.2}$$

In contrast to the typical game, returns per token in the private investment are decreasing in the total number of tokens allocated to the private investment. The subjects were informed about the profit function only indirectly by Table 5.1. This table presents the return of each token allocated to the private investment. It is easy to see in this table that the last 7 tokens contributed to one's private investment yield a return below 15, the individual return per token in the collective investment. It is, thus, a dominant strategy for each player to contribute 7 tokens to collective investment and to allocate the remaining 13 tokens to his private investment. The profit of the entire group is maximized, however, if each player contributes all of his endowment to the collective investment (as the group return of a token in the collective investment, 4 times 15, is larger than 40, the highest return of a token in the private investment).

The experiments were conducted in a computerized way with 48 students at the University of Amsterdam. We observed 12 independent groups of 4 subjects each. After each round, each subject was informed about his return from each investment and the sum of tokens contributed to the collective investment by the other players in his group. At the end of the experiment, each subject was paid in cash depending on his cumulated profit after the 25 rounds of the game.

Table 5.1. Return from tokens allocated to the private investment

Token	Return from that token	Token	Return from that token
1st	40	11th	20
2nd	38	12th	18
3rd	36	13th	16
4th	34	14th	14
5th	32	15th	14
6th	30	16th	10
7th	28	17th	8
8th	26	18th	6
9th	24	19th	4
10th	22	20th	2

On average we observe, with respect to the dominant strategy, an over–contribution to the collective investment of about 25 percent. Figure 5.1 shows the time path of the average contributions to the collective investment. In each round the average contribution is above 7, the dominant strategy solution. Furthermore, the average contribution of each independent group is above the dominant strategy solution. Thus, we observe a statistically significant over-contribution to the public good (χ^2 test, 1 percent significance level). It is unlikely that this over-contribution results from accumulated errors. In this game with an interior dominant strategy solution, subjects might make errors to both directions around the dominant strategy.[2] The observed over-contribution seems less important than in the typical public goods experiments, but it is statistically significant. Vergnaud, Willinger, and Ziegelmeyer (1999) replicated this experiment in France and found the same results. Also Sefton and Steinberg (1996), van Dijk, Sonnemans, and van Winden (1997), and Falkinger, Fehr, Gächter and Winter-Ebmer (2000) confirm this result in similar experiments.[3]

[2] Anderson, Goeree, and Holt (1998) apply their logit equilibrium model to the game presented in Keser (1996) to show that the interior dominant strategy solution need not imply that, on average, errors cancel out.

[3] Laury and Holt (*forthcoming*) provide a survey on public goods experiments with equilibrium solutions in the interior of the strategy space.

Fig. 5.1. Time path of the average contributions to the collective investment (Keser 1996)

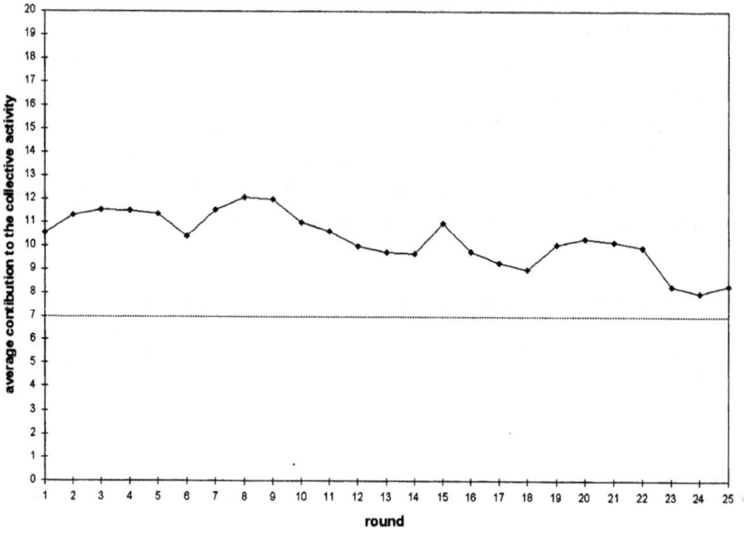

5.2.2 Uncertain group payoffs

In the typical public goods model the amount of the public good provided depends on the contribution of all players, and this provision level is realized with certainty. In real life, we observe many situations where the public good provision is uncertain. Consider, for example, work teams (such as a soccer team) where the individual compensation is tied to group results but the correlation between effort and results is imperfect. Motivated by such considerations, Dickinson (1998) presents experiments on public goods games with uncertain group payoffs.[4] He introduces two variations of the typical public goods model that he calls the "uncertainty" model and the "incentive" model. In the uncertainty model the public good is provided with a fixed probability below one. In the incentive model the probability of the provision of the public good increases in the contribution level.

The parameters of his model are $n = 5$, $e = 15$, and $T = 7$. The profit function of player i is

$$\Pi_i\left(x_i, \sum_{j=1}^{5} y_j\right) = x_i + pk \sum_{j=1}^{5} y_j \tag{5.3}$$

where p is the probability with which the public good is provided, and k the individual return per token in the collective investment. In the baseline experiment

[4] The uncertainty in his model is different from the one in threshold models in which a certain level of contributions is needed for the provision of a public good (e.g., Isaac, Schmidtz, and Walker 1988). A survey of experimental results on threshold public goods models is given by Ledyard (1995)

$p = 1$ and $k = 0.5$, and in the uncertainty experiment $p = 0.7$ and $k = 0.5$. In the incentive experiment, the probability with which the public good is provided depends on the sum of all players' contributions to the collective investment, $p = 0.01 \sum y_j$, and $k = 0.666$. Under the assumption of risk-neutrality it is, in the baseline and the uncertainty model, a dominant strategy for each player to contribute nothing to the public good. In the incentive model there exist two Nash equilibria, one equilibrium in which no player contributes anything to the public good, and another equilibrium in which each player contributes all of his token endowment to the public good. In all three models the collectively optimal outcome is obtained if each player contributes all of his token endowment to the public good.

The experiments were conducted as classroom experiments at the University of Arizona. In each of ten sessions, 5 subjects first played a sequence of 7 rounds of the baseline model, then a sequence of seven rounds of the uncertainty model, and then a sequence of 7 rounds of the incentive model. On the aggregate, the contribution levels in the uncertainty and in the incentive model show no significant difference with respect to the contribution level in the baseline model. In all three models, subjects make significantly positive contributions to the public good. In each of the three models contributions show the typical downward trend. Thus, the typical overcontribution result applies also to situations where the group payoff is uncertain.

5.3 Reciprocity as an instrument to achieve cooperation

Many explanations for the voluntary contributions phenomenon can be found in the literature. Most of them are in terms of generalized preferences, such as warm glow preferences, altruism, or reciprocal altruism. Warm glow preferences imply that the pure act of contributing to a public good increases a subject's utility (Andreoni 1990), while altruistic preferences imply that a subject puts positive value on the payoff of others (Becker 1974). We talk about reciprocal altruism when a subject's preferences on the payoffs of others depend also on the behavior, motivations, and intentions of the others. "If somebody is being nice to you or others, you are inclined to be nice to him; if somebody is being mean to you or others, you are inclined to be mean to him." (Rabin 1998, p. 21). While this definition of reciprocity is motivational, Axelrod (1984) defined reciprocity in terms of behavior without reference to preferences: cooperation is reciprocated with cooperation and defection is reciprocated with defection. In the following, I have this definition in mind when I talk about reciprocity. In public goods experiments we often observe subjects to behave reciprocally. We argue that reciprocity is used as an instrument to achieve cooperation with others. This is elaborated in Keser and van Winden (2000) where we present an interpretation of subjects' behavior in terms of conditional cooperation that is characterized by both reciprocity and forward-looking aspects. This interpretation finds strong support in strategies submitted by subjects for participation in an international computer tournament (Keser 2000a).

5.3.1 Conditional cooperation

In Keser and van Winden (2000) we present experiments in which the repetition of the public goods game is effectuated in two different ways. In the so-called *partners situation*, players interact in the same groups during the entire game, while in the so-called *strangers situation* the groups are randomly formed anew in each round.[5] The game-theoretical prediction is the same in both situations: for the typical public goods game, it is zero contribution to the collective investment in each round. The public goods game has the parameters $n = 4$, $e = 10$, $T = 25$, and the profit function

$$\Pi_i\left(x_i, \sum_{j=1}^{4} y_j\right) = 10x_i + 5\sum_{j=1}^{4} y_j \tag{5.4}$$

The experiments were organized in a computerized way with 160 subjects at the University of Amsterdam. With 40 subjects in the partners situation we observed 10 independent partners groups of 4 subjects each, and with 120 subjects in the strangers situation we observed 6 independent strangers populations of 20 subjects each. After each round of the game, each subject was informed about his return from each investment and the sum of tokens contributed to the collective investment by the other players in his group. At the end of the experiment, each subject was paid in cash according to his cumulated profit after the 25 rounds of the game.

We observe that partners contribute on average 45 percent of their endowment to the public investment. This is significantly above the strangers' average contribution of 19 percent of their endowment (Mann-Whitney U test, 5 percent significance level). This difference is significant from the first round on. Figure 5.2 shows the time paths of the average contributions in the partners and the strangers situation. The contribution level of partners is in each repetition above the contribution level of strangers. Interestingly, only in the strangers situation do we observe a continual downward trend. In the partners situation contributions fluctuate on a relatively high level until they decrease strongly toward the end of the game.

---

[5] Andreoni (1988) inspired the comparison of subjects' behavior in the partners and in the strangers public goods situation. His hypothesis is that partners should contribute more than strangers. A rational player in the partners situation could—in contrast to the strangers situation—have a strategic interest in the sense of Kreps, Milgrom, Roberts, and Wilson (1982) in contributing his tokens to the public investment. If, for example, he is not sure whether or not the others in his group are conditionally cooperative, he could have an interest, in early repetitions of the game, to build a reputation of being a conditionally cooperative type himself in order to free-ride on the other players' contributions toward the end of the game. In contrast to this hypothesis, Andreoni's experimental result show a higher contribution level in the strangers situation than in the partners situation. He has no explanation for this counter-intuitive result, which is based on only two independent strangers observations. It is, thus, not surprising that several other studies have followed to examine the partners-strangers phenomenon (Weimann 1994; Croson 1996; Palfrey and Prisbrey 1996; Burlando and Hey 1997). A survey is given by Andreoni and Croson (*forthcoming*).

Fig. 5.2. Time paths of the average contributions to the collective investment of partners and strangers (Keser and van Winden 2000)

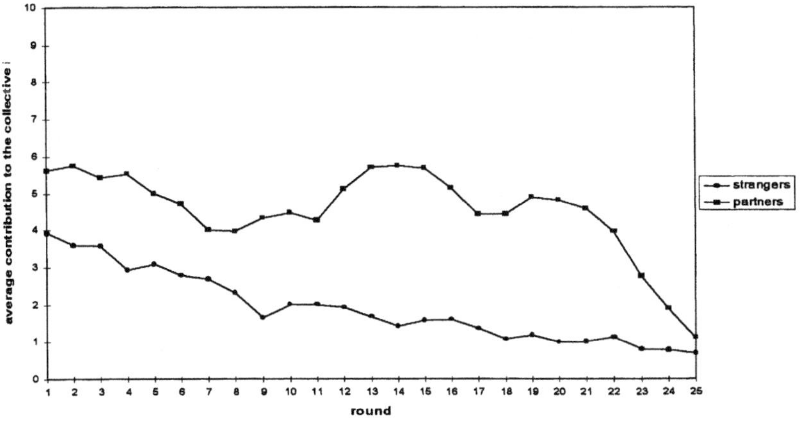

We suggest an interpretation of subjects' behavior in terms of *conditional cooperation*. We distinguish between two aspects: one is *future-oriented behavior*, the other is *simple reactive behavior*. As future-oriented behavior we define aspects of subjects' behavior that are induced by their perception of future interaction. Evidence of this type of behavior particularly shows up in the partners situation where the contribution level tends to fall sharply in the final rounds. Possibly, near the end of the game, subjects realize that investment in their relationship with the others is not worthwhile any longer. Or, they anticipate such reasoning by the others. Other evidence of future-oriented behavior is provided by the fact that already in the first round of the game we observe a significant difference in the contribution levels of partners and strangers. An explanation can be found in Keser (2000a), discussed below, where subjects are observed to signal in the first rounds their willingness to cooperate, and then reciprocate the observed contribution of the others until almost the end of the game. Intuitively, it is plausible that the propensity to signal a willingness to cooperate is stronger in a partners situation, where subjects interact in the same group during the entire game, than in a strangers situation, where groups are randomly formed in each round. Furthermore, the literature suggests that individuals show a propensity to identify with the group they belong to. As a consequence, an interest in group success is substituted for or added to their interest in individual success (see, for example, Brewer and Kramer 1986; Dawes and Thaler 1988; Dawes, Van de Kragt, and Orbell 1988; Simon 1993; Taylor and Moghaddam 1994). Obviously this factor is more relevant for the partners situation than for the strangers situation.

The second aspect of conditional cooperation concerns reactive behavior. Supportive in this respect is the above-mentioned observation in Keser (2000a) that subjects' behavior in a public good game is oriented toward the average behavior of the other group members in the previous round. This kind of behavior is in line with the principle of reciprocity that was used by Axelrod (1984) as an explanation for the observed cooperation in a prisoner's dilemma situation where subjects tend to reciprocate cooperation with cooperation and defection with defection. In Keser and van Winden (2000) we formalize reciprocity in a qualitative decision rule:[6] if a subject intends to change his decision from one round to the next, he changes it in the direction of the other group members' contribution in the previous round. This means that he increases his contribution if it was below the average of the others, and he decreases his contribution if it was above the average. We observe that subjects significantly tend to obey this rule. Interestingly, this evidence appears equally strong in both the partners and the strangers situation (about 80 percent of the observed changes are in the right direction).

Note that only in the strangers condition do we observe a large number of free-riders (defined, in a weak sense, as subjects who contribute nothing to the collective investment in the majority of rounds). Free riders' behavior does not violate our qualitative rule of reciprocity as they do not change their decisions from one round to the next. Their contribution is below or equal to the average contribution of the others. At the same time, those subjects who have contributed more than others tend to decrease their contributions. This offers an explanation of the observed continual decay in the average contribution level in the strangers situation.

Thus, we give a dynamic interpretation of subjects' behavior in the public good situation in terms of conditional cooperation. In contrast to some static theories of cooperative behavior, as the theory of reciprocity (Rabin, 1993), the theory of equity (Bolton and Ockenfels 2000), or the theory of inequality aversion (Fehr and Schmidt 1999), with which our experimental results are also compatible, our theory can explain the observed differences in the behavior of partners and strangers.

5.3.2 Strategic behavior

Selten (1967) presents a strategy method of experimentation that directly reveals subjects' strategies. Subjects, preferably with some experience in playing the considered game, are asked to design complete and exact behavioral plans that prescribe a decision for each situation that may arise in the game. The experiment presented in Keser (2000a) is an application of this strategy method to the above presented public goods game with an interior dominant strategy solution (as in Keser 1996).

I invited academic economists, mathematicians and psychologists all over the world to participate in a strategy tournament. They received an invitation brochure in which the game and the tournament instructions were described in detail. Fifty scientists from 13 different countries submitted their strategies for playing the public goods game. The strategies were submitted as flow-charts which were translated by myself into computer code. Each participant submitted three strategies, one strategy for each of three consecutive simulation rounds. In a simulation, the submitted strategies were combined in all possible groups of 4 strategies to play the 25-period

[6] This definition is inspired by the learning direction theory first presented by Selten and Stoecker (1986). See also Selten (1998).

game. The success of a strategy in a computer simulation was measured by its average profit over all plays in which it was involved. After a simulation, results were communicated to the participants. Each participant received an anonymous list of ranked simulation profits and records of 20 randomly chosen plays. The record of a play documented, for each round of the game in question, the strategy's allocation decision, its payoff from each investment, and the number of tokens contributed by the entire group to the collective investment. In each simulation round, one of the participants was randomly chosen for cash payment depending on his strategy's success. Furthermore, the knowledge that the list of rank simulation profits would be published after the final simulation should have provided a good incentive for participants to aim at high payoffs.

We observe that the average contribution to the collective investment increases from one simulation to the next. In all three simulations we observe, however, the same pattern. Initial contributions are highest. They decrease during the first few rounds, to remain then almost constant, until they decrease drastically in the final rounds. The average contributions in the final round almost coincide with the dominant strategy solution.

The analysis of the strategies submitted for the final simulation reveals several typical properties, each characterizing a majority of strategies It is not necessarily the case, however, that each strategy has all of these properties. Strategies have a 3-phase structure. In an initial phase they contribute their entire endowment to the collective investment. In an end phase, which lasts 1 to 6 rounds, they play the dominant strategy contributing 7 tokens to the collective alternative, whatever the history of the game so far. The behavior in the intermediate phase can be described by reciprocity. The contribution of strategy i to the collective investment in round t, $y_{i,t}$, is determined as

$$y_{i,t} = ROUND\left(\frac{\sum_{j \neq i} y_{j,t-1}}{n-1}\right) + \alpha_i \quad \text{with } \alpha_i \in \{-1, 0, 1, 2, 3\}. \tag{5.5}$$

A strategy's contribution to the collective investment is based on the average contribution of the other players in the previous round. Since decisions can be made as integers only, the observed averages have to be rounded to the nearest integer. Furthermore, we observe that an integer α_i is added, which is constant over time but different for each strategy i. A positive α_i is chosen by more strategies than a negative one. This means that strategies following this rule rather contribute a little more than less than the observed average contribution of the other players in the previous round. Furthermore, strategies pay attention never to contribute fewer than 7 tokens to the collective investment. Similarly to other strategy experiments (in particular, Selten, Mitzkewitz, and Uhlich 1997), we observe that a strategy with more typical properties tends to be more successful than a strategy with less typical properties.

We have to be aware of the fact that strategic behavior cannot be supposed to fully reflect spontaneous behavior of subjects. In the strategy experiment, subjects are forced to analyze the game, at least to some extent, and to construct decision rules for the entire game. When subjects interact spontaneously, they neither have the time nor consider it their task to analyze the game in detail. Decision rules may be made up from one round to the next. Thus, spontaneous behavior is likely to be more erratic and driven by feelings of sympathy or dislike toward the others than strategically planned behavior. We consider the strategy experiment a complement, not a substitute for, spontaneous game-playing experiments. Obviously, in the public goods situation, reciprocity plays a role in both strategic and spontaneous experiments. The typical strategic behavior is compatible with the model of conditional cooperation presented in Keser and van Winden (2000). The strategy experiment further reveals that reciprocity is considered as an instrument to lead others to cooperation. The own willingness to cooperate is signalled in the first round by maximal contribution to the collective investment. This result is in keeping with those of earlier strategy experiments on the prisoner's dilemma and oligopolies (Axelrod 1984; Selten, Mitzkewitz, and Uhlich 1997; Keser 1992; see also Selten 1998).

5.4 Punishment

In the previous section we have seen evidence for reciprocity in public goods experiments. Reciprocity shows in an orientation of a subject's contribution level at the observed contribution of others. It is used as an instrument to achieve cooperation with others. Reciprocity of this kind can show in other aspects of behavior which are not captured by the typical public goods model. Reciprocity may, for example, be expressed by punishing others even if this incurs costs to the one who punishes. In other words, also punishment may be considered an instrument to achieve cooperation with others. Ostrom, Gardner, and Walker (1992) allow for costly punishment in a common pool resource experiment (see Section 6 below for a description of the common pool resource game). They observe that subjects make use of this opportunity, which increases the overall level of cooperation. Fehr and Gächter (1999) allow for costly punishment in a public goods experiment. Their baseline public goods game without punishment has the parameters $n = 4$, $e = 20$, $T = 10$, and the profit function

$$\Pi_i\left(x_i, \sum_{j=1}^{4} y_j\right) = x_i + 0.4 \sum_{j=1}^{4} y_j \tag{5.6}$$

In their public goods game with punishment, there is a second decision stage, after the contribution decision in each period. Each player is informed about the individual contributions to the public good and, then, has the opportunity to punish each of the other group members. Player j can punish group member i by assigning him punishment points, p^i_j. For each punishment point assigned to i, the first stage payoff of player i is reduced by 10 percent. The first stage payoff of player i is never reduced below zero. Thus, the number of effective punishment points imposed on player i is given by $P^i = \min\left(\sum_{j \neq i} p^i_j, 10\right)$. Player i's costs for punishing other players are given by $\sum_{j \neq i} c(p_i^j)$, where $c(p_i^j)$ is strictly increasing in p_i^j as presented in Table 5.2. The profit function of player i in the punishment model is

$$\Pi_i(.) = \left(x_i + 0.4 \sum_{j=1}^{4} y_j \right) [1 - \frac{1}{10} P^i] - \sum_{j \neq i} c(p_i^j) \tag{5.7}$$

The game theoretical solution prescribes in both games zero contribution to the collective investment. In the punishment game, punishment should never occur.

Table 5.2. Punishment levels and associated costs for player i punishing player j

punishment points p_i^j	0	1	2	3	4	5	6	7	8	9	10
costs of punishment $c(p_i^j)$	0	1	2	4	6	9	12	16	20	25	30

The experiments were organized in a computerized way at the University of Zürich. The authors examined both a partners situation where subjects stay in the same group during the 10 rounds and a strangers situation where subjects are randomly re-matched in each round. 10 groups of 4 subjects were in the partners situation and 3 populations of 24 subjects were in the strangers situation. In each session, subjects played first 10 rounds of one game (baseline or with punishment) and then, without having been informed about that before, 10 rounds of the other game (with punishment or baseline). In the baseline game subjects are informed about the total contribution of the group to the collective investment; in the punishment treatment subjects are informed about all individual contributions to the collective investment in the group and about the aggregate punishments imposed on them by the other group members.

In the experiments we observe in both the partners and the strangers situation that the existence of punishment opportunities causes a large rise in the average contribution level. In the partners (strangers) situation the contribution level increases from 35.5 (18.5) percent in the baseline game to 85 (57) percent in the punishment game. In the punishment game, subjects can "force selfish subjects to adjust contributions towards those levels that they consider as appropriate." (Fehr and Gächter 1999, p. 26) This is typically the contribution level of the others group members. We observe that a subject's negative deviation from the average contribution is strongly punished. The more his contribution falls below the average contribution of the others group members the more heavily he is punished.

5.5 Games with a flexible interaction structure

In the literature on the public provision of public goods, Tiebout (1956) challenged in a path-breaking article the conjecture by Musgrave (1939) and Samuelson (1954) that public goods cannot be allocated efficiently. He considers a world of local public goods to demonstrate that public goods might be efficiently allocated if agents are fully mobile and can move to those communities that best satisfy their preferences. In Ehrhart and Keser (*in preparation*) we present experiments to examine the private provision of public goods in a kind of Tiebout world, in which each agent belongs to a community but has the opportunity to migrate to another community or create a new one. In our experiments, where subjects may make voluntary contributions to the funding of a public good within their community, we observe that agents frequently migrate to other communities, although mobility is costly. The observed contribution level is significantly above the theoretical prediction and, under certain conditions, closer to the socially efficient level than the observed contribution level in experiments without mobility.

These experiments allow us to obtain a better understanding of individual decision–making than in public goods experiments without mobility. We observe that the more cooperative subjects are continually on the run from the less cooperative ones. However, the less cooperative ones keep following them around. Both free-riding and cooperation appear to be active principles, in the sense that free-riders seek to take advantage of the contributions of others and that cooperators try to form groups with other cooperators.

The experiments are based on a typical public goods game with the parameters $n \leq 9$, $e = 10$, and the linear profit function

$$\Pi_i\left(x_i, \sum_{j=1}^{n} y_j\right) = x_i + k(n)\sum_{j=1}^{n} y_j \qquad (5.8)$$

where $k(n)$, the return per token in the collective investment, depends on n as presented in Table 5.3. Note that for $n > 1$, the constraints $nk(n) > 1 > k(n)$ are satisfied.

Table 5.3. The return per token in the collective investment, $k(n)$, depending on the group size n

N	1	2	3	4	5	6	7	8	9
k(n)	0.70	0.65	0.60	0.55	0.50	0.45	0.40	0.35	0.33

Our experiments involve a dynamic game with a population of nine players. Each player in this population participates in a sequence of 30 rounds. In the first round, the 9 players are randomly assigned to three separate groups of three players each to play once the public good game with $n = 3$. From the second round on, each round is divided into two stages. In the first stage, each player decides whether he wants to stay with his group, switch to one of the other groups that existed in the previous round, or create a new group. Switching to another group or creating a new group incurs costs of 5 to the player. In the second stage, each player decides, in the baseline public goods game within his new group of n players, on the allocation of his token endowment between the private and the collective investment.[7] Each

[7] If in the first stage of a round a player has created a new group, he forms a 1-player group during the second stage of the current round.

player has the following information: in the beginning of the first stage of each round, when he makes his group adherence decision, he knows the size, the total and average group contribution to the collective investment, and the per capita return from the collective investment of each group in each of the prior rounds in which it existed. In the beginning of the second stage of each round, before making his allocation decision, he is informed about the size n of his new group.

In the subgame perfect equilibrium solution of this game, each player allocates, in each round, all of his tokens to his private investment. No player ever changes his group because in doing so he would only incur costs. For the entire population it is optimal, however, if from the second round on they form one group of nine players and if in each round each player contributes all of his tokens to the collective investment.

The experiment was organized in a computerized way with 90 students at the University of Karlsruhe. Thus, we observed 10 independent populations. They contribute on average 52 percent of their endowment to the collective investment; the average group size is 4.6. We observe on average 41 group changes per population.

A fair amount of movement takes place in the experiment. There is a continual growing and splitting of groups. Groups with a relatively high contribution level tend to grow but, once they are growing, contributions decrease and the groups begin to split. New groups arise and the dynamics goes on. We can show that this dynamics is due to the more cooperative subjects being on the run from the less cooperative ones who follow them around.

In Ehrhart and Keser (*in preparation*) we continue this research to examine whether the opportunity for migration has a positive effect on the level of voluntary contributions. We compare behavior in this game with *free mobility* to subjects' behavior in a game *without mobility* and in another game with *limited mobility*.

In the game without mobility, subjects play the baseline public goods game during 30 rounds in the same group of 5 players.[8] We observe that the average contribution of 49 percent of the endowment is below the average contribution in the game with free mobility. The difference, however, is small and statistically not significant (Mann-Whitney U test, 5 percent significance level).

The game with limited mobility is similar to the game with free mobility but, from the second round on, each round is divided into *three* stages. In the first stage, players decide by a majority vote whether or not their group should be closed against entry of other players in the current round. In the case of group closure each group member, independently of his individual vote, has to pay costs of 5. In the second stage, each player makes his group choice under the restriction that a closed group cannot be joined. In the third stage, each player decides on the allocation of his token endowment between the private and the collective investment.

We observe an average contribution of 64 percent of the endowment, an average group size of 4.9, and an average of 27 group changes and 7 group closures per population. The contribution level is significantly higher than in the game without mo-

[8] We have chosen this group size as in the experiments with (free and limited) mobility we observe an average group size of about 5.

bility and significantly higher than in the game with free mobility (Mann-Whitney U tests, both 1 percent significance level). We conclude that the opportunity to close one's group significantly increases the contribution level. Subjects make use of the opportunity for group closure although it is costly.[9] Another interesting observation is that if a group is closed, the contribution level in that group tends to shrink. The contribution level outside this group, however, tends to increase.

5.6 Common pool resource situations

A common pool resource (CPR) is a resource in which yield is subtractable and exclusion from appropriation is difficult. Examples of CPRs include grazing commons, high sea fisheries, and irrigation systems. Similar to the public goods situation, in a CPR situation the pursuit of self interest by individuals leads to a collectively undesirable over-exploitation - the tragedy of the commons (Hardin 1968). In Keser and Gardner (1999) we present an experiment based on the strategy method to examine behavior in a CPR situations. The game is modelled, following Ostrom, Gardner, and Walker (1994), as a twenty-fold repetition of a symmetric 8-player game ($n = 8$). Each player i is endowed with $e = 25$ tokens, which can be allocated to a safe investment, x_i, or to a CPR, y_i (with $x_i + y_i = 25$). The safe investment yields him a payoff of $r = 5$ per token. The payoff to each player i from investment in the CPR depends both on his own investment, y_i, and on the total investment, $\sum_{j=1}^{8} y_j$, in the CPR. The group payoff to the total investment in the CPR is given by the production function

$$F\left(\sum_{j=1}^{8} y_j\right) = 23\sum_{j=1}^{8} y_j - 0.125\left(\sum_{j=1}^{8} y_j\right)^2 \tag{5.9}$$

F is a concave function, which implies that at the optimal level of CPR investment the players invest some but not all of their tokens in the CPR. Each player receives a fraction of the group payoff to the total investment in the CPR proportional to y_i. Thus, the profit function of player i is given by

$$\Pi_i\left(x_i, y_i, \sum_{j=1}^{8} y_j\right) = 5x_i + \left(y_i / \sum_{j=1}^{8} y_j\right) F\left(\sum_{j=1}^{8} y_j\right) \tag{5.10}$$

In the symmetric subgame perfect equilibrium of the 20-fold repetition of this game, each player invests in each round 16 tokens in the CPR. In the symmetric group optimum, however, each player invests 9 tokens in the CPR, while economic rents are completely dissipated if each player invests 18 token in the CPR.

We observe that although the equilibrium solution organizes the data at the aggregate level (group investment generally lies between the equilibrium prediction

[9] This result is similar to the one by Fehr and Gächter (1999) who show that the costly opportunity to punish each of the other players for no or too small contributions to the collective investment is used by subjects and increases the average contribution.

and the point of complete rent dissipation), subjects don't behave in accordance with that equilibrium. However, in contrast to the strategy experiment on voluntary contributions to a public good (Keser 2000a) and strategy experiments on oligopolies (Selten, Mitzkewitz, and Uhlich 1996; Keser 1992) we observe no active attempt to achieve a cooperative goal in the CPR situation. We know from the subjects' commentaries that it is not clear to them at which appropriation level cooperation should take place.[10] The relatively large number of 8 players makes the analysis of the game rather complex.

Note that we have experimental evidence that in oligopoly situations (with 2 or 3 players), which are strategically equivalent to the common pool resource situation, symmetry makes it easier for subjects to find a cooperative point. Therefore, we observe more cooperative outcomes in symmetric than in asymmetric oligopolies (Mason, Phillips, and Nowell 1992; Keser 2000b). In the CPR situation, the subjects' difficulty in identifying a cooperative goal explains the lack of cooperative strategies.

We may conclude that in situations where the pursuit of self-interest leads to collectively undesirable outcomes (public goods, common pool resources, oligopolies) cooperative outcomes may occur without government intervention. It is, however, important that the collective interest and the cooperative goal are obvious.

5.7 Conclusion

Voluntary contributions beyond the game-theoretic prediction are a relatively robust phenomenon. The typical behavior of subjects can be characterized by reciprocity, or, conditional cooperation. Conditionally cooperative subjects seem to use reciprocity as an instrument to attain a cooperative outcome in the interaction with others. However, we also observe free riders that make no voluntary contributions to public goods and, where possible, actively seek to take advantage of contributions made by others. The coexistence of conditionally cooperative subjects and free riders in a population can explain the phenomenon of decreasing voluntary contributions. The subjects' opportunity to punish individual others or to migrate to other communities may increase the average level of voluntary contributions to public goods.

We conclude that the prediction of economic theory regarding the private provision of public goods is too pessimistic. Based on the theoretical prediction, the role of the government is often justified by the necessity to provide public goods. This justification seems to have lost some of its grounds. We probably need further experiments to explore in how far financing of public goods by lump-sum taxes can improve efficiency relative to the provision of public goods by voluntary contributions. A first step in this direction has been made by Andreoni (1993) and Chan, Godby, Mestelman, and Muller (*forthcoming*), who examine in experiments to what

[10] Ostrom, Gardner and Walker (1994) show that this can be solved, for example, by communication among subjects.

extent lump-sum taxes for the provision of public goods crowd out voluntary contributions.

References

1. Anderson, S.P., Goeree, J.K., and Holt C.A. (1998), A theoretical analysis of altruism and decision error in public goods games, *Journal of Public Economics 70*, 297-323.
2. Andreoni, J. (1988), Why free ride?, *Journal of Public Economics* 37, 291-304.
3. Andreoni, J. (1990), Impure altruism and donations to public goods, a theory of warm glow giving, *Economic Journal 100*, 464-477.
4. Andreoni, J. (1993), An experimental test of the public-goods crowding-out hypothesis, *American Economic Review 83*, 1317-1327.
5. Andreoni, J. (1995), Cooperation in public goods experiments: Kindness of confusion, *American Economic Review 85*, 891-904.
6. Andreoni, J. and Croson, R. (*forthcoming*), Partners versus strangers: Random rematching in public goods experiments, *Handbook of Experimental Economic Results*, C. Plott and V. Smith, eds., Elsevier Press, New York.
7. Aranson, P.H. and Ordeshook, P.C. (1981), Regulation, redistribution and public choice, *Public Choice 37*, 60-100.
8. Axelrod, R.M. (1984), *The evolution of cooperation*, Basic, New York.
9. Becker, G.S. (1974), A theory of social interactions, *Journal of Political Economy 82*, 1063-1093.
10. Bergstrom, T.L., Blume, L., and Varian, H. (1986), On the private provision of public goods, *Journal of Public Economics 29*, 25-49.
11. Bolton, G.E. and Ockenfels, A. (2000), ERC: A theory of equity, reciprocity and competition, *American Economic Review 90*, 166-193.
12. Brewer, M.B. and Kramer, R.M. (1986), Choice behavior in social dilemmas: Effects of social identity, group size, and decision framing, *Journal of Personality and Social Psychology* 50, 543-545.
13. Burlando, R. and Hey, J. (1997), Do Anglosaxons free-ride more? *Journal of Public Economics 64*, 41-60.
14. Chan K.S., Godby R., Mestelman S., and Muller, R.A. (*forthcoming*), Crowding out voluntary contributions to public goods, *Journal of Economic Behavior and Organization.*
15. Cornes, R.C. and Sandler, T. (1986), *The theory of externalities, public goods, and club goods*, Cambridge University Press.
16. Croson, R. (1996), Partners and strangers revisited, *Economics Letters 53*, 25-32.
17. Davis, D. and Holt C. (1993), *Experimental economics*, Princeton University Press, Princeton, NJ.
18. Dawes, R.M. and Thaler, R.H. (1988), Anomalies: Cooperation, *Journal of Economic Perspectives* 2, 187-197.
19. Dawes, R.M., Van de Kragt, A.J.C. and Orbell, J.M. (1988), Not me or thee: The importance of group identity in eliciting cooperation in dilemma situations: Experimental manipulations, *Acta Psychologica* 68, 83-97.
20. Dickinson, D.L. (1998), The voluntary contributions mechanism with uncertain group payoffs, *Journal of Economic Behavior and Organization 35*, 517-533.
21. van Dijk, F., Sonnemans, J., and van Winden, F. (1997), Social ties in a public good experiment, Working Paper, University of Amsterdam.

22. Ehrhart, K.M. and Keser, C. (1999), Mobility and cooperation: On the run, SFB 504 Discussion Paper 99-69, University of Mannheim, and CIRANO Scientific Series 99s-24, Montréal.
23. Ehrhart, K.M. and Keser, C. (*in preparation*), Mobility, exclusion, and cooperation, draft.
24. Falkinger, J. (1996), Efficient private provision of public goods by rewarding deviations from average, *Journal of Public Economics 62*, 413-422.
25. Falkinger, J., Fehr, E., Gächter, S., and Winter-Ebmer, R. (2000), A simple mechanism for the efficient provision of public goods: Experimental evidence, *American Economic Review 90*, 247-264.
26. Fehr, E. and Gächter, S. (1999), Cooperation and punishment in public goods experiments, Working Paper, University of Zürich.
27. Fehr, E. and Schmidt, K.M. (1999), A theory of fairness, competition, and cooperation, *Quarterly Journal of Economics 114*, 817-868.
28. Hardin, G. (1968), The tragedy of the commons, *Science 162*, 1243-1248.
29. Holt, C.A. and Laury, S.K. (*forthcoming*), Theoretical explanations of treatment effects in voluntary contributions Experiments, *Handbook of Experimental Economic Results*, C. Plott and V. Smith, eds., Elsevier Press, New York.
30. Isaac, R.M., Schmidtz, D. and Walker, J. (1988), The assurance problem in a laboratory market, *Public Choice 62*, 217-236.
31. Isaac, R.M., Walker, J.M., and Williams, A.W. (1994), Group size and the voluntary provision of public goods, *Journal of Public Economics* 54, 1-36.
32. Keser, C. (1992), Experimental duopoly markets with demand inertia–game-playing experiments and the strategy method, *Lecture Notes in Economics and Mathematical Systems 391*, Springer Verlag.
33. Keser, C. (1996), Voluntary contributions to a public good when partial contribution is a dominant strategy, *Economics Letters 50*, 359-366.
34. Keser, C. (2000a), Strategically planned behavior in public goods experiments, CIRANO Scientific Series 2000s-35.
35. Keser, C. (2000b), Cooperation in symmetric duopolies with demand inertia, *International Journal of Industrial Organization 18*, 23-38.
36. Keser, C. and Gardner, R., (1999), Strategic behavior of experienced subjects in a common pool resource game, *International Journal of Game Theory 28*, 241-252.
37. Keser, C. and van Winden, F. (2000), Conditional cooperation and voluntary contributions to public goods, *Scandinavian Journal of Economics 102*, 23-39.
38. Kreps, D., Milgrom, P., Roberts, J., and Wilson, R. (1982), Rational cooperation in the finitely repeated prisoners' dilemma, *Journal of Economic Theory* 27, 245-252.
39. Laffont, J.-J. (1987), Incentives and the allocation of public goods, in A.J. Auerbach and M. Feldstein (eds.), *Handbook of Public Economics*, Vol. 2, 537-569, North Holland, Amsterdam.
40. Laury, S.K. and Holt C.A. (*forthcoming*), Voluntary provision of public goods: Experimental results with interior Nash equilibria, *Handbook of Experimental Economic Results*, C. Plott and V. Smith, eds., Elsevier Press, New York.
41. Ledyard, J. (1995), Public goods: A survey of experimental research, in A.E. Roth and J. Kagel (eds.), *Handbook of Experimental Economics*, Princeton University Press.
42. Mason, C.F., Philipps, O.R., and Nowell, C. (1992), Duopoly behavior in asymmetric markets: An experimental evaluation, *Review of Economics and Statistics 74*, 662-669.
43. Montmarquette, C. (1996), L'importance relative des gouvernements: Causes, conséquences et organisations alternatives, in R. Lacroix, C.E. Forget and G. Fortin (eds.), *L'efficacité des organisations et la compétitivité de l'économie*, Congrès de l'ASDEQ 94, Montréal, 133-150.

44. Musgrave, R.A. (1939), The voluntary exchange theory of public economy, *Quarterly Journal of Economics 52*, 213-217.
45. Ostrom, E., Gardner, R., and Walker, J.M. (1992), Covenants with and without a sword: Self-governance is possible, *American Political Science Review 86*, 404-417.
46. Ostrom, E., Gardner, R., and Walker, J.M. (1994), *Rules, games, and common-pool resources*, The University of Michigan Press, Ann Arbor.
47. Palfrey, T. and Prisbrey, J. (1996), Altruism, reputation and noise in linear public goods experiments, *Journal of Public Economics* 61, 409-427.
48. Rabin, M.(1993), Incorporating fairness into game theory and economics, *American Economic Review* 83, 1281-1302.
49. Rabin, M. (1998), Psychology and economics, *Journal of Economic Literature 36*, 11-46.
50. Samuelson, P., 1954, The pure theory of public expenditure, *Review of Economics and Statistics 36*, 387-389.
51. Sefton, M. and Steinberg, R. (1996), Reward structures in public good experiments, *Journal of Public Economics 61*, 263-287.
52. Selten, R. (1967), Die Strategiemethode zur Erforschung des eingeschränkt rationalen Verhaltens im Rahmen eines Oligopolexperiments, in Sauermann, H. (ed.), *Beiträge zur experimentellen Wirtschaftsforschung*, J.C.B. Mohr, Tübingen.
53. Selten, R. (1998), Features of experimentally observed bounded rationality, *European Economic Review 42*, 413-436.
54. Selten, R., Mitzkewitz, M., and Uhlich, G.R. (1997), Duopoly strategies programmed by experienced players, *Econometrica 65*, 517-555.
55. Selten, R. and Stoecker, R. (1986), End behavior in sequences of finite prisoner's dilemma supergames, *Journal of Economic Behavior and Organization 7*, 47-70.
56. Simon, H.A. (1993), Altruism and economics, *American Economic Review* 83, 156-161.
57. Taylor, D.M. and Moghaddam, F.M. (1994), *Theories of intergroup relations: International social psychological perspectives,* Second edition, Praeger, Westport.
58. Tiebout, C.M. (1956), A pure theory of local expenditures, *Journal of Political Economy* 64, 416-424.
59. Vergnaud, J.-C., Willinger, M., and Ziegelmeyer, A. (1999), Mécanisme de contribution volontaire et effet de contexte: Théorie et évidence expérimentale, Working Paper, University of Strasbourg.
60. Weimann, J. (1994), Individual behavior in a free riding experiment, *Journal of Public Economics* 54, 185-200.

6 Comment on Claudia Keser

Claude Montmarquette

In this short but elegant paper, Keser discusses the question of public goods in the context of experimental economics. While organized as a survey, Keser mainly focuses on her own contributions to this topic. She and her coauthors offer stimulating insights to all concerned with the role of government in the economy and the problem of voluntary contributions to public goods.

The typical public goods experiment is a straightforward exercise. The Nash equilibrium is zero contribution to the public goods. On the other side, investing all its endowment on the public goods is the group optimum. The distinctive result in those experiments is a voluntary over-contribution relatively to the Nash equilibrium, but an undercontribution with respect to the optimum solution. Keser (1996) has bit a real breakthrough in this literature by presenting an experiment where a dominant strategy is for each player to contribute not all his or her endowment to the private goods. This approach eliminates the subjects' error making to explain the traditional results. Although she observes statistically significant overcontributions by the participants with respect to the Nash equilibrium, the overcontributions appear less important than what was found in the previous literature. Her model opens the way to understand individual human behavior in a more realistic setting, as a corner equilibrium can indeed be questionable when spending is limited to only two goods. To be useful for policy issues, experimental economics needs to explain real and complex situations and not only simple makeup laboratory situations. In an other experiment Keser is looking at a situation where the group optimum is a partial contribution to public goods. This is an important experiment. The assumption that the group optimum is for all players to invest their whole endowment to the public goods is unrealistic since, if realized, the economy should be producing only pure public goods.

The definition of a pure public good characterized by its nonrivalry in consumption and its nonexclusion from consumption implies for the social optimum that all people in the world should voluntarily contribute to its production. Each individual is able to consume those goods while sharing the costs of production with the others. Commitments to find a cure to a very contagious disease will be a genuine example of pure public goods. A global communication system can also be considered an international public good. At a national level, national defense, and a clean environment are the usual examples. Public goods can also be produced locally. The illumination of Berlin at night can be enjoyed by all people leaving in Berlin, but are of little interest for the habitants of Bonn. In Ehrhart and Keser (1999), the production of local public goods is examined with an experiment in which each agent belongs to a community but has the opportunity to migrate to another community or create a new one. In this kind of Tiebout world, the authors found "that free riders seek to take advantage of the contributions of others and that cooperators try to form groups with other cooperators". This study illuminates many debates around the world directly related to this context. In the U.S, and certainly elsewhere, a very hot topic is the debate among the pros and cons for a centralized or a decentralized educational system and with respect to the private/public division of responsibility for education. In Europe and in Canada, a major question is federalism or decentralized government, while in Asian und Latin American countries, the discussion focuses on whose in and whose out as free trade partners.

Contrary to a widely held view, Isaac et al (1994) found that larger group size provides public goods more efficiently than smaller group size. This question is revisited in Keser and van Winden (forthcoming) with public goods experiments using partners and strangers. In the experiments realized with partners, players interact in the same group during the entire game. With strangers, groups are randomly formed in each repetition. Thus, indirectly, the group of strangers is larger than the group of partners. Keser and van Winden's results indicate greater voluntary contributions from the partners groups than among strangers. In a partner's situation, it seems more useful to signal a willingness to cooperate. Thus, this experiment predicts that despite a smaller differential in the return between the public and the private goods investments facing them (in the public choice median voter model this corresponds to a larger per unit cost of production of the public goods), individuals in small communities are more inclined to allocate a greater percentage of their income to the public goods than those living in large communities do. Put it differently, people in small communities are more cooperative.

A particularly original contribution by Keser is her study of strategic behavior with 50 scientists from 13 countries playing the public goods game. She argues that conditional cooperation is strongly supported to explain how subjects behave and that conditional reciprocity is a strong instrument to achieve cooperation. This has two major implications. First, it might explain, why so few international public goods exist. Either for political, historical or economic reasons, conditional cooperation is not easily achieved at the world level. More generally, the rule is "defection reciprocated with defection" as we observe perennial discussions and difficulties of financing international institutions. Second, if conditional cooperation can be used to achieve cooperation, this suggests some policy design. Mobility among groups was mentioned as a possibility to enhance conditional cooperation. Perhaps key information on contributions, identification of the players, allowing discussions among participants or a structure of punishment for those who contribute below the group average contribution (discussed in Section 4 of the survey) merit consideration and exploration.

In her survey, Keser discusses also the question of uncertain group payoffs and mentions taxes. It would have been useful to link some of these parts with other sections that have been more developed. For example, how the level of trust or the uncertainty of other contributions might play in the strategy of conditional contribution. To the extent that the initial period decision lacks information about the other contributions and might be influential to the dynamics of the game, this could be an interesting question. The role of taxes in the migration study is also a subject worth considering.

A small regret concerns her too short discussion of the notion of reciprocity without reference to preferences using Axelrod's definition. Becker (1962) has long since shown that the law of demand can be derived without a utility function. Experimental works by Evans (1997), Gode and Sunder (1993) suggest that efficiency is derived from the structure of the market rather than motivation, intelligence and learning ability of human economic agents, If constraints and market structures appear more important than preferences why is the trend in experimental economics to add elements to the utility function such as altruism, fairness or distaste for inequality? A more critical discussion of this point in her survey would have been helpful for future work.

References

Becker, G. (1962). Irrational Behavior and Economic Theory, *Journal of Political Economy* **70**: 1–13.

Evans, D. (1997). The Role of Markets in Reducing Expected Utility Violations, *Journal of Political Economy* **105**: 622–636.

Gode, D. and Sunder, S. (1993). Allocative Efficiency of Markets with Zero Intelligence Traders: Market as a Partial Substitute for Individual Rationality, *Journal of Political Economy* **101**: 119–137.

Isaac, R., Walker, J. and Arlington, W. (1994). Group Size and the Voluntary Provision of Public Goods, *Journal of Public Economics* **54**: 13–16.

(Omitted references are found in Keser's article)

7 Fairness in the Labour Market*

A Survey of Experimental Results

Simon Gächter and Ernst Fehr

Abstract. In this chapter we provide a selective survey of experiments to investigate the potential of social motivations in explaining labour market phenomena. We argue that laboratory experiments are a useful instrument to explore issues in labour market theory and personnel economics. Our starting point is the observation that employment relations are frequently governed by incomplete contracts. We show that the norm of reciprocity that leads to gift exchanges is an effective contract enforcement device under conditions of contractual incompleteness. We then present evidence that gift exchange can explain various labour market phenomena that are puzzles from the viewpoint of standard economic theory. Further issues in the related field of personnel economics that have by now been subjected to an experimental scrutiny concern characteristics of the employment relation and the issues of motivation and incentives systems. We conclude by pointing out the complementary nature of experiments to more conventional methods of data gathering.

7.1 The comparative advantage of experiments in labour market research

Is the labour market best described as any other neo-classical market, like the market for groceries, or is the labour market substantially different? Much of research in labour economics has such a question in its background. As an example, take the issue of *non*-compensating wage differentials. There is a huge empirical literature on the question of whether observed wage differentials reflect merely a compensation for working conditions, skills, etc., or whether they contain elements of true rents. Clearly, the existence of true rents, i.e., non-compensating differentials, is in sharp conflict with the neo-classical view of the labour market. As a second example, take the question of whether real and/or nominal wages are rigid, which is also a central topic in macroeconomics. Sticky wages are held responsible for involuntary unemployment, real effects of monetary policy, and business cycle fluctuations. The important question therefore is: Are wages rigid because of some outside intervention – a possibility that is fully compatible with a neo-classical view of the labour market – or are there *endogenous* reasons for wage rigidities?

A further topic that is in particular studied in the related field of personnel economics (see Lazear 1995, 1998, 1999) concerns the characteristics of employment relationships and the issue of the proper motivation of employees. What are the

* Support by the Swiss National Science Foundation under the project no. 1214-05100.97 and the EU-TMR project ENDEAR (FMRX CT98-0238) is gratefully acknowledged. Armin Falk, Manfred Königstein, Dorothea Kübler, Christian Thöni and the participants of the GEW Meeting in Meissen in October 1998 provided very helpful comments.

economic consequences of the fact that most employment relations are contractually incomplete, long-term and take place mostly in non-anonymous environments? How can employees be induced to provide a satisfactory work effort? How do various incentive schemes work that were devised to overcome the motivation problem?

This paper surveys the results of many experiments that were designed to answer these questions. There are, however, various ways how one can test the issues raised in the previous paragraph. Let us illustrate these possibilities with the help of an example that figures prominently in this survey. One important theory of wage determination is the so-called "gift exchange version" of efficiency wage theory (Akerlof 1982; Akerlof and Yellen 1990). This theory is based on lots of sociological and psychological research which supports the conclusion that the labour relation can often be characterised in terms of a "gift exchange" between workers and firms: firms voluntarily pay their workers above the next best alternative and workers respond with above-minimum work effort. Such behaviour can result in sticky wages and involuntary unemployment.

A first possibility to evaluate such an argument is to conduct *survey studies* and to interview personnel managers and other labour market participants about the determinants of their wage policy. Bewley (1999) is a particularly elaborate survey study (but see also Kahneman, Knetsch and Thaler 1986; Blinder and Choi 1990; Agell and Lundborg 1995; Campbell and Kamlani 1997). A finding of these studies is, for example, that personnel managers actually point to the importance of generosity and work morale in a way that is consistent with the gift-exchange version of efficiency wage theory. A second possibility is to conduct *case studies*. A recent example is Burks (1999) who argues that gift exchange motivations are important in the motor freight industry. Third, the most common possibility for economists is to perform econometric analyses of naturally occurring *field data*. For example, Krueger and Summers (1988), who, among others, found econometric evidence of non-compensating wage differentials, speculated that they may be explained by fair wage-effort or gift exchange considerations.

All three methods have their strengths and weaknesses. Economists are often not very fond of survey methods because they prefer *revealed* rather than *reported* behaviour. Case studies tend to be 'special cases' and it may be hard to generalise from them. Econometric studies with field data often lack appropriate data. And so on.

The issues we want to investigate in this paper are very hard, if not impossible, to study with field data. For example, we will demonstrate the power of gift exchanges as an explanation for various labour market phenomena. How can we assess the relative impact of gift exchanges if we observe successful cooperation in a naturally occurring employment relationship? The survey results, if we trust them, probably offer some hints. However, in real world contracting relationships there are always various intervening factors and motivations inextricably present at the same time. In a strict sense, therefore, survey studies and case studies, as well as field data, can only produce evidence that is *consistent* with a particular theory, but other theories may be consistent with the same outcome as well.

In addition, for many of these issues, all these problems are intensified by a lack of appropriate field data. How can we unambiguously measure a gift-exchange relationship that rests on reciprocal *preferences*? How can we measure "wage flexibility" and "wage rigidity" and causally link them to gift exchange motivations? Further examples of empirical difficulties are provided by various theories on incentive schemes that depend on data of the utility function that are inherently unobservable to the researcher.

The tools of *experimental economics* offer a way out of these problems. Laboratory methods allow the mapping of a particular model with its assumptions (including preferences) and environmental conditions into an economic situation in which real people have to make real economic decisions that involve monetary payments. (In *all* experiments that we will discuss in the following, participants received monetary payments according to their decisions.) Moreover, decisions take place under *controlled conditions,* like, e.g., anonymity. By stripping down an economic situation to its essential features we can – in a nutshell – unambiguously test the behavioural importance of some arguments as an explanation for naturally occurring phenomena. For example, we will demonstrate the occurrence of sticky wages in the laboratory and *causally* link them to gift exchange considerations. Hence, the decisive comparative advantage of laboratory methods is that one can control the decision situation and thereby exclude various intervening outside factors that plague empirical work on such issues. Moreover, one can test comparative static predictions and (counterfactual) consequences of institutional changes.

Sceptics may argue that one cannot learn much from these experiments because (i) stakes are usually "low", (ii) the students that are the subjects of most experiments lack the experience of most labour market participants and that (iii) the experiments are often artificial and lack context. These are, of course, very serious issues, and experimental economists are very well aware of them. For that reason, a lot of experiments discussed below were conducted to test these objections. However, we can assure the reader already at this place that (i) different stake *levels* do not lead to strikingly different behaviour; (ii) there are some surprising subject pool effects and that (iii) context and the decision frame matter to some degree in particular in strategically complicated decision situations.[1]

Despite the comparative advantages of experimental methods we would like to point out that we view experiments as a *complementary method* to all other methods of data gathering. After all, experiments can only help to validate an argument. The relevance of laboratory findings has to be evaluated in naturally occurring situations. We believe, however, that the laboratory findings in many cases support the evidence from the other methods. Together, the different methods may help to improve the behavioural foundations of labour economics (see Agell 1999, Bowles and Ginitis

[1] See Cooper, Kagel, Lo and Wei (1999) for an interesting discussion of interaction effects of subject pool and decision context in a strategically complicated game. See Hey (1991, Part I), Davis and Holt (1993, Chaps. 1 and 9) and Friedman and Sunder (1994) for further methodological discussions.

2000, and Kaufman 1999 for many arguments and findings from the other social sciences).

In the rest of this survey we will proceed as follows. We set the stage in Section 2 by first discussing the central role of contractual incompleteness in labour relations. We will review evidence that most people use the behavioural discretion that comes with contractual incompleteness in a reciprocal way. In Section 3 we will present experiments that were designed to test the explanatory power of reciprocity for various labour market phenomena that are hard to explain from the neo-classical viewpoint: rent-sharing and non-compensating wage differentials, endogenous wage rigidities, and the absence of entrance fees. Section 4 takes a closer look at employment relationships that are, mostly, long-term and social relationships. We will present experimental studies that evaluate the relative importance of these two elements in the presence of incomplete employment contracts.

In Sections 2 to 4 we deliberately present experiments where firms can only pay fixed wages and where – with some exceptions – no incentive contracts were possible. In Section 5 we change this focus by presenting experimental tests of various incentive schemes that are also used in reality and/or that have been proposed by theorists. We concentrate on the interplay of trust and voluntary cooperation, and explicit incentives. Section 6 concludes.

7.2 Consequences of incomplete employment contracts

A central observation about labour markets is that *labour relations are typically contractually incompletely regulated.* In incomplete contracts not all relevant aspects are comprehensively determined, and/or important aspects are not enforceable by third parties like the court. Very often the employment contract just stipulates a wage payment; many details that actually determine performance are not specified in the contract (see Milgrom and Roberts 1992, Chap. 5, for an illuminating discussion of the various reasons for contractual incompleteness). Under conditions of incompletely specified obligations and only weak or absent explicit performance incentives the issue of motivation arises. How can a firm motivate their employees to put forward an efficiency-enhancing effort level if effort is not fully contractually determined? Milgrom and Roberts (1992, p. 127) make the point very clear:

> "In principle, a perfectly fashioned **complete contract** [emphasis in original] could solve the motivation problem. It would specify precisely what each party is to do in every possible circumstance and arrange the distribution of realized costs and benefits in each contingency (including those where the contract's terms are violated) so that each party individually finds it optimal to abide by the contract's terms. [...] *motivation problems arise only because some plans cannot be described in a complete, enforceable contract* [emphasis in original]."

Notice that contractual incompleteness as defined here is of course not confined to employment relations but is prevalent in many business relations as well (see, e.g., Macaulay 1992; Milgrom and Roberts 1992, Hart 1995).

An implication of contractual incompleteness is that it opens up the room for *social norms* to govern behaviour. *Reciprocity,* in particular, may influence economic actions. For example, if employees choose their effort in reaction to the "generosity" of the firm's wage offer, firms may have an incentive to pay non-market clearing "efficiency wages" and thereby making a "gift" to the employees. In essence, this is what the "fair-wage effort hypothesis", or the "gift exchange hypothesis" of efficiency wage theory stipulates.

In the following we present a version of the gift exchange game that has been introduced into the literature by Fehr, Kirchsteiger and Riedl (1993, 1998) for the purpose of testing the gift exchange hypothesis. In the version of Falk, Gächter and Kovács (1999) and Gächter and Falk (2001) the potential role of reciprocity can be tested in a multiple *one-shot* gift exchange game. No form of reciprocal altruism, or any repeated game effect in general is possible in this design. This experiment, therefore, allows determining the importance of genuine reciprocity. We will describe the basic design in some detail because many of the experiments described in this survey incorporate a similar structure.

At the beginning of an experiment subjects are randomly allocated to their roles as 'firms' and 'workers', respectively (for simplicity we will henceforth call these subjects 'firms' and 'workers', respectively). The experimental game they play is a bilateral version of the so-called *'gift exchange game'*. In the **first stage**, subjects in the role of a firm make an employment offer to a particular worker. This employment offer consists of a *wage* offer. Wages have to be integers between 20 and 120 and the available effort levels are between 0.1 and 1 with increments of 0.1. In a given period each firm is paired with one given worker. After firms have made their wage offers, subjects in the role of workers, who have accepted that offer, have to make an effort decision at the **second stage** of the game. That is, workers have to determine their *actual effort level.* A worker's choice of an effort level is associated with costs for the worker as indicated in table 7.1. All participants are informed about the feasible effort levels and the costs of effort.[2]

Table 7.1. Effort levels e and costs of effort $c(e)$

e	**0.1**	**0.2**	**0.3**	**0.4**	**0.5**	**0.6**	**0.7**	**0.8**	**0.9**	**1**
$c(e)$	20	21	22	24	26	28	30	32	35	38

After firms are informed about the effort decision of 'their' worker, the second stage is completed and payoffs can be calculated. A worker's payoff π^W at the end

[2] 'Effort' can be interpreted as the monetary equivalent of the disutility of work, which increases in the effort level. The important point of this design feature is that it sets incentives that can be thought of being 'isomorphic' to real world effort choices that are perceived as being onerous. See Fahr and Irlenbusch (2000) and Sonnemans, van Dijk and van Winden (2001) for experiments with '*real* effort'.

of the second stage is given by

$$\pi^W = \begin{cases} w - c(e) & \text{upon acceptance} \\ 0 & \text{otherwise} \end{cases} \tag{7.1}$$

where w denotes the accepted wage and $c(e)$ the costs of the worker's actual effort. In case a worker does not trade, she earns nothing. A firm's payoff π^F is

$$\pi^F = \begin{cases} (v - w)e & \text{upon acceptance} \\ 0 & \text{otherwise} \end{cases} \tag{7.2}$$

where v denotes a firm's redemption value, i.e., the maximal gross profitability of a worker for the firm (provided $e = 1$). (Functional forms for firms are chosen to exclude the possibility of losses.) In the experiments v was set to 120. Again, all subjects knew these payoff functions. After the experiment, subjects were paid according to their decisions and according to their payoff functions.

Besides the studies of Falk, Gächter and Kovács (1999) and Gächter and Falk (2001), there exist several other gift exchange experiments (discussed below). However, the crucial feature of the present design is that it completely rules out any form of individual reputation formation. In these experiments there are ten periods and in each period each firm is exogenously and anonymously matched with a *new* worker. Thus, the probability of meeting the same subject twice is zero, while in the above-mentioned other gift exchange experiments this probability was positive. Therefore, the results in our experiments cannot be explained by the expectation to meet the same partner again in the future.

This two-stage design reflects a basic feature of most *employment relationships*, namely the incompleteness of the labour contract discussed above. Firms are neither able to condition *in a legally enforceable way* their wage payment on a particular effort, nor can they condition the wage on unambiguously verifiable output measures. Therefore, workers in the real world almost always have considerable discretion in determining their actual effort. In Gächter and Falk (2001) the only enforceable effort level is the minimum effort level of 0.1, for rational and selfish workers will – *regardless* of the wage payment – always choose $e = 0.1$. Firms, therefore, have no reason to pay more than $w = 21$, which is just enough to induce a selfish worker to accept the contract.

While selfishness predicts the choice of an effort level of 0.1 that is independent of the paid wage, *reciprocity* predicts an increase of the effort choice in the offered wage. A worker may perceive a generous wage as a 'gift'. If she is reciprocally motivated, she may feel a desire to repay the gift with an above-minimal effort choice. To the extent that such a voluntary 'gift exchange' between the worker and the firm actually takes place, efficiency is increased in this game with incomplete contracting.

The results of the one-shot experiments conducted in Austria (by Gächter and Falk 2001) and in Hungary (by Falk, Gächter and Kovács 1999) are summarised in Figure 7.1. Figure 7.1 impressively shows that – contrary to the selfishness prediction – workers choose effort levels that increase in the offered wage payment.

This holds for both countries, despite some level differences. Put differently, in both countries sufficiently many people are motivated by reciprocity. This makes it worthwhile for firms to offer generous wages. Reciprocity clearly mitigates the co-operation problem in the gift exchange game. Gächter and Falk (2001) also perform a detailed analysis of the individual data and find that reciprocity is also dominant at the individual level.

Fig. 7.1. Reciprocity in the one–shot gift exchange game

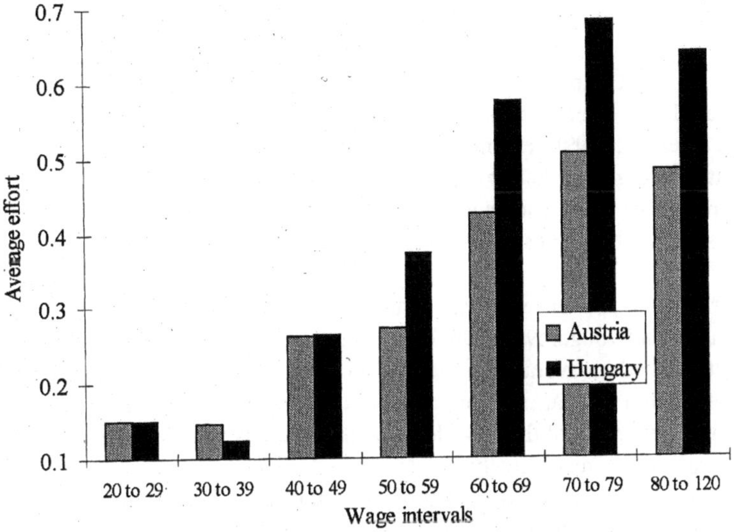

Sources: Gächter and Falk (Austria); Falk, Gächter and Kovács (Hungary).

Meanwhile – beginning with Fehr, Kirchsteiger, Riedl (1993, 1998) – this kind of reciprocal behaviour has also been observed in numerous gift exchange games under various institutional conditions and in various countries[3]. In particular, Fehr and Tougareva (1996) investigate the effect of stake size on reciprocal behaviour. Charness (1996; re-examined in Charness and Haruvy 1999) studies the role of attribution. Charness (2000) tests the "responsibility-alleviation effect", which states that "shifting the responsibility for outcomes to an external authority dampens internal impulses toward honesty, loyalty, or generosity" (p. 375). Charness, Frechette and Kagel (2001) investigate the robustness of laboratory gift-exchange with respect to different presentations of payoff functions. Fehr, Gächter and Kirchsteiger (1997) and Fehr and Gächter (1998) enlarge the possibilities for reciprocation by

[3] The gift exchange phenomenon was observed in experiments conducted in such diverse countries as Austria, Hungary, Portugal, Russia, Spain, Switzerland, The Netherlands and the USA.

adding a third stage with reward and punishment opportunities. Fehr, Gächter and Kirchsteiger (1993, 1997), and Fehr and Gächter (2001) investigate the impact of incentive contracts on reciprocal behaviour. Kirchler, Fehr, and Evans (1996), Fehr, Kirchler, Weichbold and Gächter (1998), Fehr and Falk (1999) and Brandts and Charness (2000) test the role of competition in reciprocal contract enforcement. Falk, Gächter and Kovács (1999) and Gächter and Falk (2001) – besides studying the baseline described above – also investigate the influence of repeated interaction and social approval incentives on reciprocal behaviour. Pereira, Silva and Andrade e Silva (2001) compare positive and negative reciprocity in the gift exchange game. Kirchsteiger, Rigotti and Rustichini (2000) study the impact of mood on the willingness to engage in gift exchanges. Hannan, Kagel and Moser (1999) study different subject pools. Hannan (2000) investigates the role of firm profit for employee effort. van der Heijden, Nelissen, Potters and Verbon (1998, 2001) and Lensberg and van der Heijden (1998) examine 'simple and complex gift exchanges' in yet another variant of the gift exchange game. In the following two sections we will describe some results of these studies in more detail. Before we move on, it is worthwhile to discuss briefly the issues of (i) stake levels, (ii) subject pool effects and (iii) "framing" effects.

First, it seems that reciprocal behaviour is robust even under *high stakes conditions*. Fehr and Tougareva (1996) conducted gift exchange games in Russia in which subjects earned on average up to three months' income in a two-hour session. In a control session the earnings opportunity decreased by a factor of ten. They could not detect any effect of the stake level on the frequency or strength of reciprocal and selfish responses, respectively.[4]

Second, there is the issue of subject pool effects. For example, Hannan, Kagel and Moser (1999) find that undergraduate students – although they engage in gift exchanges – behave less reciprocally than their MBA counterparts.[5] Hannan, Kagel and Moser attribute the subject pool differences to different work experiences undergraduates and MBA students might have when they enter the laboratory. Most undergraduates work in minimum wage jobs where gift exchanges are less important than in the jobs in which most MBA's work. In contrast, in Fehr, Kirchler, Weichbold and Gächter (1998), subjects were soldiers with various social backgrounds. Their behaviour was not at all different from student subjects.

Third, there is the issue of context. In some gift exchange experiments (e.g., in Fehr et al. 1998) the game was framed as an employer–employee relationship. In others, e.g., in Fehr and Gächter 2001, the game was presented as a buyer–seller re-

[4] Cameron (1999), and Hoffman, McCabe and Smith (1996) also do not find 'stake effects' in their (ultimatum game) experiments. Slonim and Roth (1998) find some slight effects that depend on experience and the stake size. See Camerer and Hogarth (1999) for a very comprehensive meta-study of stake-level effects. Their meta-study of 74 experiments reveals that in strategically simple games like ours high stakes do not lead to a different behaviour than low stakes. In strategically complex games, however, higher stakes affect behaviour.

[5] Fehr and List (2002) get a similar result in an investment game conducted in Costa Rica, where CEO's were both more trustful and trustworthier than student subjects.

lation. Although the issue of this kind of 'context–framing' has not been investigated systematically, the resulting gift exchanges are qualitatively the same. Even quantitatively, the results are very similar. Charness, Frechette and Kagel (2001) study another form of framing. They compare gift exchange games (with parameters that were very similar to those described above) where in one treatment the subjects are told the payoff functions (as in the experiments discussed above). In another treatment, the subjects are given a payoff table in addition to the payoff functions. Interestingly, the presence of payoff tables lowered (but did not eliminate) gift exchanges and increased strategic behaviour. Kirchsteiger, Rigotti and Rustichini (2000) show that the subjects' mood during the experiment also affects gift exchanges. Research on this kind of issues has just begun. It is important to understand under which conditions stable gift exchanges will occur. Yet, these latter results (and further ones discussed in Section 5) notwithstanding, there are important domains in which gift exchanges turned out to be a very robust observation.

In the gift exchange game described above, the focus has been on positive reciprocity. Generous wage payments are reciprocated with generous effort choices. The question therefore arises whether *negative reciprocity* – the willingness to *punish* greedy behaviour – is also effective in increasing effort levels in the gift exchange game. To test this, Fehr and Gächter (1998) introduced a **third stage** into their design, in which firms had – in addition to an opportunity to reward their worker (i.e., to behave positively reciprocal as well) – the possibility to *punish* a worker. Both rewards and punishments were costly. Only no punishment or no reward was costless.

The data shows that the selfishness prediction is neither borne out in the two-stage experiment (conducted as a control), nor in the three-stage experiment where the punishment and reward opportunities were present. In the two-stage games, effort levels were on average above 0.4. In the three-stage experiments, the prospects of a punishment or a reward were obviously highly credible. The average effort level in the three-stage treatment amounts to $e = 0.6$ which is significantly higher than the effort level achieved in the two-stage treatment. In both conditions effort levels were stable over time.

The observation of positive reciprocity is not restricted to the gift exchange game. Berg, Dickhaut and McCabe (1995) have designed an 'investment game' that resembles the gift exchange game. In this game, a first mover can pass on money to a second mover. The amount sent is tripled. The second mover then has to decide how much money to give back to the first mover. Pecuniary incentives are such that a selfish second mover is predicted to keep the whole amount for himself. The first mover, who anticipates this outcome, is predicted to pass nothing to the second mover. Actual outcomes are markedly different, though. First movers pass on considerable amounts to the second movers who reciprocate by giving back some money. This result has by now been replicated several times and turned out to be robust in many variations and across cultures.[6] Positive reciprocal behaviour has also been observed

[6] See Jacobsen and Sadrieh (1996); Croson and Buchan (1999); Fahr and Irlenbusch (2000); Ortmann, Fitzgerald and Boeing (2000); Buchan, Croson, and Dawes (2000); Cochard,

in related one-shot 'trust games' (see Bolle 1998; Dufwenberg and Gneezy 2000), in the one-shot sequential prisoner's dilemma game (see e.g., Bolle and Ockenfels 1998; Clark and Sefton 2001) and – in the form of conditional cooperation – in one-shot public goods experiments (Ockenfels 1998; Fischbacher, Gächter and Fehr 2001). Hoffman, McCabe and Smith (1998) and McCabe, Rassenti and Smith (1998) investigate reciprocity in a specially designed extensive form game and relate the results to insights from evolutionary psychology.[7]

Negative reciprocity can as well be observed in other games, for example in the form of rejections of greedy offers in the 'ultimatum game' (see Güth 1995b, Roth 1995 and Camerer 2001, Chap.3, for surveys). In the public goods game with punishment, negative reciprocity takes the form of punishment of free riders by the contributors (Fehr and Gächter 2000).

The 'moonlighting game' (invented by Abbink, Irlenbusch and Renner 2000, and replicated by Fehr, Falk and Fischbacher 2000, and Cox, Sadiraj and Sadiraj 2001) nicely combines possibilities for positive and negative reciprocation. In this game player A can give player B any integer amount of money $g \in [0,6]$ but, instead, he also can take from B any integer amount of money $t \in [1,6]$. In case of $g > 0$ the experimenter triples g so that B receives $3g$. If t is chosen, player A reaps t and player B loses t. After player B observes g or t, she can pay A an integer reward $r \in [0,18]$ or she can reduce A's income by making an investment $i \in [1,6]$. A reward transfers one money unit from B to A. An investment i costs B exactly i but reduces A's income by $3i$. In this game positive reciprocity occurs if $g > 0$ triggers $r > 0$. Negative reciprocity prevails if t leads to i. If players are selfish and rational the following outcome is predicted: B will always choose $r = 0$ because any other choice is costly. Therefore, A only loses if he chooses $g > 0$ and has nothing to fear if $t > 0$. As a consequence, A will choose $t = 6$.

The actual behaviour of subjects unambiguously rejects this prediction:

(i) Roughly 75 percent of player A's choose $g > 0$, although $t = 6$ is predicted.
(ii) On average, $g > 0$ elicits $r > 0$, so that positive reciprocity occurs.
(iii) If A's choose $t > 0$ they are, in general, heavily punished by $i > 0$. In less than ten percent of the cases $t = 6$ is chosen.

In summary, meanwhile there is comprehensive evidence that a majority of people behaves reciprocally even under strict one-shot conditions with no material incentives to reciprocate. Such behaviour can be observed in a variety of different

Van Phu, and Willinger (2000); Buchan, Johnson and Croson (2001); Cox (2000, 2002); Glaeser, Laibson, Scheinkman, and Soutter, (2000); Dufwenberg, Gneezy, Güth and van Damme (2001); Fershtman and Gneezy (2001); Burks, Carpenter and Verhoogen (2001), and Camerer (2001, Chap. 3) for an overview. While the gift-exchange game was inspired by the 'fair-wage effort hypothesis (Akerlof 1982), the investment game was not designed to test issues from labour economics but to test for non-selfish motivations. The findings from the gift-exchange game and the investment game correspond nicely.

[7] Reciprocal preferences may very well have evolutionary roots. Explanations in this direction comprise Güth (1995a), Huck and Oechssler (1999), Bowles and Gintis (1998), Gintis (2000) and Sethi and Somanathan (2001).

games and it has been replicated in various countries with different subject pools and under high stakes conditions. Camerer (2001, Chap. 3) provides a very comprehensive survey on the most important findings. In contractually incompletely regulated relationships there is room for behavioural discretion and most people use it in a reciprocal way. The fact that results are qualitatively similar across a range of games points to the robustness and importance of other-regarding preferences as opposed to the ubiquitous assumption of selfishness that governs most of (labour) economics.[8]

Since most employment relations are of necessity governed by incomplete contracts, the question of economic consequences for important issues in labour economics arises. First, one immediate conclusion from the above evidence is that the gift exchange version of efficiency wage theory (Akerlof 1982; and Akerlof and Yellen 1990) receives support from the laboratory. In this sense our results *complement* the findings from various survey studies mentioned in Section 1, which also corroborate the importance of gift exchanges, and the connection of "work morale" and "generosity". In the following section we further investigate the explanatory power of such "gift exchanges". Second, due to reciprocal behaviour the inefficiency problem inherent in contractual incompleteness is mitigated *for the contractual parties*, since actual effort levels are considerably above the predicted minimal (and inefficient) effort level of 0.1.

However, there is a caveat. Although reciprocity may be beneficial in a particular employment relationship, it may be detrimental for third parties. As it has been pointed out by Akerlof and Yellen (1990), fair wage-effort considerations may very well lead to involuntary unemployment (because employed workers enjoy a job rent), and, hence, result in an overall inefficiency.[9]

Falk and Fehr (1999) show that fairness considerations may indeed lead to unemployment. In their experiment a firm can in each period potentially conclude three contracts with homogenous workers. As it is usually assumed in labour market theory, the marginal product of labour is decreasing. In equilibrium, all three workers are profitable to the firm and should thus be employed. However, as the results of the experiment show, firms correctly anticipate that workers do not accept very "low" wages. Given the profitability of the "marginal" worker, firms' best response is to offer only two contracts, which *endogenously* leads to unemployment.

With the help of a three-person ultimatum game, Okada and Riedl (1999a,b) also present experimental evidence on this issue. In their design a proposer first has to make a choice between a three-person coalition and a two-person coalition, where the three-person coalition leads to a larger pie that can be distributed between

[8] Meanwhile there are several theories of reciprocity that try to explain the above-mentioned laboratory data. See Rabin (1993), Dufwenberg and Kirchsteiger (1998), Levine (1998), Falk and Fischbacher (1999), Fehr and Schmidt (1999), Bolton and Ockenfels (2000), and Charness and Rabin (2001).

[9] A similar conclusion holds for the phenomenon of corruption, where the two parties involved benefit from reciprocal bribery. However, reciprocity-based bribery may have negative externalities. On an experimental test of these arguments see Abbink, Irlenbusch and Renner (2001).

the coalition members than the two-person coalition. Hence, it would be efficient to form a three-person coalition. After the proposer has made a decision about the size of the coalition, she has to propose a division of the pie between the coalition members who can reject the proposal (resulting in zero payoffs for all parties). Okada and Riedl show that expected negative reciprocal behaviour expressed in the form of rejections of proposed divisions, often leads to inefficient coalition sizes and hence to the "social exclusion" of one bargaining partner.

7.3 Investigating important labour market phenomena

Can *reciprocity* explain various naturally occurring labour market phenomena that are hard to explain from the viewpoint of the standard model that assumes purely selfish motives? In this section we present evidence that demonstrates the power of reciprocity in explaining important labour market phenomena that have puzzled researchers for some time.

These puzzles are often very hard to resolve with the naturally occurring field data. Experimental methods, therefore, have a comparative advantage in assessing the explanatory power of social motivations that may have shaped naturally occurring field data. The empirical phenomena we address in turn are (i) rent sharing and non-compensating wage differentials, (ii) wage rigidity, and (iii) the general absence of entrance fees, which should be prevalent given that workers, for whatever reason, enjoy job rents.

7.3.1 Rent sharing and non-compensating wage differentials

In the standard neoclassical theory of wage determination a firm's profit plays no role at all for the wages workers of a given skill level receive. In equilibrium, with selfish preferences, workers are just paid their reservation wage, i.e., the value of their best alternative job opportunity. Therefore, workers do not enjoy job rents, i.e., wages above their reservation wage. However, much of empirical research on actual wage payments during the last decade has cast doubt on the empirical validity of this prediction. Recent micro-econometric evidence at the firm level supports the argument that wage payments contain some rent components. To mention just two examples, the papers by Blanchflower, Oswald and Sanfey (1996) and Hildreth and Oswald (1997) show that there is a positive relation between long-run wages and the lagged profitability of non-unionised companies or non-unionised industries, respectively. While rent-sharing theories of the labour market predict this correlation, it is not consistent with competitive theories.

Can *reciprocity* account for such a positive correlation between profitability and wages? The previously discussed gift exchange experiments already show unambiguously that workers earn rents. The reservation wage, which was set by the experimenter, was below the actual contract wage. In these experiments a majority of subjects actually is reciprocally motivated and it therefore pays for the firm to share the rent. Falk, Gächter and Kovács (1999) analyse rent sharing at some detail and find that equitable sharing is very important in explaining both observed wages and effort levels.

Rent sharing is also predicted by social psychological equity theory. According to equity theory people feel entitled to – and hence aim at – a share of the 'output' that equals their 'input share' used in the production of that output. Social psychological research has already established several decades ago the importance of equity in labour relations (see, e.g., Adams 1965, and Walster and Walster 1978; in economics, equity theory is discussed in Selten 1978 and Güth 1994). Königstein (2000, Chap. 1 and 3) and Gantner, Güth and Königstein (2001) present experimental evidence on this in the context of bargaining over the proceeds of joint production. In the experimental designs employed in these papers the two bargaining partners first both have to make a production decision (i.e., determine an "input") after which they bargain over the division of the jointly produced pie (i.e., the "output"). The designs are such that standard economic theory and equity theory make distinct predictions. All three papers report considerable support for equity theory over standard economic predictions, although it turns out that different people employ different equity standards.[10]

In summary, these findings suggest that to the extent that contracts are incomplete and/or wages are determined via bargaining between employers and employees, some rent sharing will occur. Equity standards and reciprocal behaviour are expected to significantly affect the bargaining outcome.

A related finding to rent sharing is the existence of inter-industry wage differentials. Even after controlling for a large number of job-, and worker-related characteristics, and demographic variables, large and statistically significant industry wage differences remain. Moreover, these differences exist for union as well as for non-union workers and seem to be remarkably similar (i) across countries with different labour market institutions, (ii) across occupations and (iii) across time. These observations clearly violate the 'law of one price', because, apart from compensated differences, homogeneous work should have the same price. In violation of the 'law of one price', two particularly interesting facts are that (a) high profit industries tend to pay high wages and (b) if one occupation in an industry is highly paid, all other occupations in that industry also tend to pay high wages (Dickens and Katz 1987; Krueger and Summers 1988; Katz and Summers 1989). If workers' perception of what constitutes a fair wage level is positively correlated with firms' profit opportunities, high profit firms are forced to pay a higher wage to elicit a *given* level of effort. Moreover, if higher profit opportunities are associated with a higher marginal product of effort, firms with high profit opportunities have an incentive to elicit higher effort levels. Both reasons may be responsible for the observed positive correlation between profits and wages in the field data. Hence, it may well be that rent sharing contributes to non-compensating wage differentials.

As shown in the previous sub-section, in experiments with incomplete labour contracts rent sharing *is* a common phenomenon. To investigate the impact of rent

[10] Ruffle (1998) also finds evidence for equity theory in the context of dictator and ultimatum games in which the recipient produces a pie according to her success in a skill contest.

sharing on wage differentials, Fehr, Gächter and Kirchsteiger (1996) have conducted gift-exchange experiments in a competitive market environment. To test for the consequences of different profit opportunities experimental firms differed according to the profitability of a given job. There were three levels of job profitability (i.e., the redemption value v in the firm's payoff function described above): v was high, intermediate or low. Firms with a high level of job profitability earned more per employed worker than firms with intermediate and low levels, respectively. To test for inter-temporal stability, the experiment was repeated 16 times. Theoretically, under the standard assumption of selfishness, firms' profitability should not have any impact on wage payments, i.e., there should be no wage differentials. Figure 7.2 gives the results.

Fig. 7.2. Wage differentials over time for different levels of job profitability for the firm

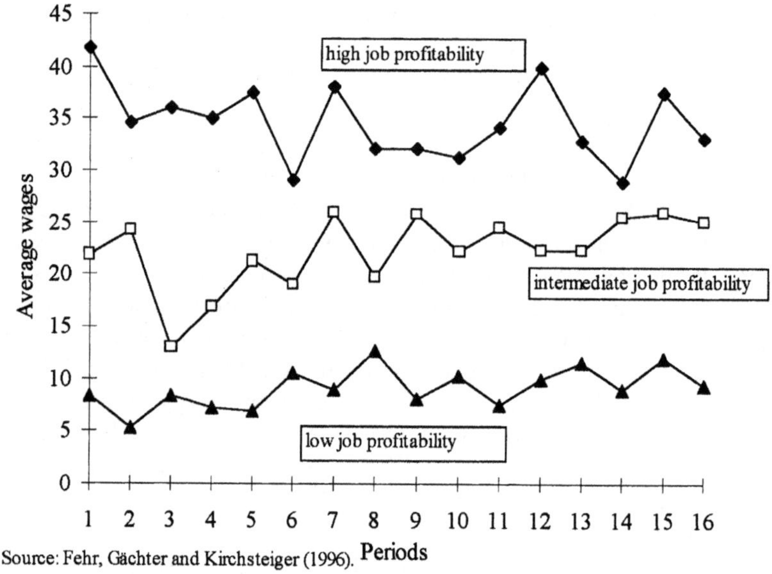

Source: Fehr, Gächter and Kirchsteiger (1996).

In sharp contrast to the neoclassical prediction, profit opportunities actually do influence wage payments. In the experiments, firms that were assigned high levels of job profitability paid higher wages than firms with intermediate and low levels of job profitability, respectively. Furthermore, the wage differentials are stable over time. By design, neither unobservable heterogeneity in working conditions, nor unobservable heterogeneity in skill levels, can be made responsible for these wage differentials. Hence, in support of arguments made by, e.g., Krueger and Summers (1988), we conclude that fair-wage effort considerations and the implied rent sharing can indeed explain non-compensating wage differentials.

It should be noted that the fair-wage effort hypothesis is not the only efficiency wage theory that can explain wage differentials. The so-called "shirking version of efficiency wage theory" that has been developed by e.g., Shapiro and Stiglitz (1984) and others, can also explain wage differentials. The shirking version is essentially a theory of involuntary unemployment that arises because of a *moral hazard* problem. In these models, firms pay incentive-compatible efficiency wages to prevent workers from shirking. Fehr, Kirchsteiger and Riedl (1996) have developed a simplified version of the shirking model and subjected it to an experimental test. As in Fehr, Gächter and Kirchsteiger (1996), firms differ in the assigned levels of job profitability. In contrast to the previous design, however, firms can verify shirking with a certain probability and punish shirking workers with a wage reduction.

The efficiency wage model of Fehr, Kirchsteiger and Riedl (1996) contains many testable predictions. For our present purposes the most important prediction is that there are non-compensating wage differentials: the higher a firm's job profitability, the higher is the optimal wage that is paid by the firm. The reason is that firms with higher job profitability demand higher effort levels and therefore have to pay higher wages to prevent shirking. The experimental results confirm this prediction.

In summary, two theories that predict wage differentials – the fair-wage effort hypothesis and the shirking version of efficiency wage theory – receive support in the laboratory. Hence, they are valuable candidate theories for the explanation of observed wage differentials outside the laboratory.

7.3.2 Wage rigidities and the role of competition

The presence of wage rigidities is one of the most important open questions in modern macroeconomics. Sticky wages have not only been made responsible for involuntary unemployment but also for business cycle fluctuations and real effects of monetary shocks. As long as rigid wages are not the result of some governmental regulation or of union power, they are hard to explain from a neoclassical point of view. The challenge is to find *endogenous* reasons why wages may be sticky. One of the many arguments that have been proposed in this direction is gift exchange theory (e.g., Akerlof 1982). Given that a gift exchange mechanism is at work, firms have no interest in lowering wages.

All our gift exchange experiments have produced results that are consistent with this argument. Wage *levels* are a function of rent sharing, but for a given job profitability, wages are sticky. As Figure 7.2 shows wages do not decline to the predicted level.

What is the impact of competition on wage rigidity? Fehr, Kirchler, Weichbold and Gächter (1998) report the first experiment that assesses the impact of competition on wage rigidity and gift exchanges. In this study, the gift exchange game is played in three different treatments. The first is a *'Bilateral Gift Exchange treatment'*, in which a given worker-firm pair remains paired for ten periods (as in Falk, Gächter and Kovács 1999 and Gächter and Falk 2001). The second treatment is a *'Gift Exchange Market'* in which there is an excess supply of labour and in which firms make wage offers in a one-sided oral auction. To assess the impact of contractual incompleteness on the wage formation process a *'Complete Contract Market'* is conducted in which there is no incomplete contract anymore because the effort level has been exogenously set to $e = 1$. Hence, the worker has no effort discretion anymore and has only to decide about acceptance or rejection of a wage offer.

In the gift exchange treatments the observed reciprocal behaviour is very similar to the one reported in Figure 7.1. Moreover, reciprocal responses are almost identical in the 'Bilateral Gift Exchange' and the 'Gift Exchange Market'. Second, average wage levels are also almost identical in these two treatments. Thus, competition seems to have a negligible effect on the formation of prices in markets with incomplete employment contracts. In the 'Complete Contract Market', however, where the effort level is exogenous and where, hence, there is no scope for positive reciprocity, wages actually decline over time.

The experiments by Fehr and Falk (1999) investigate wage rigidities in a particularly strong setup. In their experiments both firms and workers can engage in bidding, i.e., in their experiments wages are formed in a *'double oral auction market'*. Both workers and firms can make wage offers and demands, respectively. Firms are not forced to accept the lowest wage offer. In all other respects the experiments are similar to the ones by Gächter and Falk (2001) described in Section 2. Fehr and Falk (1999) compare two treatments: a double auction market with *incomplete contracts*, i.e., one where firms cannot condition their wage payment on an effort level and where workers do have effort discretion, and a double auction market with *complete contracts.* In these experiments the effort level is held fixed by the experimenter. The interpretation is that a homogeneous good of known and enforceable 'quality' is traded. This is the standard setup of dozens of market experiments (see Holt 1995 for an overview). Figures 7.3 and 7.4 show the most important results.

First, as Figure 7.3 demonstrates, workers indeed engage in considerable underbidding, but *firms refuse to accept low offers.* The reason is, once again, the workers' reciprocal behaviour: once a worker is employed, her effort decision depends positively on the received wage. This gives firms – even in such a highly competitive environment as a double auction – an incentive to pay generous and stable "efficiency" wages.[11] Figure 7.4 is testimony to the fact that the former result is not due to an impeded functioning of markets. With complete contracts, where workers do not have the possibility to behave positively reciprocally (though they still have the opportunity to reject wage offers), wages actually decline to very low levels. Firms now do take advantage of worker's underbidding.

Several survey studies corroborate these findings (see, e.g., Agell and Lundborg 1995; Campbell and Kamlani 1997, Bewley 1999). According to these studies, firms are even reluctant to hire under-bidders because they fear this would have a detrimental influence on work morale. This finding is fully compatible with the laboratory results. Both the survey results as well as the experimental findings do not support Solow's (1990) argument that there may exist a social norm against underbidding. If there is such a norm it is, as Figure 7.4 shows, overpowered by

[11] See Dufwenberg and Kirchsteiger (2000) for a theoretical account of this finding.

Fig. 7.3. Workers' offers and mean contract wages in the market with *incomplete* contracts

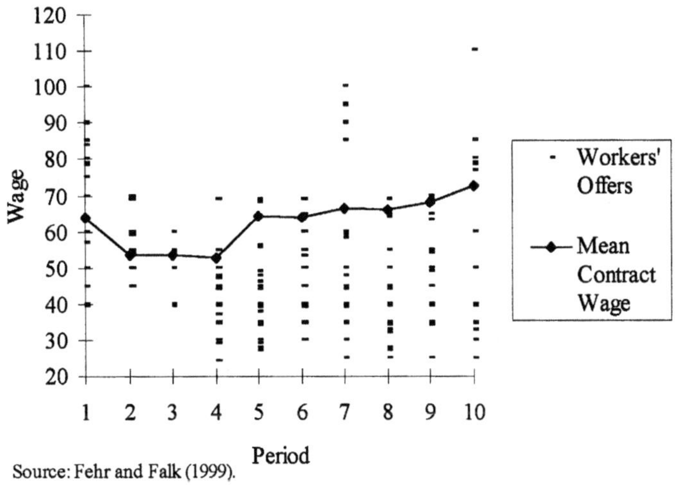

Source: Fehr and Falk (1999).

Fig. 7.4. Workers' offers and mean contract wages in the market with *complete* contracts

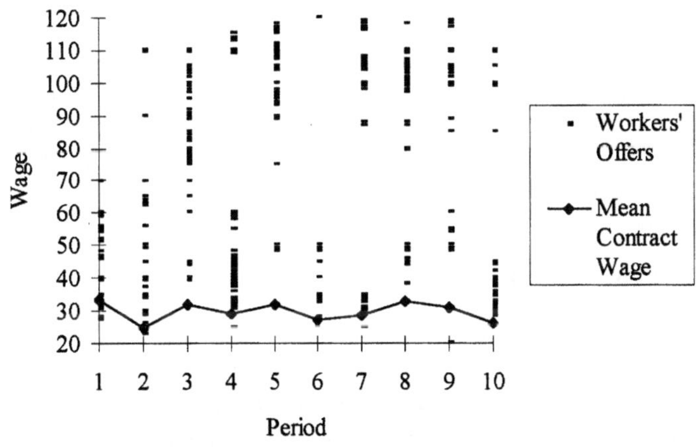

Source: Fehr and Falk (1999).

competitive forces. In the experiments with incomplete contracts (Figure 7.3) wage declines are prevented by reciprocity and not by a social norm against underbidding.

In contrast to the market experiments of Fehr, Kirchler, Weichbold and Gächter (1998), and Fehr and Falk (1999), Burda, Güth, Kirchsteiger, and Uhlig (1998) investigate the issue of wage rigidity in the context of a two-period *ultimatum game*. In their experimental setup there is an exogenously given wage – to be interpreted as a "competitive wage" – that declines from period 1 to period 2. The surplus of an employment relationship minus the competitive wage is constant between the two periods. Firms offer complete employment contracts by making take-it-or-leave-it wage offers to workers who do not have effort discretion. If a worker rejects a wage offer the firm can "hire" another worker at the exogenously set competitive wage. According to standard theory, firms are predicted to take advantage of the declining competitive wage and to offer lower wages in period 2. The experimental results are roughly in line with this prediction. Hence, in these ultimatum game experiments with complete contracts, wages also do not exhibit downward rigidity.

In summary, with *complete* contracts competition leads to wages that are close to the ones predicted by standard economic theory. In this respect the results from the market experiments are grossly in line with those of numerous other market experiments (see Holt 1995 for an overview). In ultimatum games with complete contracts wages are downwardly flexible as well. With *incomplete* employment contracts, however, wages are – due to reciprocal behaviour within an employment relationship – very insensitive to the amount of competition. These results suggest that labour markets that are characterised by complete contracts will roughly work as predicted by neo-classical labour market theory. However, labour markets, where employment relationships are inherently contractually incomplete, will exhibit wage rigidities. This outcome is expected even if the labour market is in all other respects completely unregulated and competitive.[12]

7.3.3 The absence of entrance fees

If workers, once they are on the job, earn rents because rents are necessary to ensure profitability-enhancing effort choices (i.e., workers earn 'efficiency wages'), the workers should be willing to make an up-front lump-sum payment to buy these rents. In other words, in a competitive market, they should be willing to pay an 'entrance fee' into the job at a price that equals the rent earned later on. Since this entrance fee is a lump-sum payment that is, moreover, paid up-front, it should not affect performance incentives on the job. Therefore, if efficiency wage considerations generate *ex post* rents, firms in competitive markets are predicted to charge entrance fees. Since, however, we do in general not observe entrance fees in real-world labour markets, workers do in fact not earn true *ex post* rents (see Carmichael 1985 for a formulation of this statement). This is a fundamental point. If true, there cannot be involuntary unemployment that arises solely from efficiency wage considerations. No worker earns a rent and, hence, the market clears.

[12] See Burks (1999) for an interesting case study from the motor freight industry.

If labour market participants would indeed all be selfish, it is difficult to find reasons for the absence of entrance fees, if workers actually earn on-the-job rents. If, however, fairness and reciprocity motivate sufficiently many labour market participants, they may denounce an entrance fee as very unfair. Entrance fees, if observed, could then lead either to a rejection of the contract, or to very low performance levels. Put differently, entrance fees – although they are up-front lump-sum payments – would not be behaviourally neutral. Hence, the absence of entrance fees could therefore also be due to anticipated negative behavioural effects of such payments.

It is hard to test such (counterfactual) arguments outside the laboratory. Therefore, Fehr, Gächter and Kirchsteiger (1993) have tested consequences of entrance fees in a labour market experiment where firms had an incentive to pay efficiency wages (with the implication of on-the-job rents) to minimise shirking on the job (see Shapiro and Stiglitz 1984 and the experiment by Fehr, Kirchsteiger and Riedl 1996). The market institution was a posted-bid market. The experimental design also explicitly allowed for 'up-front lump-sum payments' from the workers to the firms. The experimental parameters were such that 'up-front lump-sum payments' should show up if the entrance fee argument is correct. However, the design also allowed for positive 'up-front lump-sum payments' from the firms to the workers (i.e., the 'opposite' of an entrance fee).

The experimental results are again compatible with reciprocity and reject the implications of the selfishness assumption. On average, no entrance fees were observed. To the contrary, firms offered substantial *positive* up-front payments to the workers. Firms that actually tried to collect entrance fees did not succeed at all. Their contracts were either rejected or workers' performance was at its lowest possible level. Moreover, the higher the positive up-front payment to the workers the higher was the effort choice. Hence, although these payments are up-front and lump sum, they are not behaviourally neutral if people are reciprocally motivated. Again, since the majority of people is motivated by reciprocity considerations, it is not in the interest of the firms to demand entrance fees. These results suggest that reciprocity can explain the co-existence of on-the-job rents and the absence of entrance fees.

7.3.4 The employment contract as a long-term and social relation

Although some economic transactions resemble the anonymous one-shot games studied above, many economically important cooperation problems, most notably the employment relation, are markedly different. They do *not* take place only once and under such a restricted interaction structure as in the above experiments. In labour relations people interact repeatedly, which offers them many possibilities for reciprocation, reputation formation, and social exchange.

Laboratory experiments offer the unique possibility of changing the institutional conditions under which behaviour takes place in a controlled way. In the following we present evidence on the impact of two such institutional conditions on voluntary cooperation in incompletely regulated social relationships. In particular, the experiments reviewed below had the purpose of determining the relative importance of

(i) repeated interaction, and (ii) social exchange incentives that characterise many employment relationships. The benchmark for all these institutional variations is provided by behaviour under one-shot interactions.

7.3.5 The efficiency of long-term interaction

In the parlance of game theory long-term labour relations can be modelled as 'repeated games'. In contrast to our one-shot games, in *infinitely* repeated games it is well known from so-called 'folk theorems' that cooperation is compatible with selfishness (in the context of employment contracts see, e.g., MacLeod and Malcomson 1998). Even in *finitely* repeated games, it is possible to sustain cooperation over some time, provided rationality and selfishness are not 'common knowledge' (see Kreps, Milgrom, Roberts, and Wilson 1982).

In the last sections we have seen that a majority of people is reciprocally motivated. This suggests that some people also behave reciprocally in the repeated games; but now even those who are completely selfish may have material incentives to cooperate. This mixture of reciprocal and material incentives to cooperate may actually have interesting interaction effects. For instance, it may give the selfish subjects an incentive to imitate the reciprocal ones.

Thus, it is a challenge to understand *how* reciprocal and selfish subjects behave in a repeated interaction. Our experiments may help to pin down the empirically relevant regularities of behaviour in repeated gift-exchange situations. From an economic viewpoint the most important question is whether the mere fact of repeated play can actually help to attenuate the efficiency problem.

The experiments by Falk, Gächter and Kovács (1999) and Gächter and Falk (2001) address exactly this question in the context of the gift exchange game. As already mentioned, in both studies the baseline treatment was a so-called 'One-Shot-treatment', which is a sequence of one-shot games, played in each period by different worker-firm pairs. In both studies other treatment conditions consisted of *finitely* repeated gift exchange games in which each subject interacted ten times with the same opponent. The comparison of these two treatments allows the separation of the impact of a repeated interaction with the same opponent on cooperation from a pure reciprocity effect.

Figure 7.5 shows the result of the one-shot interactions and of three different repeated game interaction treatments (to be explained in more detail in the next subsection). There is actually a high benefit of a repeated interaction. Average effort levels in the repeated games are about 0.75 as compared to 0.5 in the one-shot interaction. Hence, contributions in the repeated game treatments clearly improved efficiency relative to the 'One-Shot-treatment'.[13]

Gächter and Falk (2001) qualitatively replicate this result. The main difference to Falk, Gächter, and Kovács (1999) is that in the repeated game they find an

[13] In public goods experiments similar results are observed in comparisons of one-shot and repeated interactions. Repeated interactions clearly improve cooperation rates in most experiments. See Croson (1996), Keser and van Winden (2000) and Keser (2001) for further results and a discussion.

Fig. 7.5. Average effort over time in a gift exchange game in repeated and random interactions in anonymous and non–anonymous conditions

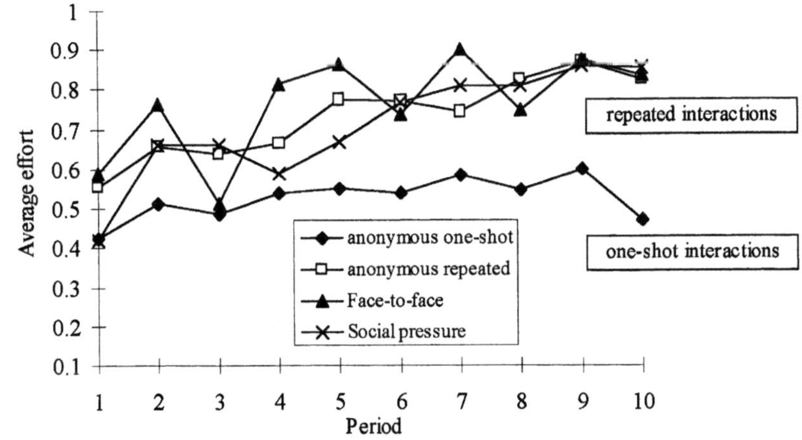

Source: Falk, Gächter, and Kovács (1999).

'endgame effect', i.e., a considerable drop in effort levels in the final period. Although wages did not fall, the average effort fell to about the levels of the one-shot game. The average effort level in the final period of the repeated game and the average effort in the final period of the one-shot game are not statistically significantly different. In a detailed statistical data analysis at an aggregate and individual level, Gächter and Falk (2001) show that some subjects in the repeated game actually *imitated* reciprocal play and reverted to their selfish strategy by the last period. The majority of subjects (at least 50 percent) is driven by a reciprocal motivation. As an upper bound, the behaviour of at most 30 percent is compatible with selfish reputation formation.

Cochard, Van Phu and Willinger (2000) are also interested in the effects of repetition on cooperative behaviour. They compare a finitely repeated investment game (of 7 rounds) and a sequence of seven one-shot investment games. They find, on average, that in the repeated game senders send more and receivers return more than in the one-shot games. They also find a severe drop in returned amounts in the final period of the repeated game, although the sender's investment levels were not different between conditions. Thus, the results from the repeated and one-shot gift-exchange games and the respective investment games correspond nicely.

The experiments by Falk, Gächter and Kovács (1999), Gächter and Falk (2001), and Cochard, Van Phu and Willinger (2000) show that a repeated interaction is itself able to mitigate the contract enforcement problem. To achieve a treatment comparison with one-shot contracts, the duration of the employment relation has been set exogenously in these experiments. This is in contrast to Anderhub, Königstein and Kübler (1999) who, in their experimental design, *endogenise* the length of the employment contract. Moreover, they investigate the relationship between firm-specific human capital investment and the employment duration. The formation of firm-specific human capital can provide a rationale for a long-term employment relation that is independent of the rationale given by the presence of reciprocal behaviour under incomplete contracts.

Anderhub, Königstein and Kübler (1999) endogenise contract length in a two-period game by giving firms the possibility to offer a 1-period contract (a 'short-term contract') or a 2-period contract (a 'long-term contract'). A firm can employ one worker two times under a short-term contract (i.e., rehire the worker in period 2), sack a worker after period 1 and hire a new one in period 2, or employ the same worker with a long-term contract. Workers bid for jobs and those workers who got a job have to decide on a firm-specific investment that benefits the worker by reducing his production cost. Parameters are such that investment is unprofitable if the worker is only employed for one period. The game-theoretic solution of the model proposes that investment is independent of contract length. Thus, the model is an example for the efficiency of spot markets. Theoretically long-term contracts do not increase firm-specific investment. In contrast to the game-theoretic solution the main hypothesis of Anderhub, Königstein and Kübler (1999) proposes a positive influence of contract length on investment decisions. The evidence supports their hypothesis: investment rates of experienced subjects are 69 percent for short-term contracts and 97 percent for long-term contracts (game theory predicts 100 percent in both cases). The authors conclude that job security may increase investment into firm-specific human capital even in environments where theoretically spot markets generate full efficiency. Thus, these results suggest that dismissal rules that grant job security may improve welfare (for econometric field evidence see, e.g., Bertola 1990).

7.3.6 The social embeddedness of the labour relation

A natural feature of many employment relationships is that they are also characterised by *social* interactions. In most instances work does not take place in a social vacuum, i.e., under completely anonymous conditions. Instead, employers and employees personally interact with each other. Something similar holds true in teamwork.

In general, a substantial amount of economic production takes place in personalised settings. Sociologists, like Granovetter (1992), have therefore stressed the 'embeddedness' of economic transactions in social structures in which social incentives are important as well. Blau (1964) points out that many incompletely regulated social relationships are characterised by a social exchange. In the work context, in particular, behaviour may be based on a social exchange of good performance against social approval. Consistent with this argument, human resource economists often stress the importance of social influences on work motivation. In team work 'peer pressure' can help to sustain work morale. Kandel and Lazear (1992), Rotemberg (1994), and Barron and Paulson Gjerde (1997) provide formal models in which voluntary cooperation can be observed in exchange for social approval.

How do social exchange incentives work in the gift exchange game? Are they capable of mitigating the cooperation problem? To ascertain the impact of social approval incentives and to separate them from repeated game effects, Falk, Gächter and Kovács (1999) have designed four treatment conditions. In all treatments the gift exchange game described in Section 2 was used. The first treatment was the pure *anonymous one-shot treatment* that we have already described above. All other treatments were finitely repeated games, i.e., the same firm-worker pair played the gift exchange game for ten periods. The second treatment just consisted of a ten-times repeated gift exchange game under *anonymity*. The third and the fourth treatment condition lifted anonymity. In the *third condition*, a particular firm-worker pair was seated *face to face*. Communication was not allowed neither during the experiment, nor afterwards. Thus, the exchange of social approval or disapproval was only possible through facial expressions. In the fourth condition, the *social pressure* treatment, subjects were also seated face to face. Subjects were told that they are not allowed to communicate during the experiment, but that they have to talk about their decisions at the end of the experiment. This discussion provided the possibility for verbal social exchange. These treatment conditions are a minimal setup to study the effects of social approval or disapproval without having communication as a coordination device available (see Bohnet and Frey 1999 and Falk, Gächter and Kovács 1999 for further discussion).

Figure 7.5 above contains the main results. In our discussion about the benefits of a long-term interaction, we have already observed that a repeated interaction considerably mitigates the cooperation problem. Surprisingly, adding social approval incentives did not change the outcome very much. Average effort levels increased only slightly. Since the design is 'additive' in the sense that – everything else equal – only one factor is added in a new treatment, this shows that, economically, the decisive step in mitigating the cooperation problem seems to be the repeated interaction. At least in these experiments, the social exchange incentives were of minor importance.

7.4 Work motivation and incentive schemes

In the previous sections we have seen a host of findings that underscore the importance of reciprocity-based voluntary cooperation. These results from the lab nicely complement the arguments by organizational scientists on the importance of "loyalty" (Simon 1997), "consummate cooperation" as opposed to "perfunctory cooperation" (Williamson 1985), "morale" and "good will" (Bewley 1999), "intrinsic motivation" (Frey 1997) and "organisational citizenship behaviour" (Organ 1988).

The importance of voluntary cooperation in modern labour relationships raises the question how *explicit performance incentives* affect voluntary cooperation. Economic theory has made a lot of progress in characterising optimal incentives schemes and contracts.[14] However, standard theory has neglected the importance of social motivations and the determinants of voluntary cooperation. In addition to the question how explicit incentives influence behaviour, the question of interaction effects between performance incentives and reciprocity-based voluntary cooperation comes up. Understanding the interplay of voluntary cooperation and explicit performance incentives is an important practical matter, because both performance incentives and voluntary cooperation are important in labour relations. In the following we concentrate on experiments that shed light on this interplay of voluntary cooperation and explicit incentives.[15]

We start with Fehr and Gächter (2001) who have extended the gift-exchange design by incorporating a very simple incentive device.[16] Firms could offer a contract $(w, f, \hat{e})$ that stipulated a wage w, a desired effort $\hat{e}$ and a fine f the worker had to pay if it could be verified that she has shirked, i.e., $e < \hat{e}$. With probability $0 < s < 1$ shirking was detected. Under the assumption of risk neutrality, a worker will not shirk (i.e., $e = \hat{e}$) if

$$w - c(\hat{e}) \geq s(w - f) + (1 - s)w \quad \Leftrightarrow \quad sf \geq c(\hat{e}) \tag{7.3}$$

holds.[17]

Parameters f and s were such that the maximally incentive-compatible effort was above the minimum but below the maximal feasible effort. In this framework, where voluntary cooperation is defined as an effort above the best-reply effort, Fehr and Gächter (2001) test two hypotheses: (i) reciprocity-based voluntary cooperation and financial incentives add up and (ii) financial incentives crowd out voluntary cooperation. The first hypothesis is supported if workers' effort choice only depends on the generosity of the firms' wage offer; the second hypothesis holds true if people perceive the fine as a threat and mistrust that is incompatible with voluntary

[14] See Gibbons (1998) and Prendergast (1999) for recent comprehensive surveys. Milgrom and Roberts (1992; in particular Chaps. 7-13) and Lazear (1995, 1998) provide textbook accounts.

[15] Investigating properties of incentive systems in the lab is a fertile area of research. DeJong, Forsythe, Lundholm and Uecker (1985), Berg, Daley, Dickhaut and O'Brien (1992), Epstein (1992), and Keser and Willinger (2000) investigated standard principal-agent games. Chaudhuri (1998) and Cooper, Kagel, Lo and Wei (1999) studied the 'ratchet effect'; Bull, Schotter and Weigelt (1987) tested tournaments and piece rates; Irlenbusch and Sliwka (2001) and Oosterbeek, Sloof and Sonnemans (2001) investigated 'career incentives'. Dickinson (2001) examined the relative merits of rewards and punishments in various incentive schemes. van Dijk, Sonnemans and van Winden (2001) studied incentives in real effort experiments.

[16] For related studies see Benz, Fehr and Frey (2001) and Fehr, Klein and Schmidt (2001) who investigate multitask relationships and Fehr and Rockenbach (2001) who study sanctions in the investment game.

[17] The left-hand side of the inequality is the worker's payoff from non-shirking and the right-hand side is the expected payoff of shirking if we assume that $e = e_0$ in case of shirking and $c(e_0) = 0$. Since, for simplicity, f does not depend on the amount of shirking, a worker who decides to shirk will always shirk fully, i.e., $e = e_0$.

cooperation. To judge possible crowding effects, Fehr and Gächter (2001) have also replicated the gift-exchange game without the fines (i.e., where firms could only offer $(w, \hat{e})$).

The data support the second hypothesis: while in the treatment without fines the previous results from the numerous gift-exchange experiments are replicated, voluntary cooperation breaks down in the incentive treatment. Instead, agents choose best-reply effort levels in many cases. Thus, it appears that the material incentives have led to a crowding out of voluntary cooperation.

Yet, is this result due to the material incentives *per se*, or is it just the framing of the incentive that is inimical to voluntary cooperation? To test this argument, Fehr and Gächter (2001) ran a treatment, where the incentive was framed as a bonus that was forfeited in case of detected shirking. Parameters were such that the incentive structure was exactly *identical* to the fine treatment (in the experiment no value-laden terms like fine or bonus were used). Thus, if crowding out of voluntary cooperation is due to the material incentives per se we should get a similar result as with fines, since the bonus is just a differently framed incentive device. If fine and bonus are perceived differently, despite being the same materially, then we might not observe a crowding out of voluntary cooperation. The data support the latter reasoning. With a bonus as an incentive device, voluntary cooperation was largely left intact.

An interesting observation from these experiments concerns *efficiency* as measured by the surplus (the sum of profits of worker and firm). Here it turned out that efficiency was highest in the experiments without explicit incentives, and lowest with fines as incentive devices. However, the firms' profits were highest with fines and lowest without any incentives.

Profit sharing is another possibility to align interests between an employer and an employee. An employee who receives a profit share has an incentive to provide an above-minimum effort level because his effort choice has an impact on the profit. This mitigates the efficiency problem associated with contract enforcement. Put differently, it is exactly this incentive that is lacking in incomplete contracts in which firms can only pay a fixed wage.

Building on previous experiments by Güth, Klose, Königstein, and Schwalbach (1998) and Fehr and Gächter (1998), Anderhub, Gächter, and Königstein (2001) have investigated this idea in a principal-agent framework.[18] Their design is as follows. A firm can offer the worker a work contract that consists of three elements: a fixed wage w, a return share s ($s \in [0,1]$), and a desired effort level $\hat{e}$, which is nonbinding (as above). An agent, after having accepted a contract, then has to choose an effort level. This effort produces a return of $r(e)$. The payoffs to the worker and the firm, respectively, are as follows:

$$\pi^W = sr(e) + w - c(e) \quad \text{and} \quad \pi^F = (1-s)r(e) - w. \tag{7.4}$$

[18] See Güth, Königstein, Kovács and Zala-Mezõ (2001) and Königstein, Kovács and Zala-Mezõ (1999) for extensions to a design with multiple agents, and Nalbantian and Schotter (1997) for an experiment on profit sharing at the group level.

The fixed wage w can be positive or negative. For example, $w > 0$ and $s = 0$ is a contract in which the firm just offers a fixed wage to the worker and keeps the whole return (this is the situation we have analysed so far). At the other extreme, if $s = 1$ and $w < 0$, this is tantamount to 'selling the return to the worker' at a price of $w < 0$. Hence, this design allows for a great variety of contracts. In the subgame perfect equilibrium, however, the contract $[s = 1, w* < 0$ such that $-w* = c(e^{max}) - r(e^{max})]$ is the solution: If all parties are rational and selfish, they will realise that it is the worker with his effort decision, who solely produces the return. The return is highest if the effort is highest (i.e., $e = e^{max}$). This is also the efficient outcome. If the worker gets the full return (i.e., with a profit share of $s = 1$) she has no reason to provide less than full effort. The maximal price that the firm can ask for is the difference between this maximal return and the effort costs. A selfish worker, in turn, will be willing to pay any price $w < 0$ that leaves him with a non-negative payoff (i.e., $r(e) - c(e) \geq 0$). In other words, in equilibrium, the firm will appropriate the whole surplus.

Two main results of the experiment are in line with these predictions. First, it is indeed the case that in the overwhelming number of concluded contracts the firms offer return shares of $s = 1$. Second, the workers' effort behaviour is in most cases 'incentive compatible' in the sense that the workers provide *at least* the effort level that is individually rational given the incentives set by the particular profit share. Hence, in these experiments a high degree of efficiency is reached.

The prediction that firms will ask for the maximal price, i.e., the whole surplus, is not borne out by the data. Most contract offers were such that they shared the resulting surplus about equally by proposing an appropriate $w < 0$. Workers indeed rejected contracts if the price they had to pay was 'unfairly high' and would have left them with almost zero profit. This finding is very much in line with related experimental results on the 'ultimatum game' (see Güth 1995b, and Roth 1995 for overviews) and the evidence on rent sharing discussed above. Keser and Willinger (2000), in their 'principal-agent' experiment, also found that the agents behaved in concordance with the incentives set by the principals and that they rejected 'unfair contracts'.

Do these results imply that there is no reciprocity anymore in this contracting game? The data do not allow us to draw such a conclusion. A further analysis shows that workers deviated in a reciprocal way from their best-reply effort level. In line with the previous findings discussed above, the more generous the contract offer of the firm, the higher has been the effort choice of the worker (Güth, Klose, Königstein and Schwalbach 1998 get a similar result in their principal-agent experiment). This result allows connecting to the above findings. It appears that this kind of profit sharing is a performance incentive that leaves the reciprocal motivation intact.[19]

[19] In a further exploration of the data collected by Anderhub, Gächter and Königstein (2001), Königstein (1999) investigates optimal contract design based on actual as opposed to theoretical behaviour of agents. He estimates the empirical acceptance function and the empirical effort function and thereafter determines the payoff consequences of alternative contracts. He finds that the principal's income is maximised by a mixed contract with an

A further study is by Schotter (1998) who investigated the role of trust in the achievement of equilibria in an incentive system. The experiment was one where the incentive system was team profit sharing, which induces two equilibria (a 'high' and a 'low' effort equilibrium) that differ in their *vulnerability*. Roughly, vulnerability can be defined as the extent of 'riskiness' of an equilibrium in terms of how much an agent who provides a high level of effort is hurt by a lower effort put forward by his companion workers. The basic idea of the experiment is that workers' trust in high effort choices of others may help them to co-ordinate on a 'high effort', but 'vulnerable' equilibrium. The more 'trust' workers have, the more likely are 'high but vulnerable' effort choices.[20] In various treatments Schotter (1998) showed that this argument is indeed borne out by the data. Schotter concluded that "worker trust and system vulnerability" are complementary. This has important implications for the design of work places and performance systems. In concordance with the previous results reported above, it is not only the incentive properties of the incentive mechanisms that matter but also the social norms and the norms of trust workers hold and develop with their fellow workers.

Gneezy and Rustichini (2000a) conducted a very nice field experiment to test the interplay between explicit incentives and voluntary cooperation. Their subject pool were ten Israeli day-care centres for young children, where the parents are supposed to pick up their kids at 4 p.m. Many parents arrive late, which forces the teachers to stay. Simple economic theory suggests that the introduction of a fine will do away with the problem. To test this prediction, Gneezy and Rustichini (2000a) ran a field experiment in cooperation with the managers of the day-care centres (but without the knowledge of the parents). They recorded the late-arrivals in all ten day-care centres for four weeks. After four weeks, six day-care centres announced a small fine for arriving late. In the other four day-care centres, which served as the control group, the patterns of late arrivals were just observed and no fine was introduced. After twelve weeks the fine was abolished in all six day-care centres. Late arrivals were just recorded (in all ten day-care centres). Figure 7.6 documents the results of this field experiment.

The results show that the pattern of late-arriving parents is stable over time in the control group. In the first four weeks the pattern of late arrivals is the same in both

intermediate level of profit share and fixed wage, rather than by a contract with a very high profit share but low fixed wage. Specifically, keeping the agent's income constant, it is optimal to choose an intermediate policy-mix rather than an extreme one. Although this result may depend on the specifics of the experiment of Anderhub, Gächter and Königstein (2001), by identifying the behaviourally relevant acceptance and incentive functions, this result points to a general avenue for behavioural research in principal-agent games.

[20] In these experiments 'trust' should arise endogenously. Before playing the profit sharing game, all subjects had to play a coordination game with many Pareto-rankable equilibria. Some subjects first had to play the 'minimum effort game' where experimental play reliably leads to the Pareto-inferior equilibrium (see Ochs 1995 for an overview). In contrast, other subjects first played a 'median effort game' where usually Pareto-better equilibria are reached. Schotter conjectures that the former leads to a 'low trust' climate in the subsequent profit sharing game, whereas the latter induces high trust. Schotter replicates the results from various co-ordination game experiments and shows that either type of co-

Fig. 7.6. Average number of late–coming parents, per week

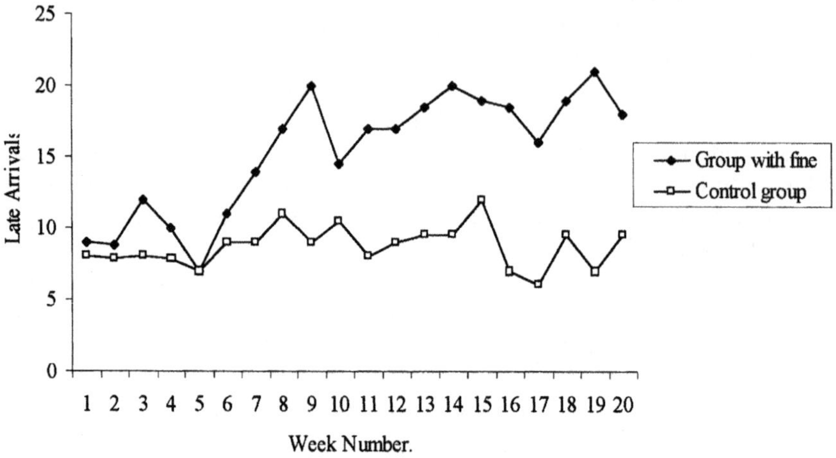

Source: Gneezy and Rustichini (2000a)

the control group and the treatment group. However, after the day-care centres of the treatment group introduced the fines, the number of late-arrivals *increased,* instead to decrease as is predicted by economic theory. After the fine was abolished, late-arrivals remained at the increased levels. Gneezy and Rustichini (2000a) argue that fines, as well as rewards, may change the perception of the psychological contract: While the day-care centres operated on a basis of good will before the fines were introduced, parents may have perceived the fine as a price: "Once a commodity, always a commodity" (p. 16).

In another related study Gneezy and Rustichini (2000b) come to a similar conclusion. In this paper, they investigated performance incentives in two different tasks (using different subject pools). The tasks were (i) answering 50 questions taken from an IQ-test (called the "IQ Experiment") and (ii) collecting monetary donations for societies of cancer research (called the "Donation Experiments"). In the IQ experiment they studied different levels of payments: no payment, 10 cents, 1 New Israeli Shekel (NIS), and 3 NIS; in the donation experiment subjects received either no payment, or 1 or 10 percent, respectively, of the collected amount. In both experiments, economic theory predicts a monotonic relationship between the level of incentives and the respective performance. The results are striking. In the IQ experiment, subjects in the no payment condition answered on average 28.4 questions correctly. In the low incentive condition, performance dropped to 23.07 correct questions. With NIS1 and NIS3 the number of correct answers increased to 34.7 and 34.1, respectively. A similar result is found in the donation experiment: With no payment, sub-

ordination game is a good predictor of behaviour in the hypothesised direction in the profit sharing game.

jects collected on average 238.6 NIS. With a payment of 1 percent, the collected donations dropped to 153.6 NIS and amounted to 219.3 NIS if subjects received 10 percent of the donated money. Gneezy and Rustichini (2000b, p. 807, emphasis theirs) summarize their findings as follows: "The result has been that the usual prediction of higher performance with higher compensation, *when one is offered,* has been confirmed: but the performance may be lower *because of* the introduction of the compensation." The reason might be that very low payments are perceived as "insulting".

It is worthwhile to set the findings from this section into perspective to the results on the repeated gift-exchange experiments discussed above. There we have seen that the mere fact of having a 'long-term' relation considerably increases voluntary cooperation, without any explicit performance incentives that may have dysfunctional effects. One reason might be that the incentives that are provided by a repeated interaction are perceived as "reciprocity-compatible" in the sense that they leave the reciprocal motivations intact. Moreover, a repeated interaction may foster social ties that attenuate shirking incentives (van Dijk, Sonnemans, van Winden 2000). In addition, those not motivated by reciprocity have an incentive to imitate reciprocity. Thus, simply having a long-term employment relation may mitigate the shirking problem. In our opinion, these laboratory findings support arguments in the business literature that praise the benefits of long-term employment relationships (e.g. Pfeffer 1999; Miller, 1992, Chaps. 9 and 10).[21]

A summary of the basic message of all experiments in this subsection suggests that in incomplete contracts not only the material incentives are important but also the *perception* of the terms of the contract is crucial (see also Frey 1997). This makes things less straightforward than economic theory suggests. Understanding the incentives, *as people perceive them,* surely is an important task for future research.

What are the implications for the design of optimal contracts (see also Königstein 2001)? The results reviewed above show that material incentives can have counterproductive effects.[22] While this suggests that one should take crowding out effects seriously, it does not mean that material incentives will in general impair efficiency. The presence of fairness-related voluntary cooperation indicates that incentives should be designed such that they do not inhibit voluntary cooperation. More generally, optimal contracts should take the perception of the "psychological contract" into account and not only focus on the material incentive effects.

7.5 Concluding remarks

In this paper we have surveyed recent laboratory experimental research that is inspired by issues that are important in labour and personnel economics. In doing this, we have concentrated on four topics: (i) the behavioural consequences of incomplete employment contracts and the importance of gift-exchange motivations;

[21] See Gächter and Falk (2002) and Fehr and Falk (2001) for further discussion.

[22] A similar logic may hold for contract enforcement through the law. See Frey (1997, Chap. 6) and Bohnet, Frey and Huck (2001) for a theoretical model and experimental evidence.

(ii) how the behavioural regularities can explain important labour market phenomena; (iii) characteristics of employment relations, and (iv) the interplay of various incentive schemes with trust and voluntary cooperation.

The starting point of our review has been the contractual incompleteness of most actual labour relations. Incompleteness leaves room for behavioural discretion. With selfishly motivated labour market participants many of these relationships are bound to reap only inefficiently low gains from trade whereas a more 'co-operative behaviour' would lead to higher gains from trade. We have in particular investigated the role of *reciprocity* as a contract enforcement device and as a means to overcome inefficiencies inherent in contractual incompleteness. However, in principle, all experiments on social motivations and on the conditions of successful co-operation are of relevance here. By now, there is an abundance of evidence that most people are not only motivated by their selfish material gain. Much of this evidence has been gained from carefully conducted, simple stylised games, like the ultimatum- and the dictator game, the prisoner's dilemma and voluntary contribution games, trust- and investment games, and so on (see Kagel and Roth 1995 and Camerer 2001 for the most comprehensive overview to date). Many experiments reviewed in this paper – in particular those on incentive schemes – can also be seen as a 'test' to what extent social motivations identified in simple and stylised games, transfer to the more complex economic incentive structures that may be relevant in labour market contexts.

Open issues in labour economics have inspired most of the experiments reviewed in this survey. One of the fascinating aspects of research in this area is that the empirical methods can be used in a *complementary* way to provide better behavioural foundations of labour economics (Agell 1999; Kaufman 1999; Bowles and Gintis 2000). Economic theory and empirical methods like case studies, interviews with labour market participants, conventional econometric analysis of field data, and laboratory research, can help identifying – in an interdisciplinary way – the principles that govern employment relations and the labour market.

References

1. Abbink, Klaus, Bernd Irlenbusch and Elke Renner (2000): "The Moonlighting Game. An Experimental Study on Reciprocity and Retribution", *Journal of Economic Behavior and Organization* 42, 265-277.
2. Abbink, Klaus, Bernd Irlenbusch and Elke Renner (2001): "An Experimental Bribery Game", *Discussion paper*, University of Erfurt.
3. Adams, John (1965): "Inequity in Social Exchange", in: Leonard Berkowitz (ed.), *Advances in Experimental Psychology* 2. New York: Academic Press.
4. Agell, Jonas (1999): "On the Benefits from Rigid Labour Markets: Norms, Market Failures, and Social Insurance", *Economic Journal* 109, F143–F164.
5. Agell, Jonas and Per Lundborg (1995): "Theories of Pay and Unemployment: Survey Evidence from Swedish Manufacturing Firms", *Scandinavian Journal of Economics* 97, 295 - 307.
6. Akerlof, George (1982): "Labor Contracts as Partial Gift Exchange", *Quarterly Journal of Economics* 97, 543-69.

7. Akerlof, George and Yellen, Janet (1990): "The Fair Wage-Effort Hypothesis and Unemployment", *Quarterly Journal of Economics* 105, 255 - 283.
8. Anderhub, Vital, Manfred Königstein, and Dorothea Kübler (1999): "Firm-specific Investment of Workers and Length of Contract. An Experimental Investigation", *mimeo,* Humboldt-University.
9. Anderhub, Vital, Simon Gächter, and Manfred Königstein (2001): "Efficient Contracting and Fair Play in a Simple Principal-Agent Experiment", forthcoming in *Experimental Economics.*
10. Barron, John, and Kathy Paulson Gjerde (1997): "Peer Pressure in an Agency Relationship", *Journal of Labor Economics* 15, 234-254.
11. Benz, Matthias, Ernst Fehr and Bruno Frey (2001): "Multitask Relationships, Incentives, and Intrinsic Motivation", *mimeo,* University of Zurich.
12. Berg, Joyce, John Dickhaut, and Kevin McCabe (1995): "Trust, Reciprocity, and Social History", *Games and Economic Behavior* 10, 122-142.
13. Berg, Joyce, Lane Daley, John Dickhaut and John O'Brien (1992): "Moral Hazard and Risk Sharing: Experimental Evidence", in: Mark Isaac (ed.), *Research in Experimental Economics Vol. 5.* Greenwich: JAI Press Inc.
14. Bertola, Guiseppe (1990): "Job Security, Employment and Wages", *European Economic Review* 34, 851-886.
15. Bewley, Truman (1999): *Why wages don't fall in a recession.* Cambridge: Harvard University Press.
16. Blanchflower, David, Andrew Oswald, and Peter Sanfey (1996): "Wages, Profits, and Rent-Sharing", *Quarterly Journal of Economics* 111, 227-252.
17. Blau, Peter (1964): *Exchange and Power in Social Life.* New Brunswick: Transaction Publishers.
18. Blinder, Alan and Don Choi (1990): "A Shred of Evidence on Theories of Wage Stickiness", *Quarterly Journal of Economics,* 105, 1003-1016.
19. Bohnet, Iris and Bruno Frey (1999): "The Sound of Silence in Prisoner's Dilemma and Dictator Games", *Journal of Economic Behaviour and Organization* 38(1), 43–57.
20. Bohnet, Iris, Bruno Frey and Steffen Huck (2001): "More order with less law: On contract enforcement, trust, and crowding", *American Political Science Review* 95(1), 131-144.
21. Bolle, Friedel (1998): "Rewarding Trust – An Experimental Analysis" *Theory and Decision* 45, 83-98.
22. Bolle, Friedel and Peter Ockenfels (1990): "Prisoners' dilemma as a game with incomplete information", *Journal of Economic Psychology* 11, 69-84.
23. Bolle, Friedel and Alexander Kritikos (1998): "Self–Centered Inequality Aversion versus Reciprocity and Altruism", *Discussion Paper,* Europa–Universität Viadrina, Frankfurt(Oder).
24. Bolton, Gary and Axel Ockenfels (2000): "ERC – A Theory of Equity, Reciprocity, and Competition", *American Economic Review* 90(1), 166-193.
25. Bowles, Samuel and Herbert Gintis (2000): "Walrasian Economics in Retrospect", *Quarterly Journal of Economics* 115, 1411–1439.
26. Bowles, Samuel and Herbert Gintis (2001): "The Evolution of Strong Reciprocity", *Mimeo,* University of Massachusetts.
27. Brandts, Jordi and Gary Charness (2000): "Do Market Conditions Affect Preferences? Evidence from Experimental Markets with Excess Supply and Excess Demand", *mimeo,* CSIC Barcelona.
28. Buchan, Nancy, Eric Johnson and Rachel Croson (2001): "Trust, Reciprocity and Altruism: An International Experiment", *mimeo.*

29. Buchan, Nancy, Rachel Croson and Robyn Dawes (2000): "Direct and Indirect Trust and Reciprocity", *mimeo.*
30. Burda, Michael, Werner Güth, Georg Kirchsteiger, and Harald Uhlig (1998): "Employment Duration and Resistance to Wage Reductions: Experimental Evidence", *Discussion Paper 74,* Humboldt University.
31. Burks, Stephen (1999): *The Origins of Parallel Segmented Labor and Product Markets: A Reciprocity-Based Agency Model with an Application to Motor Freight.* PhD Dissertation, University of Massachusetts.
32. Burks, Stephen, Jeffrey Carpenter and Eric Verhoogen (2001): "Playing Both Roles in the Trust Game", forthcoming in *Journal of Economic Behaviour and Organization.*
33. Camerer, Colin (2001): *Behavioral Game Theory: Experiments on Strategic Interaction.* Forthcoming: Princeton University Press.
34. Camerer, Colin and Robin Hogarth (1999): "The Effects of Financial Incentives in Experiments: A Review and Capital-Labor-Production Framework", *Journal of Risk and Uncertainty* 19(1-3), 7-42.
35. Cameron, Lisa (1999): "Raising the Stakes in the Ultimatum Game: Experimental Evidence from Indonesia", *Economic Inquiry* 37(1), 47-59.
36. Campbell, Carl and Kunal Kamlani (1997): "The Reasons for Wage Rigidity: Evidence from a Survey of Firms", *Quarterly Journal of Economics* 112, 759-789.
37. Carmichael, Lorne (1985): "Can Unemployment be Involuntary?" *American Economic Review* 75, 1213-1214.
38. Charness, Gary (1996): "Attribution and Reciprocity in a Simulated Labor Market: An Experimental Investigation", *Mimeo,* UC Berkeley.
39. Charness, Gary (2000): "Responsibility and Effort in an Experimental Labor Market", *Journal of Economic Behavior and Organization* 42: 375-384.
40. Charness, Gary and Ernan Haruvy (1999): "Altruism, Equity, and Reciprocity in a Gift-Exchange Experiment: An Encompassing Approach", forthcoming in: *Games and Economic Behavior.*
41. Charness, Gary and Matthew Rabin (2001): "Social Preferences: Some Simple Tests and a New Model." *Mimeo,* University of California at Berkeley.
42. Charness, Gary, Guillaume Frechette and John Kagel (2001): "How Robust is Laboratory Gift-Exchange?" *Mimeo.*
43. Chaudhuri, Ananish (1998): "The ratchet principle in a principal agent game with unknown costs: an experimental analysis", *Journal of Economic Behavior and Organization* 37, 291-304.
44. Clark, Kenneth and Martin Sefton (2001): "The Sequential Prisoner's Dilemma: Evidence on Reciprocation", *Economic Journal* 111, 51-68.
45. Cochard, François, Nguyen Van Phu and Marc Willinger (2000): "Trust and reciprocity in a repeated investment game", *mimeo,* Université Louis Pasteur Strasbourg.
46. Cooper David, John Kagel, Wei Lo and Qingliang Gu (1999): "Gaming Against Managers in Incentive Systems: Experimental Results with Chinese Students and Chinese Managers", *American Economic Review* 98(4), 781-804.
47. Cox, James (2000): "Trust and Reciprocity: Implications of Game Triads and Social Contexts", *mimeo,* University of Arizona.
48. Cox, James, Klarita Sadiraj and Vjollca Sadiraj (2001): "Trust, Fear, Reciprocity, and Altruism", *mimeo.*
49. Cox, James (2002): "Trust, Reciprocity, and Other-Regarding Preferences: Groups vs. Individuals and Males vs. Females", in: Amnon Rapoport and Rami Zwick: *Experimental Business Economics.* Dordrecht: Kluwer Academic Publishers.

50. Croson, Rachel (1996): "Partners and strangers revisited", *Economics Letters* 53, 25-32.
51. Croson, Rachel and Nancy Buchan (1999): "Gender and Culture: International Experimental Evidence from Trust Games", *American Economic Review, Papers and Proceedings* 89(2), 386-391.
52. Davis, Douglas and Charles Holt (1993): *Experimental Economics*. Princeton: Princeton University Press.
53. DeJong, Douglas, Robert Forsythe, Russell Lundholm and William Uecker (1985): "A Laboratory Investigation of the Moral Hazard Problem in an Agency Relationship", *Journal of Accounting Research* 23 (Supplement), 81-120.
54. Dickens, William and Lawrence Katz (1987): "Inter-Industry Wage Differences and Industry Characteristics", in: Kevin Lang and Jonathan Leonhard (eds.), *Unemployment and the Structure of Labor Markets*, New York: Basil Blackwell.
55. Dickinson, David (2001): "The Carrot vs. the Stick in Work Team Motivation", *Experimental Economics* 4(1), 107-124.
56. Dufwenberg, Martin and Georg Kirchsteiger (1998): "A Theory of Sequential Reciprocity", *Working paper*, Stockholm University.
57. Dufwenberg, Martin and Georg Kirchsteiger (2000): "Reciprocity and wage undercutting", *European Economic Review* 44(4-6), 1069-1078.
58. Dufwenberg, Martin and Uri Gneezy (2000): "Measuring Beliefs in an Experimental Lost Wallet Game", *Games and Economic Behavior* 30, 163-182.
59. Dufwenberg, Martin, Uri Gneezy, Werner Güth, and Eric van Damme (2001): "Direct vs. Indirect Reciprocity", *Homo Oeconomicus* 18, 19-30.
60. Epstein, Seth (1992): "Testing Principal-Agent Theory", in: Mark Isaac (ed.), *Research in Experimental Economics Vol. 5*. Greenwich: JAI Press Inc.
61. Fahr, René and Bernd Irlenbusch (2000): "Fairness as a constraint on trust in reciprocity: earned property rights in a reciprocal exchange experiment", *Economics Letters* 66, 275-282.
62. Falk, Armin and Ernst Fehr (1999):"Fairness and Unemployment", *mimeo*, University of Zürich.
63. Falk, Armin, Ernst Fehr and Urs Fischbacher (2000): "Testing Theories of Fairness – Intentions Matter", *Working Paper* No. 63, Institute for Empirical Research in Economics, University of Zurich.
64. Falk, Armin, Simon Gächter, and Judit Kovács (1999): "Intrinsic Motivation and Extrinsic Incentives in a Repeated Game with Incomplete Contracts", *Journal of Economic Psychology* 20(3), 251-284.
65. Fehr, Ernst and Armin Falk (1999): "Wage Rigidity in a Competitive Incomplete Contract Market", *Journal of Political Economy* 107, 106-134.
66. Fehr, Ernst and Armin Falk (2001): "Psychological Foundations of Incentives", forthcoming in *European Economic Review*.
67. Fehr, Ernst and Simon Gächter (1998): "How Effective are Trust- and Reciprocity-Based Incentives?" in: Avner Ben-Ner and Louis Putterman (eds.), *Economics, Values, and Organization*. Cambridge: Cambridge University Press.
68. Fehr, Ernst and Simon Gächter (2000): "Cooperation and Punishment in Public Goods Experiments", *American Economic Review* 90, 980-994.
69. Fehr, Ernst and Simon Gächter (2001): "Do Incentive Contracts Crowd Out Voluntary Cooperation?", *Working Paper No.* 35, Institute for Empirical Economic Research, University of Zurich.
70. Fehr, Ernst, Simon Gächter, and Georg Kirchsteiger (1993): "Reciprocity versus Competitive Forces: The Impact of Entrance Fees in an Experimental Efficiency Wage Market", *Working Paper*, University of Vienna.

71. Fehr, Ernst, Simon Gächter, and Georg Kirchsteiger (1996): "Reciprocal Fairness and Noncompensating Wage Differentials", *Journal of Institutional and Theoretical Economics* 152, 608-640.
72. Fehr, Ernst, Simon Gächter, and Georg Kirchsteiger (1997): "Reciprocity as a Contract Enforcement Device: Experimental Evidence", *Econometrica*, 65(4), 833-860.
73. Fehr, Ernst, Erich Kirchler, Andreas Weichbold, and Simon Gächter (1998): "When Social Norms Overpower Competition – Gift Exchange in Experimental Labor Markets", *Journal of Labor Economics* 16, 324-351.
74. Fehr, Ernst, Georg Kirchsteiger and Arno Riedl (1993): "Does Fairness Prevent Market Clearing? An Experimental Investigation", *Quarterly Journal of Economics* 108, 437-460.
75. Fehr, Ernst, Georg Kirchsteiger and Arno Riedl (1998): "Gift exchange and reciprocity in competitive experimental markets", *European Economic Review* 42, 1-34.
76. Fehr, Ernst, Alexander Klein and Klaus Schmidt (2001): "Fairness, Incentives, and Contractual Incompleteness", *Working Paper No.* 72, Institute for Empirical Economic Research, University of Zurich.
77. Fehr, Ernst and John List (2002): "Do Explicit Incentives Reduce Trustworthiness? – An Experiment with CEOs", *mimeo*, University of Zürich.
78. Fehr, Ernst and Bettina Rockenbach (2001): "The Hidden Cost of Economic Incentives", *mimeo*, University of Zurich.
79. Fehr, Ernst and Klaus Schmidt (1999): "A Theory of Fairness, Competition and Cooperation", *Quarterly Journal of Economics* 114, 817-868.
80. Fehr, Ernst and Elena Tougareva (1996): "Do High Stakes Remove Reciprocal Fairness – Evidence from Russia", *mimeo*, University of Zurich.
81. Fershtman, Chaim and Uri Gneezy (2001): "Discrimination in a Segmented Society: An Experimental Approach", *Quarterly Journal of Economics* CXV, 351-377.
82. Fischbacher, Urs, Simon Gächter and Ernst Fehr (2001): "Are people conditionally cooperative? Evidence from a public goods experiment", *Economics Letters* 71, 397-404.
83. Frey, Bruno (1997): *Not Just For the Money. An Economic Theory of Personal Motivation.* Cheltenham: Edward Elgar Publishing.
84. Friedman, Daniel and Shyam Sunder (1994): *Experimental Methods. A Primer for Economists.*Cambridge: Cambridge University Press.
85. Gächter, Simon and Armin Falk (2001): "Reputation and Reciprocity – Consequences for the Labour Relation", forthcoming in: *Scandinavian Journal of Economics.*
86. Gächter, Simon and Armin Falk (2002): "Work motivation, Institutions, and Performance" in : Amnon Rapoport and Rami Zwick: *Experimental Business Economics.* Dordrecht: Kluwer Academic Publishers.
87. Gantner, Anita, Werner Güth and Manfred Königstein (2001): "Equitable choices in bargaining games with joint production", *Journal of Economic Behavior and Organization* 46, 209-225.
88. Gibbons, Robert (1998): "Incentives in Organizations", *Journal of Economic Perspectives* 12, 115-132.
89. Gintis, Herbert (2000): "Strong Reciprocity and Human Sociality", *Journal of Theoretical Biology* 206, 169-179.
90. Glaeser, Edward, David Laibson, José Scheinkman and Christine Soutter (2000): "Measuring Trust", *Quarterly Journal of Economics* CXIV, 817-868.
91. Gneezy, Uri and Aldo Rustichini (2000a): "A Fine is a Price", *Journal of Legal Studies* XXIX, 1-17.
92. Gneezy, Uri and Aldo Rustichini (2000b): "Pay Enough or Don't Pay at all", *Quarterly Journal of Economics* CXV(3), 791-810.

93. Granovetter, Mark (1992): "The Sociological and Economic Approaches to Labor Market Analysis: A Social Structural View", in: Mark Granovetter and Richard Swedberg (eds.), *The Sociology of Economic Life*. Boulder: Westview Press.
94. Güth, Werner (1994): "Distributive Justice. A Behavioral Theory and Empirical Evidence", in: Hermann Brandstätter and Werner Güth (eds): *Essays on Economic Psychology*, Berlin: Springer.
95. Güth, Werner (1995a): "An evolutionary approach to explaining cooperative preferences by reciprocal incentives", *International Journal of Game Theory* 24, 323-344.
96. Güth, Werner (1995b): "On ultimatum bargaining experiments – a personal review", *Journal of Economic Behavior and Organization* 27, 329-344.
97. Güth, Werner, Wolfgang Klose, Manfred Königstein, and Joachim Schwalbach (1998): "An Experimental Study of a Dynamic Principal-Agent Relationship", *Managerial and Decision Economics* 19, 327-341.
98. Güth, Werner, Manfred Königstein, Judit Kovács, Enikö Zala-Mezõ (2001): "Fairness Within Firms: The Case of one Principal and Multiple Agents", *Schmalenbach Business Review (Zeitschrift für betriebswirtschaftliche Forschung)*, 53, 82-101.
99. Hannan, Lynn (2000): "The Effect of Firm Profit on Fairness Perceptions, Wages and Employee Effort", *mimeo*, J. Mack Robinson College of Business, Georgia State University.
100. Hannan, Lynn, John Kagel, and Donald Moser (1999): "Partial Gift Exchange in Experimental Labor Markets: Impact of Subject Population Differences, Productivity Differences and Effort Requests on Behavior", forthcoming in *Journal of Labor Economics*.
101. Hart, Oliver (1995): *Firms, Contracts, and Financial Structure*. Oxford: Clarendon Press.
102. Hey, John (1990): *Experiments in Economics*. Oxford: Basil Blackwell.
103. Hildreth, Andrew and Andrew Oswald (1997): "Rent sharing and wages: evidence from company and establishment panels", *Journal of Labor Economics* 15, 318-337.
104. Hoffman, Elizabeth, Kevin McCabe, and Vernon Smith (1996): "On Expectations and the Monetary Stakes in Ultimatum Games", *International Journal of Game Theory* 25, p. 289 - 301.
105. Hoffman, Elizabeth, Kevin McCabe, and Vernon Smith (1998): "Behavioral Foundations of Reciprocity: Experimental Economics and Evolutionary Psychology", *Economic Inquiry* 36, 335-371.
106. Holt, Charles (1995): "Industrial Organization: A Survey of Laboratory Research", in: John Kagel and Alvin Roth (eds.), *Handbook of Experimental Economics*. Princeton: Princeton University Press.
107. Huck, Steffen, and Jörg Oechssler (1999): "The indirect evolutionary approach to explaining fair allocations", *Games and Economic Behavior* 28, 13-24.
108. Irlenbusch, Bernd and Dirk Sliwka (2001): "Career Concerns in a Simple Experimental Labour Market", *mimeo*, University of Erfurt.
109. Jacobsen, Eva and Sadrieh, Abdolkarim (1996): "Experimental Proof for the Motivational Importance of Reciprocity", *Discussion Paper No. B-386*, University of Bonn.
110. Kagel, John and Alvin Roth (1995): *The Handbook of Experimental Economics*. Princeton: Princeton University Press.
111. Kahneman, Daniel, Jack Knetsch and Richard Thaler (1986): "Fairness as a Constraint on Profit Seeking: Entitlements in the Market", *American Economic Review* 76, 728-741.
112. Katz, Lawrence and Lawrence Summers (1989): "Industry Rents: Evidence and Implications", *Brookings Papers on Economic Activity (Microeconomics)*, 209-290.
113. Kaufman, Bruce (1999): "Expanding the Behavioral Foundations of Labor Economics", *Industrial and Labor Relations Review* 52(3), 361-392.

114. Keser, Claudia (2001): "Cooperation in Public Goods Experiments", in: Friedel Bolle and Marco Lehmann-Waffenschmidt (eds.): *Surveys in Experimental Economics. Bargaining, Cooperation and Election Stock Markets*. Physica Verlag.
115. Keser, Claudia and Marc Willinger (2000): "Principals' principles when agents' actions are hidden", *International Journal of Industrial Organization* 18, 163-185.
116. Keser, Claudia and Frans van Winden (2000): "Conditional Cooperation and Voluntary Contributions to Public Goods", *Scandinavian Journal of Economics* 102, 23-39.
117. Kirchler, Erich, Ernst Fehr, and Robert Evans (1996): "Social exchange in the labor market: Reciprocity and trust versus egoistic money maximization", *Journal of Economic Psychology* 17, 313-341.
118. Kirchsteiger, Georg, Luca Rigotti and Aldo Rustichini (2000): "Your Morals are Your Moods", *CentER Working Paper* No. 2000–122.
119. Königstein, Manfred (1999): "Optimal Contracting With Boundedly Rational Agents", forthcoming in: *Homo oeconomicus.*
120. Königstein, Manfred (2000): *Equity, Efficiency and Evolutionary Stability in Bargaining Games with Joint Production.* Lecture Notes in Economics and Mathematical Systems 483. Berlin et al.: Springer.
121. Königstein, Manfred, Judit Kovács, Enikö Zala-Mezõ (1998): "Fairness in One Principal-Multiple Agents-Situations – Post-experimental Questionnaire Analysis", *mimeo*, Humboldt-University Berlin.
122. Kreps, David, Paul Milgrom, John Roberts and Robert Wilson (1982): "Rational Cooperation in the Finitely Repeated Prisoners' Dilemma", *Journal of Economic Theory* 27, 245-252.
123. Krueger, Alan and Lawrence Summers (1988): "Efficiency Wages and the Inter-Industry Wage Structure", *Econometrica* 56, 259-94.
124. Lazear, Edward (1995): *Personnel Economics.* Cambridge: The MIT Press.
125. Lazear, Edward (1998): *Personnel Economics for Managers.* New York: John Wiley & Sons, Inc.
126. Lazear, Edward (1999): "Personnel Economics: Past Lessons and Future Directions", *Journal of Labor Economics* 17(2), 199-236.
127. Lensberg, Terje, Eline van der Heijden (1998): "A Cross-Cultural Study of Reciprocity, Trust and Altruism in a Gift Exchange Experiment", *CentER for Economic Research Working Paper No.* 9877.
128. Levine, David (1998): "Modeling Altruism and Spitefulness in Experiments", Review of Economic Dynamics 1, 593-622.
129. Macaulay, Steward (1992): "Non-Contractual Relations in Business: A Preliminary Study" in: Mark Granovetter and Richard Swedberg (eds.), *The Sociology of Economic Life*. Boulder: Westview Press.
130. MacLeod, Bentley and James Malcomson (1998): "Motivation and Markets", *American Economic Review* 88, 388-411.
131. McCabe, Kevin, Stephen Rassenti, and Vernon Smith (1998): "Reciprocity, Trust, and Payoff Privacy in Extensive Form Bargaining", *Games and Economic Behavior* 24, 10-24.
132. Milgrom, Paul and John Roberts (1992): *Economics, Organization and Management.* New Jersey: Prentice Hall International.
133. Miller, Gary (1992): *Managerial Dilemmas: The Political Economy of Hierarchy.* Cambridge University Press.
134. Nalbantian, Haig and Andrew Schotter (1997): "Productivity under Group Incentives: An Experimental Study", *American Economic Review* 87, 314-341.

135. Ochs, Jack (1995): "Co-ordination Problems", in: John Kagel and Alvin Roth (eds.), *Handbook of Experimental Economics*. Princeton: Princeton University Press.
136. Ockenfels, Axel (1999): *Fairness, Reziprozität und Eigennutz – ökonomische Theorie und experimentelle Evidenz*, Tübingen: J.C.B. Mohr (Paul Siebeck).
137. Okada, Akira and Arno Riedl (1999a): "Inefficiency and Social Exclusion in a Coalition Formation Game: Experimental Evidence", *mimeo*, CREED University of Amsterdam.
138. Okada, Akira and Arno Riedl (1999b): "When Culture Does Not Matter: Experimental Evidence from Coalition Formation Ultimatum Games in Austria and Japan", *mimeo*, CREED University of Amsterdam.
139. Olson, Mancur (1965): *The Logic of Collective Action. Public Goods and the Theory of Groups*. Cambridge: Harvard University Press.
140. Oosterbeek, Hessel, Randolph Sloof and Joep Sonnemans (2001):"Promotion rules and skill acquisition: an experimental study" *mimeo*, CREED University of Amsterdam.
141. Organ, Dennis (1988): *Organizational Citizenship Behavior*. Lexington, Mass.: Lexington Books.
142. Ortmann, Andreas, John Fitzgerald and Carl Boeing (2000): "Trust, Reciprocity, and Social History: A Re-examination", *Experimental Economics* 3(1), 81-100.
143. Pereira, Paulo, Nuno Silva, and João Andrade e Silva (2001): "Positive and negative reciprocity in the labor market", *mimeo*, ISEG, Technical University of Lisbon.
144. Pfeffer, Jeffrey (1998): "Six Dangerous Myths about Pay", *Harvard Business Review* May-June, 109-119.
145. Prendergast, Canice (1999): "The Provision of Incentives in Firms", *Journal of Economic Literature* XXXVII, 7 – 63.
146. Rabin, Matthew (1993): "Incorporating Fairness into Game Theory and Economics", *American Economic Review* 83, 1281 - 1302.
147. Rotemberg, Julio (1994): "Human Relations in the Workplace", *Journal of Political Economy* 102, 684-717.
148. Roth, Alvin (1995): "Bargaining Experiments", in: Alvin Roth and John Kagel (eds.), *Handbook of Experimental Economics*. Princeton: Princeton University Press.
149. Ruffle, Bradley (1998): "More Is Better, But Fair Is Fair: Tipping in Dictator and Ultimatum Games", *Games and Economic Behavior* 23, 247 – 265.
150. Schotter, Andrew (1998): "Worker trust, system vulnerability, and the performance of work groups" in: Avner Ben-Ner and Louis Putterman (eds.), *Economics, Values, and Organization*. Cambridge: Cambridge University Press.
151. Schotter, Andrew and Keith Weigelt (1992): "Asymmetric Tournaments, Equal Opportunity Laws, and Affirmative Action: Some Experimental Results", *Quarterly Journal of Economics* 107, 511-539.
152. Selten, Reinhard (1978): "The Equity Principle in Economic Behavior". In: Hans Gottinger and Wolfgang Leinfellner (eds.), *Decision theory and Social Ethics*. Dordrecht: Reidel.
153. Sethi, Rajiv and E. Somanathan (2001), "Understanding Reciprocity", forthcoming in: *Journal of Economic Behavior and Organization.*
154. Shapiro, Carl and Joseph Stiglitz (1984): "Equilibrium Unemployment as a Worker Discipline Device", *American Economic Review* 74, 433-444.
155. Simon, Herbert (1997): *Administrative Behavior. A Study of Decision-Making Processes in Administrative Organizations*. 4th Edition. New York: The Free Press.
156. Slonim, Robert and Alvin Roth (1998): "Learning in High Stakes Ultimatum Games. An Experiment in the Slovak Republic", *Econometrica* 66, 569-596.
157. Solow, Robert (1990): *The Labour Market as a Social Institution*. Oxford: Basil Blackwell.

158. van der Heijden, Eline, Jan Nelissen, Jan Potters, and Harry Verbon (1998): "The poverty game and the pension game: The role of reciprocity", *Journal of Economic Psychology* 19, 5-41.
159. van der Heijden, Eline, Jan Nelissen, Jan Potters, and Harry Verbon (2001): "Simple and Complex Gift Exchange in the Laboratory", *Economic Inquiry* 39, 280-297.
160. van Dijk, Frans, Joep Sonnemans, and Frans van Winden (2000): "Social Ties in a Public Goods Experiment", forthcoming in: *Journal of Public Economics.*
161. van Dijk, Frans, Joep Sonnemans, and Frans van Winden (2001): "Incentive systems in a real effort experiment", *European Economic Review* 45, 187-214.
162. Walster, E. and G. Walster (1978): *Equity - Theory and Research.* Boston: Allyn and Bacon.
163. Williamson, Oliver (1985): *The Economic Institutions of Capitalism.* New York: Free Press.

8 Comment on Simon Gächter and Ernst Fehr

Manfred Königstein*

The survey by Simon Gächter and Ernst Fehr gives a nice account of recent experiments in the field of labour economics. Compared to the thousands of empirical studies in labour economics that use field data – i.e., data collected within natural environments as opposed to the laboratory – there are, so far, only a few experimental investigations. And these experiments do not yet cover all topics of modern labour economics as they are outlined e.g. in Ashenfelter and Hallock (1995). However, Gächter and Fehr show how laboratory investigations can add to the evidence of field studies or even provide answers when field studies remain silent. Experiments are no substitute for field studies, but important complementary research tools. The two authors themselves have in fact done much of the work in this area of experimental research. The main topics covered by the survey may be labelled "wage determination" and "effort incentives". Within this comment I will summarize some of the results provided in the article and outline a few directions for further research.

Labour relations are complex relationships. The motives of interacting individuals are unknown, and there are many aspects of labour relations that could be relevant for observed behavior. This holds for both interactions within the field as well as interactions within the laboratory. Within the lab, however, the conditions for subjects' decisions can be manipulated easily. For instance, payoff schemes may be changed to influence motivation. In the field such manipulations are difficult, if not impossible. So experiments may address research questions that are infeasible outside the lab due to a lack of control. Furthermore, in the lab environmental variables may be adjusted one at a time, whereas in the field, quite often, many things change at the same time. So it may be is easier in the lab to attribute a behavioral response to a specific cause. In summary, experiments allow to test very specific theories. Hence, they may lead to refined theoretical concepts and increase the ability to discriminate between controversial causes of economic phenomena. Some of the experiments described in the survey are good examples of this potential of labour experiments.

8.1 Wage determination

Experiments allow to compare the empirical wage level that arises in economic interaction, with its theoretical level. In field studies this is generally infeasible, since one lacks information on variables that determine the theoretical wage level (e.g. outside option values of the conflicting parties). Experiments are therefore important tests for theories of wage determination. In principle, the wage policy has to

* For helpful comments I thank Simon Gächter. Financial support by the Deutsche Forschungsgemeinschaft, SFB 373, and the EU, TMR Research Network ENDEAR (FMRX-CT98-0238) is gratefully acknowledged.

take its consequences on workers' effort choices into account (see below). So both issues, wage determination and effort incentives, are quite closely connected.

A robust phenomenon in lab experiments is that the wages paid to subjects in the role as workers are higher than predicted by economic theory; specifically, there is rent sharing between employers and employees. This holds in the bilateral gift exchange game (Gächter and Falk (2001) as well as in ultimatum bargaining with joint production (Königstein (2000)).

Theoretical reasons for rent sharing might be, for instance, fairness concerns of the conflicting parties. Or the employer may be willing to prevent shirking by paying the worker a rent which is lost if the relationship terminates - this argument relies on a long-term relationship. Furthermore the degree of rent sharing might depend on bargaining power.

Experiments show that a long-term relationship is sufficient, but not necessary for rent sharing. It occurs even when parties interact only once (Falk, Gächter and Kovács (1999)). Gächter and Fehr attribute this to "reciprocity" as an important motivational force driving subjects' behavior. Subjects are willing to sink money in order to reward good behaviour or punish bad behaviour of others. Employers anticipate reciprocal activities of workers. So, paying a rent to a worker may actually be beneficial to the employer himself.

Interestingly, employers pay rents even when there is competition among workers (Fehr, Kirchler, Weichbold and Gächter (1998)). Furthermore, in market experiments more profitable firms pay higher wages than less profitable firms (Fehr, Gächter and Kirchsteiger (1996)). However, the influence of competition on the degree of rent sharing depends on the incompleteness of the work contract: If work effort is incompletely enforceable, employers do not hire "underbidders"; thus, wages are above the competitive level. But, if effort is enforcable, wages are close to the competitive level (Fehr and Falk (1999)).

These studies are examples how lab exeriments can be used to address fine-tuned empirical questions. It is obvious how these findings relate, e.g., to issues of monitoring in firms; note that imperfect monitoring is one theoretical reason for incomplete enforceability of work effort. Thus, these experiments might feed back into theoretical work and field studies. They offer some justification for a downward rigidity of wages. Furthermore, the finding of rent sharing in work contracts offers a microeconomic explanation for non-compensating wage differential between industries that are found in field studies. Finally, one might be interested in determining a firm's optimal wage policy in this environment; i.e., the wage policy that maximizes a firm's profit given the observed restrictions on workers' behavior. However, little work has been done on this issue so far (e.g. Königstein (forthcoming)).

8.2 Effort incentives

The question here is: "What is the impact of monetary reward schemes on employees' choices of effort levels"? The starting point for Gächter and Fehr is again the gift exchange game. It exhibits the most simple monetary reward scheme one can think of: a pure fixed wage payment. Experiments show that higher fixed wages trigger higher effort levels and thus increase efficiency even in one-shot games (Gächter and Falk (2001)). Effort is even higher in long-term interactions (Falk, Gächter and Kovács (1999)) or if the employer has the possibility to punish (reward) the worker ex-post for low (high) effort (Fehr and Gächter (1998)).

Since fixed wage payments induce higher efficiency levels than theoretically predicted, this implies at the same time that the comparative advantage of performance based reward schemes is reduced. Gächter and Fehr report some studies in which both kinds of contracts, fixed wage contracts as well as profit sharing contracts, were feasible and in fact observed (Güth, Klose, Königstein and Schwalbach (1998)). One result of these studies is that generous contracts of either type are able to induce higher than equilibrium effort.

Different types of performance based reward systems trigger different consequences. For instance, offering profit sharing is quite effective in inducing effort (Anderhub, Gächter and Königstein (forthcoming); but, to threaten workers (within the offered contracts) with ex-post punishment in case of shirking - this is another kind of performance based reward system - is detrimental for work effort (Fehr and Gächter (2000)). The threat of punishment may lead to a crowding out of intrinsic effort motivation.

Many further questions can be addressed in experiments on effort incentives. For instance, the effectiveness of reward schemes depends, in general, on the possibilities of monitoring, the space of feasible contracts, and the time horizon. While each of these points shows up in some study a more thorough and systematic investigation is needed. Furthermore, little work has been done one the multi-agent case. That many employees belong to the same level of a firm's hierarchy is common. So, the multi-agent case may be viewed even more natural than the single agent framework. With multiple agents there might be technological spillovers of one worker's effort decicion on the performance of other workers. For instance, the interaction might be characterized as a prisoners' dilemma game or a coordination game. In general a worker's effort will depend on the social production technology and on the type of work contract. With team production performance based reward schemes may nevertheless rely solely on individual performance measures. On the other hand they may include or be solely based on group information. Such issues have been addressed in a few experiments on team incentive systems. For instance, in Nalbantian and Schotter (1997) subjects are exposed to group reward schemes that were exogenously fixed by the experimenter. It might be interesting to investigate the situation where the choice of incentive scheme is left to subjects.

In addition the multi-agent case may trigger questions of both horizontal fairness (fairness between workers) as well as vertical fairness (fairness between employer and workers). More generally, in a multi-layered hierarchy it is not clear what forms an employee's social reference group.

Another interesting topic to be studied further is the provision of incentives within multi-tasking environments (see e.g. Benz, Fehr and Frey (2001) and Fehr,

Klein and Schmidt (2001)). Furthermore, an issue that to my knowledge has not yet been addressed in experiments is the case of multiple principals.

Questions of effort incentives and reward schemes are fundamental for personnel economics and organizational economics. So the survey by Gächter and Fehr extends the field where experiments may be fruitfully applied toward the domain of management science. I view this as a very promising research direction. Labour relations are established inside firms and may be characterized as interactions between a few persons. Such conflicts seem particularly well suited for laboratory studies, since in the lab there are typically only a few persons who interact with one another.

There is certainly room for more studies on labor economics issues. The survey by Gächter and Fehr provides an overview of recent studies and serves to identify new research directions. Applications of experimental methods within the field of labour economics are still scarce, but hopefully they will become more widespread in the near future.

References

Anderhub, V., Gächter, S. and Königstein, M. (forthcoming). Efficient Contracting and Fair Play in a Simple Principal-Agent Experiment, *Experimental Economics*.

Ashenfelter, O. and Hallock, K. (eds) (1995). *Labor Economics*, Vol. 1 of *International Library of Critical Writings in Economics*, Edward Elgar, Hants and Vermont.

Benz, M., Fehr, E. and Frey, B. (2001). Multitask Relationships, Incentives, and Intrinsic Motivation, mimeo, University of Zurich.

Falk, A., Gächter, S. and Kovács, J. (1999). Intrinsic Motivation and Extrinsic Incentives in a Repeated Game with Incomplete Contracts, *Journal of Economic Psychology* **20**: 251–284.

Fehr, E. and Falk, A. (1999). Wage Rigidity in a Competitive Incomplete Contract Market, *Journal of Political Economy* **107**: 106–134.

Fehr, E. and Gächter, S. (1998). How Effective are Trust- and Reciprocity-Based Incentives?, *in* A. ben Ner and L. Putterman (eds), *Economics, Values, and Organization*, Cambridge University Press, Cambridge.

Fehr, E. and Gächter, S. (2000). Do Financial Incentives Crowd Out Voluntary Cooperation?, Working Paper No. 35, Institute for Empirical Research in Economics, University of Zurich.

Fehr, E., Gächter, S. and Kirchsteiger, G. (1996). Reciprocal Fairness and Noncompensating Wage Differentials, *Journal of Institutional and Theoretical Economics* **152**: 608–640.

Fehr, E., Kirchler, E., Weichbold, A. and Gächter, S. (1998). When Social Norms Overpower Competition – Gift Exchange in Experimental Labor Markets, *Journal of Labor Economics* **16**: 324–351.

Fehr, E., Klein, A. and Schmidt, K. (2001). Fairness, Incentives and Contractual Incompleteness, Working Paper No. 72, Institute for Empirical Research in Economics, University of Zurich.

Gächter, S. and Falk, A. (forthcoming). Reputation and Reciprocity: Consequences for the Labour Relation, *Scandinavian Journal of Economics*.

Güth, W., Klose, W., Königstein, M. and Schwalbach, J. (1998). An Experimental Study of a Dynamic Principal-Agent Relationship, *Managerial and Decision Economics* **19**: 327–341.

Königstein, M. (2000). *Equity, Efficiency and Evolutionary Stability in Bargaining Games with Joint Production*, Lecture Notes in Economics and Mathematical Systems, Springer, Berlin et al.

Königstein, M. (forthcoming). Optimal Contracting With Boundedly Rational Agents, *Homo Oeconomicus*.

Nalbantian, H. and Schotter, A. (1997). Productivity under Group Incentives: An Experimental Study, *American Economic Review* **87**: 314–341.

9 Cooperation in Environmental Commons

Axel Ostmann*

Abstract. Common property is open to lack of care. Many natural resources, locally and globally, cannot be satisfactorily organised individually. In such cases the group of (potential) users has to deal with an unfavourable incentive structure, motivating the individual user to harvest or to pollute, respectively, to an unsustainable extent. In the survey presented here experience from a variety of experimental commons dilemma situations is reported. Evaluating and comparing the results of these experiments enhances our knowledge under what conditions people can successfully manage a common and under what condition they fail to do so.

9.1 Endangered resources and the commons

Common property is open to lack of care. Aristotle (Barker 1952) in his Politeia starts his controversy with Platon, Sokrates, and Phaleas with a discussion of the issues of individual vs. collective property rights.

> (Book II, ch. 3, §4): ... What is common to the greatest number gets the least amount of care. Men pay most attention to what is their own: they care less for what is common; or, at any rate, they care for it only to the extent to which each is individually concerned. Even where there is no other cause for inattention, men are more prone to neglect their duty when they think that another is attending to it ...

In the Aristotelian view the problem of the commons is reduced care. But since individualistic organisation may also generate or increase problems like egotism, greed, and quarrels an unrestricted private property system would be dangerous too:

> (Book II, Ch. 5, §5ff): ... The present system [of private property] would be far preferable, if it were adorned by customs [in the social sphere] and by the enactment of proper laws [in the political]. It would possess the advantages of both systems, and would combine the merits of a system of community of property with those of the system of private property. [It would be the ideal]; for property ought to be generally and in the main private, but common in one respect [i.e. in use]. ... When everyone has his own separate sphere of interest, there will not be the same ground for quarrels; and the amount of interest will increase, because each man will feel that he is applying himself to what is his own. And on such a scheme, too, moral goodness [and not, as in Plato's scheme, legal compulsion] will

* The author is greatly indebted to Andrew Muller who made many valuable suggestions for improvements.

> ensure that the property of each is made to serve the use of all, in the spirit of the proverb which says "Friends' goods are goods in common" ... It is clear from what has been said that the better system is that under which property is privately owned but is put to common use; and the function proper to the legislator is to make men so disposed that they will treat property in this way.

Self-interest and striving for appropriation are only endangering the rights of the collective if not moderated and balanced by other (social) motives.

> (Book II, Ch. 3, §9) ... Self-love is rightly censured, but what is really censured is not so much love of oneself as love of oneself in excess – just as we also blame the lover of money [not so much for loving money as for loving it in excess] ...

In the Aristotelian view politics has to balance the motivational forces by well-adapted rules and education. Education has to propagate measured behaviour and measured emotions.

> (Book II, chapter 7, §8): ... It is more necessary to equalize men's desires than their properties; and that is a result which cannot be achieved unless men are adequately trained by the influence of laws. ... (§11) There are some crimes which are due to lack of necessities; ... But want is not the only cause of crimes. Men also commit them simply for the pleasure it gives them, and just to get rid of an unsatisfied desire. Vexed by a desire which goes beyond the simple necessities of life, they will turn criminals to cure their vexation. ... (§20) The source from which a remedy for such evils may be expected is not the equalisation of property, but rather a method of training which makes the better sort of natures unwilling, and the poorer sort unable, to indulge in covetousness.

In modern times the viewpoint has changed in favour of an unrestricted individualism. The homo oeconomicus and rational actor paradigm usually starts with individual incentives bare of social motives and emotions. Such a rationale of action shows how difficult it is for individuals, that are nothing but self-interested, to organise collective action. As Olson (1965) has taught us, organisations have to motivate or to force (the large the group the more) their members to contribute enough for the task to fulfil.

> (Olson 1965, p. 2) Rational, self-interested individuals will not act to achieve their common or group interests ... even if there is an unanimous agreement in the group about the common good and methods of achieving it.

The assumed individualistic orientation of common property users makes it not easy to aggregate the individual interests into a "intérêt general" (Condorcet, Arrow, Sen have discussed this issue). And even when the common interest is accepted by all actors the individual incentives may motivate the actors for waiting that the partners will sacrifice or contribute in favour of the group. The famous Swiss novelist Gotthelf describes the corresponding behaviour in the following words:

> (Gotthelf 1973, p. 133): Indeed not one had thought that his doings would result in a damage to the common; and moreover actually not one had an understanding of responsibility for the whole entirety. ... Everybody has his/her own interest at heart, whatever may happen to the entirety. ... He is a person of the moment, he takes a small momentary advantage, asks not how much damage is done the next day, or how many dollars will be lost the next day for the sake of a few cents profit today. [1]

In the late 60s a larger part of the public in the industrialised countries started to notice that the actual practice in appropriating (and polluting) natural resources may lead to critical shortage or even destruction within a few generations. In 1972 Meadows and his colleagues tried to quantify such limits to growth (Meadows, Meadows, Randers and Behrens 1972). In this environment actors face not only lack of care but also exhaustion and destruction. The population explosion and the finiteness of the world became perceived dangers. The famous article of Hardin (1968) on the tragedy of the commons originates from this historical situation. Perceiving the finiteness of natural resources is not really a modern issue. Let us again consider a respective argument of Aristotle:

> (Book II, chapter 6, §10): ... It is strange that Socrates should distribute landed property in [a fixed number of] equal lots, without making any corresponding arrangements to secure a [fixed] number of citizens. He imposes no restriction on the number of children who may be brought into the world ... (§12). One would have thought that it was even more necessary to limit population, and to prevent reproduction from exceeding a certain level, than to limit property. ...

Note that Hardin is not the first to discuss a limiting policy in reproduction. If limiting the usage of resources (either as source of wealth or as sink of waste) is really needed for rescuing the endangered resources, then it is the focal question how to implement limits that are found to be respected. Traditionally economists favour either (if possible) a privatising policy[2] or command and control by ruling

[1] Own translation (no published English translation available) of the following text: Es meinte nämlich nicht einer, daß das, was er mache, dem Ganzen schade, und zudem hatte eigentlich auch nicht einer einen Begriff von der Sorge für das Ganze. ... Jeder hat zunächst das eigene Interesse im Auge, gehe es dem Ganzen, wie es wolle. ... Er ist ein Mensch des Augenblicks, einen kleinen augenblicklichen Vorteil nimmt er, fragt nicht, wie groß der Schaden am folgenden Tag sei, wieviel Batzen um des gewonnenen Kreuzers willen am folgenden Tage zugrunde gehen werden.

[2] The policy of tradable permits can be seen as a special form of the privatising policy. In this case a new type of good is established substituting the non-marketable resource. The good "permit" is private and a functionable market may be established if carefully designed. Usually permits define amounts of usage of some resource or of emissions or other damaging by-products usually as a share of a planned total amount (beside defining the conditions under which those amounts can be used and/or how they are to measure and to report). In many a case it is not easy to observe if the permitted amount is surpassed. In

power. Since in general in our setting important external effects cannot be excluded at reasonable cost a privatising policy has to be excluded. Moreover a command and control policy can be too costly or even impossible because of lack of a sovereign power as it usually is in multinational scenarios. What under such conditions can be done and is done is to establish negotiations, contracts, rules, and/or institutions that are designed to ensure a reasonable management of a jointly used scarce resource. Conceptually this third policy line can be considered as managing a common. How and under what conditions members of such a common can successfully manage their resource is empirically examined in the field but also in the laboratory (Ostrom 1990). The focus of this survey is on experimental research only.

9.2 Incentives and the common's dilemma

Environmental commons refer to resources. The variety of resources comprises such different cases as fertile land, strategic materials, forests, water, food, fish, or even air. Use of resources includes not only harvesting and catch activities but also activities of pollution or degradation. In a first approximation many of these scenarios can be conceptualised as a joint production process. For determining the private interests of the actors the incentive structure underlying the scenario is evaluated in terms of individual costs and proceeds. By specifying payoff functions and action spaces of the actors the scenarios can be transformed into game-theoretical models.

In all our models the individual actor decides on his or her action, or say usage, x and "produces" two types of economic consequences: a private payoff $F(x)$ and a group payoff $f(s)$ that depends on all actions in total; in the following we operationalize the term s ("all actions in total") by simply defining it as the total sum of the individual actions. In all our scenarios the group payoff is distributed among the individual in some way. For an individual actor under consideration the individual payoff u depends on the own usage x and on the summed-up usage y of all other actors; it can be written in the following form

$$u(x,y) = F(x) - qf(x+y). \qquad (9.1)$$

Let us consider *three examples* (see Table 9.1.). For fishery scenarios usage may be measured in boats invested or nets thrown out. Since the resulting catch is not only dependent on the own effort but also on what other fishermen do, the catch and the sales can be seen as a distributed consequence whereas the effort only produces private consequences. So in terms of payoffs F has the character of a cost, whereas f can be thought of as proceeds. In other scenarios, like groundwater or pollution scenarios it is adequate to conceptualise proceeds as private and costs as distributed.

Games representing the incentive structure of commons typically exhibit suboptimal equilibria. The following standard model is most frequently used to represent a common without further institutions (hidden actions and open access for a group

such cases a control problems arises, or stated otherwise: the problem arises to guarantee the private character of the good against "thieves".

Table 9.1. Example scenarios

scenarios	usage x	economic consequences	
		private F	distributed f
fishery	boats (# and size), nets (# and type)	investment, effort, catching cost	catches, sales
groundwater	extraction for irrigation	sales of products	lowering of water table
pollution	Emissions	sales of products	cleaning cost or loss in productivity

of members): individual usage or use effort x causes a private linear cost cx, $c > 0$. The total s of individual usages produces a joint outcome $f(s)$ via a normal[3] (i.e. $f(0) = 0$, $f'(0) > c$) and concave production function. Everybody of the n members receives a share $qf(s)$ proportional to his or her use effort x, i.e. the quota q is equal to x/s. Let us fix an individual and denote the total usage of his or partners by y. Then, in a first approximation[4] the payoff function u can be set as quadratic (with appropriate positive parameters a, b, c):

$$u(x,y) = -cx + qs(a - bs) = x(a - c - bs) \tag{9.2}$$

Individuals usually are limited in their opportunities by an upper limit e for x (i.e. $0 \leq x \leq e$) interpreted as endowment or wealth. With endowments not too small the equilibrium shows a larger total usage than optimal. We speak of a homogeneous setting if all individual endowments are equal. Beside the indivdual pay-off u we use the concepts given in Table 9.2.

Table 9.2. Basic concepts

Total payoff	U	U(s) = -cs+f(s)
Welfare optimum	WO	maximizer of total payoff
Best reply	B(y)	maximizer of individual payoff partners' total usage fixed
Equilibrium	EQ	usage vector with x being a best reply to y for all individuals
Efficiency function	eff(s)	eff(s) = U(s)/U(WO)
Overuse factor	of(s)	of(s) = s/WO

[3] Since the function f conceptually refers to payoffs $f(0) = 0$ may be too restrictive; in such a case one may add an additive constant A, substituting $f(s) + A$ for $f(s)$. Since for all maximisation tasks adding additive terms is an inessential change, we can drop the term in the analysis.

[4] In order to take the convexity properties into consideration a local approximation has to consider the quadratic terms. As for the production function in the analysis all constant terms can be deleted. So considering the general form $u(x,y) = -(B + cx) + (A + f(x + y))$ including fixed costs B leads to $(A - B) - cx + f(x + y)$ which for the purpose of analysis can be standardised by deleting the constant term $A - B$.

Note that the performance measures "eff" and "of" refer to a different base: "of" refers to usage, "eff" refers to payoffs. In experimental settings the most used parameters are n=8, a=23, b=0.25, c=5, and e=10 or e=25 (Ostrom, Gardner and Walker 1994, OGW). Table 9.3 shows the values of the basic concepts for this specific parameter set.

Table 9.3. Solutions for base line parameters

U	s(18-0.25s)
WO	2nx=(a-c)/b: s=36
B(y)	x = min { e , (72 - y)/2 }
EQ	(n+1)x=(a-c)/b: s=64, x=8
eff(EQ)	0.40
of(EQ)	1.78

Overuse factor and efficiency of the equilibrium only depend on the group size, and not on a, b, c:

$$of(EQ) = \frac{2n}{n+1} \quad \text{and} \quad eff(EQ) = \frac{4n}{(n+1)^2}. \tag{9.3}$$

In (Ostrom et al. 1994) the authors report on series of experiments with homogeneous setting. In the experiments the common is simulated for 20 or more periods. Since subjects in all periods face the same payoff function, the structure can be analysed as a repeated game. In a common pool interpretation the respective resource shows complete renewal from one period to another, i.e. the state of the resource at the beginning of each period is always the same. In case of the poor endowment ($e = 10$) subjects realised a mean efficiency of 0.38 approaching the equilibrium with time. In case of the rich endowment ($e = 25$) subjects approach the equilibrium from below realising a mean efficiency of -0.03 (mean of = 1.96). It can be concluded that also behaviourally the setting represents a commons dilemma. Even sophisticated subjects writing strategies for computer tournaments have not done better than equilibrium (Keser and Gardner 1994, efficiencies: 1.run 0.22, 2.run 0.25, 3.run 0.32; overuse factor: 1.88, 1.86, 1.82).

9.3 Communication

In real commons dilemma situations members are far from accepting the decline of the common without taking measures against (Ostrom 1990). The first they can do is to communicate informally or in formal meetings. In communication processes members can inform each other and discuss previous behaviour and joint plans. They can appeal to someone to change behaviour, they can inform their partners, and can discuss proposals. Finally, they may reach agreements, or may set standards and rules. In experiments providing costless communication facilities, Ostrom et al.

(1994) have shown that even under the condition of a single meeting the efficiency of the experimental common may show a remarkable enhancement. Nevertheless the enhancement is not stable for the more distant future (Ostrom et al. 1994, pp. 151-3). This changes with repeated communication. The authors report a mean efficiency of 0.70 for the rich and 0.98 for the poor (homogeneous) endowment setting.

It can be argued that with the introduction of communication cooperation in the whole group or in subgroups can be organised even if in the "hidden action" environment every agreement reached is not binding (Ostmann 1988). It was observed that with repeated communication most agreements have proven to be stable (in the sense that nobody broke the agreement; Ostrom et al. (1994)).

A model that allows for an evaluation of such an agreement has to include a formal analysis of the cooperative games induced (Ostmann 2001, this volume, sections 3.1 and 3.4). The induced cooperative game specifies for each coalition what sum of payoffs a coalition can ensure for its members; this amount is called the value of the respective coalition.

In the symmetric case - here in case of homogeneous endowments - the cooperative game analysis maybe seen as irrelevant, because the unique efficient symmetric agreement is provided by every cooperative solution concept, too. Nevertheless it is important that the induced games show some further properties that favour grand coalition agreements. In Meinhardt (1999) it is shown that the games induced typically are convex, that is the value added by an additional member of a coordinated coalition increases with the size of the coalition. This fact can be understood as a strong incentive to coordinate in a grand coalition agreement.

As said before for asymmetric games the cooperative solutions are not trivial. The setting of the experimental series reported in Hackett, Schlager and Walker (1994) provides an example for an asymmetric game. In a cooperative reanalysis of this experiment Meinhardt and Ostmann (1999) compare the observed stable agreements with solutions of the derived cooperative game. The experimental common of Hackett et al. (1994) has 4 poor and 4 rich members. The focal parameters of the set-up and the non-cooperative solutions are given in Table 9.4.

Table 9.4. The Hackett, Schlager and Walker (1994) parameters and non-cooperative solutions

parameters	n=8, a=33, b=0.25, c=5
endowment	e(poor)=8, e(rich)=24
WO	s=56
EQ	x(poor)=8, x(rich)=16
eff(EQ)	0.49
of(EQ)	1.71

For giving an impression of the respective cooperative game we list the values added (also called marginal values) for the game[5] in Table 9.5.

[5] By calculating the values by the rules for the alpha values as defined in Ostmann (2001) Section 3.4. we can determine the values added. In a second step it can be shown that the

Table 9.5. Values added for coalitions of p poor and r rich members

	value added by poor member					value added by rich member				
	r=0	r=1	r=2	R=3	r=4	r=0	r=1	r=2	r=3	r=4
p=0	0	12	36	60	84	4	60	132	204	-
p=1	0	20	44	68	92	16	84	156	228	-
p=2	4	28	52	76	100	36	108	180	248	-
p=3	12	36	60	84	108	60	132	204	276	-
p=4	-	-	-	-	-	84	156	228	300	-

As said before for asymmetric games the cooperative solutions are not trivial. The inhomogeneous setting of the experimental series reported in Hackett et al. (1994) is an example. In a reanalysis of this experiment (Meinhardt and Ostmann 1999) compare the observed stable agreements with cooperative solutions (like the core, the kernel and the nucleolus; for the definitions cp. Ostmann (2001), this volume). For example the kernel[6] of the derived cooperative game distributes the total maximal payoff of 784 (which refers to the welfare optimum) in shares of 56 each to the poor and of 140 each to the rich members of the common. In order to implement this solution (approximately under the condition of integer valued choices x) the poor would have to chose $x = 4$ and the rich $x = 10$.

In fact also in the inhomogeneous setting we observe a remarkable efficiency gain by communication. The mean efficiency rises from 0.46 in the 10 pre-communication periods to 0.95 in the 10 periods after communication (8 trials; overuse factor: first part 1.71, second part 1.19). Compared to the kernel the observation is substantially biased towards equality (Meinhardt and Ostmann 1999). Astonishingly many agreements show no equal treatment within roles.

9.4 Sanctions

In the previous section we considered the effect of the introduction of communication facilities. Now, in this section a second type of measures used to stop the possible decline of a commons is examined: the introduction of sanctions. Sanctions impose costs on the sanctionee that should deter him or her from behaviour that can damage the common. In the field quite different types of sanctioning systems are used. An important distinction is that between internal sanctioning where the sanctioneer is a member and external sanctioning where an agent or an agency is entrusted with the task. In case of external sanctioning usually a sanction has to be justified by some evidence, whereas internal sanctioning can even take place without evidence. The first and the second subsection refer to scenarios with internal

values added fulfil the formula $\max\{0, 4+8(3r+p-2)\}$ for poor members and $\max\{4+12p, 36+72r+24(p-2)\}$ for rich members.

[6] The kernel can be interpreted as a fair solution equalizing the individual gains above the best alternative the individuals can argue with when comparing themselves pairwise with each other.

sanctioning. In a third subsection the case of an agency is considered that has to collect evidence before sanctions can be imposed.

9.4.1 Sanctioning each other

A second institution people invent to enhance efficiency in a common is sanctioning. In an early preformal stage sanctioning is often being practiced "in the dark" – i.e. by secretely doing harm to somebody suspected. Often the suspicion that this person has damaged the common before is not based on real information. An experimental setup to study such "blind sanctioning" situations was given in Ostrom, Walker and Gardner (1992). The results of the respective experiments suggest that blind sanctioning significantly enhances efficiency, especially when such a rule is deliberately chosen.

A set-up with sanctioning that has to be justified by a corresponding inspection result has been explored in an experiment by Moir (1996). Moir compares this institution of justified sanctions with a pure monitoring institution without sanctions and with no institution introduced. Moir's experimental results suggest that justified sanctions performs best.

In all these set-ups used by Ostrom et al. (1994) and Moir (1996) both monitoring and sanctioning is costly. Every monitoring and/or sanction means an efficiency loss for the group. Since these costs cannot be balanced with an payoff advantage of the monitor/sanctioneer all these institutions leave the equilibrium usage unchanged. The equilibrium prescribes that no monitoring respectively no sanctioning takes place.

The group size in all experiments is eight, and although Ostrom et al. (1994) and Moir (1996) differ in the production function used, the values of $eff(EQ)$ and $of(EQ)$ are identical in both set-ups ($eff(EQ) = 0.40$, $of(EQ) = 1.78$). In Table 9.6 results from a variety of experiments are summarized.

The experiment OGW 1 is the homogeneous rich endowment experiment from above (Ostrom et al. 1994, exp. 4-6, p.192). It is included in the table for means of comparison. All other experiments are separated in three parts: initial periods, interplay, additional periods. The initial periods with no institution are followed by a break either for a communication round (*C*) or for an additional information given by the experimenter (*I*). After this interplay a sequence of periods followed under the new institution or in case of M1 without institutional change. In the row M 1-3 the part one results of the Moir experiments are aggregated.

The table shows that under base line conditions very different efficiencies have been observed. Compared to the Ostrom et al. (1994) experiments the Moir data show more homogeneous first part efficiencies. Moreover in the Ostrom et al. (1994) experiments the performance of the groups are very bad in the early periods. The experiments OGW 4 and OGW 5 are run as combined experiment: the 6 trials were separated after the communication round by a group decision on whether the blind sanctioning mechanism should be introduced. In the two cases the group has performed well in the first part the group decided against the institution. This subexperiment OGW 4 also is the only one of the one-shot communication experiments

Table 9.6. A Summary of several results

experiment	initial	break	final	condition	# trials	eff	of
OGW 1	10	-	10	base line	3	-0.28 / 0.21	2.06 / 1.86
OGW 2	10	-	>10	blind sanction	8	-0.38 / 0.09	n.a.
OGW 3	10	C	16	blind sanction	3	-0.14 / 0.67	n.a.
OGW 4	10	C	15	no sanction chosen	2	0.44 / 0.56	n.a.
OGW 5		C	16	blind sanction chosen	4	-0.11 / 0.90	n.a.
M 1-3	5	-	-	initial base line	15	0.59 / -	1.67
M 1	5	I	10	pure information	5	0.66 / 0.63	1.62 / 1.65
M 2	5	I	10	monitoring	5	0.63 / 0.55	1.66 / 1.72
M 3	5	I	10	justified sanctions	5	0.52 / 0.63	1.75 / 1.51

Note that the efficiency data do not coincide with the data Moir reports because he uses another efficiency measure, namely $effM = (U - U(EQ))/(U(WO) - U(EQ))$.
column "break": C stands for a communication break, I for additional information
columns "initial" and "final": numbers of initial and final periods, resp.
last two columns: first entry reports the average in the first part (initial periods), second entry refers to last part (final periods)

in which there is no large efficiency gain in the third part. The information given in the second part of the Moir experiments simply explains the option to chose for establishing the group optimal WO. The only information experiment with a significant efficiency gain in the third part uses the justified sanction institution.

From an rational actor's perspective the target efficiency of an institution has to be identified with what is induced by the incentive structure, namely $eff(EQ)$. As reported from other social dilemma experiments people in many set-ups tend to act more cooperative as prescribed by the equilibrium. Let us call **cooperation shift** (in short: cosh) the efficiency gain above $eff(EQ)$. Then, we can describe the empirical performance of an institution by the target, that part that can be explained by the incentive structure, and the additional cooperation shift. Comparing the performance of the "null target" institutions (that do not alter the unfavourable equilibrium) we find remarkable cooperation shifts for repeated communication, for one-shot communication with a self-imposed blind sanctioning regime and for the justified sanction regime. Further research (providing a larger number of trials) has to show how stable, or variable, the respective findings are.

9.4.2 Confiscating above limits

An alternative to "null target" sanctioning is to create an advantage for the sanctioneer. Assume that a limit λ is set for the individual usage x. Note that in the set-up here reported on this limit is negotiated in the communication breaks between periods. By costly inspection a member of the common may detect another member's x is above the limit. An easy rule combining sanctioning and compensation for the inspector is to confiscate the amount exceeding the limit and to give it fully or in part to the inspector. Such an institution generates redistribution of income between members based on their inspection and use activity. Experiments with such an institution are reported in Ostmann (1994) and Ostmann (1996). The respective (symmetric) incentive structure prescribes an equilibrium with a certain inspection probability and an adapted mixture of conform and extremely greedy usage.

In contrast to the Ostrom et al. (1994) and Moir (1996) experiments the underlying game structure is a dynamic game (and not a repeated game). The amount of resource available in the next period is dependent on what has been left over in the period before. The instruction describes a fishing cooperative; an individual member catches $qf(s)$ by throwing out x nets. Setting payoff units to the worth of the standard net total product $f(s)$ can be assumed as $f(s) = min\{w, s\}$, w being the actual state of the resource, i.e. the amount of fish available. The remaining fish $w - s$ was doubled up to a capacity level W. Formally the next period state w' is calculated as $w' = \min\{2(w-s), W\}$. Communication rounds between the fishing periods allow for setting a well adapted limit for individual usage. In no case the resource has been destroyed. For all observed limits the mean individual catch was below the equilibrium values. This observation indicates also for this experiment a remarkable cooperation shift enhancing the performance above target.

Table 9.7. Individual average catch x in the fishing coop (Ostmann 1996)

λ	*1*	2	*3*	*4*	*5*	*7*
cases	27	17	18	64	24	18
EQ-x	2.80	3.78	4.75	5.71	6.67	8.50
x	1.22	2.35	4.33	4.06	5.33	7.22

EQ = individual catch according to the Nash-equilibrium of the game for the respective limit λ.

As noted before the equilibrium prescribes that in case of defection a maximum catch is to be applied, but the observed catch is far from being maximal. Moreover, observed defection rates (in the aggregate 0.23) are lower than in equilibrium with the only exception of $\lambda = 2$. Under this non-equilibrium defection behaviour the inspecting member makes sacrifices to the group. Under the institution considered a need for a rule for designating a person responsible for monitoring may evolve. In the next section we consider commons that employ an inspection agency for guaranteeing that enough control is performed.

9.4.3 External inspection

Employing an external inspector in order to implement justified sanctions is costly (assume that inspection costs are a fixed amount κ). For this reason the members of the common have not only to decide for a limit of individual usage, but also on when to employ the inspection agency. In case the loss from the deviation from the planned outcome is smaller than the inspection costs the members of the common may decide that it would be inadequate to search for the defectors. A corresponding simple rule to implement into an external inspection scenario is to call for inspection only if a certain maximum total usage tolerated η is surpassed. Let us assume that the inspection contract also specifies the extent of inspection activities in such a way that a fixed and equal probability p for being inspected is set. Internally the members of the common have to decide for what sanctions have to be applied. In approximation to usual practices perceived as fair (Ostrom 1990) we assume that the sanctions comprise two parts. First a defector detected has to pay the inspection costs κ_5 and secondly a compensation fee proportionate to the deviation from the limit. Whereas the inspection costs mean a welfare loss for the group the sanctioning can be considered as redistribution of income. Formally we may assume that every (undetected) member receives an amount $\sigma(x-\lambda)$ from the compensation fee, σ being a fixed sanctioning factor. Thus the total compensation to be paid is $m\sigma(x-\lambda)$ if m is the number of members minus the number of members detected.

Theoretically both high control probability and high sanctioning factors lower the incentives to deviate from the limiting standard. In a series of experiments (Ostmann 1998, Beckenkamp and Ostmann 1999, Ostmann, Wojtyniak and Beckenkamp 1999) the respective behavioural reactions are examined for a scenario referring to the Ostrom et al. (1994) base line. The authors use the following parameters: $\lambda = 5$, $\eta = 46$, $\kappa = 40$. In terms of efficiency an inspection cost of 40 means an efficiency loss of 0.123 if the agency is called for inspection.

For judging the performance of the sanctioning system we first have to find out in what a way the incentive structure is changed by the institution introduce. The changes induce multiple asymmetric equilibria that (in a large range) exhibit increasing efficiency for both more inspection and higher sanctioning. By varying sigma it is possible to compare sanctioning regimes that differ in the strength of sanctioning. This has been experimentally studied (Ostmann et al. 1999) for a fixed inspection probability of $p = 0.125$ and for a scale of values reaching from low sanctions (σ=0) to very high sanctions ($\sigma = 2.5$) with steps of 0.5. Note that $\sigma = 0$ stands for a regime with fixed sanctions meaning that the detected defector has to pay only the inspection costs and no compensation fee.

In Table 9.8 the target intervals defined by equilibrium behaviour are confronted with the observed total usages. The main result of these series is that observed means of the cooperation shift (= signed distance to target set) is negative for all sanctioning factors with the only exception of a moderate value. Despite the fact that incentives favour an increasingly restraint behaviour subjects counter these incentives by resistance against high sanctions. Note that for high sanctions mean total usage is significantly[7] above the target (shaded cells).

In Beckenkamp and Ostmann (1999) and Ostmann and Beckenkamp (1997) the authors discuss the possible influence of cognitive and socio-emotional processes on shaping the observed behaviour. The corresponding simulation model in Ostmann and Beckenkamp (1997) is based on a process of increasing aggression and katharsis in discharge; an alternative theory applied is the theory of reactance (Brehm 1995) that emphasizes how individuals try to re-establish the feeling of personal

[7] The respective significance levels for above upper bound of target are 0.0002, 0.06, and 0.019; for *sigma* = 1.5 and *sigma* = 2.5 the 95% confidence intervals do not intersect the target

Table 9.8. Targets and observed total usage (Ostmann et al. 1999)

sigma	0	0.5	1	1.5	2	2.5
target range	60.3	58.9	55.7	55.0	53.3	52.2
	62.5	61.0	58.8	57.4	55.0	53.7
observed mean	60.8	59.4	53.5	61.7	59.3	55.4
(s.d.)	(12.6)	(12.9)	(9.1)	(11.7)	(27.3)	(9.9)
observed of	1.69	1.65	1.49	1.71	1.65	1.54
efficiency eff	0.30	0.34	0.61	0.28	0.49	0.52
observed cosh	-0.06	-0.13	0.09	-0.31	-0.13	-0.13
# trials	6	5	6	5	5	7

freedom. Whatever the exact processes are that counter the incentives set by monetary sanctions the overall conclusions from the sanctioning experiments are evident: The hope that drastic fines may lead to non-defective behaviour is an illusion, or as Ostmann et al. (1999) write: "Limiting policies that rely only on the force of incentives may lead to resistance and inefficient management".

9.5 Dynamic games

9.5.1 Simple dynamics

In the 70s Edney and his research group report on a set of simple experiments based on a dynamic resource management task. As in the fishing coop experiment a group of subjects can individually harvest from a resource pool over some periods. Only if the pool is not depleted completely in a new period it can be harvested again. The resource available in the new period is what grows from the remainder. The main message from these experiments was that without additional measures or regulations the resource will be completely depleted in short time (often even in the first period). This behaviour can be seen as the influence of the extreme incentive structures used in these experiments. Suppose there would be a last period. Then in the last period everybody of the n members may expect to get the n-th part of what grows from the remainder; in case the growth rate is smaller than the group size (as in all experiments) it is rational not to wait with the harvest. By recursion using this argument the resource will be destroyed as soon as possible (there may be limited harvesting capacity). Like Platt (1973) Edney and his group are not focusing on incentive structures but on designing arrangements that would make it more easy to act as responsible citizen. Platt's main thesis ("social trap") is that the central problem of a dynamic common is not that members show an individualistic orientation but the way how rewards and damages are arranged in time: Individuals tend to orient themselves more toward actual, noticeable, and visible stimuli than toward future possible developments. Payoff advantages by a large individual harvest are directly noticeable whereas the damage by overuse can only be seen in the next period. In the corresponding research (Edney and Harper 1976, Edney and Harper 1978b, Edney and Harper 1978a, Cass and Edney 1978, Martichuski and Bell 1991, etc.) it was tested how praise and reproach, information, and visibility of the state of the pool affect the result. In the study of Harvey, Bell and Birjulin (1993) additionally the effects of sanctions are considered. More socio-psychological research with the resource management task was done by Messick et al. (Samuelson, Messick, Rutte and Wilke 1984, Samuelson and Messick 1986, Rutte, Wilke and Messick 1987). There are also similar experiments by Knapp (1986), Popp (1988), and Ernst (1997). Since the reports on latter experiments do not allow for an analysis of the underlying incentive structure the respective results are not to consider here.

In the following we restrict our attention on the study Cass and Edney (1978). In six trials with group size 4 participants can harvest from a field of 12 cells as often as they wish. At the beginning of the experiment every cell contains 4 units ($w_0 = 12 \times 4 = 48$). A period takes three minutes; the maximum number of five rounds was not known. At the end of a period the remainder in each cell doubles but never exceeds the cell capacity of 4 units. Every group of subjects had to deal with the task under $4 = 2 \times 2$ conditions: {**p**rivate territory, **c**ommon} x {**v**isible stock resp. **h**idden stock}

In the private territory task every subject can harvest only in his/her own 3 cells whereas in the commons condition she/he can harvest everywhere. Under the visible stock condition within a period every withdrawal can be seen immediately. The welfare equilibrium prescribes to coordinate for harvesting the maximal sustainable yield of 2 units per cell in the first four periods and to empty the pool in period five: $U(WO) = 48 + 4 \times 12 \times 2 = 144$; a group optimal sustainable harvest would yield MSY=120. The equilibrium of the (hidden stock = simultaneous move) common is to take all in the first period: $U(EQ) = 48$. Table 9.9 shows the group payoff results under the 4 different conditions.

Table 9.9. Cass/Edney

condition	pv	cv	ph	ch
payoff U	120.5	103	80	59.5
U/MSY	1.00	0.86	0.67	0.50

It can be learnt from these simple experiments that under both conditions visible stock and hidden stock the efficiency of the common without further institutions is considerably lower than the efficiency of the private firms. It can be argued that under each condition the efficiency is about that what can be expected from the evaluation of the incentive structure.

Experimental research referring to resource management tasks as considered above focus only on one extreme type of transition function $g : w \to w'$, on only one rule of capture f, and only on deterministic pool sizes. In a more general view the conflict has to be analysed as a dynamic game with strategies specifying a complete plan (given the history). Dynamic programming tools can be applied to find the solutions for the WO and EQ (here: subgame pefect equilibrium). All games considered up to now can be considered as subclasses of the respective space of games. For the repeated games set-up of the Ostrom et al. (1994) task we define the rule of complete renewal $w' = w = w_0$. For the tasks of bounded growth let $w' = \min\{k, \max\{0, r(w-s)\}\}$ where the parameter r is called the growth factor r.

Other rules of growth should be considered too, eg. the rule of logistic growth $w' = (w-s)(k+s-w)$. The dynamic to consider depends on the natural dynamics of the considered resource pool. For some cases it is more adequate to consider renewal in terms of inflow h resulting in a transition function like $w' = \max\{0, (w-s+h)\}$ or $w' = \min\{k, \max\{0, (w-s+h)\}\}$ for a limited pool capacity k. The extreme case of a resource with no renewal can be subsumed under the above classes of games by setting $r = 1$ or $h = 0$ respectively. Probabilistic models can be formulated by simply substituting a random variable W for the state of the pool and reformulating the transition function g as a probabilistic transition rule G specifying probabilities $prob(w' \in B|w)$ for $w \to B$.

9.5.2 Non-renewable resources

An experimental common dealing with a non-renewable resource is studied in Gardner, Moore and Walker (1994, GMW). The respective production functions and dynamics are motivated by a water extraction scenario (from a fossilized aquifer). In the base line condition (GMW 1) a group of 10 members has the task to manage the resource for 10 periods. This setting was compared with a restriction of the number of members (GMW 2: group size 5, 20 periods) and with the institution of "limited budget". Under the limited budget condition (GMW 3) every individual was restricted to a budget allowing for a total of 25 extraction units over all ten periods. Under the first two conditions the group performed significantly worse than the target. It is an open question if this bad performance is due to the "social trap" stated as typical for dynamic resource management tasks by Platt (1973). Only under the restrictive limited budget condition the attention for the future is sufficient for meeting the target. Compared to the time horizon and even to the equilibrium under all conditions the pool is depleted too early (see Table 9.10, last column).

Table 9.10. Performance in an exhaustible resource scenario (Gardner et al. 1994)

	condition	trials	target	eff	co.sh.	duration
GMW 1	base line	3	0.59	0.30	-0.29	2,3,4
GMW 2	small group	3	0.62	0.44	-0.22	5,6,8
GMW 3	limited budget	3	0.59	0.54	-0.05	3,4,7

9.5.3 Stochastic renewal or destruction

In Suleiman and Rapoport (1989) the stochastic development of the pool size is seen as a central and characteristic feature of many resource management tasks found in the field. The problem to act within such an environment can be seen as adding uncertainty to the simpler task of a dynamic common. If we consider for the common a simple repeated game model the corresponding uncertainty setting has to be time invariant: For every period the group faces the same probability distribution for the pool size. In a series of experiments Budescu, Rapoport, and Suleiman (Rapoport, Budescu, Suleiman and Weg 1992, Suleiman and Rapoport 1989, Suleiman, Budescu and Rapoport 1994, etc.) have studied the behaviour in a one-period stochastic common varying the range / support of a uniform distribution (holding the expectation constant; $W' \sim U[w_0, w_1]$). It has consistently been shown that the resource usage increases when the level of resource uncertainty increases. Efficiency is lowered by the additional complexity of task generated by uncertainty.

A very specific, but not unrealistic stochastic common is given by the stochastic destruction scenario introduced by Walker and Gardner (1992) (cp. Ostrom et al. (1994, ch. 6)). It is assumed that with increasing total usage s the probability of destruction increases. A simple formula for representing such a rule is

$$prob(w' = 0|w) = prob(H < s) \quad \text{and} \quad H \sim U[0, w_1]). \tag{9.4}$$

From field scenarios it is often known that up to some threshold $\underline{w}$ the event of destruction is excluded, and surpassing the threshold the probability of destruction increases from a remarkable initial level at the threshold. A representation of such a rule is given by the following formula:

$$H \sim U[0, w_1]) \quad \text{and} \quad prob(w' = 0|w) = \begin{cases} 0 & \text{if } s < \underline{w} \\ prob(H < s) & \text{else} \end{cases} \tag{9.5}$$

In the experiments of Walker and Gardner (1992, WG) and Muller and Vickers (1996, MV) transition functions of the above two types are used. For their specific parameters (especially $w = 40$, $w_1 = 200$) and the (known) maximal number of periods 20 the WO referring to the first rule (WG 1) is waiting for 16 periods (s=0) and taking 36 in the last periods. For the second rule (WG 2, MV 1, and MV 2) the equilibrium total usage is constantly 36. Whereas according to the first rule there is only one equilibrium in the other case two equilibria of different type can be calculated: the "secure" equilibrium (18 periods 40, final periods 64) and the "take now" equilibrium (15 periods 53.8, final periods 64). In the experiment MV2 after 5 practice periods the subject had repeated communication breaks of 3 minutes each with the exception of the first communication break (5 minutes). As in the Ostrom et al. (1994) experiments repeated communication enhances the efficiency and the duration until destruction considerably (see Table 9.11).

9.6 Outlook

Solutions for endangered commons can be found neither by designing a rationally optimal institution, nor by simply recommending the best responsible actions. Experimental research on commons has found evidence that for explaining the be-

Table 9.11. Performance in a stochastic destruction environment

	upper target	lower target	trials	eff	median duration
WG 1	0.22	0.22	5	0.21	4
WG 2	0.97	0.17	7	0.36	6
MV 1	0.97	0.17	5	0.13	3
MV 2	0.97	0.17	5	0.66	20

haviour of their members the incentive structure underlying the common is an important, but not the only determining factor. In some cases humans perform better than explainable by the incentive structure. But there are also cases in which a person acts involuntarily or even voluntarily, against the incentive imposed on the individuals.

In scenarios providing communication facilities often remarkable cooperation shifts are observed. On the other side in a dynamically changing and/or stochastic environment humans tend to perform worse than prescribed by rational actor theories. Cognitive procedures that in other contexts have been proved to be successful may account for this failure. But also in rather static sanctioning scenarios the people deviate from the target. In this case the designer of an institution has to consider that people can resist and obstruct institutions perceived as unfair even under personal losses.

Reports on experimental commons usually restrict the attention to models assuming identical subjects. Since it is well-known that subjects can react in the same situation in quite different ways it is not enough to assume identical subjects. In other scenarios individual differences have been explained by differences in fear, in greed, in personality, in self-concept, and in social orientation. Moreover, the different behaviour may also be motivated by different attitudes toward risks as well as by different expectations or cultural standards. There is a need for a better understanding of the interaction of situational characteristics and of the personal characteristics of the agents.

References

Barker, E. (ed.) (1952). *The Politics of Aristotle*, Oxford University Press, Oxford.

Beckenkamp, M. and Ostmann, A. (1996). A member's view of a common: Cognitive and socio–cognitive factors, *in* C. Roland-Lévy (ed.), *Social and Economic Representations*, IAREP; Université René Déscartes, Paris, pp. 1203– 1220.

Beckenkamp, M. and Ostmann, A. (1999). Missing the target? Sanctioning as an ambiguous structural solution, *in* S. et al. (ed.), *Resolving Social Dilemmas*, Taylor and Francis, Philadelphia.

Brehm, J. (1995). Reactance, *in* A. Manstead and M. Hewstone (eds), *Blackwell Encyclopedia of Social Psychology*, Blackwell, London, pp. pp. 466–468.

Cass, R. and Edney, J. (1978). The Commons Dilemma: A Simulation Testing the Effects of Resource Visibility and Territorial Division, *Human Ecology* **6**: 371–86.

Dasgupta, P. and Heal, G. (1979). *Economic Theory and Exhaustible Resources*, Cambridge University Press, Cambridge.

Dawes, R. and Thaler, R. (1988). Cooperation, *Journal of Economic Perspectives* **2**: 187–97.

Edney, J. (1979). The Nuts Game: A Concise Commons Dilemma Analog, *Environmental Psychology and Nonverbal Behavior* **3**: 252–4.

Edney, J. (1980). The Commons Problem. Alternative Perspectives, *American Psychologist* **35**: 131–150.

Edney, J. and Bell, P. (1978). The commons dilemma: Comparing altruism, the Golden Rule, perfect equality of outcomes, and territoriality, *The Social Science Journal* **20**: 22–33.

Edney, J. and Harper, C. (1976). The effects of information in a resource management problem: A social trap analog, *Human Ecology* **6**: 387–95.

Edney, J. and Harper, C. (1978a). Heroism in a resource crisis: A simulation study, *Environmental Management* **2**: 523–7.

Edney, J. and Harper, C. (1978b). The Commons Dilemma: A Review of Contributions from Psychology, *Environmental Management* **2**: 491–507.

Ernst, A. (1997). *Ökologisch–soziale Dilemmata*, Psychologie Verlags Union, Weinheim.

Gardner, R., Moore, M. and Walker, J. (1994). Racing for the Water: Laboratory Evidence on Subgame Perfection (Research Report), *Workshop in Political Theory and Policy Analysis, Indiana University, Bloomington.*

Gotthelf, J. (1973). *Die Käserei in der Viehfreude*, Manesse. Original Berlin 1850: Springer, Zürich. Alias: Albert Bitzius.

Hackett, S., Schlager, E. and Walker, J. (1994). The Role of Communication in Resolving Commons Dilemmas: Experimental Evidence with Heterogeneous Appropriators, *Journal of Environmental Economics and Management* **27**: 99–126.

Hardin, G. (1968). The Tragedy of the Commons. The Population Problem has no Technical Solution; It Requires a Fandamental Extension in Morality, *Science* **162**: 1243–1248.

Harvey, M., Bell, P. and Birjulin, A. (1993). Punishment and type of feedback in a simulated commons dilemma, *Psychological Reports* **73**: 447–450.

Keser, C. and Gardner, R. (1994). Strategic Behaviour of Experienced Subjects in a Common Pool Resource Game, *Tinbergen Institute. University of Amsterdam. Discussion Paper TI 94–119.*

Knapp, A. (1986). Die Auswirkungen emotionaler Zustände auf das Lösen eines sozialen Dilemmas, *Zeitschrift für Sozialpsychologie* **17**: 160–172.

Liebrand, W. and Messick, D. (eds) (1996). *Frontiers in Social Dilemmas Research*, 1st edn, Springer, Berlin.

Liebrand, W., Lange, P. and Messick, D. (1995). Social Dilemmas, *in* A. Manstead and M. Hewstone (eds), *The Blackwell Encyclopedia of Social Psychology*, 1st edn, Blackwell, Oxford, pp. 546–551.

Liebrand, W., Messick, D. and Wilke, H. (eds) (1992). *Social Dilemmas. Theoretical Issues and Research Findings*, Pergamon, Oxford.

Lopes, L. (1994). Psychology and Economics: Perspectives on Risks, Cooperations, and the Marketplace, *Annual Review of Psychology* **45**: 197–227.

Martichuski, D. and Bell, P. (1991). Reward, Punishment, Privatization, and Moral Suasion in a Commons Dilemma, *Journal of Applied Social Psychology* **21**: 1356–69.

Meadows, D., Meadows, D., Randers, J. and Behrens, W. (1972). *Limits to growth*, New American Library, New York.

Meinhardt, H. (1999). Common Pool Games are Convex Games, *Journal of Public Economic Theory* **2**: 247–270.

Meinhardt, H. and Ostmann, A. (1999). Resolving commons' dilemmas by cooperative games, *Working Paper in Game Theory and Experimental Economics 10. ISMW. University of Karlsruhe.*

Moir, R. (1996). *The Effects of Costly Monitoring and Sanctioning upon Common–pool Resource Appropriation Ph.D. Thesis.*, McMaster University, Hamilton, Ontario.

Muller, R. and Vickers, M. (1996). Communication in a Common Pool Resource Environment with Probabilistic Destruction, *McMaster University, Dept. of Economics, Working Paper 96–06.*

Olson, M. (1965). *The Logic of Collective Action*, Harvard University Press, Cambridge, Mass.

Ostmann, A. (1988). Limits of Rational Behaviour in Cooperatively Played Normal Form Games, *in* R. Tietz, W. Albers and R. Selten (eds), *Bounded Rational Behavior in Experimental Games and Markets. Lecture Notes in Economics and Mathematical Systems*, Vol. 314, Springer, Berlin, pp. 317–32.

Ostmann, A. (1994). An Experimental Fishing Coop, *Diskussionspapier, FR Psychologie, Universität des Saarlandes. Saarbrücken.*

Ostmann, A. (1995). Water Management on the Eve of Crisis – The Case of the Canary Islands, *Diskussionspapier B–9511, Fachbereich Wirtschaftswissenschaften, Universität des Saarlandes, Saarbrücken.*

Ostmann, A. (1996). When to Defect in Commons, *in* P. K. et al. (ed.), *Operations Research Proceedings*, Springer, Berlin, pp. 505–510.

Ostmann, A. (1998). External control may destroy commons, *Rationality and Society* **10**: 135–154.

Ostmann, A. (1999). Grenzen ökonomischer Anreize für Umweltgemeingüter, *Gaia* **7**: 286–295.

Ostmann, A. (2001). *Coalitions in Multilateral Negotiations: Aspirations, Agreement, and Outcomes*. This volume.

Ostmann, A. and Beckenkamp, M. (1997). Agentenmodelle zum Umgang mit vollständig erneuerbaren Gemeingütern, *in* C. Jung, K. Fischer and S. Schacht (eds), *Distributed Cognitive Systems – Proceedings of the VKS'97 Workshop*, DFKI (German Research Institute for Artifical Intelligence), Saarbrücken, pp. 19–31.

Ostmann, A., Pommerehne, W., Feld, L. and Hart, A. (1997). Umweltgemeingüter?, *Zeitschrift für Wirtschafts– und Sozialwissenschaften* **117**: 107–144.

Ostmann, A., Wojtyniak, B. and Beckenkamp, M. (1999). Comparing and Explaining the Success of a Common Endowed with Different Degrees of Sanctioning, *Working Paper WOW2 J99–7. Workshop in Political Theory and Policy Analysis. Indiana University, Bloomington.*

Ostrom, E. (1990). *Governing the Commons (The Evolution of Institutions for Collective Action)*, Cambridge University Press, Cambridge.

Ostrom, E. and Walker, J. (1989). Communication in a Commons: Cooperation Without External Enforcement, *Workshop in Political Theory and Political Analysis. Bloomington.*

Ostrom, E. and Walker, J. (1997). Neither Markets nor States: Linking Transformation Processes in Collective Action Arenas, *in* D. Mueller (ed.), *Perspectives on Public Choice: A Handbook*, Cambridge University Press, Cambridge, pp. 35–72.

Ostrom, E., Gardner, R. and Walker, J. (1994). *Rules, Games and Common Pool Resources*, University of Michigan Press, Ann Arbor, Mich.

Ostrom, E., Walker, J. and Gardner, R. (1992). Covenants with and without a Sword: Self–governance is Possible, *American Political Science Review* **86**: 404–17.

Platt, J. (1969). What we must do, *Science* **166**: 1115–21.

Platt, J. (1973). Social Traps, *American Psychologist* **28**: 641–51.

Popp, M. (1988). Wirkung von Informationsbedingungen, emotionalem Zustand und externer Speichermöglichkeit auf das Lösen sozialer Fallen, *Arch.Psychol.* **140**: 33–51.

Rapoport, A., Budescu, D., Suleiman, R. and Weg, E. (1992). Social dilemmas with uniformly distributed resources, *in* W. Liebrand, D. Messick and H. Wilke (eds), *Social Dilemmas. Theoretical Issues and Research Findings*, Pergamon, Oxford, pp. 43–57.

Rutte, C., Wilke, H. and Messick, D. (1987). Scarcity or abundance caused by people or the environment as determinants of behavior in the resource dilemma, *Journal of Experimental Social Psychology* **23**: 208–216.

Samuelson, C. and Messick, D. (1986). Alternative structural solutions to resource dilemmas, *Organisational Behavior and Human Decision Processes* **37**: 139–155.

Samuelson, C., Messick, D., Rutte, C. and Wilke, H. (1984). Individual and structural solutions to resource dilemmas in two cultures, *Journal of Personality and Social Psychology* **47**: 94–104.

Schroeder, D. (ed.) (1995). *Social Dilemmas (Perspectives on Individuals and Groups)*, Praeger Publ, Westport, CT.

Schulz, U., Albers, W. and Müller, U. (eds) (1994). *Social Dilemmas and Cooperation*, Springer, Berlin.

Suleiman, R. and Rapoport, A. (1989). Environmental and social uncertainty in single–trial resource dilemmas, *Acta Psychologica* **68**: 99–112.

Suleiman, R., Budescu, D. and Rapoport, A. (1994). The position effect: The role of a player's serial position in a resource dilemma game, *in* U. Schulz, W. Albers and U. Müller (eds), *Social Dilemmas and Cooperation*, Springer, Berlin, pp. 55–73.

Walker, J. and Gardner, R. (1992). Probabilistic Destruction of Common Pool Resources: Experimental Evidence, *Economic Journal* **102**: 1149–1161.

Wilke, H., Messick, D. and Rutte, C. (eds) (1986). *Experimental Social Dilemmas*, Lang, Frankfurt.

Wojtyniak, B. and Beckenkamp, M. (1998). Das Nitrat–Dilemma. Strategisches Verhalten bei asymmetrischem Landbesitz, Unveröffentlichtes Vortragsmanuskript. Marburg, TEAP (Tagung experimentell arbeitender Psychologen).

Wojtyniak, B., Beckenkamp, M. and Ostmann, A. (1997). Control and Sanctions May Destroy Commons: Experimental Results and Some Microanalytical Explications, *Working Paper in Game Theory and Experimental Economics 7. ISMW. University of Karlsruhe.*

10 Comment on Axel Ostmann

R. Andrew Muller*

The commons has proved a particularly satisfying metaphor for the analysis of many social problems. The common property dilemma arises when use of a resource (the commons) subtracts from its value to others, yet exclusion of users is difficult. Environmental and natural resource problems such as greenhouse gas warming, groundwater management and fishery management are obvious applications, but the fundamental structure applies to most cases in which individual actions have a negative effect on others: highway congestion and Cournot oligopoly are two examples. Accordingly, investigating whether the outcomes of common property dilemmas are well predicted by theory is likely to yield interesting results. It appears that many aspects of the institutions governing common property will influence the way in which it is used. Laboratory experiments provide experimental control over these factors and are particularly useful at sorting out the relevant contributions of each. Professor Ostmann has provided us with an interesting and informative survey of this literature. I would like to remark first on the general relationship between common property and related environments and second on his general findings. At a technical level common property dilemmas are a sub-class of the more general class of social dilemmas, which can be defined broadly as environments in which individually rational behaviour leads to sub-optimal group outcomes. The dilemma is generally modelled in a two commodity environment. We consider a fixed set of agents with preference functions defined over their consumption of a private good and a communal good produced from a common property resource.

Each agent is endowed with a resource, which may be allocated to the production of the private good or the communal good. Allocation to the communal good is often termed appropriation. Aggregate production of the communal good is a function of aggregate appropriation. Each agent receives a share of the communal production, where in most cases the share, q_i, is equal to the agents share in resources devoted to communal production, that is

$$q_i = \frac{x_i}{x_i + y_i}, \tag{10.1}$$

where x_i and y_i represent the effort devoted to communal production by agent i and all remaining agents respectively. We identify the private resource with effort, e.g. capital and labour, which may be used to produce the private good (say food produced by farming), or the communal good (say fish produced from a fishery). The common property resource (the fishery) may be identified with the communal production function itself. The payoff function for individual i has the form $\pi_i = \pi^i(x_i, y_i)$. The simplicity of this abstract notation makes it clear that common property problems and social dilemma problems more generally encompass virtually any economic problem in which one agent is affected by the aggregate of the

* I am indebted to David Feeny.

other agents actions. In particular, the structure is equivalent to that of a homogeneous quantity setting oligopoly.

Investigating the structure somewhat more carefully, it is immediately obvious that individual i's payoff is decreasing in y_i and hence in the appropriation of any other individual, x_j. Increased appropriation by any one individual confers a negative externality on all others. The combination of the sharing rule and a concave communal production function introduces a non-linearity into the best response functions, and consequently both cooperative and non-cooperative equilibria may be in the interior of the choice set.

Common property resource (CPR) problems are particularly closely related to public goods problems. In the case of a public good, the private resource again represents effort which may be to the production of a private good or a fully non-subtractable public good. The role of the common property resource is played by the public good production function. Public goods problems differ in that the public good production function is often linear in aggregate effort and the sharing rule is replaced by $q_i = 1\,\forall i$. The new sharing rule implies that any individual contributions x_j confer a positive externality on all other agents. The payoff function for individual i has a reduced form $\pi_i = \pi^i(x_i, y_i)$.

CPR problems are even more closely related to so-called public bad problems. In these problems the marginal utility of the communal product (the public bad) is negative. The sharing rule remains $q_i = 1\,\forall i$. Payoffs are decreasing in others contributions to the public bad. For an economically interesting problem individuals must have some incentive to produce to the public bad. Usually this is modelled by a private payoff that depends positively on individual contributions to the public bad, but the problem may easily be incorporated into the general social dilemma framework by specifying a negative marginal utility for the private good instead. The public bad problem closely resembles the CPR problem in exhibiting negative externalities, but its motivation makes it reasonable to specify a linear communal production function. In this case corner solutions similar to the case of public goods are to be expected. Thus CPR problems are closely related to other social dilemmas, and experimental results concerning all three may usefully be compared.

Modifications of the two problems are also highly parallel. For example Rapoport and Suleiman (1993) and Budescu, Rapoport and Suleiman (1995) consider CPRs in which the supply of the communal good is zero if the total appropriation exceeds a specified threshold. This has a clear parallel in the case of threshold public goods, in which none of the public good is provided if total contributions fall short of the threshold. Despite this close similarity, however, the context in which CPRs are analysed is quite distinct from that of public goods and public bads. This has led to a different emphasis in the experimental literature. The experimental public good literature started from the presumption that rational economic behaviour implies free riding in a public goods context. When it was discovered that free riding was typically not complete, interest shifted to investigating to what extent this irrational result could be ascribed to social pressure, altruism, censored observations or errors in individual optimization. Institutional design to promote co-operation has not been the focal point, although certainly some experiments have closely investigated the roles of communication or modified incentives (as in the threshold public goods literature). In contrast, much work in the area of common property has been politically motivated. Co-operative (or efficient) exploitation of common property resources has been the goal. Hardins (1968) call for mutual coercion, mutually agreed upon was interpreted as a call for government intervention. Berkes, Feeny, McKay and Acheson (1989) explicitly dismissed this call, considering it to be based on a naive view of history and a neglect of the capability of local populations to develop self-sustaining institutions capable of efficiently exploiting the commons.

Thus the general research program in the area of common property has been to document successful and less successful management practices and to investigate experimentally the role of identified factors in promoting efficient exploitation. This perhaps explains the remarkable absence of attention to the roles of traditional economic incentives such as taxes, subsidies, and tradable permits as devices for managing the commons. Because renewable resources such as fisheries are frequently managed as common property, the interaction between the property rights regime and the growth characteristic of the resource stock has been of particular interest to economists. Resource allocations now take on an aspect of investment: reductions in current appropriation can lead to an increase in the stock and larger sustained yields in the future. Moreover, for some natural growth functions it is possible under open access management to lead to complete destruction of the resource base (as in the extinction of a whale fishery) even when this is not socially optimal. Thus questions of dynamic efficiency and exhaustion arise naturally. Such questions, however, have not been important in the study of public goods and bads. Professor Ostmanns survey of common property experiments reflects this emphasis on institutional design and dynamic allocation that distinguishes CPR experiments from their close analogues in the public goods and public bads literature. After briefly touching on the baseline paradigm and the effect of communication, areas in which CPR experiments overlap broadly with related literatures, he concentrates on the roles of sanctioning and monitoring in promoting efficient allocation and on experiments related to depletion and exhaustion.

Turning now to Professor Ostmanns general findings, we note that the baseline results for common property experiments differ substantially from those for linear public goods. As Prof. Ostmann notes, Ostrom, Gardner and Walker (1995) obtained below-equilibrium efficiencies and above-equilibrium appropriations, especially in their high-endowment environments. In Professor Ostmanns terms, there has been a negative co-operation shift. This is quite unlike the typical linear public goods experiment, which yields a positive shift (Ledyard, 1995). It seems that public goods are the anomaly here. Oligopoly experiments, public bad experiments, and CPR experiments tend to exhibit more individualistic behaviour. There seem to be two lines of explanation for this. On the one hand, authors like Sonnemans, Offerman and Schram (1998) have demonstrated a framing effect suggesting that cooperation is less frequent in public bad dilemmas (with negative externalities) than in strategically equivalent games cast as public goods (with positive externalities.) On the other hand, the interior equilibrium characteristic of CPR problems may also lead to fewer excess contributions.

A number of public goods experiments with interior equilibria (for example Andreoni, 1993, Chan et al., 1996, 1997) show substantially fewer or even negative excess contributions, despite being framed with a positive externality. The positive role of communication in promoting co-operation in CPR environments is entirely consistent with that found in the broader public goods literature (Ledyard, 1995). Current work in this area is focusing on partial communication and on communication through overlapping groups (Kinukawa, Saijo, and Une , 2000). Although most of these results are obtained in a linear environment, Chan, Mestelman, Moir and Muller (1999) demonstrate similar gains in a non-linear environment. It is interesting that Ostmann and his colleagues find that contributions are biased away from equilibrium and towards equality in heterogenous environments. This parallels similar findings by my colleagues and me in the context of public goods (Chan et al., 1996, 1997). The other factors investigated by Professor Ostmann suggest that co-operation may be particularly difficult to obtain in common property environments. The literature on sanctioning is relatively limited. In principle, the possibility of sanctioning uncooperative behaviour should shift the equilibrium towards the efficient outcome.

Laboratory experiments are particularly interesting in these areas, since they allow a precise test of the underlying economic theory. An interesting feature of the experiments cited by Professor Ostmann is the inclusion of transactions costs in the form of a payment for monitoring or sanctioning. This reflects the difficulty of exclusion characteristic of CPRs. All the experiments show a general inability of sanctioning regimes to achieve efficiency. Only those sanctioning programs which are justified by monitoring and which are limited in their severity seem to reduce overuse of the commons. Psychological forces leading to the rejection of unfair and arbitrary institutions seem to lie at the heart of this failure. Further research on this topic would appear to be called for. As might be expected, the dynamic and probabilistic nature of many common property resources provides another reason for pessimism about the ability of self-organizing group behaviour. Once again, the predictive power of conventional economic theory seems limited. The Ostrom, Gardner, Walker experiments demonstrate clearly that groups are unable even to achieve Nash equilibrium levels of appropriation without communication. This seems to be further confirmation of the lack of experimental support for the backward-looking induction required in many dynamic economic theories. This is consistent with many observations, most notably the bubble experiments conducted by Smith et al. (1988; see also Sunder, 1975). Still, the Muller and Vickers (1996) experiment shows that even in this hostile environment, non-binding communication can lead to dramatically improved co-ordination.

What, then, have laboratory experiments taught us about management of common property resources? I concur with Prof. Ostmanns overall assessment. First and foremost, laboratory experiments have confirmed the reality of the dilemma against those who reject it as a libel on the human race. Yet Gotthelfs pessimism is not entirely confirmed. The behaviour we observe in the laboratory is not entirely explained by economic incentives. Social institutions, communication above all, are able to achieve a dramatic increase in cooperation. Moreover, economic instruments designed to promote efficiency seem not to be efficient unless they satisfy certain basic social principles of fairness. The laboratory data confirm what might be generalizable from the field. Small, stable communities are likely to be successful in managing their commons on the basis of self-enforcing local institutions. Matters become far more difficult when differences and communication failures are induced by geographic and ethnic division. In these circumstances, perhaps more attention should be given to conventional economic incentives while recognizing that part of their success will depend on the degree that they are perceived as fair by those regulated.

References

Andrconi, J. (1993). An Experimental Test of the Public-Goods Crowding-Out Hypothesis, *American Economic Review* **83**(5): 1317–27.

Berkes, F., Feeny, D., McKay, B. and Acheson (1989). The Benefits of the Commons, *Nature* **340**(July 13): 91–93.

Budescu, D., Rapoport, A. and Suleiman, R. (1995). Common Pool Resource Dilemmas under Uncertainty: Qualitative Tests of Equilibrium Solutions, *Games and Economic Behaviour* **10**(1): 171–201.

Chan, K., Godby, R., Mestelman, S. and Muller, R. A. (1996). Spite, Guilt, and the Voluntary Provision of Public Goods when Income is not Distributed Equally, *Canadian Journal of Economics* **29**: 605–609.

Chan, K., Godby, R., Mestelman, S. and Muller, R. A. (1997). Equity Theory and the voluntary provision of Public Goods, *Journal of Economic Behavior and Organization* **32**: 349–364.

Chan, K., Mestelman, S., Moir, R. and Muller, R. A. (1999). Heterogeneity and the voluntary provision of public goods, *Experimental Economics* **2**(1): 5–30.

Hardin, G. (1968). The Tragedy of the Commons, *Science* **162**: 1243–48.

Kinukawa, S., Saijo, T. and Une, M. (2000). Partial Communication in a Voluntary Contribution Mechanism Experiment, *Pacific Economic Review*. (forthcoming).

Ledyard, J. (1995). Public Goods: A Survey of Experimental Research, *in* J. Kagel and A. Roth (eds), *The Handbook of Experimental Economics*, Princeton University Press, Princeton.

Muller, R. and Vickers, M. (1996). Communication in a Common Pool Resource Environment with Probabilistic Destruction, McMaster University, Department of Economics, Working Paper 96-06.

Ostrom, E., Gardner, R. and Walker, J. (1994). *Rules, games, and common-pool resources*, University of Michigan Press, Ann Arbor.

Rapoport, A. and Suleiman, R. (1993). Incremental Contribution in Step-level Public Goods Games with Aysmmetric Players, *Organizational Behaviour and Human Decision Processes* **55**: 171–194.

Smith, V., Suchanek, G. and Williams, A. (1988). Bubbles, Crashes and Endogenous expectations in experimental spot asset markets, *Econometrica* **56**: 1119–52.

Sonnemans, J., Schram, A. and Offerman, T. (1998). Public Good Provision and Public Bad Prevention: The Effect of Framing, *Journal of Economic BehavioUr and Organization* **34**(1): 143–61.

Sunder, S. (1995). Experimental asset markets: a survey, *in* J. Kagel and A. Roth (eds), *The handbook of experimental economics*, Princeton University Press, Princeton, pp. 445–500.

Part III

Election Markets and Experimental Stock Markets

11 Election Markets*

Experiences from a Complex Market Experiment

Gregor Brüggelambert and Arwed Crüger

Abstract. Typically, public opinion polls or statistical forecasting models are used to obtain information about the voters' expected behavior. A decade ago, these institutions have entered into competition with so-called political stock markets. The origin of these experimental markets dates back to the work of Forsythe et al. (1992). This article concentrates on four computerized political stock markets, which took place in Germany. The paper also gives a summary of the results of other markets that were organized outside of the USA. It is shown that the findings of Forsythe et al. (1992) do not generally explain the behavior of all political stock markets that were organized in the last few years. At least in the German markets, extraordinary profits were achieved less by those people who took advantage of other people's anomalies than by people who acquired an advantage from the existence of asymmetric information. Additionally, when comparing the results of the other markets, our hypothesis states that the efficiency of political stock markets is a question of the external institutional framework (e.g. the voting system, public opinion polls), rather than of internal factors like the market institutions, number of participants, investments made by the participants etc.

11.1 Introduction

To forecast election outcomes, it is common to use public opinion polls to receive a first approximation. This method typically stands in competition with distinct models of voting behavior used to form a statistical model to predict future election events (see, e.g., Fair 1996 and Gelman and King 1993), but opinion polls and even very sophisticated models of this kind are not immune to poor performance in certain environments.

A decade ago, so-called political stock markets have been introduced as a further instrument for forecasting election results. In these experimental markets, participants have to trade futures (party stocks), whose payoffs depend on the outcome of a particular election.

Since the work of Forsythe, Nelson, Neumann and Wright (1992), who are pioneers of these experimental political markets (Iowa Election Market, hereafter IEM), several other experimental election markets have been organized to forecast election

* The authors wish to thank Marlies Ahlert, Michael Berlemann, Christian Gliesmann, Christian Haslbeck, Heather Kellett, Carsten Schmidt, Martin Strobel, Reinhard Tietz, Bettina Vaupel, Carsten Vogt, Joachim Weimann, Wolfgang Wiegard and Matthias Wrede for their work on the German political stock market project. We would like to extend special thanks to Joyce Berg, Robert Forsythe, Drew Letcher, Forrest Nelson, George Neumann and Jack Wright for considerate co-operation regarding the Iowa Electronic Markets.

outcomes. The authors have run a number of markets together with other scientists of the German Election Markets Workgroup (GEMW)[1]. Other markets have been organized by several German universities and newspapers. All of these markets worked quite well, but none of them outperformed all the polls as clearly as those for the 1988 and 1992 US presidential elections, organized by Forsythe et al. (1992, 1993). As an explanation for the efficiency of these markets, Forsythe et al. (1992) separated a subgroup of 'marginal traders' to offset the 'judgment bias' that was observed in the decision behavior of other market participants. According to the judgment bias, individuals tend to overestimate the extent to which their views accurately represent the population.

In the middle of this paper, experiences of four IEM-type political stock markets, installed in Germany for elections in 1990, 1991, 1994, and 1998, are reviewed. Additionally, the paper gives an overview on the predictive results in particular from European election markets that were organized during the last decade. It is shown that these markets differ from their US counterparts in so far as they do not systematically generate predictions close to the outcome of the electorates than the polls. A closer look at the markets shows that the 'marginal trader' hypothesis, formulated by Forsythe et al. (1992), does not hold, at least in its original form, for German markets. The paper gives evidence to the hypothesis that traders with a preference for a political party were able to make extraordinary gains despite the fact that they are influenced by a judgment bias, which was first observed by Forsythe et al. (1992). In Germany, a subgroup called "political insiders" was able to make money at the expense of less informed traders. While the markets predict well, even the "political insiders" were not able to improve the forecasts of the election markets substantially in comparison to the polls. The purpose of this paper is to explain this observation.

11.2 A brief pleading for election markets as a "complex experiment"

It can be asserted that each election market is a complex event consisting of multiple decisions and observations. The political-institutional infrastructure, which undergoes changes over time, is a major determinant for each market's specific phase. Therefore, it is sometimes regretted that complex experiments (or field experiments) like political stock markets, suffer too much from insufficient experimenter control on one the hand and a lack of replicability on the other.

But, as in complex laboratory experiments, the intention of these experiments differs greatly from that of straightforward laboratory experiments that are carried out in a highly controlled environment. Laboratory experiments of this kind usually work with quite simple and artificial environmental conditions of economic models. More complex experiments, so-called natural experiments, as well as field experiments, attempt to challenge this simplification. Some of these experiments examine

[1] The GEMW consists mainly of the following universities: MLU Halle-Wittenberg, HU-Berlin, UGH-Essen and TU-Dresden.

the performance of economic models in more complex cases than in the simple structural environments, which are normally used to test parts of normative economic theory. Others are conducted to analyze decision behavior under conditions that are closer to decision problems in reality.

Our initial intention was to study decision-making behavior in a more complex environment, and it can be said that experiments of this kind are rare in comparison to laboratory experiments.[2] If we expect to receive answers to these questions, we cannot simply substitute complex experiments with controlled ones, or theory-driven experiments by problem driven research (see, e.g., Frey and Bohnet 1996 for a broader discussion).

11.3 Organization, market precision, and possible factors of success

11.3.1 Market design and trading procedures

In their original form, the IEM-type markets mentioned above are computerized financial markets in which a certain number of contracts are traded. Market participants have to pay real money that is deposited using personal accounts in the computer system. Participating traders' final payoff is determined by the amount of cash and the number of contracts held at the last opening day of the markets, usually the day before election. Each contract has a final liquidation value, which is the payoff to a particular contract depending upon the election results.

So-called 'unit portfolios' are used to put contracts into circulation. Each unit portfolio consists of one of each available contract in a given market. Usually a type of contract is signed on a single party. During the federal election in 1998 for example, a unit portfolio in the IEM-type German Election Market 1998 (hereafter GEMWf 98, "f" for federal[3]) consisted of six types of contracts, i.e., for the parties: CDU/CSU, SPD, FDP, B'90/Greens, PDS, and RoF.[4] Here RoF stands for 'Rest of Field', i.e. votes that were given to the other remaining parties in a given election, so that the sum of contracts within a unit portfolio reaches 100% of the votes. It was possible for market participants to buy or sell unit portfolios for exactly DM 1 at any time. This means that the market is a zero-sum game. To bear any risk and to have any chance of a positive return, traders have to accept and hold unbalanced portfolios, i.e. participants have to buy or sell single contracts from their unit portfolios at prices they find reasonable. It was mentioned above that the final value of each contract is determined by the election result. In the case of the GEMWf 98,

[2] Exceptions are, e.g., Tietz (1973) or Roth (1989).

[3] See Table 11.2 for a listing of abbreviations.

[4] Party abbreviations: CDU: Christian Democratic Union, CSU: Christian Social Union, SPD: Social Democratic Party of Germany, FDP: Free Democratic Party, Greens: Bündnis 90 / Die Grünen (German green party), PDS: Party of Democratic Socialism (German Socialists).

for example, the final value of one SPD contract amounts to DM .409, because this party received 40.9% of all votes.

The IEM-type markets operate as (continuous) computerized *double auction* markets. Trading takes place by issuing offers to buy (bids) or offers to sell (asks), which are maintained in bid and ask queues, if they do not directly match with an existing offer. Market information available to an individual concerning these bid and ask queues is, at any time, reduced to the highest bid offer and the lowest ask offer (for further details about IEM-type markets, see Forsythe et al. 1992, and Brüggelambert 1999).

11.3.2 Trader demographics

Traders for most markets were recruited primarily from universities. Starting with the 1998 German federal election, applicants were also accepted from outside academia. *Table* 11.1 reports some of the trader demographics of the four markets: GEMWf 90, GEMWr 91 ("r" for "regional"), GEMWf 94, and GEMWf 98. These markets are also analyzed further in the following parts of this paper. The demographic data was obtained by questionnaire (GEMWf 90 and GEMWr 91) or by periodic surveys that appeared on screen (GEMWf 94, GEMWf 98). Percentage entries are for responding traders. Since responses were voluntary and traders who did not log in to the market during the course of the survey could not be interviewed, response rates are less than 100 percent.

Table 11.1. Trader demographics

Variable	Category	Percentages			
		GEMWf 90	GEMWr 91	GEMWf 94	GEMWf 98
Gender	male	95.0	84.1	93.9	91.7
	female	5.0	15.9	6.1	8.3
Age		25.1 (mean)	25.2 (mean)	26.7 (mean)	32.6 (mean)
Discipline	economics and BA	84.9	87.2	68.0	65.0
Current status	student	86.7	88.4	70.3	54.5
	faculty	10.0	7.0	25.0	33.4
	other	3.3	4.6	4.7	12.1
Party affiliation	CDU/CSU	26.7	30.9	27.4	9.4
	SPD	11.7	16.7	18.5	25.0
	FDP	18.3	26.2	10.4	15.6
	Greens	15.0	11.9	25.9	28.1
	independent	28.3	14.3	13.4	6.3
	other			4.4	9.4
	PDS				6.2

The structure of the voter population of the markets is obviously not representative. In all markets, most of the participants were students in economics or business administration, the number of male participants clearly dominates the number of female ones and, especially relevant, party sympathy was less strong for the large parties CDU and SPD, whereas sympathy for the small parties FDP and Greens was distinctly higher than in a representative selection of German voters.

11.3.3 Market accuracy and comparability

Despite the fact that several election markets have been organized in different countries and for different election events, it is not easy to test for the predictive power of these markets. In part, this is due to the fact that each election event, to some extent, is a singleton. In addition, it is difficult to find a suitable measure for forecasting precision itself. Results may differ to a certain degree, depending on the various ways in which market performance is measured. For example, it is uncertain whether average traded prices are preferable to last traded prices for the calculation of predictive errors. Without transaction costs, the prices that should reflect all information available to traders during that day are those of last traded prices. However, political stock markets are characterized by positive transaction costs while potential profits are low. Frequently, as a consequence of these circumstances, only a small number of people or even a single person were active in the market, in particular during the late evening hours of a trading day. From this observation, we might assume that last trading prices have an individual bias.

Presumably, this was the case in the "USA Presidential Election 96" market, in which last traded prices differ considerably from average prices of the last trading day. In this market, last trading prices had suffered from an especially high individual bias during the last trading hours. The mean absolute error (MAE) of the "USA Presidential Election 96" would be considerably larger if we would have used last traded prices for this market (see *Table* 11.2). This demonstrates that average prices, rather than last traded prices, should be taken into account. However, due to the heterogeneity of the market institutions of the election markets shown in *Table* 11.2, as well as the fact that we were unable to obtain information about prices in all variations, the use of average prices was not possible in every case.

Table 11.2: Measuring forecasting precision

Market	Market institution	Trading days	Securities	Participants	Total $ volume (approx.)	MAE of political stock markets	MAE of public opinion Average	MAE of public opinion Best poll
USA (IEM)								
Presidential Election 88	ICDA	157	4[3]	192	$4,967	0.27	2.72	1.33
Senate Election 90	ICDA	149	2	199	$1,114	0.30	2.34	0.93
Presidential Election 92	ICDA	296	4[3]	1072	$20,532	0.20	2.03	1.20
Presidential Election 96	ICDA	274	4[2]	>10,000[1]	>$200,000[1]	2.14	2.44	0.10
Austria (APSM)								
Federal Election 94	ICDA	169	6	44	$1,050	1.18	1.53	1.26
Federal Election 95	ICDA	59	6	127	$11,030	2.71	2.05	1.45
Styrian Regional Parliament 95	ICDA	96	6	127	$11,030	2.93	2.32	2.32
European Parliament 96	ICDA	78	6	127	$11,030	2.29	2.04	2.00
Vienna City Parliament 96	ICDA	> 400	6	127	$11,030	1.53	2.08	1.27
Presidential Election 98	ICDA	65	5	NA	NA	1.65	2.57	2.19
Canada (UBC-ESM)								
Federal Election 93	ICDA	41	6	257	> $30,000	0.53	1.06	0.97
House of Commons 93	ICDA	41	6	257	$30,000	3.70	n.p.	n.p.
British Columbia 96	ICDA	239	6	44	$6,324	2.70	1.88	1.88
Federal Election 97	ICDA	35	6	100	> $23,000	1.28	1.39	0.73
Germany								
FEDERAL ELECTION 1990: *Bonn*	ICDA	28	6	52	$560	1.05	1.37	1.07
GEMWf 90	ICDA	24	6	62	$840	1.22	1.37	1.07
Leipzig	ICDA	18	6	26	$220	1.62	1.37	1.07

Table 11.2: (continued)

Market	Market institution	Trading days	Securities	Participants	Total $ volume (approx.)	MAE of political stock markets	MAE of public opinion	
							Average	Best poll
Saarbrücken	POW	4	7[6]	21	$150	2.19	1.37	1.07
FEDERAL ELECTION 1994:								
GEMWf 94	ICDA	153	7	400	$16,150	0.56	0.58	0.37
PEM 94	CMW	39	7	193	$2,300	0.44	0.58	0.37
FEDERAL ELECTION 1998:								
GEMWf 98	ICDA	131	6	112	$3,600	0.96	1.10	0.41
Wahl$treet	ICDA	58	6	9482	$53,300	0.83	1.10	0.41
REGIONAL ELECTIONS:								
GEMWr 91 Hesse	ICDA	16	6	44	$770	1.10	1.10	1.10
PEM 94 Bavaria	CMW	36	7[6]	100	$2,300	1.73	1.43	1.43
Saxony-Anhalt 98 GEMW	ICDA	48	6	37	$620	3.25	3.20	2.77
Saxony-Anhalt 98 Wahl$treet	ICDA	20	6	278	$1,270	3.58	3.20	2.77
Hesse 99 GEMW	ICDA	62	5	42	$456	2.18	2.53	1.76
Hesse 99 Wahl$treet	ICDA	NA	5	500	$8.105	2.72	2.53	1.76
Brandenburg 99 Wahl$treet	ICDA	NA	6	693	$11,233	1.13	1.62	1.60
Saxony 99 GEMW	ICDA	65	6	28	$632	1.00	1.90	1.87
Berlin 99 GEMW	ICDA	46	6	200	$5,006	1.15	1.60	1.03
Berlin 99 Wahl$treet	ICDA	47	6	561	$9,093	1.25	1.60	1.03
Schleswig-Holstein 00 Prognosys	ICDA	92	6	>1,200	$15,645	0.60	1.28	1.00
Baden-Wuerttemberg 01 GEMW	ICDA	40	6	44	$955	1.78	1.48	1.27
Baden-Wuerttemberg 01 Prognosys	ICDA	54	6	1,228	$17,988	2.38	1.48	1.27

Table 11.2: (continued)

Market	Market institution	Trading days	Securities	Participants	Total $ volume (approx.)	MAE of political stock markets	MAE of public opinion Average	Best poll
Rhineland-Palatinate 01 GEMW	ICDA	40	5	44	$955	1.16	0.74	0.68
Netherlands								
Municipal Council 94	ICDA	37	8	69	$1,753	1.61	n.p.	n.p.
Second Chamber 94	ICDA	85	10	279	$25,032	1.12	1.17	1.10
European Parliament 94	ICDA	122	7	132	$7,863	2.41	n.p.	n.p.
Other countries								
Denmark 90	ICDA	14	7	≅ 70	$1,500	1.25	1.05	0.60
Turkey 91	ICDA	21	5	≅ 50	$2,000	2.14	1.96	1.17

Key: MAE: Mean Absolute Error; IEM = Iowa Electronic Markets; UBC-ESM = University of British Columbia Election Stock Market; APSM = Austrian Political Stock Market; GEMW = German Election Market Workgroup; PEM =Passau Election Market. Market institutions: ICDA = IEM-type Continuous Double Auction; POW = Posted Offer auction with weekly closings; CMW = Call Market with weekly closings; n.p. = opinion polls did not provide predictions for these election events; Wahl$treet and Prognosys = commercial versions of the IEM. Entries in brackets are the number of assets that were used as a basis for the calculation for the MAE in the respective row. *Source*: Ostmann (1991), Forsythe *et al.* (1992, 1993, 1995), Ortner *et al.* (1994), Beckmann/ Werding (1996), Brüggelambert (1999), Jacobsen *et al.* (2000), Mohr/Krätzschmar (2000), Berlemann/Schmidt (2001), unpublished information was provided by Forrest Nelson (University of Iowa), Carsten Schmidt (Humboldt-University Berlin), and Martin Werding (University of Passau). See text for further descriptions.[1]As described in more details in this section, these figures do not reflect the actual size of this market.

For technical reasons, some of the figures in *Table* 11.2 can include special effects that might be misleading. For example, for the "USA Presidential Election 96," it was not possible to divide between the vote share market and the winner-takes-all market. Although more than 10,000 traders were enrolled in the whole market, only 41 traders (dollar volume $312) were active in the vote share market during the last week before election, while the winner-takes-all market was far more attractive, with more than 200 traders and a dollar volume of $6,027. Naturally, although the number of active traders may be a decisive factor of market efficiency, only enrolled traders are presented in *Table* 11.2 because information about active traders was not reported for the majority of the markets.

A further problem concerns the choice of the adequate predictive measure. While of course absolute errors are unsuitable it is not quite clear whether it is better to use mean absolute errors instead of mean squared errors or similar measures. In *Table* 11.2, mean absolute errors are used simply because other predictive measures were not available for all markets summarized in *Table* 11.2.

Despite these problems the figures in *Table* 11.2 seem to be reliable enough to start a first statistical analysis. For a first analysis of market precision, it is advisable to work with markets that were established for the same election event and compare them with the latest poll results for the same election. *Table 11.2* summarizes at least all those election markets known to the authors where market traders had to invest their own money for market participation, and which were installed for different election events outside the USA.[5] It also lists the results of four markets that were conducted for US election events (see Berg *et al.* (1997) for more information about other IEM markets organized for election events in the USA). In 1998, commercial markets started their work in Germany. In two of them (Wahl$treet and Prognosys), organized by German newspapers, participants had to invest their own money. Results of these two markets are also reported in *Table* 11.2. Performing a t-test on the equality of means for the 34 non-US election markets, for which poll results were available, leads to the result that the mean MAE (1.62, sd. 0.14) of the election markets is not statistically different from the mean MAE (1.64, sd. 0.11, $t = -0.16$) of the polls average while the mean MAE (1.30, sd. 0.11, $t = 12.04$) of the best polls is lower on a statistically significant level.

The results did not change when we took averages of the MEA for all election markets, which were conducted for the same election, thereby eliminating nine observations, resulting in values for 25 election events. If we proceed in this manner, a t-test on the equality of means for these non-US election market leads to the result that the mean MAE (1.61, sd. 0.16) of the election markets is not different from the mean MAE (1.63, sd. 0.16, $t = -0.24$) of the polls average but higher than the mean

[5] Markets on referenda like the EU referendum market organized by Bohm/Sonnegård (1999) are also not reported in *Table* 11.2. While a political stock market prediction of the outcome of a Swedish referendum on whether or not Sweden should join the European Union clearly outperform the polls in Sweden in 1994 (see Bohm/Sonnegård 1999), the situation was reversed for a referendum on whether or not Austria should join the EU (see Ortner *et al.* 1994).

MAE (1.33, sd. 0.13, $t = 2.59$) of the best polls. Although the database is small, it seems that that the election markets outside the USA did not systematically produce better predictions than the public opinion polls.

On the other hand, we observe a strong correlation between the MAE of the election markets and the MAE of the polls average (Correlation $r = 0.82$, p-value 0.00, n=34) and the MAE of the best polls ($r = 0.79$, p-value 0.00, n=34) respectively. It becomes obvious that at least for each single election, election markets face similar problems in predicting the election outcome as polls.[6] As described in Brüggelambert (1999) as well as conducted by Berlemann/Schmidt (2001) for the German markets, the poll error seems to be a very important variable for an explanation of the market behavior. In Berlemann/Schmidt (2001), this variable turns out to be the most important in the German markets. These authors are correct in asking why this variable was not included in the regression analysis of the US election market comparable study of Berg *et al.* (1997).

Although the "Presidential Election 96" was the worst of the three presidential election markets that took place at the University of Iowa between 1988 and 1996, the markets which were organized for US election events largely predicted election outcomes more accurately than the polls did.[7] This difference between US and non -US markets may, of course, be explained by several factors, some of which will be discussed here in advance before a more detailled discussion is given that starts with section 11.4.

11.3.4 Possible factors of success

Relevance of market institutions It was mentioned above that the *market institution* of an IEM-type experimental stock market is usually a *double auction* institution. Table 11.2 shows three political stock markets (see "Saarbrücken", "PEM 94", and "PEM 94 Bavaria" in *Table* 11.2) that used other market institutions to organize trading. Ostmann (1991) conducted a very small political stock market for the 1990 Bundestag election (the federal parliamentary election of Germany) at the University of Saarbrücken, which was designed as a *posted offer auction* (see *Table* 11.2). As in the Passau Election Markets (PEM) of Beckmann/Werding (1996), organized as *call markets*, trading in the market took place only once a week. As the

[6] To be fair to the polling organizations, it should also be mentioned that there is usually a lag of several days between the conducting and reporting of opinion polls. Thus, while it might take polling organizations several days to report the effects of significant events, IEM-type markets can, in principle, report instantly until the day before the election event. Additionally, pollsters usually prefer the so-called "Sunday-Question" ("For whom would you vote if election day would be next Sunday") in comparison to the so-called "secret ballot technique" where the voting act is simulated (see Berlemann/Schmidt 2001 for a discussion). The "Sunday-Question" is commonly accepted as the more reliable questioning technique. Nevertheless, it refers to another date than the election market what might be a systematic disadvantage. This disadvantage, however, should nearly disappear if latest polls are used.

[7] Information based on a personal interview with Forrest Nelson.

prediction error in Table 11.2 illustrates, the market worked quite well, despite its handicap. Moreover, a posted offer auction is usually regarded as being less efficient than the double auction (see e.g. Friedman 1992 and Holt 1995). The same applies for the call market institution that was used by Beckmann/Werding (1996) in the PEM. Taking this into account, it was surprising that the PEM did a rather good job during the federal election in 1994 (see "PEM 94" in *Table* 11.2), while this was not the case for the regional election in Bavaria (see "PEM 94 Bavaria" in *Table* 11.2).

Market size *Table* 11.2 also makes clear that, like the market institution, the number of participants seems to have little influence on the exactness of a political stock market if we compare markets that were created for the same election event. A common characteristic of all German political stock markets appears to be that their predictions did not differ substantially from those of the polls. In *Table* 11.2, we find predictive errors of six IEM-type markets run in Austria between 1994 and 1998. The same tendency is apparent in these markets, as well as in the other markets outside the USA. While the predictive power of the markets differed considerably, the majority of them made predictions with a similar accuracy as the polls for the same election events.

Table 11.2 reports on only three markets (see the three rows "Canada: House of Commons 93", "Netherlands: Municipal Council 94", and "Netherlands: European Parliament 94"), which were organized for election events for which no polls were available. However it is apparent that the error of the market is especially high for these markets, reporting MAEs of 3.7, 1.61 and 2.41, respectively.

The role of information A further look at *Table* 11.2 illustrates that German markets have achieved successful predictions, even when compared to the polls. This shows that a market incentive system is able to generate prices containing information of comparable quality to the information provided by the polls. This result is especially remarkable when we consider that market prices were not generated by a subgroup of traders who could be regarded as a representative subgroup of German voters (see e.g. *Table* 11.1). Thereby, the following is confirmed: *The election market is capable of generating information of the same quality as provided by public opinion polls, even if the traders are not a representative subgroup of the voting population.*

This phenomenon can be explained by the assumption that traders do not need to know how they intend to vote; rather, they need to know how the rest of the population intends to vote. That means that the incentive system of the market must force the participants to reveal the information they have about voters' behavior. But clearly, this is only the second part of the story. The first part is, how do they acquire this information? The following chapters deal with this question.

11.4 Key characteristics of the German markets

11.4.1 Anomalies and lucky beggars

The 'judgment bias', caused by the 'false-consensus effect' as described in Forsythe et al. (1992), was already examined for German markets (see Brüggelambert 1997a). According to this effect, individuals tend to overestimate the extent of how accurate their opinion represents the population. Traders, therefore, anticipate a larger share of the popular vote for their personally preferred party, and accordingly, they should demand more shares of this 'house stock' at given prices than traders who prefer other parties.

Intuitively, one would expect that this bias inevitably leads to a loss for those who cater to this bias. All of these traders should, on average, pay higher prices for their house stock than other participants. To be certain of this, we computed average buying prices of each preference group related to each stock. The results were surprising. There was not any evidence that traders had paid higher prices for their house stock than other preference groups (see Brüggelambert 1997a). For the most part, average prices were comparatively low.

The reason for this might be that the judgment bias observed in Germany was especially strong during periods in which the respective home stocks had reached a rather low level. If this is true, traders who suffered from a judgment bias could also take advantage of their anomaly, if the same stock then recovered. The same is also true if the liquidation value of a party share, i.e. the election outcome, lies above the closing prices of the election market. Traders with a bias for their *house stock* are able to realize higher profits with this party share than the other groups of traders who are not influenced by this bias. Of course, the opposite is also true: traders will realize greater losses if the election results are lower than the final market prices.

Table 11.3. Election outcome and predicted vote shares

Party	GEMWf 90		GEMWr 91		GEMWf 94		GEMWf 98	
	E	M	E	M	E	M	E	M
CDU/CSU	43,8	42,3	40,2	39,3	41,5	41,1	35,2	37,4
SPD	33,5	33,4	40,8	39,6	36,4	35,3	40,9	39,0
FDP	11,0	9,2	7,4	9,4	6,9	6,3	6,3	6,4
Greens	5,1	8,3	8,8	7,4	7,3	7,9	6,7	7,5
PDS	2,5	2,6			4,4	4,4	5,1	4,9
REP			1,7	2,1	1,9	2,1		
RoF	4,2	3,7	1,1	1,8	1,6	2,6	5,9	6,3

Note: Header abbreviations: E: Election result, M: Market result
Party abbreviations: CDU: Christian Democratic Union, CSU: Christian Social Union, SPD: Social Democratic Party of Germany, FDP: Free Democratic Party, Greens: Bündnis 90 / Die Grünen (German green party), PDS: Party of Democratic Socialism (German Socialists), REP: German Republicans. See Table 11.2 for further abbreviations.

Table 11.4. Preferences and returns

Party preference	GEMWf 90	GEMWr 91	GEMWf 94	GEMWf 98
CDU/CSU	3.21 (5.02) [16] {-}, yes	1.26 (4.41) [13] {-}, yes	1.78 (12.31) [41] {-}, yes	-6.73 (0.80) [3] {+}, yes
SPD	1.81 (2.84) [6] {-}, no	4.02 (9.09) [7] {-}, yes	3.15 (4.79) [28] {-}, yes	3.22 (5.05) [6] {-}, yes
FDP	0.10 (13.59) [9] {-}, no	-0.29 (3.58) [11] {+}, yes	4.56 (4.45) [14] {-}, yes	-0.49 (5.60) [3] {+}, yes
Greens	1.39 (1.64) [7] {+}, yes	-0.41 (5.76) [3] {-}, no	-0.13 (8.53) [36] {+}, yes	0.84 (3.31) [8] {+}, no
PDS			4.71 (3.20) [6] {=}	7.54 (-) [1] {-}
other			-0.84 (21.40) [12] {+}, yes	-1.66 (0.67) [2] {+}
Group of traders with sympathy for a party	2.13 (7.25) [38]	1.18 (5.54) [34]	1.73 (10.53) [137]	0.43 (4.82) [24]
Group of traders without sympathy for a special party	-4,19 (12.17) [17]	-0,15 (4.11) [6]	-2.10 (8.75) [6]	
no response	0.88 (11.36) [7]	-0.53 (0.71) [4]	0.22 (8.54) [228]	0.22 (4.39) [88]

Note: Average returns in percentages. See Table 11.2 for abbreviations. Standard deviations in round brackets; number of observations in square brackets.

Tables 11.3 and 11.4 show a first empirical examination of this postulation. In *Table* 11.3, election outcomes and vote shares as finally predicted by the four election markets under review are summarized. *Table* 11.4 presents average returns for the groups of traders with a special party preference as well as average returns for the group of traders who announced that they do not have a preference for a political party. Using the information in *Table* 11.3, *Table* 11.4 indicates whether the final market prices were lower (see '{-}' in *Table* 11.4) than the actual election outcome or higher ('{+}'). As a simple test for the above hypothesis, a 'yes' was inserted in the respective cells of *Table* 11.4 if the average returns of traders associated with a particular political party were higher (lower) than the average returns of the group of all traders with a party preference (see 'Group of traders with sympathy for a party' in *Table* 11.4) and if the final market prices were lower (higher) than the election outcomes. We refer to these traders as 'lucky beggars' because they made profit by luck and not by rational decision-making. A 'no' was inserted if the market price was greater than the election result and the group of traders earned average or greater than average returns or if the election results were higher than the market price and the group earned average or less than average returns. Ignoring all cases where final market prices equal the actual election outcomes (see '{=}' in *Table* 11.4) as well as the cases where less than three traders indicated that they are affiliated with a political party, it is shown in *Table* 11.4 that in thirteen cases the hypothesis is supported whereas in only four cases it is not.

In order to demonstrate these tests, the results from GEMWf 90 can be examined. The CDU/CSU had results for the election that were greater than the market prices and had greater than average returns, leading to a 'yes'. The Greens had election results that were less than the market price and lower than average returns, also leading to a 'yes'. Although these groups had different results, the answer is the same for our test: traders with a judgment bias had either higher profits or losses than the average of traders with a party preference.[8]

Table 11.4 also highlights that traders who are affiliated with a political party usually realize returns that are higher than returns realized by traders who do not have preferences for a particular political party. This result is, of course, not a contradiction to the marginal trader hypothesis provided by Forsythe *et al.* (1992). Marginal traders likely lack judgment bias more than they are likely to lack a party preference. Nevertheless, one might expect that returns of a group of traders who have a particular political preference should be at least close to zero, if the judgment bias of at least the larger part of this group of traders is the source of extraordinary profits made by the 'marginal traders' in the market. In contrast to that, the results in *Table* 11.4 suggest that traders with a preference for a political party have some advantages against those traders who do not. The next two sections explore these aspects more closely.

11.4.2 Marginal traders

What becomes apparent is that those who want to profit from other people's judgment bias must maintain a high information standard in order to do so. As argued by Forsythe et al. (1992: 1157), this would require arbitrageurs who know the extent of the judgment bias exhibited by traders of each political preference. Forsythe et al. (1992) believe that a small subgroup of marginal traders had sufficient intuitive grasp to offset the judgment bias of other traders in their market. On average, these marginal traders invested more money in the market, traded more shares and were active on more days than non-marginal traders. Significantly, marginal traders tended to earn higher returns. These results led to the assumption that people who invest more have a higher stake in the outcome and tend to act more rationally.

To test the marginal trader hypotheses, we used similar procedures to isolate marginal traders with desirable characteristics (see Forsythe *et al.* 1992, p. 1158). A person was selected as a 'marginal trader', if *i*) that trader had a bid or an ask in the queue at the end of a day at a price within DM 0.008 of the price of the last trade of the day, or *ii*) had a bid or ask in a queue which was accepted by another trader sometime during the day.[9]

A correlation analysis was carried out in order to show to what extent each participant's success, while playing the 'marginal trader' strategy during the whole market period, positively correlated with market returns. As reported in *Table* 11.5, there was no such correlation in the first three markets, GEMWf 90, GEMWr 91 and GEMWf 94. It came as a surprise that even typical factors of success, such as

[8] Marginal traders, in the sense of Forsythe *et al.* (1992), tend to be able to eliminate this effect ; however, this is obviously not the case in Germany. The calculations of *Table* 11.3 and 11.4 are of course only a first trial to test this assumption.

[9] Like in Forsythe *et al.* (1992) market orders were not used to identify marginal traders, because it is impossible to recognize whether the market orders represent marginal or non-marginal trading behavior.

activity and high investments, did not correlate with market returns of the subjects in these three markets. This was not the case in the GEMf 98, in which trading at the margin appeared to become a matter of success in all three categories, while, as in the earlier markets, returns did not correlate with individual investments (see *Table* 11.5).

However, we are very likely to observe an artificial correlation between individual market activity and marginality if we apply the definition proposed by Forsythe *et al.* (1992). Even if we were able to separate a subgroup of marginal traders with significantly higher returns, this might be caused by a purely mechanical correlation, which would tell us very little about the informational role played by the 'marginal trader' strategy in the election market. The observation of a correlation between activity and marginality in the election markets is very likely. It is therefore possible that traders might have realized higher returns if they had been more active in the market, whilst marginality was merely the consequence of these traders' activity (see Beckmann/Werding 1996 and Brüggelambert 1997a).

Table 11.5. Individual indicators of (potential) success

Return correlated with	GEMWf 90	GEMWr 91	GEMWf 94	GEMWf 98
Days of activity	0.06 (0.41)	-0.22 (-1.31)	-0.01 (-0.16)	0.32 (3.03**)
Number of log-ins	-0.04 (-0.32)	-0.08 (-0.46)	0.02 (0.36)	0.46 (4.68**)
Strategy *marginal trader*	-0.03 (-0.23)	-0.19 (-1.14)	-0.06 (-1.17)	0.37 (3.58**)
Individual investments	-0.06 (-0.39)	-0.28 (-1.75)	-0.05 (-0.86)	-0.02 (-0.17)
Observations	53	37	361	83

Key: Active traders only, i.e. traders with at least one log-in during the period for which the market was organized. Entries are correlation coefficients; entries parenthesis are obtained from the t-test for continuous variables. **: significant at 1% level.

Forsythe *et al.* (1992, p. 1158) do not deny that the definition of a marginal trader is somewhat arbitrary. For example, Forsythe *et al.* (1992) identified a trader as marginal if, and only if, one of the two conditions, *i*) and *ii*) mentioned above, applied for at least three days during the last three weeks of the market. Therefore, a variety of additional selection criteria for marginal traders were introduced by Brüggelambert (1997a, 1999). It is shown that for nearly all of these selection criteria, marginal traders invested greater amounts of money and demonstrated a greater level of participation. However, it is worth noting that, in contrast to the findings made by Forsythe *et al.* (1992), comparing the mean returns did not identify a group of marginal traders that was able to earn higher returns on a statistically significant level in any of these markets. Additionally, the results in *Table* 11.5 below show that in all four markets, investment amounts are not correlated with the return, and this is clearly inconsistent with the assumption that rationality rises when the stakes are higher.

11.4.3 Experts and learning

Election markets are complex environments to deal with. As traders become more and more familiar with the rules of the market, their performance should also increase. Furthermore, it could also be expected that traders who have taken part in one market perform better in a following market. Traders who perform well in the first market and better in the second are called experts. Another approach is to test the hypothesis that experienced traders might have a competitive advantage against new traders, resulting in higher returns. This advantage is called learning.

Test for the expert effect There were two occasions when follow-up markets took place: the market for the regional elections in Hesse 1991 (GEMWr 91) followed the market for the federal elections 1990 (GEMWf 90) and the market for the federal elections 1998 (GEMWf 98) followed the market for the regional elections in Saxony-Anhalt 1998 (see "Saxony-Anhalt 98 GEMW" in *Table* 11.2).

The returns of the 31 traders who participated in both the GEMWf 90 and in the GEMWr 91 were compared to see if traders have increased their performance. The average return for these traders had indeed increased slightly, but not statistically significant (Correlation r=0,042, t=0,22, d.f.=29). The assumption that traders perform better in a follow-up market and become experts can therefore not be supported.

The returns of the 30 traders who participated in both the market for the federal elections in Saxony-Anhalt 1998 and in the GEMWf 98 were compared. In this case, the average return for these traders decreased slightly, and of course there was no expert effect (Correlation r=-0,1355, t=-0,698, d.f.=27).

Test for the existence of learning We compare the returns of continuing traders with the returns of those people without any experience in election markets. In the GEMWr 91, there were 31 experienced and 6 new traders. Surprisingly, the average return of the beginners is higher than the average return of experienced traders (5,3 vs. 0,98). Due to the small number of beginners, this difference is not statistically significant (t-Test for independence of sample averages: t=0,98). The same holds true for a comparison of the market for the federal elections in Saxony-Anhalt 1998 and the GEMWf 98. The 81 newcomers had a better average return (0,197) than the 30 continuing traders (-0,125). Again, this difference does not prove to be significant (t-Test for independence of sample averages: t=0,34).

Without proof of the existence of experts or learning, and even reverse tendencies, an explanation for these results is needed. One possible explanation is the intrinsic motivation that traders gain from acting in a new and challenging environment. Once there is nothing new to explore, traders lose their motivation and perform less successfully. Another reason might be the problem of learning in a complex environment. After a certain level of knowledge has been reached, it might be very difficult to identify further chances for improvement.

11.4.4 Political insiders

All in all, the German markets have provided acceptable results and reliable prognoses. It was possible to create another subgroup that played a similar role as the marginal traders in the US markets. This group was defined for the GEMWf 94, and called 'political insiders' (see Brüggelambert 1997a). These traders were identified by a survey, asking for their sources of information and other related issues. Participants who read newspapers and news-related magazines proved to perform better. High returns were also experienced by people who believed themselves to be well informed. Participants who were sure that they were better informed about the political landscape could show returns that were higher on a statistically significant level than those of traders with a lower information level.

By performing the same tests for the GEMWf 98, we observed a similar tendency as in the comparatively large GEMWf 94 market, i.e. informed traders realized higher returns than the less informed ones. But this was true only in absolute figures. Unfortunately, the computerized questionnaire had a poor response rate (below 30%) in the GEMWf 98. Therefore, it was difficult to generate results that were statistically significant.

Summing up these experiences, we draw the conclusion that extraordinary profits in this zero sum game were not made by people who took advantage of other people's anomalies, but rather by those people who took advantage of asymmetric information, caused by individual differences in transaction costs to acquire information. The above finding that traders with a party preference on average realized higher profits that people without a sympathy for a political party also fits this observation if the hypothesis holds that persons with a party preference usually are better informed about the political landscape than persons without sympathy for a political party (see Table 11.4 as well as the discussion in the corresponding chapter).

11.4.5 Expectations

It[10] was Hayek's (1945) outstanding contribution to emphasize that we should regard the price system as a 'mechanism for communicating information'. He criticized that, in models of competitive allocations, people do not learn anything about prices (see also Grossman 1989). In political stock markets, where returns are low, we can expect that prices become a source of information, especially for people lacking adequate standards of information. They behave as if they were (uncertain) marginal traders, because they use prices as a substitute for more expensive sources of information.

We have endeavored to test this portion of the Hayek hypothesis. On each day of trade activities, we asked traders in the markets GEMWf 90 (federal parliamentary election) and GEMWr 91 (regional election) about their expected election outcome. We intended to examine whether market prices were driven by expectations, or expectations were driven by market prices.

[10] Asking for expectations was an idea suggested by and organized together with R. Tietz.

In Brüggelambert (1999) tests on Granger causality were made for pooled data.[11] The results suggested that in GEMWf 90 expectations and public opinion polls were Granger causal for prices, whereas in the GEMWr 91 market we observed causality in prices to expectations. To interpret this result, it must be pointed out that in Germany, as in presumably most other democratic states, media coverage is not as extensive during regional election events as during federal parliamentary elections. The same applies to public opinion polls. During the GEMWr 91, public opinion polls were published on only one weekend.

The results confirmed the part of the Hayek hypothesis stated above that market prices become a source of information, especially if access to alternative channels of information is difficult.

11.4.6 Public opinion polls

In Brüggelambert (1997b) it is also shown that public opinion polls were Granger-causal for market prices. While this was not true for the market analyzed by Forsythe *et al.* (1992), the same observation could be made for other markets outside the USA (see Beckmann/Werding 1996, Jacobsen *et al.* 2000). Further, it is shown in Brüggelambert (1999) that market prices were Granger-causal for the polls. This means that polls can forecast market prices as well as prices can predict the polls. The result leads us to the conclusion that while traders take much or even most of their information from polls, they were able to interpret the influence of new information on the electoral mode and therefore did not completely trust the polls. An additional indication for this assertion is the fact that other election events (regional elections as well as an European Parliament election), which took place during the trading time of the GEMWf 94 and GEMf 98, had a statistically significant influence on market prices. It seems that traders in the market used these events as indicators for trends in the public opinion.

Figure 11.1 provides a chart of market prices and polls in relation to the election outcome for the GEM 94.

For a long period of time, the average of the polls was a good predictor of the election outcome. The market had a phase of stagnation during the first part of the semester break (from day 29 to day 114), but as the election event came closer, activity and accuracy of prices increased. Due to strong volatility, the latest poll predictions do not prove to be a reliable source of information.

If it is accepted that the average of the polls should be viewed as public information, we can no longer assert that the GEMWf 94 was efficient. But we have to be careful because we do not know how good the reputation of this channel of information ex ante was. However, this is necessary if we want to describe (bounded)

[11] Unfortunately, the database was not able to differentiate between forecasts that had been given by informed traders and those made by traders who identified themselves as uninformed. Therefore, it was impossible to test the hypothesis that presumptions heavily rested on market prices for participants whose information standard is lower. This lack should be used as a stimulus for future research, i.e. asking for expectations in future election markets.

Fig. 11.1. Mean Absolute Error GEM 94: Market Prices (av.) vs. Polls (av.) and vs. Polls (latest)

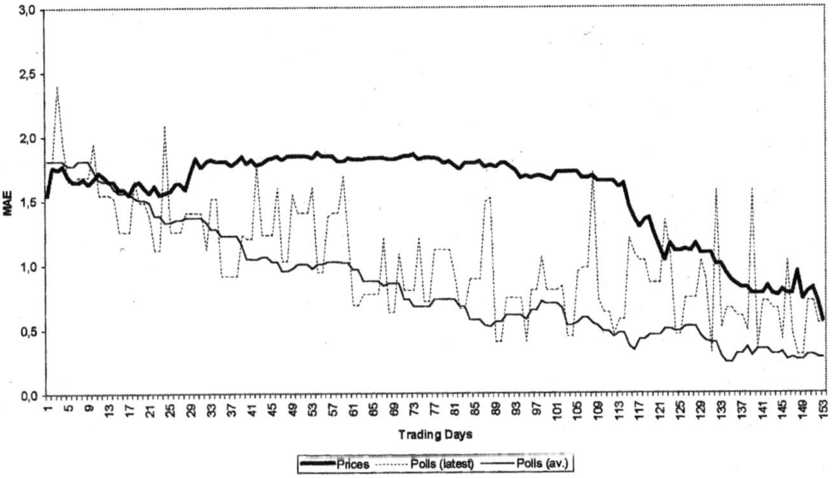

rational behavior under decision conditions in reality. We can see this in the following Figure 11.2, where the average of the polls was not as good as it was in 1994. Figure 11.2 provides a chart of market prices and polls in relation to the election outcome for the GEMWf 98. Again, all three indicators differ only slightly at the start of the trading phase, but after a short period of trading, the market provides a much better prediction quality. From day 80 on, all three indicators show a strong volatility, and end up in about the same range. This could be explained by the high uncertainty about the outcome of the 1998 election. The outcome of the 1994 election was much clearer, thus the volatility of the 1994 indicators was definitely lower.

The coalition lead is plotted in Figure 11.3. A coalition lead is the advantage in percent that is held by the ruling coalition versus the opposition. In the 1998 parliamentary elections, the CDU/CSU/FDP coalition ended up with a (negative) lead of -6.22 %.

While the market predicted an acceptable lead value at the very start, the polls (av.) underestimated the lead at first, then improved and did a perfect job at around trading day 80. Though both indicators show a similar value at the end of the market, the real lead proved to be considerably lower.

11.5 Transaction costs and efficiency

11.5.1 Incentives and environment

To test whether information is properly reflected in prices, we need a pricing model that defines the meaning of "properly". The decision maker has to be analyzed including all the influencing factors of his environment, which have to be seen in rela-

Fig. 11.2. Mean Absolute Error GEM 98: Market Prices (av.) vs. Polls (av.) and vs. Polls (latest)

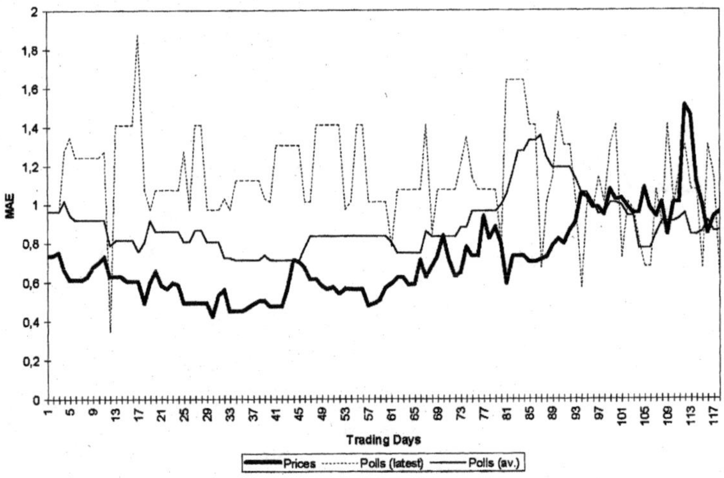

Fig. 11.3. Coalition Lead GEM 98: Market Prices and Polls (av.)

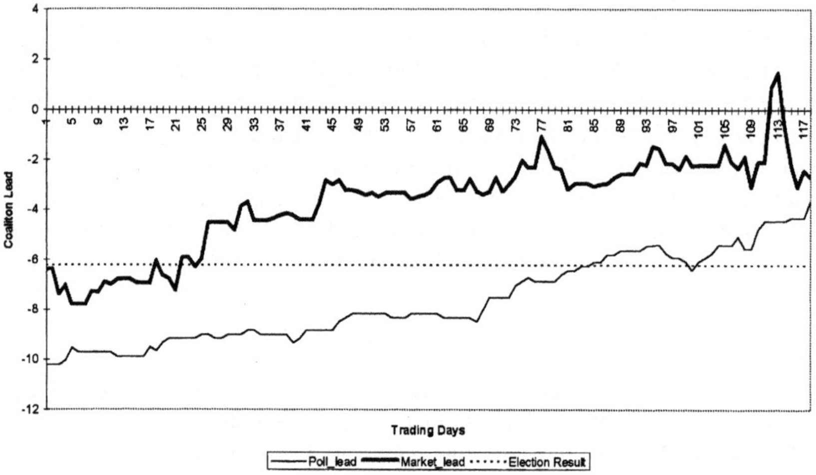

tion to his personal incentives. For election markets, we find an extremely complex social environment with small expected rewards.

Beckmann/Werding (1996, p. 189) argue that, because of low potential profits, it is doubtful that profit maximization was the primary interest of a sufficient number of participants in their field experiment. However, small expected rewards in themselves do not justify maintaining that an analysis of decision behavior under these conditions is less significant. In reality, many decisions are marked by low expected utility, which therefore initiates information processing that is in principle similar to what we expect in our markets. In this context, an appropriate example is seen in voters' behavior. Downs (1957) has shown that in a world of positive information cost, it is not rational for voters to initiate an expensive formation of opinion. It is clear to see why political advertising, ideology, campaign financing, and media consulting firms enter the picture under these conditions. It is quite obvious that voters have to use low-cost information systems like the ones we mentioned above to form their opinions. It is plausible that, given these incentives, traders in the market could use the same information sources that have been relevant to the voters in making decisions. Thus, eventually we can even learn about voters' behavior, if we reconsider the behavior of traders (see Brüggelambert 1996). The existence of positive informational costs, as well as the existence of economics to scale in information processing are responsible for the presence of experts, sound advice of good friends, credible standing, advertising, consulting groups, consumer protection agencies, accredited diplomas, product liability, asset markets, warranties, brand names, and so on. These institutions and organizations have evolved and tend to lower information cost. They serve to overcome the problem of prohibitively high expenditures necessary to determine uncertain outcomes in a highly complex environment.

11.5.2 Politics and voting systems

In order to gain more information about the factors that have an influence on the predictability of election events in general, it is necessary to go beyond the internal institutional settings of the experiment. Let us consider what might have happened in the United States. One of the major differences between the voting system in the U.S. and in Germany is that the U.S. voting system (presidential election) is a majority voting system, whereas we find a system of proportional representation (parliamentary election) in Germany.[12] Literature on electoral systems comes to the conclusion that a majority vote system has a stronger tendency to build a two-party system and ensures a clearer formation of a government than a system of proportional representation. A system of proportional representation increases competition between more than two parties, and is more likely to lead to the presence of small parties in parliament. Majority systems encourage campaigns that are focused on specific persons, since the choice of the voters is directed at candidates rather than parties. Hence, we often observe a higher influence of mass media in majority-based systems (see Katz 1980, Harrop and Miller 1987, Kaase 1994, and King 1997).

[12] Note that the other European countries - Denmark, the Netherlands, Austria, and Turkey - where the IEM was installed, also have proportional representation systems.

Firstly, this elucidates why traders in the US political stock markets have to concentrate on fewer party stocks, as opposed to traders in European political stock markets. Secondly, we find a higher influence of mass media events, such as primaries and televised debates of major candidates in the USA. Therefore, it seems correct to assume that opinion polls are of minor significance as a source of information that is easily accessible in such a climate of diversity of information channels.

It is also possible that these additional channels allow an adjustment that is temporarily closer to the political climate than polls are. To be fair to the polls, we have to concede that, due to technical problems, polls are always somewhat 'older' than continuous markets. It may be that continuous election markets can use this advantage more systematically in a majority voting system. In this environment, a continuous double auction containing a certain amount of active and well-informed traders clearly gains an advantage over a call market institution with discontinuity of trade and paucity of trading periods. This is a testable hypothesis for future research.

In Canada, a country with a majoritarian election system, an IEM-type market (UBC-ESM) with a total of six party shares outperformed the public opinion polls in 1993 (see Forsythe et al. 1995). However, it must be pointed out that Canada, although it is a country with a majority voting system, is an exception because the regional/territorial dimension allowed more than two parties to prosper (see Harrop and Miller 1987). A look at *Table* 11.2 also shows that the federal election market in Canada was not able to repeat its success in 1997. A third UBC-ESM was organized for the British Columbia provincial election. Predictive performance of this market was rather poor (see *Table* 11.2). It is possible that regional elections in Canada are affected by the same problems that regional elections in Germany have, i.e. missing informational channels because of their low attractiveness to the media. All markets that were installed in a country that uses a system of proportional representation to organize its elections, i.e. Austria, Denmark, The Netherlands, and Turkey, provided results similar to the German markets.

The informational role of these *external institutions* is significant in the decision-making process of complex experiments. By providing information, they reduce uncertainty amongst decision makers, and play a central role in market efficiency.[13] Results from complex experiments like the election markets can help to understand these aspects of real decision-making.

Jacobsen et al. (2000) studied a political stock market in the Netherlands, which was organized for three electoral dates. They also stressed the differences between the voting systems. In contrast to this paper, however, they concentrated on a type of judgment failure related to the winner's curse in common value auctions. This judgment failure may be more important for systems of proportional representation because the structure of the common values of multiparty elections makes them especially vulnerable to it. Consequently, they observed a negative correlation between vote share and price bias. This result was confirmed by the meta analysis made by Berlemann/Schmidt (2001). Like in Jacobsen *et al.* (2000) it is shown by Berlemann/Schmidt (2001) that in the German markets small contracts are overval-

[13] See North (1990) for an insightful study of this topic.

ued and large contracts are undervalued. Berlemann/Schmidt (2001) also show that the polls are not responsible for this systematic bias.

Following their first finding, Jacobsen *et al.* (2000) assumed the existence of a negative relationship between the predictive accuracy of the market and the inequality of the structure of the vote shares. The number of observations was too small to formally test this comparative statistics result. This hypothesis was also tested by Berlemann/Schmidt (2001) but not confirmed.

Despite these interesting results, we have to take into account that biased behavior, as observed by Jacobsen *et al.* (2000) and Berlemann/Schmidt (2001), should not be stable after it becomes aware of the (bounded) rational behavior of the market participants. As described by Berlemann/Schmidt (2001), the polls are not influenced by this bias. For this reason, it should be easy for rational traders to use the polls to make money from other traders' biased behavior. If, on the other hand, the results of Berlemann/Schmidt (2001) are not transferable to the markets outside of Germany, i.e., if the polls in these markets are also biased, then the problem of the direction of the causation arises. In this case, it is impossible to distinguish whether the bias is caused by a bias in the polls or by biased behavior of the traders in the market.

11.6 Summary

Participants in the election markets have attempted to deal with the problem of information costs by centralizing various sources of information. The resulting institutions economize the costs of information processing. They become increasingly relevant the greater the complexity of a given decision-making process. The institutional framework, which in itself is the product of an evolutionary process, creates organizations like polling institutes that evolve to provide relevant information to politicians and voters. The same is seen in state institutions that provide unemployment figures, inflation rates, etc. While using these informational devices, traders in the German markets were not able to aggregate more information than the polls did. Perhaps a system of proportional representation (parliamentary election) is too complex to solve this issue. Given these issues, our hypothesis states that the efficiency of political stock markets is a question of the institutional framework that exists outside the experimental design, rather than one of market institutions, number of participants or the time that the markets are open.

Besides the fact that some election markets were able to outperform polls, we should not forget that, even if they fail to do this, they serve as a continuous barometer of public opinion. The data that can be collected in these markets are of much greater detail than those available from any other existing financial market. The IEM type markets and their variants are, of course, not restricted to election events[14]. But

[14] See: http://www.biz.uiowa.edu/iem/index.html, http://ebweb.tuwien.ac.at/apsm/index.html, or http://pacific.commerce.ubc.ca./ubc-esm

even for this kind of application, we have only discussed the first steps in understanding how the market works, and especially how traders behave in an environment that is closer to reality than that of a typical laboratory experiment. In this paper we have tried to give first answers, suggestions, and directions for future research (e.g. learning behavior, long term predictability, and expectation formation).

References

Beckmann, K. and Werding, M. (1996). 'Passauer Wahlbörse': information processing in a political market experiment, *Kyklos* **49**: 171–204.

Berg, J., Forsythe, R. and Rietz, T. (1997). What makes markets predict well? Evidence from the Iowa Electronic Markets, *in* W. Albers, W. Güth, P. Hammerstein, B. Moldovanu and E. v. Damme (eds), *Understanding strategic interaction: Essays in honor of Reinhard Selten*, Springer, Berlin, pp. 444–463.

Berlemann, M. and Schmidt, C. (2001). Predictive Accuracy of Political Stock Markets: Empirical Evidence from a European Perspective, Mimeo, University of Technology and Humboldt-University of Berlin, Dresden and Berlin.

Bohm, P. and Sonnegård, J. (1999). Political Stock Markets and Unreliable Polls, *Scandinavian Journal of Economics* pp. 205–222.

Brüggelambert, G. (1997a). Von Insidern, 'marginal traders' und Glücksrittern: Zur Relevanz von Entscheidungsanomalien in politischen Börsen, *Jahrbücher für Nationalökonomie und Statistik* **216**: 45–73.

Brüggelambert, G. (1997b). Meinungsumfragen als informationstragende Institutionen: Eine ökonometrische Untersuchung der Erwartungs- und Entscheidungsbildung an Wahlbörsen, *Zeitschrift für Wirtschafts- und Sozialwissenschaften* **117**: 257–289.

Brüggelambert, G. (1999). *Institutionen als Informationsträger: Eine Untersuchung experimenteller Wahlbörsen*, Metropolis, Marburg.

Downs, A. (1957). *An economic theory of democracy*, Harper & Row, New York.

Fair, R. (1996). Econometrics and presidential elections, *Journal of Economic Perspectives* **10**: 89–102.

Finkel, S. and Schrott, P. (1995). Campaign effects on voter choice in the German election of 1990, *British Journal of Political Science* **25**: 349–377.

Forsythe, R., Frank, M., Krishnamurthy, V. and Ross, T. (1995). Using market prices to predict election results: the 1993 UBC election stock market, *Canadian Journal of Economics* **28**: 770–793.

Forsythe, R., Nelson, F., Neumann, G. and Wright, J. (1991). The Iowa presidential stock market: a field experiment, *in* R. Isaac (ed.), *Research in Experimental Economics*, Vol. 4, JAI Press, Greenwich, pp. 1–44.

Forsythe, R., Nelson, F., Neumann, G. and Wright, J. (1992). Anatomy of an experimental political stock market, *American Economic Review* **82**: 1142–1161.

Forsythe, R., Nelson, F., Neumann, G. and Wright, J. (1993). The Iowa political market, Mimeo, University of Iowa, Iowa City.

Forsythe, R., Rietz, T. and Ross, T. (1999). Wishes, expectations and actions: a survey on price formation in election stock markets, *Journal of Economic Behavior and Organization* **39**: 83–110.

Frey, B. and Bohnet, I. (1996). Experiments, theory - and reality?, *Ökonomie und Gesellschaft (Yearbook 13: Experiments in Economics)*, Campus, Frankfurt/Main, pp. 340–359.

Friedman, D. (1993). How trading institutions affect financial market performance: some laboratory evidence, *Economic Inquiry* **31**: 410–435.

Gelman, A. and King, G. (1993). Why are American presidential election campaign polls so variable when votes are so predictable?, *British Journal of Political Science* **23**: 409–451.

Grossman, S. (1989). *The informational role of prices*, MIT Press, Cambridge.

Harrop, M. and Miller, W. (1987). *Elections and voters: a comparative introduction*, MacMillan, Houndmills.

Hayek, F. (1945). The use of knowledge in society, *American Economic Review* **35**: 519–530.

Holt, C. (1995). Industrial organization: a survey of laboratory research, *in* J. Kagel and A. Roth (eds), *The handbook of experimental economics*, Princeton University Press, Princeton, pp. 349–443.

Jacobsen, B., Potters, J., Schram, A., Winden, F. and Wit, J. (2000). (In)accuracy of a European Political Stock Market: The Influence of Common Value Structures, *European Economic Review* **44**: 205–230.

Kaase, M. (1994). Is there personalization in politics? Candidates and voting behavior in Germany, *International Political Science Review* **15**: 211–230.

Katz, R. (1980). *A theory of parties and electoral systems*, Hopkins University Press, Baltimore.

King, A. (1997). The vulnerable American politician, *British Journal of Political Science* **27**: 1–22.

Mohr, W. and Krätzschmar, M. (2000). Wahlbörse im Internet – das Prognoseverfahren der Zukunft, Vortragsreihe des Institutes für Angewandte Mathematik der FH Flensburg anlässlich des World Mathematical Year 2000.

North, D. (1990). *Institutions, institutional change and economic performance*, Cambridge University Press, Cambridge.

Ortner, G., Stepan, A. and Zechner, J. (1994). Political stock markets - the Austrian experiences, Mimeo. Paper presented at the Economic Science Association Fall Meetings November 1994 - Tucson, Arizona. Technical University Vienna: Vienna.

Ostmann, A. (1991). Micro-level trading behavior and cognition: expectations, rules & actions in a small political stock market, Arbeiten der Fachrichtung Psychologie, Universität des Saarlandes: Nr. 158, Saarbrücken.

Plott, C. and Sunder, S. (1988). Rational expectations and the aggregation of diverse information in laboratory security markets, *Econometrica* **56**: 1085–1118.

Roth, A. (1989). A Natural Experiment in the Organization of Entry Level Labor Markets: Regional Markets for New Physicians in the UK, University of Pittsburgh Working Paper 245.

Smith, V. (1982). Microeconomic systems as an experimental Science, *American Economic Review* **72**: 923–955.

Smith, V. (1994). Economics in the laboratory, *Journal of Economic Perspectives* **8**: 113–131.

Sunder, S. (1995). Experimental asset markets: a survey, *in* J. Kagel and A. Roth (eds), *The handbook of experimental economics*, Princeton University Press, Princeton, pp. 445–500.

Tietz, R. (1973). Ein anspruchsanpassungsorientiertes Wachstums- und Konjunkturmodell (KRESKO), *in* H. Sauermann (ed.), *Contributions to Experimental Economics*, Vol. IV, Tübingen.

12 Expectations and Rational Actions in an Experimental Financial Market

Forrest Nelson and Reinhard Tietz

12.1 Introduction

Models of economic behavior under conditions of uncertainty typically describe the influence of subjective beliefs about future outcomes on market behavior. Tests of such models are limited by the lack of hard information regarding expectations. We report here on an experiment in which we obtain a direct measure of expectations regarding a particular natural event and detailed information regarding market transactions in a futures contract using that event as a fundamental. This unique coincidence of direct observations on expectations and concurrent market behavior permits an assessment of the consistency of behavior and expectations which is not possible from any other data as far as we know.

In models of strict rationality, risk neutral participants in a financial market will buy those financial instruments with the greatest positive relative difference between current price and the traders expectation of future prices. That is to say, knowledge of expectations and of current prices are sufficient to determine the optimal transactions. But in the market we examine, and surely in other markets as well, sub-optimal transactions arc frequent. Some explanations of these departures are provided by risk aversion, incomplete information, transactions costs, strategic behavior and outside influences. Models of bounded rationality take such departures as consistent with the theory so long as the actions taken are not contrary to the presumed objective. In what follows we will classify market actions according to the above distinctions, into strictly rational, boundedly rational, and irrational actions (cf Tietz 1992b), and use that classification as one object of our analysis.

The market setting employed in this paper is an experimental political stock market conducted at the University of Frankfurt in the Fall of 1990. Contracts traded in the market were associated with parties competing for seats in the December 2, 1990 federal parliamentary election, and traders were students of economics at the university. The experimental design and the software used for the electronic market were those developed at the University of Iowa and first reported on by Forsythe, Nelson, Neumann and Wright (henceforth FNNW), 1991a. The unique aspect of this particular experiment was the inclusion of a survey of traders on each market day regarding their beliefs of the election outcome[1]. An analysis of the relationship

[1] Our experience in other experiments, especially those with markets, has shown that decision preparation improves the consistency and thereby the degree of rationality of decisions (cf. Tietz 1992a, 1992c, 1996). We assumed that asking for expectations in our experiment might work in this direction and included the survey also for that reason.

between transactions on the political stock market and the stated expectations is the core of this paper.

The analysis here is limited in scope. Our measure of subjective expectations is confined to a point estimate only, not to other parameters of the distribution. Thus we ignore risk aversion and the effect of differences in subjective beliefs about the riskiness of the financial instruments. We also make no attempt to assess expectations regarding the interim movement of market prices, and except for certain arbitrage transactions to be explained, we make no allowance for strategic transactions. Finally, we do not account for motives other than profit gains. For example, since the objects traded are associated with political parties, participants may experience utility improvements from the buying or selling of the contracts in their favorite or most despised party quite aside from the utility gained or lost from monetary profits or losses.

Section 12.2 below briefly describes the market environment, including the market design and the expectation elicitation mechanism. Section 12.3 presents some descriptive material regarding the experience with this experiment. Summary information regarding market activity, the time series of market prices and average expectations plus opinion poll results are included here. Also reported here are more detailed summaries of the results from the expectations surveys. The section concludes with an aggreate analysis of the consistency of expectations and market behavior

The formal analysis begins in section 12.4 with the definition of critical variables which classify market actions according to degree of rationality. Univariate and multivariate analyses of the factors influencing rationality are presented in section 12.5, and an examination of the effect of rationality on the choice of actions appears in section 12.6. And, finally, section 12.7 offers some summary and concluding comments

12.2 The market environment

12.2.1 Market design

The market we examine is the Unified German Election Market (UGEM) which operated at the University of Frankfurt in the Fall of 1990[2]. This market, patterned after the Iowa Political Stock Market (FNNW, 1991a and 1991b), was an experimental and small scale but none-the-less real futures market. Participants, all of whom were students at the University, invested their own money, traded futures contracts in a structured but freely operating market environment, and earned real profits and losses as a result of their activity. The contracts they traded were futures contracts,

[2] For other analyses of this market experiment and other German election markets, see Brüggelambert 1996, 1997 a, 1997b, 1999, and Brüggelambert and Crüger (2001) in this volume. An analysis of the expectations under the assumption that decision behavior is not neutral to risk but follows portfolio theory was done by Pein 1993.

each of which was identified with a particular political party competing for parliamentary seats in the upcoming election. Contracts were redeemed or liquidated after the close of the market and the subsequent election for an amount equal to one Deutsche Mark (DM) times the share of the nation-wide popular vote won by the associated party. The opportunity for profit (or risk of loss) came from buying contracts in the market at prices lower (higher) than the party's share of the vote, or selling at higher (lower) prices.

The market operated as a double auction with traders submitting limit offers to buy (bids) or to sell (asks) at prices and quantities they specified. Bid and ask queues were maintained by the market system, and transactions were executed whenever the current high bid met or exceeded the current low ask. Traders could also execute market offers (purchases and sales), accepting the current low ask or high bid prices without entering offers into the queues. The market was fully computerized. The system maintained the bid and ask queues and trader accounts, handled all bookkeeping, and kept a comprehensive time-stamped log of trader logins, offer submissions, offer executions and transactions. The market operated continuously between the hours of 9:00 and 17:00 Monday through Friday in one computerized laboratory containing 20 networked personal computers. That permitted up to 20 simultaneous and real-time trading sessions to traders who entered and left the market place at their convenience.

Aspiring traders enrolled in the market by opening trading accounts and depositing investment monies of 5 to 50 DM. These monies were held by the market administrator until after the election at which time they were redistributed to participants in the form of contract redemptions and cash-account liquidation. Credits for the initial investments were made to the trader's market cash account. The cash account provided the necessary market liquidity – purchases were charged against it and sales were credited to it. No margin purchases or short sales were permitted. Contracts to be traded were placed in circulation via the purchase by traders of contract blocks called unit portfolios. A unit portfolio contained one unit in each of the six contracts listed in the market and was sold to (or redeemed from) traders on demand from the market system at the fixed price of 1 DM. The six listed contracts covered all parties in the election (five major parties plus a catch-all group labeled "Sonstige" (others)). Since the ultimate redemption value of each contract equaled 1 DM times the share of the vote of the represented party and the sum of the vote shares across the 6 parties represented in a unit portfolio necessarily equaled one, the price of the unit portfolio exactly equaled the sum of the redemption values paid for its components after the election. That made the market a zero sum game, save for the interest foregone on the invested funds. Of course unit portfolios were unbundled after their original issue and contracts were traded individually, so that funds invested in the market were redistributed among participants with some incurring losses and others enjoying profits.

The audit trail maintained by the electronic market system provides the source of observed market behavior. We have time-stamped records not only of actual transactions but also of the original offers which may or may not have led to transactions. Traders were promised full anonymity – market accounts were maintained under coded names and only the market administrator new the identities of the account owners. All records of those identities were destroyed after the redistribution of market proceeds.

12.2.2 The expectations survey instrument

Upon entering the market for the first time on any given day, the trader was presented with an on-screen questionnaire regarding the trader's beliefs about the share of the nation-wide popular vote each party would receive in the December election. Responses had to be given for at least three of the six listed parties before the trader was allowed to advance to the market screen. To encourage accurate responses, the sum of the vote shares across the six parties was computed and displayed as entries were made, and the trader had ample opportunity to correct any mistakes before his responses were recorded.

Fig. 12.1. Opening expectations survey screen – English translation

```
 Bourse:  Bundestagswahlmarkt 1990    | Trader no.: new1          12.05.94
 market:  all markets                 | cash bal.: DM100.000      12.43.44
--------------------------------------------------------------------------

                            Opinion Survey

                              If the election were today,       Expected
                    Your    for which party would you vote?       vote
   Party          Favorite     1st Vote          2nd Vote       Percentage
 1 CDU/CSU                                                               .
 2 F.D.P.                                                                .
 3 green                                                                 .
 4 PDS                                                                   .
 5 SPD                                                                   .
 6 other                                                                 .
 7 undecided
 8 no response                                                 Total:    .
--------------------------------------------------------------------------
Before you enter the market, we beg your indulgence with a few
questions. After entering your response to each question, press the
ENTER key. Your answer will be entered into the table above and the
next question will appear. Should you make an incorrect entry, simply
proceed through the remainder of the questions; after the last question
you will be given the opportunity to make corrections.
Please enter this survey information.
```

The actual form of the questionnaire is shown in figures 12.1–12.2[3]. The opening screen (translated into English) appeared as in *Figure 12.1*. As the trader entered

[3] The questionnaire also included items regarding 1) the trader's preferred party, and the party the trader intended to vote for on 2) the first ballot, and 3) the second ballot. Those

responses, the top portion of the screen was updated to show those responses and the last paragraph was replaced in succession with the questions appearing in *Figure 12.2.*

Fig. 12.2. Expectations questions, English translation

```
Your Favorite
Which party is your favorite? Enter its number from above and press
the ENTER key (1..7)
Please enter this survey information, press ESC to advance.
---------------------------------------------------------------------
1st Vote
If the election were held today, which of the parties listed above
would you vote for on the first vote? Enter its number from above and
press the ENTER key (1..7)
Please enter this survey information, press ESC to advance.
---------------------------------------------------------------------
2nd Vote
If the election were held today, which of the parties listed above
would you vote for on the second vote? Enter its number from above and
press the ENTER key (1..7)
Please enter this survey information, press ESC to advance.
---------------------------------------------------------------------
Expected Vote Percentage
What percentage of the popular vote do you expect the CDU/CSU party
will win in the December 2 election? If you have no estimate for the
party just press ENTER. Enter your response here and press the ENTER
key (0..100)
Please enter percentages for at least three parties.
Please enter this survey information, press ESC to advance.
---------------------------------------------------------------------
[the question above was repeated for each of the remaining 5 parties.]
---------------------------------------------------------------------
Would you like to change any of your responses entered in the table
above? If you enter Yes you will be given the opportunity to change
your answers. Press Y to change your answers, press N to continue.
Please enter this survey information, press ESC to advance.
```

For the first 10 market days we relied solely on the cooperation of traders to supply the expectation responses. By the end of the second week it had become obvious that many traders were losing patience with these questions. In particular, completion rates declined and the frequency of "nonsense responses" – a response of 0 percent for all 6 parties for example – increased. Beginning on 12 November an

responses are of incidental interest here, except for their use in checking the preference bias in vote-share expectations. The extent to which asking these questions first might have distorted the vote-share responses is not addressed.

incentive mechanism was introduced to encourage more thoughtful responses. From that date onwards, traders were paid a premium determined by the accuracy of their predictions. Specifically, the premium awarded for each expectation was computed as:

$$\text{Premium}_{ijt} = \max\left[0, 10 - \left(E_{ijt} - V_i\right)^2\right] \tag{12.1}$$

where E_{ijt} is the expectation response offered for contract i by trader j on day t; V_i is the Vote outcome for party i on election day, 2 December; E and V are in percentages; and the unit of Premium_{ijt} is the Pfenning (1/100th of a DM). The total premium payment made to trader j after the election thus consisted of the cumulative sum of Premium_{ijt} across t and i.[4]

12.3 Market experience

12.3.1 Market results

63 traders enrolled in the market, with a total investment of 1506 DM. Over the course of the 24 market days from October 29 through 30 November they engaged in transactions involving 108,233 individual shares. The total value (price times quantity) of those shares traded was 14,695.35 DM, so the average mark invested in the market turned over nearly ten times within the one month period. *Figure 12.3* contains a time series plot of daily average prices along with corresponding results from contemporaneous opinion polls and the daily average of the responses to the expectations survey. Finally, *Table 12.1* below compares the outcome of the election on 2 December, 1900 with the average of market prices on 30 November, the last day of the market. For comparison, the table also contains the average of the expectations survey responses and the results of the Opinion Poll conducted by Allensbach on that same day.

Table 12.1. Final prices, expectations and opinion polls, and the election outcome

Party	Average Expectations (30.11.90)	Allensbach Poll (30.11.90)	Market Prices (30.11.90)	Election Outcome (02.12.90)
CDU	43.4	42.5	42.8	43.8
FDP	9.3	10.0	9.1	11.0
GRUENE	7.4	8.5	8.5	5.1
PDS	2.1	2.5	3.1	2.4
SPD	34.3	34.5	33.5	33.5
SONST.	3.4	2.0	3.3	4.2

[4] The maximum potential payoff amounted to 8.40DM. Actual premium payments ranged from 0 to 6.26 and averaged 2.06 DM per trader.

Fig. 12.3. Time series graphs of market prices, expectations and opinion polls

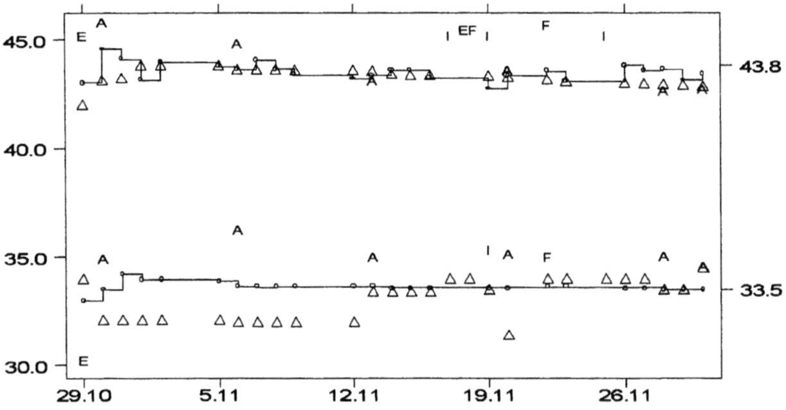

A. CDU (upper) and SPD (lower)

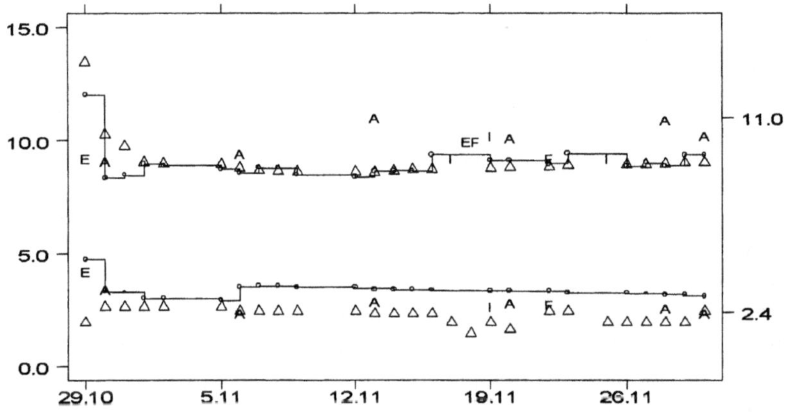

B. FDP (upper) and PDS (lower)

(Results for CDU and SPD appear in panel A, for FDP and PDS in panel B, and Gruene and Sonstige in panel C. The vertical scale is the percentage of the vote, and dates appear on the horizontal axis. Small circles connected by solid lines represent daily average prices, triangles indicate daily expectation averages, and the letters indicate opinon poll results, with A for Allensbach, E for Emnid, F for Forsa and I for Infas. Election outcomes are indicated on the right border.)

Fig. 12.3. (continued)

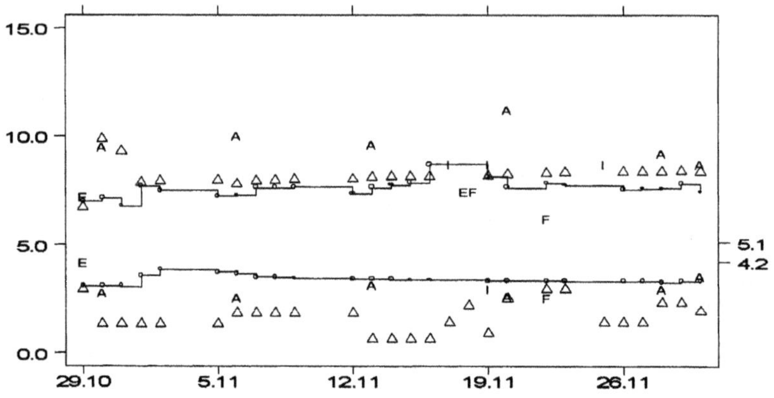

C. Gruene (upper) and Sonstige (lower)

12.3.2 Expectations survey

The data generated by the expectations survey described above included 449 responses across 54 traders. Not all of these responses were usable. To be included in the analysis to follow, we required the responses to satisfy the following criteria:

1. The trader had to have appeared in the market and supplied expectations responses on at least two days.
2. The sum of the expectations across parties had to fall in the range from 95 to 105.
3. Responses had to have been supplied for all six parties.
4. The data had to pass an inspection for nonsense responses. In particular, obvious typing errors (like the apparent exchange of two entries) and responses which were constant across 4 or more parties in sequence were classified as nonsense responses and thus eliminated.

347 observations on expectations from 49 traders remained in the data set after this screening. A comparison of these remaining cases before and after the introduction of the incentive suggested no apparent differences. Rather, the principle effect of the incentive seemed to be on response rates – 32 percent of the observations had to be eliminated prior to the introduction of the incentive, but only 18 percent afterwards.

Four traders (numbers 58, 60, 73 and 82) gave acceptable responses on only one day. They will be eliminated from particular analyses. Likewise, the one day (10/29/90) in which only one trader gave an acceptable response (see Table 12.2) may be eliminated for some purposes. Thus the fully reduced sample will consist of 342 cases (a case being one trader on one day).

Descriptive statistics for these expectation data appear in Tables 12.2–12.5 below, organized by market days. *Table 12.2* contains counts of observations by trading day. Recall that the market was closed on weekends and holidays, leaving 24 market days. *Table 12.3* contains the average expectations across traders for each day and each party. As is apparent, the first day (with a single response as noted above) is distinctly different from the remaining days. Time series plots of these average expectations are included in Figures 12.3, along with comparative plots of market prices and opinion poll results. The standard deviations of expectation responses by party and day appear in *Table 12.4*, and average absolute estimation errors (the difference between stated expectations and the election result) appear in *Table 12.5*. Finally, *Table 12.6* contains a summary across all days of mean expectations; the standard deviation of expectations; the coefficient of variation (CV); and the average absolute estimation errors. Corresponding entries for market prices are included for comparison.

Table 12.2. Frequencies of expectation reports, by day across traders

Day	Date	Freq.	Day	Date	Freq.
1	10/29/90	1	13	11/14/90	23
2	10/30/90	7	14	11/15/90	20
3	10/31/90	6	15	11/16/90	9
4	11/01/90	12	16	11/19/90	13
5	11/02/90	9	17	11/20/90	18
6	11/05/90	8	18	11/22/90	25
7	11/06/90	10	19	11/23/90	14
8	11/07/90	12	20	11/26/90	21
9	11/08/90	12	21	11/27/90	27
10	11/09/90	10	22	11/28/90	29
11	11/12/90	10	23	11/29/90	21
12	11/13/90	15	24	11/30/90	15
				Total	347

Correlations between average expectations for the six parties appear in Panel A of *Table 12.7*. The observations are days, so that the correlations refer to movements over time. The Market ran over 24 days but the first market day is excluded, leaving 23 observations for these correlations. The sign patterns of correlations in Table 12.7 suggest that CDU and PDS form one positively correlated group, FDP and GRUENE a second, and these groups are negatively correlated one with the other. Thus expectations for CDU and PDS rose or fell together, as FDP and GRUENE were falling or rising, respectively. SPD and SONSTIGE are negatively correlated with each other but uncorrelated with other parties. Part of these correlations arise from the negative time trend for CDU and PDS, and a positive time trend for FDP and GRUENE.

Similar correlations among market prices and among opinion polls[5] appear in panels B and C of Table 12.7. Remarkably, there are fewer significant correlations

[5] The values used for opinion polls were the prognoses reported by the polling organization authoring the most recent publicly realeased poll report as of that market day. 6 of these

Table 12.3. Means of expectations, by day across traders

Day	Date	Party CDU/CSU	FDP	GRUENE	PDS	SPD	SONST.	SUM
1	10/29/90	43.00	12.00	7.00	4.00	30.00	4.00	100.00
2	10/30/90	44.57	8.36	7.14	3.21	34.71	2.57	100.57
3	10/31/90	44.08	8.47	6.77	3.07	34.32	3.30	100.00
4	11/01/90	43.12	8.97	7.72	2.28	35.67	2.29	100.04
5	11/02/90	43.94	8.89	7.50	2.63	35.33	1.48	99.78
6	11/05/90	43.75	8.75	7.25	2.24	36.50	1.51	100.00
7	11/06/90	43.62	8.57	7.28	2.14	36.03	2.35	99.99
8	11/07/90	44.04	8.78	7.62	2.50	34.38	2.86	100.17
9	11/08/90	43.64	8.78	7.63	2.49	34.73	2.64	99.92
10	11/09/90	43.35	8.48	7.65	2.41	35.72	2.39	100.00
11	11/12/90	43.18	8.39	7.36	2.39	36.10	2.58	100.00
12	11/13/90	43.33	8.66	7.62	2.65	34.79	2.95	100.00
13	11/14/90	43.59	8.68	7.75	2.90	34.79	2.39	100.09
14	11/15/90	43.58	8.63	7.85	2.64	34.91	2.49	100.09
15	11/16/90	43.20	9.37	8.72	2.37	34.47	2.13	100.26
16	11/19/90	42.70	9.12	8.12	2.43	35.11	2.76	100.25
17	11/20/90	43.31	9.14	7.63	2.60	34.91	2.41	100.00
18	11/22/90	43.53	8.98	7.83	2.52	34.78	2.36	100.00
19	11/23/90	43.04	9.42	7.74	2.27	35.41	2.26	100.14
20	11/26/90	43.80	8.87	7.54	2.57	34.35	2.70	99.85
21	11/27/90	43.54	9.00	7.59	2.55	34.62	2.90	100.19
22	11/28/90	43.60	8.90	7.60	2.35	34.83	2.73	100.00
23	11/29/90	43.11	9.38	7.80	2.36	34.48	2.89	100.01
24	11/30/90	43.35	9.34	7.44	2.13	34.34	3.36	99.97
	Total	43.49	8.92	7.65	2.51	34.90	2.58	100.05

in these two tables, and all of these are negative. All of the significant correlations are in the same direction as the corresponding correlations among expectations in panel A.

Table 12.8 contains correlations between expectations, market prices and opinion poll reports within party and across time. Details of a more complete comparison of expectations with market prices and polls appear in *Table 12.9*. Here we report on the results from two equations of a vector auto-regression, the first of expectations on lagged expectations, current and lagged prices and current and lagged polls:[6]

$$E = \alpha + \beta_1 E_{-1} + \beta_2 E_{-2} + \gamma_1 P_{-1} + \gamma_2 P_{-2} + \delta_1 OP + \delta_2 OP_{-1} + e, \qquad (12.2)$$

reports were from Allensbach and one each from Forsa and Infas. Emnid and FG Wahlen also published prognoses during this election period, but their releases were on weekends while the market was closed. No market day had more than one poll published on that day.

[6] That prices appear in the expectation equation with additional lags reflects the sequencing of observations. Traders see poll reports in the morning papers or on television the evening before, then they enter the market where they reveal expectations, and finally transactions which determine the day's average prices are undertaken.

Table 12.4. Standard deviations of expectations, by day across trader

		Party					
Day	Date	CDU/CSU	FDP	GRUENE	PDS	SPD	SONST.
1	10/29/90	0.00	0.00	0.00	0.00	0.00	0.00
2	10/30/90	2.37	1.18	0.90	1.07	1.91	1.51
3	10/31/90	1.96	1.61	1.16	0.64	2.69	2.14
4	11/01/90	3.52	1.37	1.61	1.28	2.67	1.59
5	11/02/90	1.29	1.08	1.22	0.48	1.58	0.86
6	11/05/90	2.38	1.28	1.49	0.84	3.66	0.80
7	11/06/90	1.57	0.92	1.28	0.81	2.46	1.27
8	11/07/90	1.55	0.71	1.25	0.60	2.22	2.00
9	11/08/90	1.90	1.12	1.39	0.66	2.23	2.24
10	11/09/90	1.94	0.97	1.36	0.50	2.25	1.07
11	11/12/90	3.85	1.76	1.48	0.58	3.86	2.03
12	11/13/90	2.13	1.12	1.21	0.59	2.63	1.81
13	11/14/90	1.52	1.33	1.36	1.09	2.37	1.41
14	11/15/90	1.76	1.19	1.11	0.87	2.02	0.91
15	11/16/90	1.08	0.90	0.78	0.63	1.46	0.77
16	11/19/90	1.34	1.18	1.14	0.90	1.99	1.40
17	11/20/90	2.00	0.98	1.44	0.63	2.51	1.20
18	11/22/90	1.39	0.98	1.21	0.88	2.05	1.41
19	11/23/90	1.75	0.70	1.57	0.71	2.69	1.01
20	11/26/90	1.83	1.14	1.55	1.00	2.17	1.73
21	11/27/90	1.44	0.74	1.41	0.71	1.77	1.01
22	11/28/90	1.37	0.77	1.25	0.64	1.86	1.34
23	11/29/90	1.43	0.53	1.10	0.54	2.15	1.45
24	11/30/90	2.23	0.50	1.07	0.45	1.27	1.21
	Total	1.85	1.05	1.29	0.79	2.26	1.43

and the second of market prices on lagged prices, current and lagged expectations and current and lagged polls:

$$P = \alpha + \beta_1 P_{-1} + \beta_2 P_{-2} + \gamma_1 E + \gamma_2 E_{-1} + \delta_1 OP + \delta_2 OP_{-1} + e. \tag{12.3}$$

In both, E represents Expectations, P Prices and OP opinion polls. The analysis is repeated for each contract in the market. The question of interest here is the extent to which movements in expectations can predict future market price movements, and vice versa – in the spirit of "Granger-Sims Causality". Accordingly, the coefficients of the autoregressions are of less interest than are certain joint tests. The entries in the table, therefore, are the F statistics from two tests in each regression. The tests address these questions: after controlling for lagged values of the dependent variable, 1) do current and lagged values of polls still exert some influence ($H_0 : \delta_1 = \delta_2 = 0$), and 2) do current and lagged values of the other variable (prices or expectations) still have some explanatory power ($H_0 : \gamma_1 = \gamma_2 = 0$).

Table 12.5. Estimation errors (average absolute error), by day across traders

		Party						
Day	Date	CDU/CSU	FDP	GRUENE	PDS	SPD	SONST.	TOTAL
1	10/29/90	0.80	1.00	1.90	1.60	3.50	0.20	1.50
2	10/30/90	2.03	2.64	2.04	1.04	1.79	1.63	1.86
3	10/31/90	1.42	2.53	1.70	0.80	2.18	1.83	1.74
4	11/01/90	2.55	2.19	2.63	0.93	2.67	2.21	2.20
5	11/02/90	1.01	2.11	2.40	0.50	2.06	2.72	1.80
6	11/05/90	1.85	2.25	2.17	0.61	3.13	2.69	2.12
7	11/06/90	1.34	2.43	2.20	0.58	2.67	1.85	1.84
8	11/07/90	1.36	2.22	2.52	0.40	1.78	2.03	1.72
9	11/08/90	1.63	2.22	2.55	0.51	1.88	2.28	1.84
10	11/09/90	1.65	2.52	2.55	0.45	2.42	1.81	1.90
11	11/12/90	2.62	2.61	2.28	0.51	3.50	2.34	2.31
12	11/13/90	1.56	2.34	2.52	0.54	1.97	1.89	1.80
13	11/14/90	1.07	2.32	2.65	0.85	1.84	2.08	1.80
14	11/15/90	1.24	2.38	2.75	0.61	1.64	1.72	1.72
15	11/16/90	0.96	1.63	3.62	0.46	1.10	2.07	1.64
16	11/19/90	1.47	1.88	3.02	0.69	1.96	1.75	1.79
17	11/20/90	1.32	1.86	2.53	0.53	1.98	1.87	1.68
18	11/22/90	1.14	2.02	2.74	0.66	1.85	1.98	1.73
19	11/23/90	1.46	1.58	2.64	0.54	2.31	1.94	1.74
20	11/26/90	1.51	2.13	2.46	0.69	1.60	2.06	1.74
21	11/27/90	1.16	2.00	2.53	0.60	1.49	1.41	1.53
22	11/28/90	1.11	2.10	2.52	0.52	1.58	1.69	1.59
23	11/29/90	1.29	1.62	2.70	0.44	1.59	1.74	1.57
24	11/30/90	1.53	1.66	2.42	0.43	1.24	1.28	1.43
	Total	1.41	2.09	2.57	0.60	1.90	1.89	1.74

Table 12.6. Expectations and prices by parties

	Party					
	CDU/CSU	FDP	GRUENE	PDS	SPD	SONST.
Expectations across traders and days						
Mean	43.49	8.92	7.65	2.51	34.9	2.58
St. Dev.	1.85	1.05	1.29	0.79	2.26	1.43
CV (%)	4.25	11.27	16.86	31.47	6.47	55.43
Mean Abs, Err.	1.41	2.09	2.57	0.6	1.9	1.89
Prices across individual transactions						
Mean	42.85	9.10	8.43	3.11	33.47	3.33
St. Dev.	0.62	0.39	0.55	0.51	1.62	0.45
CV (%)	1.45	4.28	6.47	16.39	4.85	13.55
Mean Abs, Err.	1.02	1.91	3.33	0.71	0.27	0.88

Table 12.7. Correlations of parties across time

A. Expectations						
	CDU/CSU	F.D.P.	GRUENE	PDS	SPD	SONST.
CDU/CSU	1.0000					
F.D.P.	-0.5697	1.0000				
GRUENE	-0.6017	0.5943	1.0000			
PDS	0.6215	-0.4984	-0.3217	1.0000		
SPD	-0.2119	-0.2976	-0.1810	-0.4197	1.0000	
SONST.	-0.0371	0.0088	-0.1869	0.1665	-0.6351	1.0000
B. Market Prices						
	CDU/CSU	F.D.P.	GRUENE	PDS	SPD	SONST.
CDU/CSU	1.0000					
F.D.P.	-0.1279	1.0000				
GRUENE	-0.7526	0.0353	1.0000			
PDS	0.1163	-0.4617	-0.2220	1.0000		
SPD	0.1221	0.1912	-0.2440	0.0591	1.0000	
SONST.	0.2559	0.2131	-0.2999	-0.2528	-0.2847	1.0000
C. Opinion Polls						
	CDU/CSU	F.D.P.	GRUENE	PDS	SPD	SONST.
CDU/CSU	1.0000					
F.D.P.	-0.8119	1.0000				
GRUENE	-0.4470	0.2753	1.0000			
PDS	0.0042	-0.2213	-0.0349	1.0000		
SPD	-0.0235	0.0757	-0.7475	-0.0771	1.0000	
SONST.	-0.0321	-0.1534	-0.2788	-0.1918	-0.0495	1.0000

The sample size is 23. Correlations higher than .352 are significantly greater than zero at the 5% level, correlations higher than .277 are significant at the 10 % level.

At a 10 % level of significance, the tests would be rejected in only four of the 24 cases. But a comparison across regressions offers a suggestive pattern. Specifically, the p-values of the F statistics for the effect of lagged polls on both expectations and prices are appear to be uniformly distributed over the 0-1 interval, ranging from .07 to .98 in the Expectations equation and from .24 to .72 in the Price equation. On the other hand, the p-values for the test on prices in the expectations regressions, and expectations in the price regressions, tend to be skewed more heavily toward smaller values – they range from .07 to .36 in the expectations equation and from .001 to .18 in the price equation. Of course these statistics are not independent across parties, but the pattern provides weak evidence for the case that opinion polls have no effect on either expectations or market prices, while expectations did influence market prices and market prices did influence expectations.[7]

[7] See Brüggelambert 1999 for a more detailed comparison of polls and the market in this experiment.

Table 12.8. Correlations of expectations, prices and polls within party and across time

CDU/CSU				PDS			
	E	P	OP		E	P	OP
E	1.0000			E	1.0000		
P	0.5851	1.0000		P	0.0858	1.0000	
OP	0.1021	0.0743	1.0000	OP	-0.2549	0.0108	1.0000
F.D.P.				**SPD**			
	E	P	OP		E	P	OP
E	1.0000			E	1.0000		
P	0.9587	1.0000		P	0.7812	1.0000	
OP	-0.3987	-0.5133	1.0000	OP	-0.4745	-0.6061	1.0000
GRUENE				**SONSTIGE**			
	E	P	OP		E	P	OP
E	1.0000			E	1.0000		
P	0.6191	1.0000		P	-0.6134	1.0000	
OP	0.1213	0.3969	1.0000	OP	0.3264	-0.3101	1.0000

E = Expectations, P = Market Prices, OP = Opinion Polls. The sample size is 23 as in Table 12.7.

Table 12.9. F-statistics from vector autoregressions for expectations and prices

	Expectations Equation		Price Equation	
Party	Polls	Prices	Polls	Expectations
CDU/CSU	0.02 (0.9839)	1.10 (0.3591)	0.43 (0.6572)	2.83 *(0.0932)*
F.D.P	3.21 *(0.0714)*	3.09 *(0.0773)*	0.52 (0.6071)	11.47 *(0.0011)*
GRUENE	0.63 (0.5466)	1.22 (0.3246)	1.58 (0.2407)	1.92 (0.1836)
PDS	0.41 (0.6727)	2.10 (0.1599)	0.34 (0.7171)	2.25 (0.1418)
SPD	0.85 (0.4472)	1.81 (0.1999)	0.92 (.4212)	2.37 (0.1302)
SONSTIGE	2.39 (0.1278)	1.95 (0.1792)	0.64 (0.5418)	2.57 (0.1124)

Entries are F(2,14) statistics, with associated p-values in parentheses, for joint test of hypotheses that neither current nor first order lag values of the column variable affect the current value of the dependent variable after controlling for one lag on the latter.

12.3.3 Aggregate analysis of expectations

Here we present a simple, preliminary analysis of the efficacy of expectations as an explanation of market behavior. If the market actions taken by traders are consistent with their expectations, then at least on balance the trades resulting from those transactions should lead to subjective improvements in the trader's position. Specifically, a subjective measure of the value of a trader's portfolio is given by his cash holdings plus the sum of the value of share holdings, with those share holdings priced according to the trader's expected vote outcome. Accordingly, we compute the subjective value of each trader's portfolio at the beginning of the day, then again at the beginning of the next trading session but using the same expectations for both calculations. The difference between these two values is then a measure of the subjective improvement in the trader's portfolio resulting from the trades made over the time interval. Trades include not only market buy and sell offers executed while the trader is connected to the market but also those trades resulting from limit offers left in the offer queues when the trader's trading session ended.

The analysis began with 304 trading sessions from among the 45 traders with useable data. That permitted the calculation of 259 measures of subjective portfolio improvement. *Table 12.10* below contains results of those calculations. The average improvement is a positive 29 Pfenning per trading session, which is significantly different from zero under the assumptions of independent, normally distributed changes in portfolio values. The magnitude may appear small, but in fact it implies a .9% gain per trading day. Compounded over twenty sessions in the five week market, that would yield a gain of nearly 20% in five weeks.

The analysis below investigates the extent to which such overall measures of the relation between expectations and behavior can be detected at the level of individual market actions as well.

12.4 Classification of market actions according to degree of rationality

The principle objective of the analysis is to assess the consistency of market actions with expectations according to concepts of rational behavior. We begin here with a close examination of the actions traders could take in the market, a discussion of how such actions can be valued according to the profit motivation of traders, and finally a classification of the actions selected according to rationality.

12.4.1 Possible market actions

Recall that there were four types of offers or market actions traders could take on the market – market offers to buy (purchases) and sell (sales), and limit offers to buy (bids) and sell (asks). These 4 offer types will be referred to as M_buy, M_sell, L_buy and L_sell, respectively, in the description to follow. In the case of market offers, the trader accepted the current market price, meaning the highest price in the bid queue for a sale and the lowest price in the ask queue for a purchase. His

Table 12.10. Subjective portfolio valuations

	N	Mean	St.Dev.	Min	Max
Value at beginning of trading session	259	32.082	13.881	9.791	51.037
Value at beginning of subsequent session	259	32.374	14.011	9.854	52.946
Change in valuation	259	0.292	0.896	-8.038	3.367
t-statistic for Hypothesis of equal means	t = 5.24	258 d.f.			
Number of Sessions	Number showing improvement			Pct. improved	
259	195			75.3	

only option was the number of units to be traded. In limit offers the trader set the quantity, a time limit for the offer, and the limit price. Each limit offer was entered into a queue where it remained until it was transacted, its time limit expired, it was withdrawn by the trader, or it reached the front of the queue and was found to be infeasible[8]. Offers could be partially filled since the market system operated one unit at a time, but withdrawals, expirations and infeasible offers where removed in their entirety.[9]

Contracts were placed in circulation via the purchase from the system of "Unit Portfolios". Each such portfolio consisted of one share in each of the six contracts, and it was available at the price of 1 DM. Since liquidation values to be paid after the election were to be computed as 1 DM times the vote share of the party, and since each and every party was represented by one and only one contract, the guaranteed liquidation value of a unit portfolio was the same 1 DM. This mechanism guaranteed that the market was a zero sum game – all funds paid to the system for new unit portfolios were paid back in the form of liquidation values. More relevant to the current discussion, the mechanism also provided opportunities for arbitrage transactions. Trades in the market were for individual contracts, so that there was no guarantee that market prices would add up to exactly one DM at any point in time. If it happened that the sum of the bid prices exceeded one, a clever trader could buy a unit portfolio from the system for 1 DM and then sell each contract in it on the

[8] The criteria for feasibility was that the trader had to have a sufficient cash balance in his portfolio to purchase at least one share in a bid, and had to hold at least one share for an ask. The condition applied only when an offer moved to the front of a queue and thus was revealed to other traders.

[9] If the offered price of a limit offer overlapped with a price in the opposite queue, a transaction occurred immediately and the limit offer was in effect identical to a market offer. Otherwise it remained in the queue for later action. For purposes of assessing rationality of market actions, the question arises whether limit offers which result in immediate transactions should be treated as market offers, on the grounds that the immediacy of the transaction is the more important aspect and the residual queue order as less important. The analyses reported below were repeated using this alternative treatment; save for differences expected from the change in sizes of subsamples, there were no systematic or substantive differences in the results.

market, earning back his 1 DM along with an arbitrage profit. The only risk was that the sale of all contracts in the unit portfolio could not be completed before market prices changed – perhaps because another trader also recognized this profit opportunity and acted more quickly. Of course similar arbitrage opportunity could arise on the other side of the market as well.

Clearly transactions intended as arbitrage trades of the sort described above do not have the same motivation as other market offers, buy-and-hold strategies for example. Thus it is important to identify such activities and exclude them from the analyses of these other activities. This identification is not particularly easy since the market system allowed such arbitrage only by sales or purchases of the contracts one at a time and such actions were not identified as arbitrage transactions. Our attempt to identify arbitrage transactions was to order the observations by trader, date and time, then to look for sequences of 6 market offers covering all 6 contracts. If those 6 offers were all on the same side of the market (buy or sell), by the same trader, on the same date and for the same number of units, and if the sequence began when profit opportunity was in fact present (sum of market bids greater than 1.00 or sum of market asks less than 1.00), then we designated the six offers in this sequence as "arbitrage offers". This calculation is not perfect. An arbitrage sequence might have been aborted midstream because market prices changed in an adverse direction. Or it might have taken more than six offers to complete the sequence if the number of units was not the same in each. Combinations of arbitrage and portfolio improvement transactions might likewise have led to incomplete arbitrage sequences.

This arbitrage screening identified 31 opportunities in which the sum of bids exceeded 1.00. Arbitrage opportunities also arose on the other side – sum of asks less than 1 – but they were fewer in number and no buying sequences involving them were found in our data. In 16 of 31 opportunities, arbitrage sequences as defined above were discovered. Each such occasion might involve multiple arbitrage sequences by one or more traders. Indeed we found 83 such sequences from 15 different traders. The 83 sequences of 6 transactions, 498 offers in all, are excluded from much of thc analysis to follow.

Table 12.11 contains a tabulation of the number of observations on which the subsequent analysis will be based, with rows indicating the reasons for deletion of observations. The discussion of expectations appeared in section 12.3 above. An additional five observations were deleted because they were limit offers at prices which would have placed them immediately at the front of their respective queues, but the trader had insufficient resources to afford a transaction of even a single unit. Note that all 5 are for limit offers. Attempts to execute infeasible market offers were denied by the market software and thus never entered the database.

12.4.2 Assessment of actions with respect to profit motive

The question to be examined is the extent to which the behavior of traders is consistent with their own statements of their expectations. We look not to the composition of the trader's portfolio, or even to sequences of market actions, but rather to the

Table 12.11. Account of the number of observations

	Limit sell	Limit buy	Market buy	Market sell	Total
Original number of observations	2121	1740	714	1233	5808
Unused observations					
incomplete expectations information	552	515	93	229	1389
arbitrage	60	0	0	438	498
infeasible offers	2	3	0	0	5
Total number unused	614	518	93	667	1892
Remaining observations	1507	1222	621	566	3916

individual actions in isolation. And the view of rational behavior, that is of the consistency between stated expectations and market actions, is a narrow one. We do not account, for example, for technical trading or other strategic market actions which might be rationally taken without regard to expectations of the election outcome. Nor do we attempt to control for personal preferences and actions which might be quite rational in light of them – buying and holding shares in ones favored party even if the expectation of success is low, for example.

A standard of rational behavior consistent with either the strictly-rational or boundedly-rational models is that traders should only make those transactions from which they can anticipate a profit. If the responses given to the survey questions regarding expected election outcomes are an accurate reflection of their beliefs, then a comparison of those expectations and the prices at which market actions are taken should reveal the extent to which those market actions are rational.[10]

The expected rate of return from a market purchase offer by trader j of one unit of contract i at time period t is defined by

$$r^P_{ijt} = \frac{E_{ijt} - P^A_{it}}{P^A_{it}} \tag{12.4}$$

where E_{ijt} is trader j's expectation of the liquidation value for contract i as of time t, and P^A_{it} is the market's current low ask price for contract i at time t. Purchases of contracts with positive returns r^P_{ijt} will increase the trader's expected profits.

Similarly, the return which would be expected from a market sell offer by trader j of one unit of contract i at time period t is defined by

$$r^S_{ijt} = \frac{E_{ijt} - P^B_{it}}{P^B_{it}} \tag{12.5}$$

where again E_{ijt} is trader j's expectation of the liquidation value for contract i as of time t, and now P^B_{it} is the market's current high bid price for contract i at time t. Note that with this definition of returns for sales, the most attractive selling opportunities are those for contracts with negative values of r^S_{ijt}.

[10] Note that this is a narrow definition of rationality. It is the definition, however, that we are able to assess with the data available from this experiment.

Returns expected for limit offers are similar except that they depend on the limit price chosen by the trader. Specifically,

$$r_{ijt}^{B} = \frac{E_{ijt} - P_{ijt}^{bid}}{P_{ijt}^{bid}} \tag{12.6}$$

for bids and

$$r_{ijt}^{A} = \frac{E_{ijt} - P_{ijt}^{ask}}{P_{ijt}^{ask}} \tag{12.7}$$

for asks, where P_{ijt}^{bid} and P_{ijt}^{ask} are the prices chosen by the trader for the bid or ask, respectively, rather than the market prices. As with market offers, bids at prices such that r_{ijt}^{B} is positive, and asks at prices for which r_{ijt}^{A} are negative, add positively to expected profit.

When a trader arrives at the market place he faces a set of market prices, P_{it}^{A} and P_{it}^{B}, and has his own expectations E_{ijt} for each of the contracts in the market, $i = 1, \ldots, 6$. And from each offer submitted we know the type and price of the offer. From this information we can compute the expected returns for each submitted offer. In addition we can compute the expected returns from market buy and market sell offers, r_{ijt}^{P} and r_{ijt}^{S}, for each of the six contracts, whether or not the offer was for that contract and/or of that type. We can in turn use those returns to determine the most attractive purchase and the most attractive sale available to the trader as of the point in time at which the offer was entered. Specifically, let r_{jt}^{*P} be the larger of 0 and the maximum return on any purchase at market price. That is,

$$r_{jt}^{*P} = \max\left(0, r_{1jt}^{P}, r_{2jt}^{P}, \ldots, r_{6jt}^{P}\right). \tag{12.8}$$

For purposes of this calculation, if the trader has not enough cash to buy at least one share of a contract, the corresponding value for r_{ijt}^{P} is treated as zero. Note that the minimum value for r_{jt}^{*P} is zero since the trader always has the option of not making any purchase. In a similar fashion, the most attractive sale is for the contract with the largest negative value for r_{ijt}^{S}. Define r_{jt}^{*S} as this smallest return:

$$r_{jt}^{*S} = \min\left(0, r_{1jt}^{S}, r_{2jt}^{S}, \ldots, r_{6jt}^{S}\right). \tag{12.9}$$

Here r_{ijt}^{S} is set to zero when trader j holds none of contract i at time t and thus cannot make a sale. Accordingly, the largest possible value for r_{jt}^{*S} is zero.

12.4.3 Classification of offers according to rationality

For each offer submitted by a trader, we can compute the expected return for that offer, r_{ijt}^{A}, r_{ijt}^{B}, r_{ijt}^{P} or r_{ijt}^{S}, depending on the type of the offer submitted. And we can compute the best possible returns for market purchases and sales, r_{jt}^{*P} and r_{jt}^{*S}. From these terms we are prepared to classify the offers according to consistency with the profit motive as follows.

Considering only market purchases, the best action to take is to select that contract which has the highest return and make a purchase in it. Since a market purchase for a contract with $r^P_{ijt} = r^{*P}_{jt}$ is the best possible purchase from the profitability point of view, such a purchase is strictly rational. But suppose the trader chooses to purchase instead another contract which has a positive but lower expected return than r^{*P}_{jt}. Such behavior is less rational but still reasonable, since by itself it amounts to an improvement compared to the status quo. We would classify this action as one with a lower degree of rationality. Purchases for which r^P_{ijt} are negative would decrease expected profit and would therefore be deemed irrational.

Consider next a limit offer to buy. Any such bid at a price P^{bid}_{ijt} which yields $r^B_{ijt} \geq r^{*P}_{jt}$ offers a chance for at least as large a profit as the best possible market purchase, but with less certainty that the offer will be accepted by another trader. Thus it is impossible to say that this action is any more or less rational than the market purchase for which $r^P_{ijt} = r^{*P}_{it}$. On the other hand, if $r^{*P}_{it} > r^B_{ijt} \geq 0$ then the proposed bid is inferior to the best market purchase though still supportive of the profit motive, while if $0 > r^B_{ijt}$, then the action is contrary to the motive of improving profits; that is to say, it would be classified as irrational.

Similar arguments apply to market and limit offers to sell, with the difference that sales are rational for contracts with negative expected returns.

From this heuristic discussion we define the rationality key "RKey" according to the entries in *Table 12.12*. We employ the classification of trader actions according to RKey in what follows. Note that this classification ignores interesting combination of actions. For example, selling a contract whose expected return is positive may be perfectly rational if it affords the liquidity to purchase another contract with an even higher expected return. Combinations of actions such as this are beyond the scope of this work. Throughout the remainder of this paper, the "rationality of traders" will be taken to imply the definitions of Table 12.12.

Table 12.12. Classification of offers with respect to rationality

	Action Taken			
RKey (Classification)	Ask (limit sell)	Bid (limit buy)	Purchase	Sale
0 (irrational)	$r^A_{ijt} > 0$	$r^B_{ijt} < 0$	$r^P_{ijt} < 0$	$r^S_{ijt} > 0$
1 (boundedly rational)	$0 \geq r^A_{ijt} > r^{*S}_{jt}$	$0 \leq r^B_{ijt} < r^{*P}_{jt}$	$0 \leq r^P_{ijt} < r^{*P}_{jt}$	$0 \geq r^S_{ijt} > r^{*S}_{jt}$
2 (strictly rational)	$r^{*S}_{jt} \geq r^A_{ijt}$	$r^{*P}_{jt} \leq r^B_{ijt}$	$r^{*P}_{jt} \leq r^P_{ijt}$	$r^{*S}_{jt} \geq r^S_{ijt}$

12.5 Influences on the degree of rationality

12.5.1 Univariate analysis

In the tables to follow, the variable "RKey" is cross-tabulated against various other variables. In *Table 12.13* the comparison is with offer type. As can be seen there, buying offers (L_buy and M_buy) have a higher order of rationality than do selling offers (L_sell and M_sell). This effect is similar to that found by Camerer and Weber 1992.

Table 12.13. Comparison of rationality key against offer type

	RKey			
Offer Type	0	1	2	Total
L_sell	564	402	541	1507
	37.4	26.7	35.9	100.0
L_buy	233	445	544	1222
	19.1	36.4	44.5	100.0
M_buy	162	174	285	621
	26.1	28.0	45.9	100.0
M_sell	210	152	204	566
	37.1	26.9	36.0	100.0
Total	1169	1173	1574	3916
	29.9	30.0	40.2	100.0

Entries are cell frequency/row percentage. Pearson $\chi^2(6) = 134.56$, p-value $= 0.000$

In *Table 12.14* we examine the pattern of RKey across contracts. The lowest degree of rationality occurs with CDU and SPD, and the highest with PDS and Sonstige. The contrast here corresponds with both vote share (CDU and SPD received 43.8 percent and 33.5 percent of the nationwide vote respectively, while PDS won only 2.4 percent and the other small parties – Sonstige – 4.2 percent) and with the party biases of the UGEM traders. This pattern could be due to a trading bias, with traders making emotional decisions about their favorite party but colder and more rational decisions about others. (See FNNW 1992 and Brüggelambert 1999 for further evidence of trading biases in these and similar markets.) Or it could be due to liquidity factors – more money is tied up with the purchase of one share in CDU than one in PDS and thus traders may have had greater constraints on their decisions regarding the larger parties. Or it could be due to the subjective sense that there are greater profit possibilities in the small parties since price movements of the same order of magnitude will cause a greater variability in expected returns for small parties. This latter effect is supported by the greater value of CV for expectations in small parties. C.f. Table 12.6. More evidence on all of these factors can be found in the multivariate analysis below.

The time of an offer might also have had some effect on the rationality of the decision leading to it. Included here are experience effects of trades across different days, and sequencing effects involving trades within the day. *Table 12.15* examines the frequency of the RKey categories across weeks – the frequency of strictly rational actions (RKey=2) seems to have risen from the first week through the fifth, with a small exception in the fourth. *Table 12.16* examines the experience effect with a direct control for individual experience, specifically the day of this transaction

Table 12.14. Comparison of the rationality key with contracts

Contract	RKey 0	1	2	Total
CDU/CSU	245	343	159	747
	32.8	45.9	21.3	100.0
F.D.P	211	234	297	742
	28.4	31.5	40.0	100.0
GRUENE	224	157	271	652
	34.4	24.1	41.6	100.0
PDS	98	143	236	477
	20.6	30.0	49.5	100.0
SPD	210	248	202	660
	31.8	37.6	30.6	100.0
SONSTIGE	181	48	409	638
	28.4	7.5	64.1	100.0
Total	1169	1173	1574	3916
	29.9	30.0	40.2	100.0

Entries are cell frequency/row percentage. Pearson $\chi^2(10) = 396.75$, p-value $= 0.000$

relative to the day the trader first entered the market, rather than from the aggregation across all traders. Though the chi-square test suggests a significant dependence across trader experience and degree of rationality, there is no clear pattern.

Table 12.15. Comparison of the rationality key with market week

week	RKey 0	1	2	Total
1	147	163	186	496
	29.6	32.9	37.5	100.0
2	266	270	346	882
	30.2	30.6	39.2	100.0
3	272	256	368	896
	30.4	28.6	41.1	100.0
4	187	212	258	657
	28.5	32.3	39.3	100.0
5	297	272	416	985
	30.2	27.6	42.2	100.0
Total	1169	1173	1574	3916
	29.9	30.0	40.2	100.0

Entries are cell frequency and row percentage. Pearson $\chi^2(8) = 8.07$, p-value $= 0.426$

The timing of offers within the day is the focus of *Table 12.17*. Traders may be more careful with the first offer they place when arriving at the market than the

Table 12.16. Comparison of the rationality key with trader experience

	RKey			
Trader Experience	0	1	2	Total
1st day	154.0	195.0	209.0	558.0
	27.6	35.0	37.5	100.0
day 2-5	409	395	518	1322
	30.9	29.9	39.2	100.0
day 6-10	269.0	219.0	342.0	830.0
	32.4	26.4	41.2	100.0
day 11-15	170	182	265	617
	27.6	29.5	43.0	100.0
day 16-20	130	114	175	419
	31.0	27.2	41.8	100.0
day 21-23	37	68	65	170
	21.8	40.0	38.2	100.0
Total	1169	1173	1574	3916
	29.9	30.0	40.2	100.0

Entries are cell frequency/row percentage. Pearson $\chi^2(10) = 26.47$, p-value $= 0.003$

fiftieth offer. Or, said another way, the first offer may more likely be the outcome of a rational calculus involving expectations and prices, while later decisions are more likely to come from technical trading considerations. Another possibility is that expectations may have changed by the time later offers are submitted. Accordingly, in Table 12.17 we have grouped offers into sets depending on the order in which they are issued – the first offer of the day, offers number two through five, offers 6 through 10, 11 through 25, 26 through 50, and finally greater than 50. As revealed by the table, decisions later in they day clearly have a lower degree of rationality than those early in the day.

An important caveat with all of these comparisons is that the observations are not independent. Dependencies exist along several dimensions – across days but within trader, within days, and certainly within days and traders. And a related observation is that those traders with a lot of market activity carry a much greater weight since the unit of observation here is an offer.

12.5.2 Multivariate analysis

All of the investigations above are bivariate comparisons. It is of more interest to do a multivariate analysis. We report below the results from an ordered logit model for the dependent variable RKey described above.[11] The model is

$$y^* = \beta' X + u, \qquad \text{RKey} = \begin{cases} 0 & \text{if } \quad y^* < \alpha_1 \\ 1 & \text{if } \alpha_1 < y^* < \alpha_2 \\ 2 & \text{if } \alpha_2 < y^* \end{cases} \tag{12.10}$$

[11] Cf. eg. Nelson (1987).

Table 12.17. Comparison of the rationality key with time of day

	RKey			
Offer Within Day	0	1	2	Total
offer 1	66	95	141	302
	21.9	31.5	46.7	100.0
2-5	257	322	431	1010
	25.5	31.9	42.7	100.0
6-10	224	274	372	870
	25.8	31.5	42.8	100.0
10-25	355	308	419	1082
	32.8	28.5	38.7	100.0
25-50	184	111	142	437
	42.1	25.4	32.5	100.0
>50	83	63	69	215
	38.6	29.3	32.1	100.0
Total	1169	1173	1574	3916
	29.9	30.0	40.2	100.0

Entries are cell frequencies/row percentages. Pearson $\chi^2(10) = 71.32$, p-value $= 0.000$.

y^* is a latent variable; only RKey and the exogenous variables in the vector X are observed. The parameters to be estimated are the regression coefficients β and the "cut points" α_1 and α_2. No intercept term is included in the model since it is not identified independently of the two cut points, and the variance of u is normalized to 1 since it is not identified independently of the scale of β, α_1 and α_2. In the analysis employed here it is assumed that the error term u follows a $\mathcal{N}(0,1)$ distribution.

Whether an offer placed in the market is rational or not depends on the type of offer, and the direction and level of influence of those factors which explain the degree of rationality also differ across offer types. Accordingly, the model is estimated separately for each of the four offer types, Limit-Sell, Limit-Buy, Market-Buy and Market-Sell. Results appear in *Table 12.18*, with coefficient estimates for each offer type appearing in a separate column. Entries in the second row for each independent variable are standard errors.

The first variable in the table (lnoffseq) is the logarithm of the offer sequence number – the same variable as was used in Table 12.17 but without the grouping. For all four offer types the coefficient is negative, though it is not always large relative to its standard error. The implication is that offers made early in the day are more rational, or perhaps more careful, than offers placed later in the day.

The second variable (favorite) is a dummy variable defined to be 1 or 0 depending on whether or not, respectively, the offer being placed is for a party designated in the beginning-of-day survey as being the trader's favorite party. This factor has a negative effect on rationality for selling offers (both L_sell and M_sell) and a positive effect for buying offers (L_buy and M_buy), though the coefficient in the limit-buy equation is not large relative to its standard error. This suggests that traders are more rational with purchases of their favorite party than with purchases of other

Table 12.18. Factors affecting rationality of offers – ordered logit model

Offer Type:	L_sell	L_buy	M_buy	M_sell
No. Obs.	1507	1222	621	566
$\chi^2(10)$	432.6	171.0	267.7	302.3
p value	0.000	0.000	0.000	0.000
lnLklhd	-1423.44	-1190.43	-527.17	-465.09
Psuedo R^2	0.1319	0.0670	0.2025	0.2453
lnoffseq	-0.3056 (0.0482)	-0.1379 (0.0605)	-0.1582 (0.0867)	-0.1160 (0.0814)
favorite	-0.5829 (0.1432)	0.0741 (0.1528)	1.1328 (0.2455)	-0.8883 (0.4537)
cash	-0.0234 (0.0086)	-0.0184 (0.0090)	0.0315 (0.0106)	-0.0322 (0.0162)
shares held	-0.0137 (0.0013)	0.0097 (0.0014)	0.0173 (0.0021)	-0.0231 (0.0037)
partysize	-0.0478 (0.0035)	0.0001 (0.0034)	0.0301 (0.0053)	-0.0720 (0.0072)
spread	14.6278 (6.3661)	12.7022 (8.7337)	-1.1799 (27.2934)	23.4956 (19.9597)
r^{*P}_{jt}	0.1599 (0.3354)	-0.4074 (0.2884)	1.5148 (0.6074)	4.0057 (0.8896)
r^{*S}_{jt}	0.5876 (0.2006)	0.1154 (0.2399)	1.9934 (0.3292)	-0.8551 (0.4171)
ln(size)	0.1907 (0.0583)	0.2102 (0.0544)	0.0078 (0.1002)	0.2383 (0.1228)
invest	-0.0041 (0.0046)	-0.0213 (0.0052)	-0.0355 (0.0094)	0.0271 (0.0081)
_cut1	-2.7182 (0.2344)	-1.9136 (0.2330)	-1.0449 (0.3932)	-1.0042 (0.4299)
_cut2	-1.3296 (0.2253)	-0.0852 (0.2261)	0.6539 (0.3918)	0.7363 (0.4273)

A separate equation was estimated for each offer type. Entries in the header include the number of observations used in each equation; a Chi Square statistic for testing the hypothesis that all coefficients in the model save the cut points, are zero; the p-value for this Chi Sq. statistic; the value of the log-likelihood; and a measure of goodness of fit of the equation. Coefficient estimates, and their standard errors in parentheses, appear in the body of the table. Exogenous variables are described in the text.

parties. And on the other hand they are less rational in sales of their favorite party than they are with other parties. Perhaps traders are suspicious of their own biases, fearing that their expectations of their favorite party are too high. Thus their market actions are at prices generally lower than would be presumed based solely on stated expectations. Note that the "promotion of one's favorite party" by paying excessive prices would work in the opposite direction, so that the evidence here is that these traders did not generally participate in this sort of activity.

Variable three (cash) represents the balance in the trader's cash account. One might expect that when cash balances are low, traders might be more rational with purchases but less rational with market sales as they execute some sales merely for the sake of increasing their liquidity position. Thus the sign pattern should run as follows:

$$\beta(\text{M\_buy}) < \beta(\text{L\_buy}) < \beta(\text{L\_sell}) < \beta(\text{M\_sell}). \qquad (12.11)$$

In fact the pattern in the estimated coefficients is the opposite. We have no explanation.

Variable four (shares held) is the number of shares held by the trader in the party for which this offer is being submitted. The estimated coefficients are strongly positive for both type of buying offers and strongly negative for both types of selling offers. The difference between limit and market offers on each side is negligible. Clearly, when traders hold many shares in a party they are more rational with further purchases, but they may not be so rational with sales.

The variable partysize is measured as the mean, across market days, of the daily average of transaction prices for that party. The size of the party, and thus the price of a contract, may influence the rationality of offers in a number of ways. First, there may be liquidity effects, since the purchase of large parties require bigger investments. For example, a cash constrained trader seeking a sale to replenish his cash holding might be more inclined to sell a few shares of larger parties than many shares of small ones. Second, there may have been a sense among traders that the variability in election outcomes may not be proportional to the size of the party – one percent increase or decrease in the vote for PDS may be as likely as a one percent change in the vote for CDU – and thus the relative profit potential was seen as higher for small parties. The coefficient estimates are consistent with both arguments.

The variable "spread" measures the difference (in DM) between the market high bid and the market low ask at the point in time when the offer was placed. A wide spread makes it more difficult to place rational market offers, so that the coefficients of "spread" should be expected to be negative for market offers, and zero or positive for limit offers. In fact the only significant coefficient is in line with this argument.

r^{*P}_{jt} is the maximum achievable return among all feasible market purchases, and r^{*S}_{jt} is the negative of the return for the most profitable market sell offer.[12] Both variables were defined in section 12.4 above. When r^{*P}_{jt} is high there is much room for profitable and rational market purchases, so that the coefficient of this variable

[12] Recall that the largest possible value for r^{*S}_{jt} is zero, and the profitability of market sales increases as r^{*S}_{jt} becomes more negative.

should have a large positive value for market purchases, the M_buy entry. Likewise, the coefficient of r_{jt}^{*S} should have the largest negative value for M_sell. The two respective coefficients are consistent with that pattern. It is not obvious why r_{jt}^{*P} should have any effect on rationality of sales, or of r_{jt}^{*S} on rationality of purchases, yet those two coefficients are both strongly positive. Finally, the sizes of r_{jt}^{*S} and r_{jt}^{*P} should have no effect on limit offers. Indeed, three of those four coefficients are small relative to their standard errors. That the estimated coefficients are not all consistent with the hypothesized pattern may be for either of two reasons. First, the sizes of r_{jt}^{*P} and r_{jt}^{*S} should have a large influence on which offer type is selected, and the conflict between offer type and rationality may have lead to these sign patterns. The effect of r_{jt}^{*P} and r_{jt}^{*S} on the selection of offer type will be investigated in section 12.6 below. Secondly the sizes of r_{jt}^{*P} and r_{jt}^{*S} should influence the spread between the two cut points of the model, and this was not allowed for in these estimates.

If the size of the offer being placed is large, one would expect traders to be more rational – game-playing and mistakes are more costly with large offers. Since limit offers allow for or even encourage extreme prices (high for sales, low for buys)[13], measuring offer size in monetary terms could lead to differences in expected signs between limit and market offers. The number of shares, on the other hand, is neutral with respect to the difference between limit offers and market offers, and to buy versus sell offers. Accordingly we measure offer size by the logarithm of the number of shares in the offer in variable nine (ln(size)). The number of shares was first truncated to feasible sizes – ln(size) = ln(min(shares offered, portfolio holdings)) for sales and ln(size) = ln(min(shares offered, Cash balance/price)) for purchases. The signs of the coefficients of ln(size) are all consistent with the hypothesis above, though for M_buy offers the coefficient is quite small relative to its standard error.

The final variable (invest) measures the total amount of money invested by the trader in the market as of the time of this offer. The coefficients are negative for all offer types except for M_sell offers – aside from this case traders with large investments appear to be less rational than those with small investments. Perhaps traders with large investments undertake more strategic actions, the profitability of which is not so easily captured with the expectations measured here and the rates of return computed from them. This finding appears to be stronger for buying offers than for selling offers. Overall, the results present a reasonably consistent pattern of behavior. Changes in the degree of rationality of market actions agree with changes in the number of offers placed within the day, preferences over parties, portfolio size, party size, offer size and the size of investments. Results of cash holdings could not be explained, however, and the effects of maximum achievable returns posed small problems.

The qualitative implications of the influence of exogenous factors on rationality are determined by the signs of coefficients as described above, but it is hard to infer anything about the magnitudes of the effects from the coefficients alone. *Table 12.19*

---

[13] It is common, for example, to see traders posting limit offers to buy a very large number of shares of each contract in a market at a price of or nearly at zero.

contains the estimated marginal effects of exogenous variables on the probability of alternative values of RKey. Specifically, from equation (12.10) above we see

$$P(\text{RKey} = 0) = \Phi(\alpha_1 - \beta' X), \quad (12.12)$$

$$P(\text{RKey} = 1) = \Phi(\alpha_2 - \beta' X) - \Phi(\alpha_1 - \beta' X), \quad (12.13)$$

and

$$P(\text{RKey} = 2) = 1 - \Phi(\alpha_2 - \beta' X), \quad (12.14)$$

so the marginal effects of a change in exogenous variable k on the three outcome probabilities are as follows:

$$\frac{dP(\text{RKey} = 0)}{dX_k} = -\beta_k \phi(\alpha_1 - \beta' X), \quad (12.15)$$

$$\frac{dP(\text{RKey} = 1)}{dX_k} = \beta_k \phi(\alpha_1 - \beta' X) - \beta_k \phi(\alpha_2 - \beta' X), \quad (12.16)$$

$$\frac{dP(\text{RKey} = 2)}{dX_k} = \beta_k \phi(\alpha_2 - \beta' X). \quad (12.17)$$

$\Phi(\bullet)$ and $\phi(\bullet)$ are the unit normal distribution function and density function, respectively. The marginal effects depend on the values of the exogenous factors; the values used in Table 12.19 are the means across the entire sample of 3921 offers, and those means, and the standard deviations, appear in the second column of the table.

The entry 0.110 in the first row of the table, for example, indicates that if the natural log of the offer sequence number falls from the mean of 2.14 to 1.14, roughly the third offer of the day rather than the eighth, then the probability of an irrational (RKey = 0) limit-sell offer falls by 0.110, and the probability of a rational offer (RKey = 1 or RKey = 2) rises by $(0.031 + 0.079) = 0.110$. The marginal effects are not directly comparable across variables since the units of measurement are different. Multiplying the marginal effects by the standard deviation of the corresponding variable, however, permits cross-variable comparisons. By that indicator, "shares held" has the largest marginal effect – if s_k represents the standard deviation of variable k and e_{ijk} is the marginal effect of variable k on outcome i for offer type j, then $s_k * \max(\text{abs}(e_{ijk}))$ is 0.41 for "shares held". The variable with the second largest impact is "partysize" ($s_k * \max(\text{abs}(e_{ijk})) = 0.30$) while "$r_{jt}^{*P}$" has the smallest impact ($s_k * \max(\text{abs}(e_{ijk})) = 0.01$). Generally, the magnitudes of these marginal effects makes it apparent that the likelihood of a rational action depends a lot on the circumstances facing the trader when that action is taken.

Table 12.20 further illustrates the quantitative effect of exogenous variables on the rationality of actions. Reported here are predicted probabilities of the three RKey outcomes for each of the four possible market actions. Probabilities in the first panel are computed from equations (12.12) – (12.14) using the coefficients in Table 12.18 above and the sample means for the values of the exogenous variables. For example, at the sample mean the predicted probability of irrationality of the action chosen

Table 12.19. Marginal effects of exogenous factors on rationality probabilities

Exogenous Variable	Mean (St.Dev.)	RKey	Offer Type L_sell	L_buy	M_buy	M_sell
lnoffseq	2.14	0	0.1100	0.0350	0.0735	0.1207
	(1.10)	1	-0.0312	0.0833	0.0225	-0.0869
		2	-0.0787	-0.1182	-0.0959	-0.0338
favorite	0.1466	0	0.2098	0.0667	0.1401	0.2303
	(0.3538)	1	-0.0596	0.1588	0.0429	-0.1658
		2	-0.1502	-0.2255	-0.1830	-0.0645
cash	7.14	0	0.0084	0.0027	0.0056	0.0092
	(7.13)	1	-0.0024	0.0064	0.0017	-0.0067
		2	-0.0060	-0.0091	-0.0073	-0.0026
shares held	46.49	0	0.0049	0.0016	0.0033	0.0054
	(76.11)	1	-0.0014	0.0037	0.0010	-0.0039
		2	-0.0035	-0.0053	-0.0043	-0.0015
partysize	17.99	0	0.0172	0.0055	0.0115	0.0189
	(15.99)	1	-0.0049	0.0130	0.0035	-0.0136
		2	-0.0123	-0.0185	-0.0150	-0.0053
spread	0.0048	0	-5.2651	-1.6740	-3.5164	-5.7794
	(0.0069)	1	1.4957	-3.9849	-1.0758	4.1601
		2	3.7694	5.6589	4.5922	1.6192
r^{*P}_{jt}	0.1261	0	-0.0576	-0.0183	-0.0384	-0.0632
	(0.1595)	1	0.0163	-0.0436	-0.0118	0.0455
		2	0.0412	0.0619	0.0502	0.0177
r^{*S}_{jt}	-0.2295	0	-0.2115	-0.0672	-0.1413	-0.2322
	(0.2583)	1	0.0601	-0.1601	-0.0432	0.1671
		2	0.1514	0.2273	0.1845	0.0650
ln(size)	1.68	0	-0.0686	-0.0218	-0.0458	-0.0753
	(1.12)	1	0.0195	-0.0520	-0.0140	0.0542
		2	0.0491	0.0738	0.0599	0.0211
invest	33.15	0	0.0015	0.0005	0.0010	0.0016
	(12.08)	1	-0.0004	0.0011	0.0003	-0.0012
		2	-0.0011	-0.0016	-0.0013	-0.0005

Entries in the four right-hand side columns are $dP(\text{RKey} = I)/dX_k$ and are evaluated at the mean of all exogenous variables across the full sample. The means and, in parentheses, standard deviations for the exogenous variables appear in column 2.

ranges from 0.057 for L_buy offers up to 0.445 f or M_sell offers.[14] The interesting comparison is the change in these probabilities across different values of the exogenous variables. The second panel reports the same probability calculations, but this time setting the exogenous variables at values unfavorable to rationality.

[14] Note that the apparent discrepancy between these entries and the simple counts of actions by RKey and offer type in Table 12.13 is due to the nonlinearity in the probability formulas; the probability at the mean is not equal to the mean of the probabilities.

Specifically, each exogenous variable is moved one quarter of its sample standard deviation away from the mean in the direction which decreases the probability of a rational action, that direction being determined by the sign of the corresponding coefficient in Table 12.18. Similarly, the third panel contains probabilities computed at values of the exogenous variables moved a quarter of a standard deviation from the mean in a direction favorable to rational action. The effects are striking; a change in the value of each exogenous variable, from one quarter of a standard deviation below its mean to one quarter of a standard deviation above, uniformly decreases the probability of irrational action (RKey = 0) by a factor of 5 or more. Again we see that the consistency between the expectations of traders and their market actions depends greatly on the circumstances they face at the time of that action.

Table 12.20. Predicted probabilities of action rationality at various levels of the exogenous variables

	Offer Type			
	L_sell	L_buy	M_buy	M_sell
Probabilities with exogenous variables at the sample mean				
$P(\text{RKey}=0)$	0.325	0.057	0.157	0.445
$P(\text{RKey}=1)$	0.500	0.541	0.599	0.501
$P(\text{RKey}=2)$	0.175	0.402	0.244	0.055
Probabilities with exogenous variables 0.25 of a standard deviation from the sample mean in a direction unfavorable for rationality				
$P(\text{RKey}=0)$	0.622	0.125	0.478	0.877
$P(\text{RKey}=1)$	0.333	0.626	0.472	0.121
$P(\text{RKey}=2)$	0.045	0.248	0.050	0.002
Probabilities with exogenous variables 0.25 of a standard deviation from the sample mean in a direction favorable for rationality				
$P(\text{RKey}=0)$	0.112	0.017	0.018	0.062
$P(\text{RKey}=1)$	0.456	0.366	0.330	0.519
$P(\text{RKey}=2)$	0.432	0.617	0.651	0.419

12.6 Determinants of market behavior

The previous section took the type of market action (Limit-Sell, Limit-Buy, Market-Sell, Market-Buy) as given and investigated the extent to which the offer placed by the trader was consistent with his stated expectations. It is abundantly clear that the pattern of rationality and of the factors affecting that rationality vary across offer type, so that offer type and rationality are intertwined. We see from Table 12.13 for example, that 37 percent of all sell offers, both market and limit, are irrational (RKey = 0) while only 20 percent of limit-buy and 26 percent of market-buy offers are contrary to the profit motive. And from Table 12.18 one would infer that buy offers tend to be more rational if the contract involved is for the trader's favorite party, while traders are less rational with sell offers involving their favorite party. Thus an understanding of the factors affecting the choice of offer type is critical in assessing the consistency of expectations and market behavior. Accordingly, in this section we turn to the issue of how traders decide on the type of market action – what factors make them choose to submit limit offers in place of market offers, or to buy shares rather than sell. Those decisions are also affected by expectations as well as other factors.

The model employed in this section is a multinomial logit model:

$$P(\text{offer is type } i) = \frac{exp(D_i)}{exp(D_1) + exp(D_2) + exp(D_3) + exp(D_4)} \tag{12.18}$$

where

$$D_i = \Sigma_j \beta_{ij} X_j \qquad \text{for } i = 1,2,3,4 \tag{12.19}$$

and the X_j's are factors thought to affect the offer type decision.

The unit of observation in this model is an offer, but the factors included in X are restricted to those determined by the circumstances of the market and of the trader just prior to any decision about the nature of the offer – what contract, what price and the number of shares, as well as the offer type. Results appear in *Table 12.21* below.

The factors we consider include the maximum potential profitability on both the buy and sell side, the amount of cash on hand, the division of the trader's portfolio between shares and cash, trader age and time of day effects. Each exogenous factor is represented as three rows in the table, with the coefficients for the Limit-Buy, Market-Buy and Market-Sell equations appearing in the three rows. Columns contain the coefficient estimate and its standard error. Interpretation of the coefficients requires comparing them to each other and to 0 – the normalized value of the coefficients in the Limit-Sell equation. Overall statistics for each factor, that is test statistics for the hypothesis that $\beta_{1j} = \beta_{2j} = \beta_{3j} = \beta_{4j}$, are not presented.

The first four exogenous variables represent the potential profitability of Market-Buy and Market-Sell offers. "r_{it}^{*P}" and "r_{it}^{*S}" are the best possible returns for purchases and sales, respectively, as defined in equations (12.8) and (12.9). r_{it}^{*P} ranges from 0 upwards and r_{it}^{*S} from 0 downwards, with zero in each case indicating that no market offer of that type is profitable according to the trader's expectations and market prices. "$d(r_{it}^{*P} = 0)$" and "$d(r_{it}^{*S} = 0)$" are dummy variables representing the $r_{it}^{*P} = 0$ and $r_{it}^{*S} = 0$ conditions, respectively. In the Market-Buy equations, the coefficient of r_{it}^{*P} should be positive, and that of $d(r_{it}^{*P} = 0)$ should be negative. And in the Market-Sell equations the coefficients of r_{it}^{*S} and $d(r_{it}^{*S} = 0)$ should both be negative. The signs of the remaining coefficients are less predictable, but they should generally be smaller. All coefficient estimates except for that of r_{it}^{*P} in the Market-Buy equation are consistent with this predicted pattern, but they are not always the most significant terms in the various equations.

Table 12.21. Factors influencing the choice of offer type: Multinomial logit model

Offer Type	L_buy	M_buy	M_sell
r_{it}^{*P}	0.2686 (0.2476)	-0.1011 (0.3178)	-1.6976 (0.4937)
r_{it}^{*S}	0.9367 (0.1978)	-0.7262 (0.2641)	-0.3048 (0.2325)
$d(r_{it}^{*P}=0)$	-0.6263 (0.1693)	-1.1091 (0.2790)	-0.1797 (0.1842)
$d(r_{it}^{*S}=0)$	-0.1296 (0.1054)	0.9008 (0.1448)	-0.2078 (0.1445)
cash share	0.7697 (0.1930)	0.6543 (0.2428)	-0.4772 (0.2694)
invest	-0.0119 (0.0036)	0.0168 (0.0052)	-0.0087 (0.0047)
ln offseq	0.1395 (0.0387)	-0.1113 (0.0491)	0.2504 (0.0511)
ln trdr age	-0.0455 (0.0531)	-0.5738 (0.0683)	-0.3295 (0.0640)
no. bids	-0.0045 (0.0175)	-0.0790 (0.0214)	-0.0296 (0.0231)
no. asks	0.0153 (0.0149)	0.1300 (0.0162)	0.0187 (0.0198)
ave sprd	-14.4098 (9.0058)	-121.5562 (16.8586)	-75.0714 (14.0330)
constant	0.0617 (0.2322)	-0.5499 (0.3127)	-0.0448 (0.2917)

No. obs. = 3916 Ln Lklhd $= -4800.62$ Pseudo $R^2 = 0.0588$

$\chi^2(33) = 599.9$ P value = 0.000

Offer type L_sell is the comparison group. Entries in the header include the number of observations used; a Chi Square statistic for testing the hypothesis that all coefficients in the model except the constants are zero; the p-value for this Chi Sq. statistic; the value of the log-likelihood; and a measure of goodness of fit of the model. Coefficient estimates, and their standard errors in parentheses, appear in the body of the table. Exogenous variables are described in the text.

The variable "cash share" represents the allocation of a trader's investment between cash and contracts. One would expect that as the share of a trader's investment held in his cash account rises, he might be more inclined to buy shares than to sell, so the coefficients of "cash share" in the Limit-Buy and Market-Buy equations should be positive while in the Market-Sell equation it should be small or negative. Those sign patterns are realized, and they are significant. The variable "invest" is the level of the trader's investment. We have no a-priori predictions of the effect of this variable. Estimated coefficients suggest that traders with high investments tend most often to make Market-Buy offers, least often to make Limit-Buy offers, with the other two types in between.

The next two variables measure the effect of time. “ln offseq” is the logarithm of the within-day sequence number of a trader’s offer and thus indicates whether the offer is among the first by this trader on this day or among the later ones. “ln trdr age” is the logarithm of the number of days since the trader first entered the market and represents market experience. Both variables are in logarithmic units to diminish the marginal effect of large values. For example, one trader entered 136 offers in a single day; it seems unlikely that the difference between the 126th and 136th would have been as great as the difference between the first and the tenth. Coefficient estimates suggest that traders most often begin the day with market-buy offers (β=-0.113) and then become more likely to make limit-sell (β=0), Limit buy (β=0.1395) and market-sell (β=0.2504) offers later in the day. More experienced traders seem disinclined to place market offers on either side, favoring limit offers instead.

“no. bids” and “no. asks” measure the number of limit-bid and limit-sell offers, respectively, that a trader had in the offer queues when he began his first trading session of the day. In the market-buy equation, the coefficient of “no. bids” is large and negative, while that of “no. asks” is large and positive. Apparently traders with many limit-buy offers become reluctant to buy on the market, while those with many outstanding limit-sell offers become anxious to buy on the market.

The penultimate set of estimates are for the variable “ave sprd”, which is the distance between the high bid and low ask prices, averaged over all six contracts. Wide bid-ask spreads could indicate a thin market or much market uncertainty, and either condition might lead traders to place limit offers rather than market offers. In fact all coefficients are negative with that for the Market-Buy equation the most negative, indicating that when the bid-ask spread is wide traders are most likely to submit limit-sell offers and least likely to submit market-buy offers.

The last two rows are estimates of the constant terms in the three equations. Since other variables were not centered at their means or other interesting values, the values of these constants are of no particular interest.

12.7 Conclusions

The objective of this analysis was to examine the consistency between the expectations reported by traders in a market and the market transactions undertaken by those traders. If expectations reports are truthful and meaningful, and if the trader is motivated by profit, then the actions taken should be those which, when evaluated according to the stated expectations, yield the greatest expected return.

A precursory examination of the data reveals that only 40 percent of market actions are the optimal ones, given the traders expectations, while another 30 percent are consistent with profit seeking but sub-optimal, and the last 30 percent are inconsistent. This high degree of seemingly irrational behavior might appear troublesome, except for a number of things. First, the classification of actions according to rationality used in the analysis implicitly presumes that the only strategy followed by traders is that of "buy and hold". If traders employ a wider range of strategies, purely technical trading for example, or transactions meant to take advantage of expected temporary movements in prices, then many of the "irrational actions" may have been misclassified. Second, the analysis neglects actions taken for purposes other than profit seeking. The contracts traded in this market were associated with political parties, and some traders might gain enough satisfaction from holding shares in their favorite party to make them willing to forgo some profit. Third, the array of transactions available to traders is sufficiently broad that the calculations needed to determine optimal actions may be overwhelming. That is to say, many apparently suboptimal trades might simply represent mistakes. And finally, the trader's current portfolio may prevent optimal actions. For example, a trader in an illiquid position might undertake apparently sub-optimal sales in order to gain the liquidity necessary for subsequent optimal actions.

These considerations motivated the analysis of factors related to the degree of optimality of market actions. When suboptimal actions are observed, are the conditions surrounding the action consistent with strategic behavior, motives other than profit, liquidity constraints, etc., which would explain away the seemingly irrational behavior? Indeed a number of such explanations were discovered. Purchases seem to be more consistent with expectations than sales. Transactions involving small parties are more rational than those involving large parties. Traders exhibited more irrational behavior in the early days of the market than they did in later days. The first transactions undertaken within a trading session were more often rational than those undertaken late in the session. The degree of rationality is different for transactions involving the trader's favorite party than it is for transactions on other parties. The degree of rationality declines as the holdings of a party increase. And the greater is the potential return, the more rational are market actions.

The consistency between expectations and market actions was thus revealed to be quite strong, particularly after controlling for mitigating factors. And that leads to final conclusion of the paper – traders are able to provide truthful and coherent statements of their expectations, and they are driven by the motive of earning profits.

References

Brüggelambert, G. (1996). Marginal traders und die Hayek–Hypothese: Erfahrungen mit einer computerisierten Börse, *in* de Gijsel et al. (ed.), *Ökonomie und Gesellschaft*, Vol. 13, Campus, Frankfurt/New York, pp. 214–295.

Brüggelambert, G. (1997a). Meinungsumfragen als informationstragende Institutionen: Eine ökonometrische Untersuchung der Entscheidungs- und Erwartungsbildung an politischen Börsen, *Zeitschrift für Wirtschafts- und Sozialwissenschaften* **117**: 257–289.

Brüggelambert, G. (1997b). Von Insidern, ‚marginal traders' und Glücksrittern: Zur Relevanz von Entscheidungsanomalien in politischen Börsen, *Jahrbücher für Nationalökonomie und Statistik* **216**: 45–73.

Brüggelambert, G. (1999). *Institutionen als Informationsträger: Erfahrungen mit Wahlbörsen*, Metropolis, Marburg.

Brüggelambert, G. and Crüger, A. (2001). Experiences from a complex market experiment, Surveys, *in* F. Bolle and M. Lehmann-Waffenschmidt (eds), *Experimental Economics: Bargaining, Cooperation and Election Stock Markets*, Physica-Verlag, Heidelberg/New York.

Camerer, C. and Weber, M. (1992). Recent developments in modelling preferences: uncertainty and ambiguity, *Journal of Risk and Uncertainty* **5**: 325–370.

Forsythe, R. and Lundholm, R. (1990). Information Aggregation in an Experimental Market, *Econometrica* **58**: 309–347.

Forsythe, R., Frank, M., Krishamurtey, V. and Ross, T. (1995). Using Market Price to Predict Election Results: The 1993 UBC Election Market, *Canadian Journal of Economics* **28**: 770–793.

Forsythe, R., Nelson, F., Neumann, G. and Wright, J. (1991a). Forecasting the 1988 Presidential Election: A Field Experiment, *in* R. M. Isaac (ed.), *Research in Experimental Economics*, Vol. 4, JAI Press, Greenwich, pp. 1–44.

Forsythe, R., Nelson, F., Neumann, G. and Wright, J. (1991b). Forecasting Elections: A Market Alternative to Polls, *in* T. Palfrey (ed.), *Laboratory Research in Political Economy*, University of Michigan Press, Michigan, pp. 69–112.

Forsythe, R., Nelson, F., Neumann, G. and Wright, J. (1992). The Anatomy of an Experimental Political Stock Market, *American Economic Review* **82**: 1142–1161.

Nelson, F. (1987). Logit, Probit and Tobit, *in* Eatwell, Milgate and Newman (eds), *The New Palgrave: A Dictionary of Economics*, The Macmillan Press Ltd., London.

Pein, R. (1993). Portfolioannalyse eines Marktexperimentes, unpublished Diploma-thesis,Frankfurt am Main.

Tietz, R. (1992a). An Endowment effect in market experiments?, *in* S. Lea, P. Webley and B. Young (eds), *New Directions in Economic Psychology, Theory, Experiment and Application*, Edward Elgar, Aldershot, pp. 99–121.

Tietz, R. (1992b). Semi-normative theories based on bounded rationality, *Journal of Economic Psychology* **13**: 297–314.

Tietz, R. (1992c). The Shift of Supply and Demand Functions due to the Spiral of Planning, Discussion Paper, Frankfurter Arbeiten zur experimentellen Wirtschaftsforschung A 32, J.W.Goethe-Universität, Frankfurt am Main.

Tietz, R. (1996). Experimentelle Wirtschaftsforschung-Wege zur Modellierung eingeschränkter Rationalität, *in* de Gijsel et al. (ed.), *Ökonomie und Gesellschaft*, Vol. Jahrbuch 13 of *Experiments in Economics – Experimente in der Ökonomie*, Campus, Frankfurt /New York, pp. 120–155.

13 What Do Market Makers Achieve?

Evidence from a Large Scale Experimental Stock Market

Jörg Bochow, Peter Raupach, and Mark Wahrenburg

13.1 Introduction

Research on the microstructure of securities markets benefits from a large amount of empirical data. Nonetheless, some relevant questions can only be answered with the help of experiments. Growing competition between different stock exchanges raises the general question of finding the most efficient way to organize securities trade. This paper presents results from a large scale experimental market which was designed to compare different market structures with regard to their ability to efficiently process information and to ensure high liquidity. The past years have witnessed a tendency towards fully computerized markets like the German Xetra trading system which offer a continuous double auction trading platform. However, these markets often experience problems in providing a satisfactory level of liquidity. Some stock exchanges tried to cure the lack of liquidity by introducing market makers. For example, the German stock exchange introduced so called *designated sponsors* into the *Neuer Markt* segment within Xetra. Their task is to maintain a liquid market by continuously standing ready to buy and sell securities. Other markets like the option trading segment at EUREX rely on multiple competitive market makers as a source of liquidity. Yet it is empirically not clear to what extent the introduction of market makers achieve its intended purpose. The reason is that empirical studies on this issue are often unable to trace differences in liquidity back to the existence of market makers. Any comparison of different real life securities markets suffers from the notorious problem that markets differ in many more dimensions than just in the existence of market makers. It is therefore difficult to argue that any observed liquidity difference is due to market making. Other institutional aspects such as trading volume, minimum tick sizes, information privileges of some market participants etc. may also contribute to differences in market liquidity.

Experimental economists recently began to compare different trading mechanisms using laboratory experiments. These experiments produced valuable insights into the ability of markets to process and aggregate information. However, laboratory experiments are less well suited to study market liquidity issues because the experimental setting has only a weak resemblance with real-world markets in terms of the number of participants and trading volume.

This paper studies the impact of market making in a different experimental setting by using a large scale market operating in the internet. During the soccer World Cup 1998, 50000 participants traded virtual stocks on the participating teams and speculated on the success of the individual teams. The 32 stocks were traded using three different trading mechanisms: some markets operated as a continuous auction markets while other markets operated as dealer markets with either one monopolistic market maker (specialist) or three competitive market makers. The paper investigates the impact of market structure on market liquidity. The organization of the paper is as follows. Section 2 provides a short overview of previous research results. Section 3 describes the experimental design. Section 4 reports our main findings and section 5 concludes with a summary and open issues for further research.

13.2 Previous research

One may wonder why liquidity is so important to investors and stock exchanges. For investors, and especially for managers of investment funds, high liquidity means to be able to buy or to unwind their positions within a short time interval and at relatively low costs. For the stock exchanges, it is crucial to be able to provide the liquidity demanded by investors as only few stock exchanges are expected to survive during the next years of keen competition. As there exist different trading mechanisms it is interesting to identify which mechanism offers the highest liquidity.

Unfortunately, liquidity can hardly be measured with a single observable number because there are several dimensions associated with it, i.e. depth, breadth and resiliency.[1] To target this problem several measures are introduced as proxies. The liquidity ratio, for example, is computed as the ratio of trading volume to absolute price change over some fixed interval.[2] Another measure is the relative odds ratio which bases on the chances of a certain trading volume to cause certain critical price deviations. The most used measure, however, is the bid-ask spread. It reflects the cost of a round trip, i.e. buying and selling immediately.[3] A bid-ask spread that is small indicates low costs of immediacy and high liquidity of a stock. The size of the spread is commonly assumed to be influenced by the three components, i.e. adverse selection cost, inventory cost and order processing cost.[4] Every market participant faces these costs, especially market makers who act as counterparts every time another market participant wants to trade. Whenever a market maker trades with a better-informed market participant, he loses on the trade on average. As he cannot distinguish between uninformed and informed traders, he uses the spread to compensate for the losses he suffers when trading with informed traders. Inventory costs are incurred by the market maker as he has to bear the risk of a highly unbalanced portfolio. Finally, order processing costs arise as compensation for the market maker‘s service, e.g. his opportunity cost of time.

Several empirical studies compare the liquidity of different stock exchanges. Stock exchanges may be divided into four groups (with the risk of oversimplifying the issue): call markets, continuous auction markets (Paris Bourse, IBIS) and dealer markets. Within the group of dealer markets there exist those with a monopolistic

[1] Hasbrouck (1990), p. 235; Hasbrouck/Schwartz (1988), p. 10

[2] Kluger/Stephan (1997), p. 19.

[3] Amihud/Mendelson (1986); Grossman/Miller (1988)

[4] See for example Laux (1993), p.238-240.

specialist acting as a market maker (e.g. NYSE), and markets with competing market makers (e.g. NASDAQ). Pagano/Röell (1990) and De Jong/Nijman/Röell (1995) analyze the spread of French shares that are listed both at the Paris Bourse and at the London Stock Exchange (LSE), a market maker system. They observe that the spread is lower at the Paris Bourse than at the LSE. Lee (1993) compares the spread of NYSE-listed stocks that are also traded at NASDAQ. He reports lower spreads on the specialist market of the NYSE . Christie/Huang (1994) similarly find a decrease in trading costs for stocks that were first traded at NASDAQ and then moved to NYSE.

The results of the studies mentioned, however, do not enable a clear conclusion as to which market structure provides most liquidity. The differences among market structures may also be attributable to different listing standards, which can be divided into quantitative and qualitative type.[5] Quantitative standards include firm size, distribution of ownership and earnings record. Qualitative standards are designed to protect shareholders from agency problems and to ascertain corporate responsibility and accountability to them. Other market characteristics like trading volume also differ between stock exchanges. The differences observed in the spreads may be ascribed to the firm and market characteristics rather than to trading mechanisms.

In order to overcome that problem, some studies used matched samples to control for different stock characteristics. Booth et al. (1995) utilize a matched sample of stocks that are traded on NASDAQ and on IBIS, a German computerized continuous auction system. They conclude that the spreads are higher on the market maker system. Affleck-Graves/Hedge/Miller (1994) observe that the quoted spreads on NYSE and on NASDAQ are comparable in size but not in their components. They find the adverse selection component to be higher for the sample of NYSE. However, their result may be flawed, as one measure among others for matching the sample is likely to be correlated with the bid-ask spread.[6] Huang/Stoll (1996) match their sample with such criteria as industry code, share price, market value of equity , book-to-market ratio and leverage. They report higher execution costs on NASDAQ than on NYSE. Bessembinder/Kauffman (1996) obtain similar results. Keim/Madhavan (1996) also find that NYSE offers lower transaction costs than NASDAQ. Stoll (1993) utilizes revenue and expense data of brokerage firms and states that indirect trading costs implicit in the spread and the commissions carried by investors are higher on NASDAQ than on NYSE.

The empirical studies mentioned above seem to indicate higher execution costs in dealer markets compared to continuous auction systems. Furthermore, the specialist market seems to provide better liquidity than the competitive market maker system. Nevertheless, the results depend on the matching procedures implemented to create similar characteristics of the shares to be analyzed. There is, however, a potential selection bias as different shares may be attracted by different trading mechanisms. It is possible that liquid shares are traded in continuous auction or

[5] Affleck-Graves/Hedge/Miller (1994), p.1476.

[6] See Theissen (1997), p. 4.

specialist markets *because* they are liquid and do not need many market makers.[7] In addition, differences in brokerage fees or in the quality of the order service (clearing and settlement) may distort the results.

The problems mentioned can be tackled in experimental stock markets. These do not suffer from a selection bias because the experimental setting is precisely controlled by the experimentator. Most previous stock market experiments focus on the aggregation of information and how it is processed under different trading mechanisms. Some papers also conduct a detailed comparison of liquidity aspects. Interestingly, the research often finds results opposite to the empirical evidence. Friedman (1993a,b) reports in his experiments a lower spread for the continuous auction market than for the call market, while the trading volume at the continuous auction market is higher than for the call market. Schnitzlein (1996) analyzes the Kyle (1985) model in an experimental setting. He compares a call and a continuous auction trading and finds that the call market is more liquid, measured by the average price change per unit order flow, and uninformed traders incur lower losses. Krahnen/Weber (1998, 1997) study a double auction with market maker systems which differ in the number of market makers. They observe lower spreads and a higher trading volume when they increase the number of market makers.

Theissen's study (1997) is closest to our analysis. He compares the information processing and the liquidity supply in the call market, continuous auction market and the dealer market. Using various measures for liquidity as proposed in the literature, he observes that execution costs are lowest in the call market and highest in the dealer market. Unlike Theissen (1997), we do not set up a call market, but we include a specialist market. Furthermore, the trading periods and the number of participants of our study by far exceed the setting of his work. A general problem of the experimental studies mentioned is the small number of trading participants (usually 8-15) and the low trading volume. It is unclear to what extent the results carry over to a real world stock market.

13.3 Experimental design

13.3.1 Basic principles

The WM-Stock-Exchange (WM = Soccer World Cup) is a computer-based trading system especially developed for this experimental stock exchange. After registration, everybody was allowed to participate in the experiment. Registration and order placements of the participants were realized via internet and were automatically processed within seconds. The participants' trading results depended on the performance of the shares they bought in anticipation of the results their favorite teams would achieve.

[7] Theissen (1997), p. 5

13.3.2 Price formation and trading rules

The exchange operated similarly to well-known election stock markets. Registration at the WM-Stock-Exchange was possible at any time. Each participant received an initial portfolio of 100 shares of each of the soccer teams, a current account with an opening balance of 0, and a limit to overdraw of up to 250 000 WM (the virtual currency of the WM-Stock-Exchange). The current account was used to settle all transactions. As new shares were issued for each additional player, and the fundamental value of the shares did not change through the registration of new participants, there was no direct influence on the stock prices. The participants could buy and sell shares with the exception of short selling which was forbidden. The stock holdings are limited by the overdraft limit of the current account.

The price of the shares was determined by supply and demand in a continuous market setting. Whenever a team left the tournament (or at the end of the championship) its shares were repurchased by the stock exchange at a predetermined liquidating dividend. The repurchase price depended on the performance of every team. It was calculated as follows: for every victory, a dividend was paid which increased after every round. A tie always resulted in an even split of the dividend between both teams. In the first tournament round, a dividend of 100 WM was paid for every victory. In the second round of the tournament, when a team qualified for the quarter final, it received an additional dividend of 150 WM, and for winning the quarter finals one of 300 WM. Winning the semi-finals yielded 600 WM. The winner of the third place gained an extra 450 WM dividend and the winner of the final, the World Cup Winner, received further 1200 WM. For example, the repurchase price of a team's share with two victories and a tie in the first tournament round and a defeat thereafter was 100 + 100 + 50 WM. The repurchase price of a particular share could have reached a maximum value of 2550 WM if the underlying team had won all matches during the tournament. The minimum repurchase price of a particular share was 0 WM. No dividends were paid out to participants until a team quit the tournament. As soon as a team finished its last game, its shares were suspended from trade and repurchased by the stock exchange.

13.3.3 Market design

The number of the participating soccer teams at the World Cup was 32. Virtual shares of each team were traded between June 1st, 1998 and July 12th, 1998. During that time the stock exchange was opened daily from 12 am to 11 pm. Of those 42 trading days 32 covered the actual time of the World Cup that ran from June 10th to July 12th. All matches took place during trading periods. Thus, the participants were able to response immediately to new information (e.g. goals, player sent off). This makes it possible to analyze the impact of new information on market liquidity.

The participants could submit either limit or market orders. Outstanding orders could be cancelled at any time as long as they had not been executed. There were no transaction costs. Every participant had access to the following continuously updated information: the five best bid and ask prices along with their respective order sizes[8], the own stock holdings and current account balance, the own outstanding orders, and their ranking among the other participants. After every transaction, both transacting parties received a message with the transaction details. The participants did not know what shares were traded in which particular trading mechanism, and whether or not there were any differences between these mechanisms. They were only told that they participate in an experiment designed to study different trading mechanisms.

Table 13.1. Allocation of stocks to their market structure

Continuous auction	Specialist market	Competitive market maker
England	Brazil	Germany
France	Italy	Argentine
Netherlands	Belgium	Yugoslavia
Spain	Croatia	Nigeria
Denmark	Norway	Romania
Austria	Scotland	Paraguay
Bulgaria	Iran	South Korea
Columbia	Mexico	USA
Japan		
Morocco		
Tunisia		
South Africa		
Saudi Arabia		
Cameroon		
Chile		
Jamaica		

The trading mechanisms put into place are the continuous-auction market, the specialist market, and the competitive market maker system. The continuous-auction market used here resembles the trading mechanism of the stock exchanges in Paris and Tokyo. As there was no intermediary in this market structure, liquidity was provided only through the limit orders of the participants. The specialist market with a monopolistic market maker resembles the trade procedure at the NYSE, while the competitive market maker market with 3 competing market makers corresponds closely to the new trading rules at NASDAQ. The specialist and the market maker in our experiment were obliged to set bid and ask prices with a minimum size of 100 shares to indicate their readiness to purchase or sell at any time. Thus, their quotes guaranteed a nonempty order book and the immediate execution of market orders. Each participant could induce trade by placing a limit or a market order. His counterpart was either the market maker or another ordinary participant. Trade between two ordinary participants occurred if their offers met within the market maker's spread, or if a sudden burst in supply or demand exceeded the order volume

[8] aggregated among orders of the same price

of the market maker. The specialist and the market maker in our experiment did not enjoy any information privileges as compared to other traders.

The allocation of football teams to trading mechanisms was based on the ranking of FIFA (Federation of International Football Association) on December 1997. The objective was to assign teams randomly to trading mechanisms and at the same time to ensure a similar distribution of expected team strength (measured by the rank) among the different markets. The assignment ensured that the sums of the rankings for the particular market structures were relatively equivalent across trading mechanisms. Table 13.3.3 shows the allocation of the teams to the trading mechanism in which their shares were traded. There are more teams in the auction market because of the non-trivial cost of market making that was paid out to market makers (detailed in following section).

13.3.4 Tasks and remuneration of market makers

At a dealer market the market maker has an important function. As he is obliged to quote bid and ask prices at any time, he significantly influences the process of price discovery. The spread is supposed to be the tool he uses to generate his profit and simultaneously provide liquidity to the market. In order to induce a market maker behavior that is comparable to real stock markets, the market makers were paid for their service using a performance-related payment schedule. Each market maker was assessed according to three criteria: profit per trade session, size of the average percentage market spread, and the ability to keep inventory at a constant target level. At the end of a trade session his inventory was supposed to deviate only by an average of 2 percent from his beginning level. All market makers were ranked according to these criteria at the end of the experiment. Each ranking carried equal weight in determining the overall performance of a market maker. The most successful market maker received an hourly wage of 25 DM. The most unsuccessful one received 10 DM. The remaining market makers were paid wages between 25 and 10 DM, so that the average remuneration was 16.50 DM which corresponded to the hourly wage of a student. The overall realized individual compensation of market makers varied between 770 DM and 3037.50 DM. All market makers were informed about their duties and the performance-related payment schedule. By applying three different performance measures (i.e. profit, average percentage market spread size, inventory fluctuations) we believed that the market makers would behave similar to real market makers.

Each of the market makers was responsible for trading 4 different shares. For one particular share he acted as monopolistic market maker. His initial inventory consisted of 100 000 shares which was 1000 times the initial holdings of the other participants. His current account had an overdraft limit which roughly enabled him to double his inventory as of the beginning of the experiment. For the other 3 stocks he acted as one of three competing market makers. His opening balance consisted of 33 333 shares of each stock and again an adequate amount of credit to roughly double the number of shares. Thus, both dealer markets were identical in their market power with regard to inventory size. Special care was taken to ensure that cooperation and communication among market makers was impossible. There were 8 market makers in our settings who covered 16 stocks. They worked in shifts, 3 persons taking turns in the role of one maket maker every 6 hours. In total, 24 students from the universities of Dortmund, Bochum, and Witten/Herdecke were recruited. Their performance was individually calculated. To get used to their role, the market makers had a learning period from June 1st until the beginning of the World Cup on June 10th, 1998. During that time, their trading was not taken into account when measuring their performance at the end of the experiment.

13.3.5 Remuneration of participants

The goal of experimental markets is to create a trading environment close to reality. To achieve this, one has to design a remuneration scheme for the participants. That is why many experimental stock exchanges pay all participants according to their performance. Election stock markets do not remunerate participants but use financial incentives by requiring the participants to invest real money in the stocks. Some organizers of experimental stock exchanges reject any financial incentives for the participants. They argue that the participants will behave like investors at real stock markets even without remuneration. They think monetary incentives could destroy the intrinsic motivation and could induce the participants to turn the experiment against the organizers.

Some papers study the impact of remuneration on behavior within experiments. Kroll/Levy/Rapoport (1988) show that the choice of a portfolio of risky stocks is significantly influenced when a high remuneration is paid. However, Kachelmeier/Shehata (1992) receive exactly opposite results in a related experiment. They show that even the promise of large payoffs does not lead to a change in the decision behavior. Oehler/Unser (1998) compare several experimental stock exchanges, which are either designed with or without an incentive scheme. They conclude that the difference in the results is insignificant. Despite the reservations mentioned above, the evidence so far does not give a clear picture whether the type of compensation significantly influences the results of an experimental stock market.

Various reasons prevented the usage of monetary incentives within our experiment. The most important were legal concerns (the experiment could be regarded as illegal betting) and the administration effort necessary to process payment for over 50 000 participants. Instead, we used incentives such as prizes for the best performing participants. The most successful trader of every trading day received investment fund shares worth DM 750. His success was determined by the absolute increase in value of his portfolio. The player with the highest portfolio value at the end of the WM-Stock-Exchange received a holiday trip worth DM 10 000.

These prizes presumably had an ambivalent effect on the participants' trading behavior. On the one side, they increased the traders' commitment and seriousness, thus improving the quality of the experiment. On the other hand, participants were tempted to follow risky trading strategies. It had been observed in stock investment games that the most successful participants used very risky trading strategies. It is difficult to assess what influence the risky trading strategies do have on the return generating process. From a theoretical point of view, there is little reason to fear a negative influence on the quality of share prices. Many basic theories in the field of market microstructure do not depend on the risk preferences of the market participants. In addition, the experience with experimental election markets shows that the stock exchanges are able to process information efficiently even with irrational trading behavior of a large number of participants: Forsythe et al. (1992) show that a political stock market forecasted more accurately the American presidential elections than any polls although the majority of participants demonstrably displayed irrational behavior in the form of a judgemental bias.

13.4 Results

13.4.1 Number of participants and orders

From June 1st to the beginning of the World Cup on June 10th there were 15 445 registrations. The largest increase in the registration of participants took place in the first round of the tournament between June 10th and June 26th. At the end of the first round there were 45 051 registrations, 90% of the final number. In total, our experiment attracted 50038 participants until July 12th. Overall, there were 2 516 146 orders placed of which 54% were limit-orders, 29% market-orders and 17% cancellations. 68% of the orders were placed in the first tournament round and 32% in the final round.

Fig. 13.1. Distribution of order types

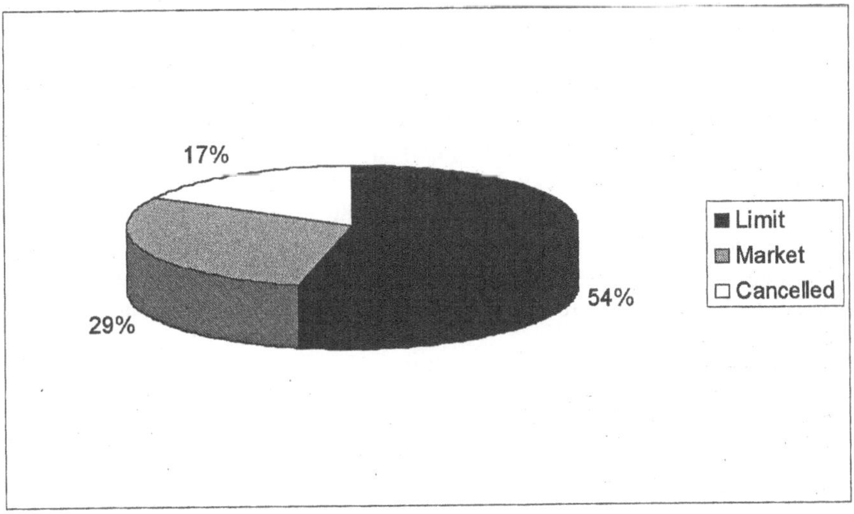

The number of transactions show a similar picture: 1 458 267 transactions were handled in total, 70% during the first and 30% in the final round. These figures show that the number of orders and the transaction volume were comparable to real stock exchanges.

In the following, we restrict our analysis to the period of the first round from June 10th to June 26th. We exclude the first 10 days before the tournament started, and the complete second round of the tournament. We do not consider the first ten days because market makers and participants presumably behaved differently due to learning effects. The second round is excluded because of likely disturbances in the stock price process due to the elimination of the teams. When a team left the tournament its shares were repurchased as described in section 13.3.2. This situation corresponds to the liquidation or bankruptcy of a firm in a real market. The price- and spread-process of a stock expected to be liquidated presumably has different characteristics than stocks of sound companies. When comparing the results of an experimental stock market with reality one has to ensure that liquidation effects are excluded from the analysis. Therefore, we concentrate on the first tournament round. For the same reason, the last trading day of the 16 teams not qualifying for the second round is removed from the data.

13.4.2 Grouping of stocks into homogeneous segments

Previous research has found that there exist a complex relationship between trading volume, stock volatility and the bid-ask spread.[9] To ensure that the observed differences in liquidity do not result from other market characteristics like trading volume and volatility, we compare bid-ask spreads separately for 3 different market segments within each trading mechanisms. The objective is to group stocks into segments with a relatively homogeneous level of trading volume and volatility. Any observed differences in liquidity are then likely to be caused only by the differences in trading mechanisms. Huang/Stoll (1996) classify their observations into segments by volatility only. This method, however, does not lead to groups with homogeneous trading volume within one segment. Therefore, we take a different approach. The stocks of each trading mechanism are grouped into the segments according to their closing prices before the start of the tournament on June 9th. As the stock price in our setting is closely connected with trading volume and volatility, we are able to create segments that show an accurate classification in both dimensions. Stocks with high stock prices at the start of the tournament are expected by the participants to earn large dividends and are called the favorites. The remaining groups are called midfield and outsider teams.

13.4.3 Comparison of volume and stock price volatility

We first compare trading volume across segments and trading mechanisms.

On average, both dealer markets show a greater trading volume than the continuous auction market, but the difference is small compared to previous studies. Across the segments, the biggest differences occur in the outsiders segment where

[9] For example, see Pagano/Röell (1990) and De Jong/Nijman/Röell (1995)

Table 13.2. Allocation of the stocks according to their prices at the start of the tournament

Market segment	Continuous auction	Specialist	Competitive market maker
Favorites	England	Brazil	Germany
	France	Italy	Argentine
	Netherlands		
	Spain		
Midfield	Denmark	Belgium	Yugoslavia
	Austria	Croatia	Nigeria
	Bulgaria	Norway	Romania
		Scotland	
Outsiders	Columbia	Iran	Paraguay
	Japan	Mexico	South Korea
	Morocco		USA
	Tunisia		
	South Africa		
	Saudi Arabia		
	Cameroon		
	Chile		
	Jamaica		

Table 13.3. Average trading volume (Number of shares traded * transaction price) per stock/day in million WM

Segment	Continuous auction	Specialist	Competitive market maker
Mean	216	264	269
Favorites	249	281	336
Midfield	231	236	265
Outsiders	196	304	228

especially the specialist market shows a high trading volume. The reason for this could lie in the fact that this segment consisted of only two teams one of which was Mexico which performed much better than most of the participants had expected at first. This, however, cannot solely be attributed to the market making. The low volume in the outsiders segment is a result of the fact, that, except for Chile, none of the teams reached the round of the last 16, so fewer data were collected. Overall, we observe a relatively homogeneous degree of trading volume both across segments and trading mechanisms.

A similar picture can be found when looking at the volatility.

The volatility is calculated by deriving the volatility from the times series of 5 second returns over 5 minute windows and annualized by multiplying $\sqrt{1.980.000} = \sqrt{250 * 11 * 60 * 12}$. By multiplying $\sqrt{12}$ we obtain a volatility over a time interval of one minute, with $\sqrt{11 * 60}$ we get a volatility over a trading day and with $\sqrt{250}$ we obtain an annualized volatility of 250 trading days. This method is consistent with common approaches of annualizing the volatility of daily returns. To

Table 13.4. Annualized volatility (5-minute-window) in percent (Median)

Segment	Continuous auction	Specialist	Competitive market maker
Overall median	457.63	362.05	348.72
Favorites	278.62	150.81	150.43
Midfield	369.10	362.05	245.93
Outsiders	562.43	373.2	460.73

get a more robust description of volatility, we use the medians instead of the sample means. Although the figures look high at first sight, they are in line with empirical high frequency data from real stock exchanges. For example, the equivalently derived annualized volatility of the S&P500 index is 116%.[10] The continuous auction market reveals the highest volatility, whereas the specialist and the dealer market show almost identical volatilities. Across the segments the volatility increases from the favorites to the outsiders segment. The volatility level in the favorites segment is low, because nearly all favorites (except for Spain) qualified for the second round. In the other segments participants had no homogeneous expectations over the stock performance during the first tournament round. We observe higher volatility in the outsiders segment than in the other segments. This result indicates that volatility may be regarded as a proxy of uncertainty. To sum up, the analysis of trading volume and volatility does not display any significant differences between the trading mechanisms within the segments built. Therefore, any differences in liquidity can be linked with different trading mechanisms.

13.4.4 The bid-ask spread

In the following, we concentrate our analysis on 3 questions, on which previous research has failed to give clear answers:

Hypothesis 1 *Market making improves liquidity.*

The effect of market making on liquidity is still questionable. Krahnen/Weber (1998) find higher spreads in auction markets whereas De Jong/Nijman/Röell (1995) and Theissen (1997) find lower spreads in an auction market compared to dealer markets. A further question arises about what kind of market making serves liquidity best:

Hypothesis 2 *A specialist market provides more liquidity to the market than a competitive market maker market.*

Empirical studies like Affleck-Graves/Hedge/Miller (1994), Huang/Stoll (1996), Bessembinder/Kauffman (1996) or Keim/Madhavan (1996) all find lower spreads in a specialist market whereas only the experimental study by Krahnen/Weber (1998) reports the opposite. A third hypothesis deals with the different impact of market making in liquid and illiquid markets:

---

10 See Locke/Sayers (1993)

Hypothesis 3 *The market maker's contribution to liquidity is higher in illiquid market segments than in other market segments.*

We analyze these hypothesis by comparing market spreads between the trading mechanisms in total and across the segments. For each team we first calculate the market spread according to the definition of Demsetz (1968):

$$\text{Market-Spread}_{t_i} = \frac{1}{2} * \frac{\text{Ask}_{t_i} - \text{Bid}_{t_i}}{\text{Bid}_{t_i} + \text{Ask}_{t_i}}. \tag{13.1}$$

Ask_{t_i} and Bid_{t_i} indicate the best available limit orders at time t for stock i. The time series of bid and ask quotes are extracted from order and transaction data. We transform them into time series with equal spacing of 5 second intervals. In the following, we use the market spread as a proxy for liquidity as proposed in the literature.

Table 13.5. Average market spreads in percent

Segment	Continuous auction	Specialist	Competitive market maker
Mean	1.97	1.65	1.51
Favorites	1.45	0.85	0.72
Midfield	1.90	1.85	1.15
Outsiders	2.53	1.98	2.52

A comparison of the mean of the percentage market spreads between the continuous auction market and the specialist and competitive market maker markets reveals considerable differences. On average, the spread in specialist markets is 16,2% lower as compared to the continuous auction market. The competitive market maker market achieves a further reduction and shows an average spread which is 23.4 % lower than the continuous auction market. The decrease holds uniformly across all segments. We use Wilcoxon scores to test whether the observed differences are significant at a 99% confidence level and find that they are indeed without any exception. The fact that even small differences are rated as significant is due to the large data sample which contains between 97702 to 132315 observations. Our results thus confirm the findings of Krahnen/Weber (1997) that market making improves liquidity significantly.

Comparing the specialist and the competitive market maker market, we find higher liquidity in the competitive market maker market. However the differences are much smaller. Furthermore, the competitive market maker market does not dominate the specialist market in all segments. Although differences are significant in each category when using the Wilcoxon scores, the picture is not as clear as between continuous auction and competitive market maker markets. We can therefore reject the hypothesis, that a specialist market provides more liquidity than a market makers system. Unlike previous empirical research by Affleck-Graves/Hedge/Miller (1994), Huang/Stoll (1996), Bessembinder/Kauffman (1996) or Keim/Madhavan

(1996), our findings favor the competitive market maker market over a specialist market.

It may be that recent reforms in the trading mechanism of the NASDAQ may lead to this contradicting result. In 1997 NASDAQ changed the trading rules allowing other market participants besides market makers to submit limit orders. Barclay et al. (1998) find significant improvement in liquidity after these reforms. Our trading mechanism of the competitive market maker market is equivalent to the new trading rules on NASDAQ, whereas all empirical studies which compare NASDAQ with NYSE spreads are based on the former trading rules. From that point of view, the result is not contradictory. Instead, our finding suggests that NASDAQ was right in changing the trading rules, which had been criticized by some authors.

One concern may be that the improved liquidity of competitive market maker markets may come at the expense of a reduced profitability of market making as compared to specialist markets. Lamoureux/ Schnitzlein (1997) report from an experimental market that dealer profitability and market efficiency are inversely correlated. The greater market liquidity of the monopolistic dealer market is achieved through losses of the market maker. Theissen (1998) supports this in an empirical study on the *Neuer Markt* segment at the Deutsche Börse. Even though our setup contains explicit instructions and incentives for the market makers so that they behave like professional market makers at real stock exchanges, the question remains whether the improved supply of liquidity in the competitive market maker market is achieved at the expense of their profitability. To answer this, we compare the average daily profits of market makers in the specialist and the competitive market maker markets. For the latter, we compute the aggregate profits of all 3 competing market makers.

Table 13.6. Mean of daily profits of market makers

Segment	Specialist	Competitive market maker
Mean	-25211	53489
Favorites	-47396	57600
Midfield	-6104	-70081
Outsiders	-29529	174321

Table 13.6 shows that the additional liquidity in the competitive market maker market does not lead to a reduction in profitability. In contrast, only market makers in the competitive market maker market make positive profits on average. A detailed explanation for the losses of the specialists is outside the scope of this paper. Differences in the performance of the underlying teams may contribute to the differences in this experiment.

After analyzing the overall influence of market makers, we concentrate our analysis on the impact of market making across different segments. We want to identify which segment profits most from the service of market makers. If hypothesis 3 is correct, market makers should have the biggest influence on the market segments with high spreads.

Table 13.7. Percentage spread improvement through market making (mean of market spreads in the continuous auction market in parenthesis)

Segment	From continuous auction to specialist	From continuous auction to competitive market maker	From continuous auction to specialist and competitive market maker
Mean	16.2 (1.97)	23.4 (1.97)	19.8 (1.97)
Favorites	41.4 (1.45)	50.3 (1.45)	45.9 (1.45)
Midfield	2.6 (1.90)	39.5 (1.90)	21.1 (1.90)
Outsiders	21.7 (2.53)	0.4 (2.53)	11.1 (2.53)

However, table 13.7 demonstrates that the size of the spread improvement decreases with the absolute size of the spread. Hypothesis 3 has to be rejected. Market making seems to have the biggest effect in segments, which are already relatively liquid without market makers. Existing literature names two reasons why market makers widen their spreads: adverse selection costs and inventory holding costs. Since insiders are excluded by our experimental design,[11] inventory holding costs should be responsible for the decrease in spreads when more market maker are added to the market. The result of this analysis –which has to be confirmed by a detailed analysis of the individual market maker spreads– suggest that competitive market makers may be able to reduce the inventory holding costs by sharing the risks associated with holding inventory. Our findings are in line with Campbell et al. (1991). They show that liquidity and the quality of information aggregation decrease when information becomes more volatile. Consistent with this finding, the outsiders within the experiment have much higher volatility and spreads. In empirical studies Madhavan/Smidt (1998), Madhavan/Sofianos (1998) and Hansch/Naik/Viswanathan (1998) all find evidence that market maker quotes are driven by inventory considerations.

Another reason for the smaller spreads in the competitive dealer market may be attributable to the trades amongst dealers. Reiss/Werner (1998), for example, find evidence for the London Stock Exchange that the inter market maker trading is responsible for the observed differences.

13.4.5 The impact of new information on spreads

The experimental setup of the WM-Stock-Exchange gives the unique opportunity to analyze the impact of information arrival on market liquidity. Events such as goals

[11] Of course, we cannot preclude the existence of participants with superior knowledge about football in our market. However, their impact is likely to be of minor importance as compared to the impact of insiders in real world stock markets.

and sent offs represent sudden new information to the market participants. They are very similar to "information shocks" in the theoretical literature. We are interested in the general influence of new information on the liquidity of different markets, and whether market makers are able to reduce the spreads and volatility in information intensive time periods.

Hypothesis 4 *Market making has a significant influence on liquidity after an information event.*

We test this hypothesis by looking at the spreads before and after new information arrives. If the market maker plays a significant role, the average spread after the information event should increase by a greater factor in the continuous auction market than in the market maker markets. We define an information event as follows:

An information event occurs, when a team scores or receives a goal.

Other events such as bookings or sent off's were not treated as information since their effect is not directly linked with team success.

Table 13.8. Number of information events

Segment	Continuous auction	Goals	Specialist	Goals	Competitive market maker	Goals
Total		128		60		54
Favorites	England	7	Brazil	6	Germany	8
	France	10	Italy	10	Argentine	7
	Netherlands	9				
	Spain	12				
Subtotal		38		16		15
Midfield	Denmark	6	Belgium	6	Yugoslavia	6
	Austria	7	Croatia	6	Nigeria	10
	Bulgaria	8	Norway	6	Romania	6
			Scotland	8		
Subtotal		21		26		22
Outsiders	Columbia	4	Iran	6	Paraguay	4
	Japan	5	Mexico	12	South Korea	7
	Morocco	10			USA	6
	Tunisia	5				
	South Africa	9				
	Saudi Arabia	9				
	Cameroon	7				
	Chile	8				
	Jamaica	12				
Subtotal		69		18		17

During the first round, a total of 242 goals were registered. Around the time of each information arrival we look at the market spreads from 5 minutes prior until

15 minutes after the event[12]. We group the time windows of all events according to their trading mechanisms and compute averages. Explorative data analysis shows a significant influence of market making on spread behavior surrounding information arrival:

Fig. 13.2. Average spreads 5 minutes before to 15 minutes after information events

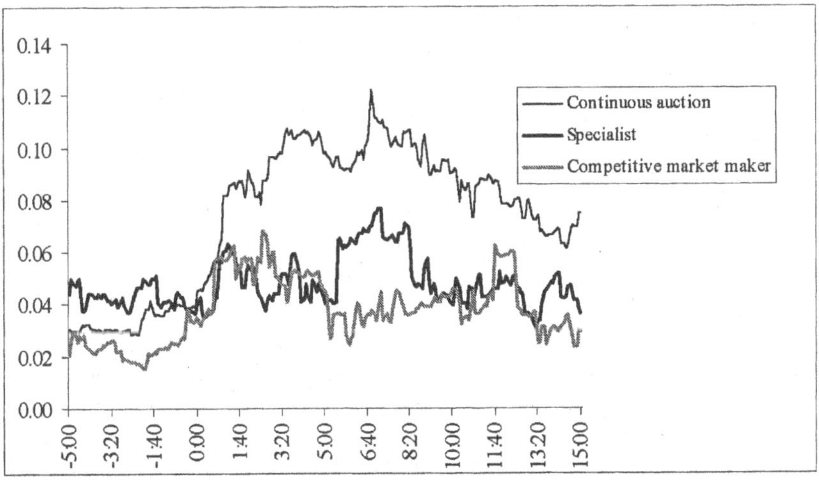

The spread increases across all trading mechanisms right after the information event. The increase is especially pronounced in the continuous auction market. Unlike other trading mechanisms, this market structure shows no clear decrease within the 15 minute period after the information event. The influence of the market makers can thus clearly be seen. The calculation of the average size of the spread in both intervals substantiates the same result:

In the 5 minutes preceding the information event, the spread is already higher than the overall average spread. Comparing table 13.5 with table 13.9, the means of the pre-event spreads for the three trading mechanisms are 71 % (continuous auction), 129 % (specialist market), and 57 % (competitive market maker) above their overall averages. This indicates that the market rationally anticipates the arrival of new information.

After an information event, the spreads jump to a higher level. The increase is especially high in the continuous auction market (on average 260 %) as compared to the dealer markets (160 % and 180 %). The favorites segment again reveals the biggest differences between the trading mechanisms. Without market makers, the spread jumps up by 153 %, with market makers the increase is only 36 % for the competitive market maker market and the spread decreases in the specialist market.

12 As opposed to the post-event measuring period, the pre-event period was cut to 5 minutes because shortening of measuring windows led to a smaller number of overlapping intervals. Thus, the assumption of independence of spreads among different goals is more realistic.

Table 13.9. Mean of market spread before and after the information event (in percent)

Segment	Period	Continuous auction	Specialist	Competitive market maker
Mean	Pre-event	3.38	3.78	2.38
	After-event	8.75	6.00	4.27
Favorites	Pre-event	1.11	3.87	0.47
	After-event	2.81	3.46	0.64
Midfield	Pre-event	2.90	3.59	1.57
	After-event	12.93	7.86	1.75
Outsiders	Pre-event	6.13	4.90	5.09
	After-event	10.50	6.69	10.41

In the outsiders' segment, we do not observe a clear difference between the auction market (71 % spread increase) and the dealer markets (36 % and 104 % spread increase). This is consistent with the above finding that market making seems to be more effective in segments where new information does not lead to very high volatility. Comparing the two dealer markets, the competitive market maker system again performs better on average than the specialist system. With the exception of the outsider segment, after-event spreads are lower in the competitive market maker segment.

To test whether the spreads of the various trading mechanisms are significantly different, we compute the spread growth ratio for each stock and then group these ratios according to their market structure. The ratio $\alpha_{i,j}$ is defined as the average spread in the after-event phase divided by the average spread in the pre-event period phase:

$$\alpha_{i,j} = \frac{\text{avg\_Spread(after-event)}_{i,j}}{\text{avg\_Spread(pre-event)}_{i,j}} \tag{13.2}$$

with $i = i$-th information event, $j = j-$th stock.

If there is a significant difference between the continuous-auction market and the competitive market maker market, the average ratio of the competitive market maker market, $\overline{\alpha}_{mm3}$, should be smaller than the average ratio of the continuous-auction market, $\overline{\alpha}_{mm0}$. Therefore, the difference between these two ratios, $d_{mm0,mm3} = \overline{\alpha}_{mm0} - \overline{\alpha}_{mm3}$, should be positive. We use the Wilcoxon-Scores to test whether these differences are significant.

The growth ratios of the continuous-auction market are generally larger than in the dealer markets with only one exception (continuous auction vs. competitive market maker in the outsiders segment). However, the differences are not significant since the p-values remain above 0.05.[13] Among the dealer markets no single trading mechanism dominates the other. The specialist market outperforms the market maker system in two segments, but none of the differences is significant.

The relative good performance of specialist markets compared to market maker markets after an information event is somewhat surprising in light of its inferior

[13] The p-ratios for the individual segments are also far above 0.05 and are not reported here.

Table 13.10. Mean of difference between spread increases after information event (Wilcoxon Scores, Zero Hypothesis: identical growth ratios, p-Value in parenthesis)

Segment	Continuous auction vs. Specialist	Continuous auction vs. competitive market	Specialist vs. Competitive market maker
Mean	1.00 (0.28)	0.79 (0.53)	-0.21 (0.89)
Favorites	1.64	1.17	-0.47
Midfield	2.27	3.34	1.07
Outsiders	0.35	-0.33	-0.68

overall performance shown earlier in table 13.5. In contrast to the overall analysis, the specialist market performs slightly better in two categories than the competitive market maker market after an information event. In short, a monopolistic market maker seems to be good in turbulent times, but bad in normal times. This evidence supports the theories of Leach/Madhavan (1993) and Seppi (1997) who claim that a monopolistic specialist can extract new information better from the observed order flow as compared to competitive market makers. One reason is that the order flow observed by competitive market makers is soiled by the orders of other market makers such that the extraction of the value of new information is more difficult to evaluate. According to our evidence, specialists seem to learn the impact of new information more quickly and therefore are able to reduce the spread faster after information events as compared to competitive market makers.

13.5 Discussion and further research

Our analysis of the experimental WM-Stock-Exchange shows significant differences in market liquidity between continuous-auction and dealer markets. The results can be summarized as follows: First, the introduction of market makers improve the liquidity of a market significantly. Second, the competitive market maker system performs slightly better than the monopolistic market maker (specialist market). Third, the impact of market making decreases when markets become more volatile. Fourth, when new information arrives at the market, bid-ask spreads increase and market making is very effective in ensuring a quick reduction of the spread after the information event.

The results raise new questions on market makers behavior. For example, the reason why market making is less effective in volatile market segments is largely left unanswered. As there are no insiders at our experiment, only inventory costs may explain the wider spreads. Alternatively, trades among market makers may also be responsible for the observation. Only a future analysis of individual market maker behavior can clarify these issues.

The data from the WM-Stock-Exchange enables us to investigate the trading behavior of each participant. It might be interesting to analyze whether and under what conditions some of them have taken over the role of market makers. Research from Forsythe et al. (1992) and Brüggelambert (1999) in the field of political stock markets support this hypothesis. But further research is required to gain more insight into the individual behavior of market makers and participants in order to gain a deeper understanding of the price discovery process of a continuous auction market and dealer markets.

References

Affleck-Graves, J., Hedge, S. P. and Miller, R. E. (1994). Trading mechanisms and the components of the bid-ask spread, *Journal of Finance* **49**(4): 1471–1488.

Amihud, Y. and Mendelson, H. (1986). Asset Pricing and the Bid-Ask Spread, *Journal of Financial Economics* **17**: 223–249.

Barclay, M. J., Christie, W. G., Harris, J. H., Kandel, E. and Schultz, P. H. (1999). The effects of market reform on the trading costs and depths of NASDAQ stocks, Working Paper.

Bessembinder, H. and Kauffman, H. M. (1996). A Comparision of Quotations, Trading Costs, and Volatility for NYSE and NASDAQ-Listed Stocks, NYSE Working Paper 96-03, May.

Booth, G. G., Iversen, P., Sarkar, S., Schmidt, H. and Young, A. (1995). Market Structure and Bid-Ask Spreads: NASDAQ vs. German Stock Market, Working Paper, 3rd draft, June.

Brüggelambert, G. (1999). *Institutionen als Informationsträger: Erfahrungen mit Wahlbörsen*, Metropolis, Marburg.

Campbell, J., Lamaster, S., Smith, V. L. and Van Boening, M. (1991). Off-Floor Trading, Disintegration, and the Bid-Ask Spread in Experimental Markets, *Journal of Business* **64**(4): 495–522.

Christie, W. G. and Huang, R. D. (1994). Market Structure and Liquidity: A Transaction Data Study of Exchange Listings, *Journal of Financial Intermediation* **3**: 300–326.

De Jong, F., Nijman, T. and Röell, A. (1995). A Comparison of the cost of trading French shares on the Paris Bourse and on SEAQ International, *European Economic Review* **39**: 1277–1301.

Demsetz, H. (1968). The cost oft transacting, *Quarterly Journal of Economics* **83**: 33–53.

Forsythe, R., Nelson, F., Neumann, G. and Wright, J. (1992). Anatomy of a Political Stock Market, *American Economic Review* **82**: 1142–1161.

Friedman, D. (1993a). How Trading Institutions affect Financial Market Performance: Some Laboratory Evidence, *Economic Inquiry* **21**: 410–435.

Friedman, D. (1993b). Privileged Traders and Asset Market Efficiency: A Laboratory Study, *Journal of Financial and Quantitative Analysis* **28**: 515–534.

Grossman, S. J. and Miller, M. H. (1988). Liquidity and Market Structure, *Journal of Finance* **43**: 617–633.

Hansch, O., Naik, N. Y. and Viswanathan, S. (1998). Do inventories matter in dealership markets? Evidence from the London Stock Exchange, *Journal of Finance* **53**(5): 1623–1656.

Hasbrouck, J. (1988). Trades, quotes, inventories, and information, *Journal of Financial Economics* **22**: 229–252.

Hasbrouck, J. (1990). Security Markets, Information and Liquidity, *Finanzmarkt und Portfoliomanagement* **4**: 230–242.

Huang, R. D. and Stoll, H. R. (1996). Dealer versus Auction Markets : A Paired Comparison of Execution Costs on NASDAQ and the NYSE, *Journal of Financial Economics* **41**: 313–357.

Kachelmeier, S. and Shehata, M. (1992). Examing risk preferences under high monetary incentives: Experimental evidence from the people's republic of China, *American Economic Review* **82**(5): 1120–1141.

Keim, D. B. and Madhavan, A. (1996). Transaction Costs and Investment Style: An Inter-Exchange Analysis of Institutional Equity Trades, Working Paper, September.

Kluger, B. D. and Stephan, J. (1997). Alternative Liquidity Measures and Stock Returns, *Review of Quantitative Finance and Accounting* **8**: 19–36.

Krahnen, J. P. and Weber, M. (1997). Market Making in the Laboratory: Does Competition Matter?, Working Paper, September.

Krahnen, J. P. and Weber, M. (1998). Does information aggregation depend on Market Structure? Market Makers vs. Double Auction, Working Paper, August.

Kroll, Y., Levy, H. and Rapoport, A. (1988). Experimental Tests for the Separation Theorem and the Capital Asset Pricing Model, *American Economic Review* **78**(3): 500–519.

Kyle, A. S. (1985). Continuous Auctions and Insider Trading, *Econometrica* **53**: 1315–1335.

Lamoureux, C. G. and Schnitzlein, C. R. (1997). When it's not the only game in town: The effect of bilateral search on the quality of a dealer market, *Journal of Finance* **52**(2): 683–712.

Laux, P. A. (1993). Trade Size and the Theories of the Bid-Ask Spread, *Journal of Financial Research* **16**(3): 237–249.

Leach, J. and Madhavan, A. (1993). Price experimentation and security market structure, *Review of Financial Studies* **6**: 375–404.

Lee, C. M. (1993). Market Integration and Price Execution for NYSE-Lsted Securities, *Journal of Finance* **48**: 1009–1038.

Locke, P. and Sayers, C. (1993). Intra–day futures price volatility: Information effects and variance persistence, *Journal of Applied Econometrics* **8**: 15–30.

Madhavan, A. N. and Smidt, S. (1998). An analysis of changes in specialist inventories and quotations, *Journal of Finance* **48**(5): 1595–1627.

Madhavan, A. N. and Sofianos, G. (1998). An empirical analysis of NYSE specialist trading, *Journal of Financial Economics* **48**: 189–210.

Oehler, A. and Unser, M. (1998). Information Intensity and Operational Efficiency in an Experimental Call Market, Paper prepared for the 7th DFG-Colloquium Eltville February 1998.

Pagano, M. and Röell, A. (1990). Trading Systems in European Stock Exchanges: Current Performance and Policy Options, *Economic Policy* **10**: 63–115.

Reiss, P. C. and Werner, I. M. (1998). Does risk sharing motivate interdealer trading?, *Journal of Finance* **53**(5): 1657–1703.

Roll, R. (1984). A Simple Implicit Measure of the Bid/Ask Spread in an Efficient Market, *Journal of Finance* **39**: 1127–1139.

Schnitzlein, C. R. (1996). Call and Continuous Trading Mechanisms Under Asymmetric Information: An Experimental Investigation, *Journal of Finance* **51**: 613–636.

Seppi, D. (1997). Liquidity provision with limit orders and a strategic specialist, *Review of Financial Studies* **10**: 103–150.

Stoll, H. R. (1993). Equity Trading Costs In-The-Large, *Journal of Portfolio Management* **19**(4): 41–50.

Theissen, E. (1997). Market Structure, Informational Efficiency and Liquidity: An Experimental comparison of Auction and Dealer Markets, Working Paper, 4th draft, September.

Theissen, E. (1998). Der neue Markt: Eine Bestandsaufnahme, Working Paper, No. 16.

14 Comment on Gregor Brüggelambert and Arwed Crüger, Forrest Nelson and Reinhard Tietz, and Jörg Bochow, Peter Raupach and Mark Wahrenburg
What Can We Learn From Experimental Asset Markets?

Michael Berlemann

14.1 Introduction

When electronic market research started in the end of the 1980's the primary objective was to conduct electronic markets to "produce" and analyze individual market data that can hardly be observed in real-world markets. Using these data it becomes possible to test several hypotheses that are common in microeconomic models or to study the efficiency of different market institutions. The first markets, conducted at University of Iowa on the occasion of political elections in the United States, turned out to be quite successful in predicting the elections' outcomes. Thus a second strand of research evolved, focussing on the forecasting quality of electronic markets.

The three papers by Brüggelambert and Crüger, Bochow et al. and Nelson and Tietz are all dealing with electronic markets, the authors conducted and analyzed during the last decade. While the papers by Bochow et al. and Nelson and Tietz focus on analyzing individual market behavior and the market institution, Brüggelambert and Crüger also discuss the forecasting aspect of electronic markets. When discussing the papers in the following I will concentrate on those aspects I suppose to be somewhat problematic. Thus I shall point out that - from my point of view - they all deliver highly interesting results.

14.2 Brüggelambert and Crüger

The markets, Brüggelambert and Crüger are reporting on, are strongly related to politics. Let us first focus on the aspect of experimental market behaviour. As Brüggelambert and Crüger claim, election markets are somewhat different from most other experimental studies because of their complexity. "Ordinary" laboratory experiments are typically designed to test a well-specified economic model and owe a high degree of control by the experimenter. I agree with Brüggelambert and Crüger when stating that experimental election stock markets are field experiments and that we have to accept the resulting lack of controllability and replicability therefore. But - as the authors claim - we should be very careful when testing hypotheses on the basis of data that were generated by field experiments. The hypotheses, we are willing to test by field experiments, are typically not well founded by economic theory since the framework is often too complex to be analyzed properly.

From my point of view the hypothesis of the existence of judgement-bias offsetting marginal traders, formulated by Forsythe et al. (1992), is an example for a somewhat questionable hypothesis that is not well founded by economic theory. It is somewhat mysterious what makes a trader to be a marginal one and what we can learn from the marginality-concept. This becomes obvious when taking a closer look at the design of the empirical test of the marginality-hypothesis. I agree with Brüggelambert and Crüger when criticizing the definition of marginal traders to be arbitrary. But if there is no proper possibility to identify a marginal trader or the used definition is likely to produce an artificial correlation between individual market activity and marginality, we should not carry out such tests - regardless of the results we get.

There is a second hypothesis that should be questioned. Brüggelambert and Crüger suppose experts, i.e. traders that took part in an election market some short time before, to gain higher profits than newcomers. I do not share the authors' surprise that this hypothesis is not confirmed empirically. Even if the market itself is a complex environment, the trading-rules and the possible strategies are clear. After the completion of the first trades each trader can be supposed to get along with these rules and there is little room for additional learning. Instead, the differences in the traders' individual payoffs are more likely to result from different degrees of political information, as the authors argue in section 3.4 themselves.

A second aspect the authors deal with is the quality of the market forecast with respect to the election outcome. Brüggelambert and Crüger do some empirical work on the question whether market predictions were able to perform out polls in the past. As it is shown in Berlemann (1999) and in Berlemann and Schmidt (2001) forecasts resulting from election markets are likely to produce better results than conventional polls from a theoretical point of view. To test for this hypothesis the authors compare the mean average errors of the forecast of election markets and polls. As much as 34 non-American elections have been taken into account for this purpose. By using a t-test on equality of means Brüggelambert and Crüger do not find statistical significant differences between election market forecasts on the one hand and the average poll prediction on the other. When comparing the markets' forecasting results to the best poll, the polls perform significantly better. There are several questions that arise in respect to this empirical finding.

In the first place it is not clear why the American election markets were excluded from the analysis. Especially the US markets performed quite well so that the results can be supposed to be influenced by this arbitrary decision. One reason for the exclusion might be the fact that the election system in the United States is somewhat different from other countries. I agree with the authors' statement that "each election event, to some extent, is a singleton" and that the predictive power is not easy to compare therefore. But that is not only true for the American markets but also for other ones. These markets were conducted in countries like Germany, Austria, Canada, the Netherlands, Denmark and Turkey. The voting systems in these remaining countries are different, too. Consequently, we should be very careful when comparing the results of markets from different countries. To carry this argument to extremes: it is even hard to compare data from election markets that were conducted in the same country, f. ex. because of the changing number of competing parties in the course of time.

This leads us to the question whether it is appropriate to assume the mean average forecast errors to be normally distributed - a necessary condition for the applicability of the t-test. In the light of the above discussion on national and international differences between electoral systems and political conditions this assumption seems not to be reasonable. For a somewhat smaller sample Berlemann (1999) had to neglect the hypothesis of normal-distributed absolute and squared errors. In this case we should make use of non-parametric tests as f.ex. the u-test.[1] In Berlemann's (1999) analysis the average rank of absolute errors and the rank of squared errors turned out to be lower in election markets than in conventional polls. For squared errors the hypothesis that election markets performed better than conventional forecasts could not be rejected at a significance level of $\alpha = 95\%$ while the difference of ranks was not significant for absolute errors. To be able to conduct parametric test the sample should be quite homogeneous. Even if election markets were organized in a good number of countries, in only a few of them (Germany, United States) enough markets were conducted to run empirical tests on a national and thus at least somewhat comparable basis. In a meta-study of German political stock markets Berlemann and Schmidt (2001) found market predictions to be significantly more accurate than the average polls when using a squared error measure. It is also somewhat questionable to compare the market forecasts to the best of all published polls since, if only enough polls were published, the probability that at least one of them is more accurate than the market forecast is close to 1.

Brüggelambert and Crüger also discuss why the non-US-markets seemed to perform somewhat poorly in comparison to the US-markets. From my point of view this is - at least not exclusively - a question of institutional differences in voting and party systems. A major reason why US-markets performed out the polls might be that the US-polls are somewhat less precise than in other countries. Because of historical reasons the US-polling institutes are not allowed to manipulate the raw data ex-post. In contrast to that German polling institutes correct the raw data quite heavily for different sorts of biases. Without these corrections most of the forecasts would have been highly misleading (compare the description of the correction procedure used by "Institut für Demoskopie Allensbach" provided by Hentschel and Tennstädt (1985)).

14.3 Nelson and Tietz

Similar as Brüggelambert and Crüger, Nelson and Tietz report results from a political stock market, the market on the occasion of the 1990 German Federal Election. The authors focus on an analysis of micro-behavior of the traders. On the one hand they try to assess how rational the traders behaved when trading in the market - an important aspect since the assumption of (boundedly) rationally behaving agents

[1] Compare Mann and Whitney (1947).

is a standard assumption of economic models. On the other hand Nelson and Tietz try to answer the question which are the factors determining the rationality of transactions.

Let us first focus on the aspect of judging the rationality of traders' behavior. Nelson and Tietz classify the traders' market actions into three different categories: strictly rational, boundedly rational and irrational actions. To be able to do so, the market participants were asked in the beginning of each trading day when entering the market to reveal their individual beliefs on the expected election result. Nelson and Tietz classify those market transactions as strictly rational, realizing the highest possible expected return (thereby using the individual expectations of the traders). Observed market transactions that did not realize the highest possible expected return but still were expected to earn positive profits are called boundedly rational while all other transaction are judged to be irrational. Using these categories the authors find about 30 percent of all market transactions to be irrational.

There are two sources of critique with respect to these results. On the one hand it is somewhat unclear why certain market transactions were excluded from the sample at least when focussing on the overall degree of rationality of transactions. Clearly arbitrage transactions are driven by the profit motive and thus should be classified as strictly rational. Including these transactions into the overall result the share of the transactions, classified as irrational, decreases to some 26 percent. On the other hand the applied classification system is somewhat problematic as the authors admit themselves when summarizing their results. This is especially true with respect to the classification of speculative transactions. A trader who expects the price of a certain party-share to rise in the future might buy it although he expects the "fundamental" value of the contract to be smaller than the actual price (compare Berlemann (1999)). Such speculative transactions would be classified as irrational while they clearly base upon the profit motive. Even if I have to admit that there is no obvious way of detecting speculative transactions it might be supposed that the classification of these transactions as irrational leads to the relatively high degree of irrationality Nelson and Tietz find in their analysis.

It might also be useful to have a closer look at the market data of traders, which not entered an expectation for each party and thus were excluded from the analysis. It is well possible that some traders felt highly informed on certain parties while they did not knew very much about other ones. Thus it would be interesting to analyze whether these market participants concentrated trading in shares on parties they revealed an expectation on.

As already stated earlier, Nelson and Tietz also care about the factors determining the rationality of the market transactions. There is not much to criticize with respect to the referring analysis. The authors identify a number of circumstances influencing the transactions' rationality. I will not try to summarize them here. One finding is that the degree of rationality seems to have increased in the course of time, i.e. the traders acted more rational the closer the election event came. On the one hand this might be interpreted as some kind of learning - on the other hand this finding might be a consequence of the above described problems of the classification system, especially with respect to speculative transactions. It is obvious that the incentive to organize speculative transactions decreases in the course of time since these transactions require to sell the referring contracts before the market is closed. Thus this finding might primarily be due to classification problems.

14.4 Bochow, Raupach and Wahrenburg

The main focus of the experiment, Bochow et al. review, is the effect of different market institutions on market liquidity. Three types of markets have been analyzed: a continous-auction market and two markets with different numbers of marketmakers (one, three). The most empirical results, Bochow et al. present, are in line with theory and thus seem to confirm the theoretical considerations. In the following I will concentrate on discussing some differences between the typical design of election marktes and the WM-market and the consequences resulting from them with respect to the interpretation of the results. The experiment, Bochow et al. review, is different from election market experiments in several respects.

The first and possibly most obvious difference is that the market was conducted on the occasion of the world soccer championship in France 1998 and thus had neither a financial nor a political background. On the one hand this seems - at least at first glance - not to generate any problems because the event, the traders have to build expectations on, should not matter. On the other hand sport events like a soccer championship seem to be more speculative than elections. In addition to that we can expect the traders to show a somewhat higher degree of judgement bias than in election markets or in real-world financial markets.

Different from election markets the true value of the traded contracts was not conditional on a unique event (e.g. the election outcome). Rather the final value of a contract depended on the result of each match of the relevant team. Thus, information about the final value of a contract was revealed in the course of time. This is a setting that is quite different from both, real-world financial and election markets.

The most important difference between election markets and the soccer market experiment by Bochow et al. is the motivation of the traders. In the beginning of the soccer market experiment the traders got an initial endowment of virtual money that could be used for market transactions. But - different from election market experiments - there was no direct link between the success of a trader in terms of gained profits and his payoff. There were only few possibilities to get some financial reward. The daily winners, i.e. the traders whose portfolio realized the highest surplus in value each day, won some investment fund certificates and the overall winner was rewarded by a free holiday trip. It is obvious, that in such an environment a risky strategy has to be chosen in order to gain some financial reward. Due to the high number of participants (50038) the reward structure of the WM-market is supposed to induce extremely risk taking by the participants.

Altogether the design of the WM-market shows remarkable differences to real-world financial markets (as well as to election markets) and some doubts remain whether the results of the experiment can be transferred to reality therefore. Especially the incentives of the market design towards excessive risk taking seem to be disturbing. Bochow et al. defend their market design by referring to the market experiment by Forsythe/Nelson/Neumann and Wright (1992). Although a high number of traders showed a "judgemental bias" in that market, the market did quite well predict the election outcome of the presidential election. But this fact does not support the thesis, that financial incentives do not affect market behaviour and market outcome.

On the one hand the financial incentives in the election market experiment, Forsythe et al. (1992) refer to, were totally different from those in the WM-market by Bochow et al., because the traders invested their own money. It is highly questionable whether the market would have performed that well in predicting the election outcome under some different sort of financial incentives.

On the other hand we have to distinguish between market behaviour and market results. Even if the election market would have predicted the election outcome well under some different financial incentives this does not mean that we would have observed the same market behaviour. It is well possible that the need to choose more risky strategies or the use of purely virtual money results in a somewhat higher market activity and thus comparatively high levels of market liquidity for instance. The results we get for the effect of different market institutions (with or without marketmakers) on market liquidity may thus be artificial and misleading.

One quite surprising result of the WM-market was that the average daily profit of a marketmaker was negative in four out of six cases. The average daily profit in the markets with only one marketmaker was negative for all subgroups: the favourite-, the midfield- and the outsider-markets. In the markets with three marketmakers positive average profits were earned on the favourite- and the outsider-markets. The great number of negative profits-earning marketmakers may be a sign for the use of risky strategies. Again there was no direct link between the absolute performance of a marketmaker (in terms of the value of his portfolio) and his financial reward. Instead the marketmaker was paid at least 10 DM an hour. This payoff could be improved up to 25 DM an hour by a good relative performance compared to the other marketmakers. The fact that there was a minimum earning per hour seems to have encouraged the marketmakers to follow risky strategies. Again it is well possible that the results of the WM-market are misleading in this respect.

14.5 Summary and outlook

Altogether the papers by Brüggelambert and Crüger, Nelson and Tietz and Bochow et al., included into this volume, provide a very useful overview on the possibilities how to evaluate data generated from experimental markets. These data can be used to learn about market institutions and market behavior. Besides that such experiments are useful mechanisms to aggregate and reveal information and thus can be used to derive good predictions for events like elections but also for other, genuinely economic events (compare e.g. inflation forecast markets described in Berlemann (2001)). Even if market experiments are belonging to the less controllable experiments the generated data can be of great value, because comparable data on real-world markets are typically not available. To be sure that the conclusions we draw are as reliable as possible we should take care of a proper theoretical derivation of the hypotheses we want to test on the basis of the experimental market data. In addition to that we should assure that the traders' incentive structure in the conducted markets is comparable to real-world markets.

References

Berlemann, M. (1999). Wahlprognosen: Politische Wahlbörsen versus traditionelle Meinungsforschung, Dresden Discussion Paper Series in Economics, Nr. 1/99.

Berlemann, M. (2001). Wahlprognosen: Forecasting Inflation via Electronic Markets: Results from a Prototype Experiment, Dresden Discussion Paper Series in Economics, Nr. 6/01.

Berlemann, M. and Schmidt, C. (2001). Predictive Accuracy of Political Stock Markets. Empirical Evidence from a European Perspective, Dresden Discussion Paper Series in Economics, Nr. 5/01 and Discussion Paper 57/2001, Sonderforschungsbereich 373, Humboldt University Berlin.

Forsythe, R., Nelson, F., Neumann, G. and Wright, J. (1992). Anatomy of an Experimental Political Stock Market, *American Economic Review* **82**: 1142–1162.

Hentschel, H. and Tennstädt, F. (1985). Election Forecasts. Problems and Solutions, Revised manuscript of a paper presented at the conference on "Opinon Polls and Election Forecasts" held by the Centro de Investigaciones Sociologicas (CIS) and the Universidad Internacional de Menendez Pelayo (UIMP), 26/27 September 1985, Sevilla.

Mann, H. and Whitney, D. (1947). On a test of wether one of two random variables is stochastically larger than the other, *Annals of Mathematical Statistics* **18**: 50–60.

Contributors

Dr. Michael Berlemann
Technische Universität Dresden
Fakultät Wirtschaftswissenschaften
VWL, insb. Geld, Kredit und Währung
Mommsenstr. 13
D–01062 Dresden
BERLEMAN@RCS.URZ.TU-DRESDEN.DE

Dipl.-Stat. Jörg Bochow
Blitztrade GmbH
Joseph-Meyer-Str. 13-15
D–68167 Mannheim
JOERG.BOCHOW@BLITZTRADE.DE

Prof. Dr. Friedel Bolle
Europa-Universität Viadrina
Lehrstuhl für Volkswirtschaftslehre insb. Wirtschaftstheorie (Mikroökonomie)
Postfach 776
D–15207 Frankfurt / Oder
BOLLE@EUV-FRANKFURT-O.DE

Dr. Gregor Brüggelambert
KPMG Economics Global Transfer Pricing Services
Am Bonneshof 35
D–40474 Düsseldorf
GBRUEGGELAMBERT@KPMG.COM

Dr. Arwed Crüger
KPMG Economics Global Transfer Pricing Services
Marie-Curie-Str. 30
D–60439 Frankfurt a. M.
ACRUEGER@KPMG.COM

Prof. Dr. Ernst Fehr
Universität Zürich
Institut für Empirische Wirtschaftsforschung
Blümlisalpstr. 10
CH–8000 Zürich
EFEHR@IEW.UNIZH.CH

Prof. Dr. Simon Gächter
Universität St. Gallen
Forschungsinstitut für Empirische Ökonomie und Wirtschaftspolitik
Varnbuelstrasse 14
CH–9000 St. Gallen
SIMON.GAECHTER@UNISG.CH

Prof. Dr. Werner Güth
Max-Planck-Institut zur Erforschung von Wirtschaftssystemen
Abteilung für Strategische Interaktion
Kahlaische Str. 10
D–07745 Jena
GUETH@MPIEW-JENA.MPG.DE

PD Dr. Claudia Keser
IBM T. J. Watson Research Center
P.O. Box 218
Yorktown Heights, NY 10598
USA
CKESER@US.IBM.COM

PD Dr. Manfred Königstein
Humboldt-Universität Berlin
Institut für Wirtschaftstheorie III
Spandauer Str. 1
D–10178 Berlin
MKOENIG@ODIN.WIWI.HU-BERLIN.DE

Prof. Dr. Marco Lehmann-Waffenschmidt
Technische Universität Dresden
Fakultät Wirtschaftswissenschaften
VWL, insb. Managerial Economics
Mommsenstr. 13
D–01062 Dresden
LW@RCS.URZ.TU-DRESDEN.DE

Prof. Claude Montmarquette, Ph.D.
Departement de Sciences Economiques et CRDE
Université de Montréal
CP 6128 et CIRANO
2020 rue Université Montréal
Canada
MONTMARC@CIRANO.QC.CA

Prof. Andrew Muller, Ph.D.
Dept. of Economics
McMaster University
Hamilton, Ont. L8S 4M4
Canada
MULLERA@MCMASTER.CA

Prof. Forrest Nelson, Ph.D.
Dept. of Economics
University of Iowa W386 PBB
Iowa City
IA 52242
USA
FORREST-NELSON@UIOWA.EDU

PD Dr. Axel Ostmann
Universität Karlsruhe
Institut für Statistik und Mathematische Wirtschaftstheorie
Zirkel 2
D–76128 Karlsruhe
AXEL@COPS.UNI-SB.DE

Dr. Peter Raupach
Goethe-Universität Frankfurt a. M.
Fachbereich Wirtschaftswissenschaften
BWL, insb. Bankbetriebslehre/Banking
Mertonstr. 17
D–60054 Frankfurt a. M.
RAUPACH@WIWI.UNI-FRANKFURT.DE

Prof. em. Dr. Dr. h.c. mult. Reinhard Selten
Laboratorium für experimentelle Wirtschaftsforschung
Universität Bonn
Adenauerallee 24–42
D–53113 Bonn
RSELTEN@WIWI.UNIBONN.DE

Prof. Dr. Mark Wahrenburg
Goethe-Universität Frankfurt a. M.
Fachbereich Wirtschaftswissenschaften
BWL, insb. Bankbetriebslehre/Banking
Mertonstr. 17
D–60054 Frankfurt a. M.
WAHRENBURG@WIWI.UNI-FRANKFURT.DE

Prof. em. Dr. Reinhard Tietz
Universität Frankfurt
Steinhausenstr. 23
D–60599 Frankfurt/M.
TIETZ@WIWI.UNI-FRANKFURT.DE

Contributions to Economics

Frank Bohn
Monetary Union and Fiscal Stability
2000. ISBN 3-7908-1266-8

Jaime Behar
Cooperation and Competition in a Common Market
2000. ISBN 3-7908-1280-3

Michael Malakellis
Integrated Macro-Micro-Modelling Under Rational Expectations
2000. ISBN 3-7908-1274-9

Stefan Baumgärtner
Ambivalent Joint Production and the Natural Environment
2000. ISBN 3-7908-1290-0

Henri Capron, Wim Meeusen (Eds.)
The National Innovation System of Belgium
2000. ISBN 3-7908-1308-7

Tobias Miarka
Financial Intermediation and Deregulation
2000. ISBN 3-7908-1307-9

Chisato Yoshida
Illegal Immigration and Economic Welfare
2000. ISBN 3-7908-1315-X

Nikolaus Thumm
Intellectual Property Rights
2000. ISBN 3-7908-1329-X

Max Keilbach
Spatial Knowledge Spillovers and the Dynamics of Agglomeration and Regional Growth
2000. ISBN 3-7908-1321-4

Alexander Karmann (Ed.)
Financial Structure and Stability
2000. ISBN 3-7908-1332-X

Joos P. A. van Vugt/Jan M. Peet (Eds.)
Social Security and Solidarity in the European Union
2000. ISBN 3-7908-1334-6

Johannes Bröcker/Hayo Herrmann (Eds.)
Spatial Change and Interregional Flows in the Integrating Europe
2001. ISBN 3-7908-1344-3

Kirstin Hubrich
Cointegration Analysis in a German Monetary System
2001. ISBN 3-7908-1352-4

Nico Heerink et al. (Eds.)
Economic Policy and Sustainable Land Use
2001. ISBN 3-7908-1351-6

Friedel Bolle/Michael Carlberg (Eds.)
Advances in Behavioral Economics
2001. ISBN 3-7908-1358-3

Volker Grossmann
Inequality, Economic Growth, and Technological Change
2001. ISBN 3-7908-1364-8

Thomas Riechmann
Learning in Economics
2001. ISBN 3-7908-1384-2

Miriam Beblo
Bargaining over Time Allocation
2001. ISBN 3-7908-1391-5

Peter Meusburger/Heike Jöns (Eds.)
Transformations in Hungary
2001. ISBN 3-7908-1412-1

Claus Brand
Money Stock Control and Inflation Targeting in Germany
2001. ISBN 3-7908-1393-1

Erik Lüth
Private Intergenerational Transfers and Population Aging
2001. ISBN 3-7908-1402-4

Nicole Pohl
Mobility in Space and Time
2001. ISBN 3-7908-1380-X

Pablo Coto-Millán (Ed.)
Essays on Microeconomics and Industrial Organisation
2002. ISBN 3-7908-1390-7

Ludwig Schätzl/Javier Revilla Diez (Eds.)
Technological Change and Regional Development in Europe
2002. ISBN 3-7908-1460-1

Alberto Quadrio Curzio/Marco Fortis (Eds.)
Complexity and Industrial Clusters
2002. ISBN 3-7908-1471-7

GPSR Compliance

The European Union's (EU) General Product Safety Regulation (GPSR) is a set of rules that requires consumer products to be safe and our obligations to ensure this.

If you have any concerns about our products, you can contact us on ProductSafety@springernature.com

In case Publisher is established outside the EU, the EU authorized representative is:

Springer Nature Customer Service Center GmbH
Europaplatz 3
69115 Heidelberg, Germany

Batch number: 10725973

Printed by Printforce, the Netherlands